Documenting the Famine of 1932–33 in Ukraine:

Archival Collections on the Holodomor Outside the Former Soviet Union

Documenting the Famine of 1932–33 in Ukraine:

Archival Collections on the Holodomor Outside the Former Soviet Union

edited by Myroslav Shkandrij

KIУС CIUS Canadian Institute of Ukrainian Studies Press
Edmonton 2023 Toronto

Canadian Institute of Ukrainian Studies Press
University of Alberta
Edmonton, Alberta
Canada T6G 2H8

University of Toronto
Toronto, Ontario
Canada M5S 2C3

ISBN: 978-1-894865-68-5 (pbk.)

Library and Archives Canada Cataloguing in Publication

Title: Documenting the famine of 1932-33 in Ukraine : archival collections on the Holodomor outside the former Soviet Union.
Other titles: Archival collections on the Holodomor outside the former Soviet Union
Names: Documenting the Famine of 1932-33 in Ukraine: Archival Collections on the Holodomor Outside the Former Soviet Union (Conference) (2019 : Edmonton, Alta.), author. | University of Alberta, publisher. | University of Alberta. Canadian Institute of Ukrainian Studies, issuing body.
Description: This collection of articles resulted from a conference entitled "Documenting the Famine of 1932-33 in Ukraine: Archival Collections on the Holodomor Outside the Former Soviet Union," which was held at the University of Alberta on 1-2 November 2019. | Includes bibliographical references and index.
Identifiers: Canadiana 20230220797 | ISBN 9781894865685 (softcover)
Subjects: LCSH: Ukraine—History—Famine, 1932-1933—Archival resources—Congresses. | LCSH: Ukraine—History—Famine, 1932-1933—Sources—Congresses. | LCGFT: Conference papers and proceedings.
Classification: LCC DK508.8375 .D63 2023 | DDC 363.809477/09043—dc23

The Holodomor Research and Education Consortium (HREC) gratefully acknowledges the Temerty Foundation for its ongoing support of Holodomor studies, including the two conferences that inspired this volume.
A grant for this publication has been provided by the Julian and Savella Stechishin Endowment Fund at the Canadian Institute of Ukrainian Studies (CIUS), University of Alberta.

Printed in Canada

Table of Contents

International Reception

New research perspectives

Preface

The present collection of articles resulted from a conference entitled "Documenting the Famine of 1932–33 in Ukraine: Archival Collections on the Holodomor Outside the Former Soviet Union," which was held at the University of Alberta on 1–2 November 2019. They were first published as a separate issue of the periodical Ukraina Moderna (no. 30, 2021). Interest in the topic has led to their republication in the present book.

Since the appearance in 1986 of Robert Conquest's The Harvest of Sorrow: Soviet Collectivization and the Terror-Famine, which first brought serious attention to issues related to the famine of 1932–33 (the Holodomor), scholars have sought out archival sources, transforming the research landscape. Organizers of the 2019 conference, with the aim of exploring and bringing to light little-known sources, invited a number of scholars who have worked in archival collections.

The resulting conference presented a survey of various archival collections. Participants mapped out what has been accomplished and reflected on future avenues of investigation. Among the collections discussed were those associated with ministries of foreign affairs in countries that had diplomatic relations with the Soviet Union in the 1930s. Several papers dealt with Holodomor-related diplomatic records in the archives of France, Japan and the United States, which are lesser known compared to those in Italy and Poland, for example.

Researchers who have worked with archives of immigrant and diaspora communities in Europe and North America shared their knowledge of relevant materials in the collections of Ukrainian, Jewish, and Mennonite communities that had emigrated from Soviet Ukraine. The archives of these groups, which had maintained contact with and aided their compatriots in Soviet Ukraine, cast a new light on the events of 1932–33. A number of papers in this volume describe these archival collections and analyze materials that can be found in these lesser-known and under-researched primary sources.

The present volume builds on the work of earlier researchers. In Ukraine, the earliest collection of documents appeared while the country was still a part of the Soviet Union. Ruslan Pyrih compiled and published Holod 1932–1933 rokiv na Ukraini: ochyma istorykiv, movoiu dokumentiv (Kyiv, 1991) one year before the Soviet Union collapsed. He later prepared a much larger collection entitled Holodomor 1932–1933 rokiv v Ukraini: dokumenty i materialy (Kyiv, 2007). In Russia, important collections include Tragediia Sovetskoi derevni: kollektivizatsiia i raskulachivanie: dokumenty i materialy v 5 tomakh, 1927–1939 (Moscow, 1999–2003), edited by Viktor Danilov, and Sovetskaia derevnia glazami

VChK-OGPU-NKVD: dokumenty i materialy v 4 tomakh (Moscow, 1998–2012), edited by Alexis Berelowitch and Viktor Danilov. Since the publication of these materials, the correspondence between Joseph Stalin and his close lieutenant Lazar Kaganovich has been published, and a number of anthologies have featured important documentary materials in translation. Researchers today are expanding the search for new sources and developing new approaches based on those already identified. A useful survey of the scholarship can be found in Contextualizing the Holodomor: The Impact of Thirty Years of Ukrainian Famine Studies, edited by Andrij Makuch and Frank E. Sysyn (Edmonton and Toronto, 2015).

The present volume is divided into four sections:

The first examines new explorations of archival collections. Andrii Bolianovskyi describes the documents of the US State Department that deal with collectivization and famine in Ukraine in the years 1929–34. Inna Gogina discusses representations of the 1932–33 Ukrainian famine in the USC Shoah Foundation's Visual History Archive. John Vsetecka examines survivor testimonies in the archive of the US Commission on the Ukraine Famine. Olga Klymenko's article explores the Maniak Collection, which consists of accounts of the Famine written in Ukraine in the late 1980s as part of a project spearheaded by journalist Volodymyr Maniak. Hiroaki Kuromiya reflects on the importance of Japanese documents on the Holodomor. Colin P. Neufeldt provides a survey of archives in North America that address the Mennonite perspective on events of 1932–33.

The second section deals with new research on the responses of Western governments to events in Ukraine in 1932–33. Olga Andriewsky investigates collections of eyewitness and survivor testimonies that were amassed in the early Cold War period (1947–55). Serge Cipko analyzes the Canadian reaction to the famine based on government statements and newspaper reports, and Paolo Fonzi discusses what Germans knew about the famine and how they perceived it.

The third section considers the international reception to news of collectivization and famine. Iryna Dmytrychyn charts the now notorious voyage enchanté of Édouard Herriot and how it influenced perceptions in France and Western Europe. Gennady Estraikh examines the reporting in the leading Yiddish daily newspaper of the day, New York's Forverts, and the US Jewish community's response to the privation described by travelers and eyewitnesses. Roman Wysocki describes the work of the Ukrainian Bureau in London in publicizing developments in Ukraine. Mykola Ivanovych Soroka analyzes how information about the events of 1932–33 was received by the new Russian émigré community in interwar Poland.

In the fourth and final section, Larysa Zasiekina explores new research perspectives and provides insights into how individuals reconstructed the psychological traumas that resulted from their experiences. The volume ends with an essay by Mirosław Czech and Ola Hnatiuk, which describes Ukrainian reactions in interwar Europe to the Holodomor. The article situates these reactions within the political landscape of interwar European politics and indicates recent sources and discoveries that require further study.

To date, many aspects of collectivization and famine and their aftermath have barely been broached, particularly the international repercussions, the psychological effects on survivors, the responses in creative writings and memoirs, and the impact on collective and cultural memory. It is hoped that this volume will encourage the publication of primary sources and further research, new approaches, and the exploration of long-overlooked issues related to the Holodomor.

Myroslav Shkandrij

New Exploration of Archival Collections

Collectivization and Famine in Ukraine in US Department of State Documents, 1929–34[1]

Andrii Bolianovskyi

While many countries maintained diplomatic relations with the Soviet Union after 1922, the United States of America did not. It established diplomatic relations only in November 1933, but its Department of State, headed by Henry Simson from 1929 to early 1933, and later by his successor Cordell Hull, regularly collected information about the Soviet Union, mainly from tourists, specialists, and various other American citizens who had traveled to the USSR, including some who had been invited by the Soviet government and who lived there in the early 1930s. On their way home, a number of these individuals visited diplomatic missions of the United States in European countries bordering the Soviet Union, especially Poland and Latvia.

American diplomats wrote reports about their meetings with Ukrainians, describing what they had heard and their impressions of what they had seen in the Soviet Union, and collected information that was available in other countries. Some of them wrote analytical notes based on information they believed to be worthy of reporting to Washington. These documents have never been fully studied. James Mace was the first researcher who collected archival documents from the US State Department during his work for the report to Congress by the Commission on the Ukraine Famine.[2] The American historian W. Wayne Morris also worked with State Department documents for his book *Stalin's Famine and Roosevelt's Recognition of Russia*, which is focused primarily on US policy toward the Soviet Union, especially the circumstances surrounding the Roosevelt administration's decision to recognize the USSR in 1934. In a

---

[1] I wish to extend my special thanks to Bohdan Klid and Myroslav Shkandrij for their assistance during the preparation of this article.

[2] US National Archives and Records Administration in Washington [cited herein as US NARA]. Record Group No. 0220 (Temporary Committees, Commissions, and Boards), Entry no. A1 40325 A; A1 40325 B; A1 40325 C — Commission On the Ukraine Famine, 1986–88. Boxes 1 to 3. For the published version of the materials collected by James Mace and his conclusion for the US Congress, see *Investigation of the Ukrainian Famine, 1932–1933: Oral History Project of the Commission on the Ukraine Famine*, ed. James E. Mace and Leonid Heretz (Washington: U.S. G.P.O., 1990), vols. 1–3.

separate section, he provides documentation revealing that the US State Department was well informed about the famine. According to Morris, the US foreign policy department had enough information to conclude that there was mass malnutrition in 1932 and the spring of 1933 and that there was convincing evidence of a high mortality rate caused by famine.[3] Marko Carynnyk also examined Americans' awareness of the famine in Ukraine in 1932–33.[4] However, the subject of collectivization and the Holodomor in US Department of State documents for the years 1930–33 remains an under-researched topic.

In February 1918 the US broke off diplomatic relations with Bolshevik Russia, but the US State Department never stopped following events in Russia, Ukraine, and other republics that emerged after the collapse of the Russian Empire. From the moment of the Soviet Union's creation, the Department of Eastern European Affairs at the US State Department studied the situation in these republics. Initially, all information about Ukraine and other Eastern European countries was received by this department; then, depending on the decision of its management concerning the importance of this information, it was reported to the Secretary of State or stored in the department's archives.[5]

The US Department of State was well informed about the 1921–22 famine in Ukraine. At the time, the Soviet leadership, under pressure from the domestic political and economic crisis in the country and in order to solve the country's socio-economic problems, acknowledged the fact of famine and agreed to accept assistance for the starving. Some US charities responded to the Kremlin's calls for help. The American Relief Administration (ARA) and the American Mennonite Assistance to Famine in Ukraine (with branches in Kyiv, Zaporizhzhia, Kharkiv, Odesa, and other Ukrainian cities), provided assistance to certain categories of starving people.

In the summer of 1922 ARA, headed by Herbert Hoover, Secretary of Commerce in the government of President Warren Harding, provided food, medical supplies, and clothing for ten million people in the Russian Soviet Federative Socialist Republic (RSFSR) and another two million in the Ukrainian SSR. The Soviet authorities requested Western countries to send aid to the Russian republic but interfered with its delivery to Ukraine, at least initially. Although in August 1921 the West knew from Soviet sources

---

[3] W. M. Morris, *Stalin's Famine and Roosevelt's Recognition* of Russia (Lanham, Md.: University Press of America, 1994), 99–126.

[4] M. Carynnyk, "Blind Eye to Murder: Britain, the United States and the Ukrainian Famine of 1933," in *Famine in Ukraine, 1932–1933*, ed. Roman Serbyn and Bohdan Krawchenko (Edmonton: Canadian Institute of Ukrainian Studies, 1986), 109–38.

[5] L. Leshuk, *US Intelligence Perceptions of Soviet Power, 1921–1946* (London and Portland, Ore.: Frank Cass, 2003), 21–55.

about the catastrophic conditions in Ukraine, Soviet representatives either denied that the country was starving or downplayed the scale of the disaster. Moscow initially insisted that all assistance go to the Volga region and assured the West that Ukraine could take care of itself and could even help Russia. Western leaders preferred to ignore the humanitarian catastrophe in Ukraine, even though they knew that millions were starving in that country. The situation improved at the end of the year, thanks partly to the lobbying of the American Jewish community. The American Jewish Joint Distribution Committee (JDC) pressured ARA to set up distribution centers in Ukraine to ship supplies to friends and relatives living there. In response to news sent by Ukrainian Jews, the JDC also urged ARA to investigate the famine situation in Ukraine. The relief mission was able to persuade the Soviet Union to allow its delegation to visit Ukraine in December 1921. The result was the Hutchinson-Gold agreement and a separate agreement, signed by ARA and the government of the Ukrainian Socialist Soviet Republic, which led to the expansion of US assistance to Ukraine.[6]

ARA's activities in Ukraine were closely monitored by staff in the State Political Directorate (GPU) of the Ukrainian SSR, who recorded details of the provision of this assistance. One message from September 1923, for example, mentions the fact that free dining rooms that had been set up in Ukraine often had posters announcing, "The food provided in this canteen by the American Relief Administration is a voluntary gift of the American people for the children of Ukraine."[7]

From 1930 to 1934 all information about collectivization, the Holodomor in Ukraine, and the famine in other Soviet republics was personally studied by Robert F. Kelley, head of the Eastern European Affairs Division of the US State Department. Many top State Department officials in Europe were also well informed about the tragic events. They included the following high-ranking US diplomats with long-standing experience: Philander L. Cable, former US Charge d'Affaires ad interim in Cuba, Havana, and, later, Buenos Aires, US Charge d'Affaires ad interim in Warsaw, 1932–35 (succeeded by Sheldon Leavitt Crosby); Jerome Klahr Huddle, US Consul General in Warsaw; Ernest Lloyd Harris, US Consul General in Vienna, 1929–35; John Work Garrett, US Ambassador to Italy, 1929–33; Frederic

---

[6] For more details, see H. H. Fisher, *The Famine in Soviet Russia, 1919–1923: The Operations of the American Relief Administration* (New York: Macmillan, 1927).

[7] "Sov[ershenno] sekretno. V Gospolitupravlenie Ukrainy (INO). Doklad o deiatel'nosti Inostrannykh Organizatsii Pomoshchi Golodaiushchim za period s 15-go avgusta po 1-oe sentiabria 1923 goda," in *Informatsiino-dovidkovyi zal Haluzevoho derzhavnoho arkhivu Sluzhby bezpeky Ukraïny u Kyievi (HDA SBU). Kolektsiia dokumentiv 01.02, Dokumenty karal'no-represyvnoï systemy SRSR, 01.02.03 — Holodomory, 01.02.03.01. 1921–1923 rokiv, 01.02.03.01.02. Dokumenty taiemnoho dilovodstva*, fol. 84 (22.11.2011).

Mosley Sackett, US Ambassador to Germany, 1930–33; George Strausser Messersmith, US Consul General in Berlin, 1930–34; Raymond Herman Geist, First Secretary of the US Embassy in Germany, 1929–39; and Frederick W. Coleman, head of the US Embassy in Latvia.

Apart from these officials, many other members of the diplomatic staff in US embassies and consulates in the above-mentioned countries, as well as in Lithuania, Estonia, and other countries, were informed about the famine in Soviet Ukraine.

The first informative reports filed by American diplomats to the US State Department about Bolshevik policies that were causing mass deaths in Ukraine date to 1929–30. These came largely from translated articles from the official newspapers of the All-Union Communist Party (Bolshevik) (AUCP[B]) or the Communist Party (Bolshevik) of Ukraine (CP[B]U), which were published in the RSFSR or the Ukrainian SSR. For the most part, they contained information on changes in the republican or local party leaderships, official data on communist reforms and their consequences in rural areas, and quotes from speeches delivered by Bolshevik leaders. They helped to provide a picture of realities as seen through "Bolshevik eyes."

The diplomatic reports included mainly information on the situation in the Ukrainian SSR in the context of conditions in other Soviet republics. On December 18, 1929, for example, the American Consulate in Tallinn sent a letter to Frederick W. Coleman in Riga titled "Conditions in Soviet Russia. November, 1929." The letter drew attention to "The Agrarian Crisis," which was described as follows: "In the country districts the reign of terror still continues. From every side reports are received concerning the execution of so and so many people. Nervousness is felt in all quarters. On the other hand it is of interest to state, that it is officially recognized to a certain extent that there exists a 'kulak' terror which is directed against the Soviet system."

The letter devotes special attention to Ukraine in a paragraph titled "The Separatist Movement in the Ukraine." The situation in Ukraine was connected in a direct way to Ukraine's struggle for independence. The letter states: "In the report admitted by the Consulate covering conditions in Soviet Russia during October, 1929, mention was made of indications of a decided separatist movement in the Ukrainian Soviet republic. Events which took place during November, 1929, to which much prominence was given in the European press, revealed the existence of an important organization in the Ukraine, which had for their purpose the *establishment* of the independence of the Ukrainian Republic. It was ascertained that these organizations stood in close touch with Ukrainian circles in Poland, and with the Polish Government itself [this is most likely a reference to the contacts between the population of the Ukrainian SSR and Ukrainians living in Western Ukraine—A.B.]. There have always been separatist tendencies in the Ukraine, but hitherto they have been scattered and unorganized. The movement which the Soviet Government now claims to have uncovered appears to have been very extensive in nature and fairly well developed."[8]

At the same time, the US State Department also received some notes containing detailed summaries of certain aspects of the Bolsheviks' national, economic, and social policies in Ukraine. Their varied subject matter ranged from brief references to the collapse of the policy of Ukrainization and the fabricated case of the Union for the Liberation of Ukraine in 1930[9] to a note on "Ukrainian Economic Affairs" based on information obtained from a report from the General Consulate of Poland in Kharkiv dated April 8, 1930.[10]

A very interesting report on the subject of collectivization and the deportation of Ukrainian peasants to remote, inhospitable areas in Russia, stamped "Strictly Confidential," is dated March 21, 1930. This document alleges that the Soviet leadership in Russia was instituting a policy of destroying the national fabric of Ukraine through mass expulsions of prosperous Ukrainian farmers to Siberia. The author of the note, Philander L. Cable, US Chargé d'Affaires ad interim in Warsaw, informs the US Secretary of State in Washington of recently released information that had appeared in the press throughout the world over the past month. This information warned of "a wholesale transfer of Ukrainian peasants, principally these who were formerly successful farmers, from their country of birth to other parts of the Soviet Union." The American diplomat states that according to the same sources, "900,000 Ukrainians will be moved during the Five-Year Plan and that during 1930 approximately 86,000 Ukrainians will be sent to Kazakhstan (Don District), 54,000 to the Far East, and 30,000 to Siberia." Cable adds that "it is argued that such a notion is contemplated not only with the view of placing good farmers in

---

[8] American Consular Service. American Consulate. Tallinn, Estonia, December 18, 1929. Subject: Conditions in Soviet Russia. November 1929. An Honorable Frederick W. B. Coleman, American Minister, Riga, Latvia. Harry R. Carlson, American Consul, in US NARA, T-1249, roll 36, fr. 0402–0403.

[9] "The Trial of the Counter-Revolutionary 'Association for the Liberation of the Ukraine' (Summary of Indictment)," *Izvestiia*, February 27, 1930 (no. 57), in US NARA, RG 59, Stack area 250, Row 30, CDF, 1930–1939, Box 6612, Doc. No 860E.01/141-175; 860E.01BII/14-860E.652/I.

[10] Enclosure to Dispatch No. 3205 of May 9th, 1930. American Legation, Warsaw, Poland. Translation of Extracts from a Report of the Polish Consulate General of Charkov [Kharkiv], dated April 8, 1930. Ukrainian Economic Matters, in US NARA, RG 59, Stack area 250, Row 30, CDF, 1930–1939, Box 6612, Doc. No. 860E.01/141-175; 860E.01BII/14-860E.652/I.

uncultivated districts, but also with the purpose of breaking down the racial solidarity that exists in Soviet Ukraine."[11]

Starting in 1931, US diplomats began to report to the State Department on insufficient food supplies in both rural areas and cities of Ukraine. On April 24, 1931 F. W. Coleman, head of the US Embassy in Latvia, reported this in a letter to the US Secretary of State, a copy of which was sent to the US Embassy in Paris. Referring to the content of three letters from Kharkiv, Kyiv, and Pyriatyn, which were published in a Russian émigré newspaper, he states that addressees were receiving food parcels from abroad, "presumably of the maximum permissible weight, 10 kg each, of foodstuffs, including flour, butter, and fat pork." Authors of thank-you letters write that "there are no such products in Ukraine in Kharkov." However, given the censorship prevailing in the USSR, Coleman made the assumption that "this should in fact mean that 'we have no food supply at all in Kharkov' — whatever this may mean."[12]

In 1932 Washington also began receiving reports that revealed how Bolshevik policy was causing an artificial famine in Ukraine. For example, on March 14, 1932 the US Legation in Latvia sent a note to the State Department containing information obtained from Tikhon Klenovich and his wife, both US citizens, who arrived in Riga after a week-long trip to Ukraine. The note, entitled "Grain Raids on the Villages," mentions that in cases where peasants had not met their grain delivery targets "police detachments would come and accompany the trucks to some villages. There is a complete search that would be made and hidden ahead and bread seized. Large quantities were sometimes obtained..." After offering the information that the grain was taken directly to railway stations to fill railroad cars, the authors of the note mention that the local authorities allocated part of the harvest to local security officers, who forcibly removed grain from peasants and their families: "The trucks were also summoned to Kherson and Odessa on several occasions to do special hauling for the OGPU." Describing the conditions in the village where Tykhon Klenovych had once lived, the author mentions the "insufficient supply to the village" and states, among other things: "The cooperative had a very limited supply of food. [...] The monthly diet was 50 grams [...] In November and December, meat was sold only three times in the cooperative. [...] Eggs cost 7 rubles for a dozen."

---

[11] Warsaw, Poland. March 21, 1930. Strictly confidential. The Honorable The Secretary of State, Washington. Philander L. Cable, Chargé d'Affaires ad interim, in US NARA, T-1249, roll 34.

[12] Legation of the United States of America. Riga, Latvia, April 24, 1931. The Honorable Secretary of State, Washington. [Signed:] F. W. B. Coleman, in US NARA, T-1249, roll 36, fr. 1405–1406.

The note contains an interesting observation about the village bordering on the one in which Klenovych had lived for a time. The entire population of that village had died, but in order to conceal this fact and in view of the complex sanitary conditions in the village, the Soviet authorities declared it an epidemic zone and quarantined it with a categorical entry ban imposed on anyone going there who might witness the mass deaths from starvation.[13]

The US government did not deem it necessary to respond formally to such information. State Department staff members adhered to a policy of non-interference in the internal affairs of other states. The US, which did not have diplomatic relations with the Soviet Union at the time, wanted to establish diplomatic relations after the election of the new president Franklin Delano Roosevelt, and considered it necessary to deepen economic relations and trade with the USSR. Meanwhile, for Stalin the US was a potentially important source of technology for industrialization. In pursuing a policy aimed at strengthening industry, especially the military industrial complex, the Soviet Union was interested in increasing foreign exchange operations to obtain funds to pay for patents, the salaries of foreign specialists, and the purchase of equipment abroad in order to transform the USSR from a predominantly undeveloped agrarian country into a developed industrial one. However, as a result of the global economic crisis, grain prices fell. Stalin therefore ordered the People's Commissariat of the Economy, the People's Commissariat of Foreign Trade, and the People's Commissariat of Supply of the USSR, together with *Eksportkhleb* (the Soviet trade organization that was responsible for the export of grain from the USSR), to increase the volume of foreign grain exports at lower prices. On December 29, 1931, at a meeting of the Currency Commission of the Council of People's Commissars of the USSR, it was decided to establish new quotas for the export of grain, food, and other food products as well as industrial raw materials to the West during the first quarter of 1932.[14]

---

[13] Enclosure No. 1 to dispatch No. 186 from the Legation at Riga, Latvia. Confidential. Memorandum of a conversation on conditions in Soviet Russia between members of the Legation staff and Mr. and Mrs. Tichon Klenovich, residents of the United States, who resided for five months in Russia, where Mr. Klenovich was employed as the manager of the garage on a state grain farm. The conversation took place at Riga on March 14, 1932. See US NARA, T-1249, roll 35, fr. 01509g–01517.

[14] "To oblige the People's Commissariat of Supply of the USSR in the 1st quarter of 1932 to export the remainder of grain production from the harvest of 1931 up to 4.5 million tons to ports, with the distribution by crops and in accordance with the decision of the government, counting [...] all released grain products under the instructions of the People's Commissariat of Foreign Trade and *Eksportkhleb*, not including substandard bread which will be returned to the People's Commissariat of Supply" (Sov[ershenno. sekretno. Protokol zasedaniia

While millions of people were dying in Ukraine because of the lack of food, the Communist International (Comintern) was allocating millions of dollars from grain exports from Ukraine to preparations for a "world proletarian revolution." The US State Department was well aware of this. A letter sent from the American Legion to the US State Department, dated November 4, 1932, contains the following information obtained from a confidential source: "The financial budget of the 20th Plenary Session of the Executive Committee of the Communist International, held in Moscow in September 1932, testifies that $756,900 for the purposes of Communist propaganda and preparatory activities to the Soviet intervention was interpreted as 'subsidies to party newspapers, printing and cultural and educational work.'"[15]

Most of the information received by the US State Department about the famine of 1932–33 in Ukraine arrived in the period between the spring of 1933 and the end of that year. On April 4, 1933, for example, Sheldon Leavitt Crosby, US Chargé d'Affaires ad interim in Warsaw, sent a special message to the Secretary of State in Washington, quoting various sources from February of that year. Citing an extract from a Ukrainian newspaper, he writes that from the Bolshevik press one can "see that passive resistance, as well as sabotage, occurs in three-quarters of Ukraine, North Caucasus, and the Crimean Republic—or in other districts with a minority population." The note states that during a meeting of the Central Committee of the AUCP(B), Nikolai Goloded (Mikalaj Haladzied), head of the Council of People's Commissars of the Belarusian SSR, admitted that "White Russia follows the example of the Ukraine in conducting a serious struggle against Moscow."[16] In fact, instead of the geographical names "Belarus" and "Ukraine," the speaker uses the terms "Belarusian counterrevolution" and "Ukrainian counterrevolution," which were more familiar to the Bolsheviks in that context.

In the US, those who took a pragmatic approach did not consider it immoral to ignore the existence of the famine because at the time they

---

valiutnoi komissii pri S.N.K. Soiuza S.S.R. ot 29 dekabria 1931 g. Predsedatel' [V. Kuibyshev], in *Rossiiskii gosudarstvennyi arkhiv ekonomiki v Moskve*, f. 8043, op. 11, d. 29, l. 268–74).

[15] The American Legion, Williamson County. November 4, 1932. The President, The White House Washington, D.C. Fred D. Goddard. Past County Commander. The American Legion, in US NARA, T-1241 — Records of the Department of State relating to political relations between the United States and the Soviet Union 1930–1929, roll 2, fr. 0040.

[16] Embassy of the United States of America. Warsaw, April 4, 1933. No. 151. Subject: Transmitting reports on conditions in Russia. Sheldon Leavitt Crosby, Chargé d'Affaires ad interim; American Embassy, Warsaw, Poland. April 4, 1933. Enclosure No. 1 to dispatch No. 151. File Translation. Source: confidential. Soviet Russia and its International Organization, in US NARA, T-1249, roll 35.

deemed it more important for the US leadership to ensure the development of export-import operations with the USSR. The Soviet Union's foreign trade and currency operations in 1932–33 placed special emphasis on the development of trade relations with the US. In a report dated August 11, 1933 on the results of export operations to the US for the first six months of the year, A. Rozenshein, the head of the Import Department of the Amtorg Trading Corporation, writes that the reporting period was characterized by "work with a certain cycle of working issues to expand our exports to the United States."[17]

In these circumstances, new reports on the famine in Ukraine continued to be sent to Washington. On August 23, 1933, for example, a memorandum on conditions in Ukraine was sent from Riga. It was written on the basis of information received from a US citizen named Varvara Yakunchikova after her departure from the Soviet Union, where she had visited her sister (who was married to a journalist in New York). It states: "Starvation in Russia at the present time is more acute than it was in 1921–22. Cannibalism is reported from all sides, especially in the Southern regions (the Ukraine and the Northern Caucasus) and Siberia, where food is particularly scarce. 'White' bread, which is actually of a grey color, may be obtained in Moscow and Leningrad only. The crop of 1933 is excellent but there is no one to collect it."[18]

State Department documents contain information providing evidence of the Soviet Union's practice of dispatching officials and employees in urban areas to help gather the harvest on collective farms in 1933 because of the shortage of farm laborers. According to a State Department document, this shortage was caused in part by mass deportations to the Far North of hundreds of thousands of Ukrainian peasants and the mass deaths of peasants who had starved to death: "In the Ukraine, for example, a large percentage of the farmers have been banished to the North, and the remaining peasants are too undernourished and too weak to execute much work. It has therefore become the practice of the government to send its city employees to the fields to help in the harvesting of the grain."[19]

On August 23, 1933, along with a letter from the US Embassy in Warsaw to the US State Department, US Consul General in Warsaw J. Clare Gaddle

---

[17] See the half-year report of the People's Commissariat of Foreign Trade of the USSR on the realization of products by the Amtorg Trading Corporation, 11 avgusta 1933 g., N'iu-York. NKVT—t. Frunkinu, t. Rabinovichu, t. Goldshteinu, t. Dvolaitskomu. Gosamtorg—tov. Vorob'evu, in Rossiiskii gosudarstvennyi arkhiv ekonimiki (Russian State Archive of the Economy, RGAE), f. 413, op. 13, d. 645, l. 37–38.

[18] Strictly confidential. Memorandum "Conditions in Soviet Russia," in US NARA, T-1249, roll 40, fr. 0013.

[19] Ibid., fr. 0013–0014.

sent a note about the journey of American citizen Whiting Williams to Kharkiv, Kyiv, and other Ukrainian cities, and about the mass mortality caused by the lack of food that he witnessed in Ukraine. Describing what he saw, he refers to the death of millions of Ukrainians. However, in his note he calls them "Russians" because at the time, as well as earlier and later, many documents of the Department of State and other US government agencies often identified Ukraine with Russia; hence, Ukrainians were called Russians.

Special attention in the note was devoted to famine conditions. In this section the note states: "He says what he saw only during his two-week visit, namely that he personally saw the bodies of deceased workers and peasants as a result of death from starvation. He saw people who died in the streets for this reason. As a separate example, he mentioned a baby girl whose death he had seen; he watched as she starved to death. He saw peasants falling from the weakness caused by hunger while working in a grain field to get food. From his conversations with Russian peasants and workers and with foreigners in the places in the areas he visited, he concluded that during the last year not hundreds or hundreds of thousands but millions of Russians had died of starvation and that food was lacking."

It is noteworthy that even the author of the note, J. Clare Huddle, who was an experienced American diplomat, did not believe that all this was true. Commenting with some skepticism on the story of this American citizen who had spent time in Ukraine, he nonetheless found the account plausible in view of the eyewitness's credentials: "It's hard to believe that his statements [...] are not exaggerated. In spite of this, Mr Williams' qualification as a columnist and his reputation are grounds for considering his claim as authoritative."[20]

On September 20, 1933 Robert Kelley, head of the Department of Eastern European Affairs at the US State Department, commenting on Huddle's note, declared that he now understood why censorship in the USSR strictly controlled all letters to the West and why many honest Western journalists traveling to that country could not write the truth about the famine in Ukraine and neighboring Soviet republics. He also mentioned the strict control over foreign correspondents in Russia, who were denied permission to visit and inspect the harvest in the main agricultural regions of Ukraine. Such was the situation with William G.

[20] American Consulate General. Warsaw, Poland, August 23, 1933. Strictly confidential! Subject: Conditions in the Russian Ukraine. Observations of Mr. Whiting Williams. [To] The Honorable The Secretary of State. J. Klahr Huddle. American Council General, in US NARA, T-1249, roll 40, fr. 0035–0044.

Chamberlain, who had worked for years as a correspondent in Russia for *the Christian Science Monitor*.[21]

This explains why the famine was not reported in early 1933 or was under-reported by American journalists. The situation changed in the summer of 1933, when the American press wrote about the millions of Ukrainians who had starved to death in the USSR. In his report published in *The New York Times* on August 25, 1933, for example, correspondent Frederick T. Birchall, using information obtained from persons who had visited the USSR shortly before, wrote that between three and four million people had died of starvation in Ukraine. Ukrainian colleagues, writing in the Ukrainian-language press published in the US, also began reporting more on the famine in Ukraine. For example, an article published on August 24, 1933 on the front page of the newspaper *Svoboda* (Jersey City, New Jersey), features a stark caption: "Two million Ukrainian peasants have starved to death since the start of the year." The article, based on an account of a mathematics professor named Ostap Menda, describes the horrific picture and catastrophic consequences of the Holodomor in Ukraine: "Crazed, starving relatives cut and eat their children. [...] Many Ukrainian villages have been completely depopulated because some peasants chose to look for food elsewhere, while others starved to death, or Moscow sent them somewhere for hard labor to the Far North and Siberia. On the streets of villages and on the roads were many bodies of dead people who had starved [to death]. They rot because they have no one to bury them, and they infect the air."[22]

In 1933 American Mennonites were among the first who tried to assist the starving population of Ukraine. As in the 1921–22 famine period in the Bolshevik-ruled Ukrainian lands, in 1933 they also decided to seek help from the US government for their fellow believers living in the USSR. In March 1933 the Central Mennonite Committee in Hillsboro, Kansas, wrote to Cordell Hull, US Secretary of State, on behalf of their religious community: "We receive thousands of letters pleading in the most pitiable manner for bread. According to testimonies verified by thousands of letters, the people are dying in large numbers for want of food. The conditions must be decidedly worse than in 1921–1922, when America carried on very extensive relief operations in that country."[23]

---

[21] Department of State. Division of Eastern European Affairs. September 20, 1933. S — Mr. Secretary. U — Mr. Phillips. A-P — Mr. Payer. Robert F. Kelley, in US NARA, T-1249, roll 40, fr. 0045.

[22] *Svoboda*, August 24, 1933, 1.

[23] Mennonite Central Committee. American Mennonite Agency for Foreign Relief. Executive Office: Scottland, Pa. Hillsboro, Kans., March 27th, 1933. Hon. Cordell Hull, Secretary of State, Washington. D.C. [Signed:] S. P. Hubert, in US NARA, T-1249, roll 31, fr. 0148.

The State Department responded very "dryly": "In reply, you are informed that although the Department appreciates the anxiety of American citizens whose relatives in Russia are suffering from lack of food, it is of the opinion that there are no measures which this Government may appropriately take at the present time in order to facilitate relief work being carried on in Russia."[24]

At the same time as the press was reporting on the fears that massive numbers of Ukrainian peasants were dying as a result of the Kremlin's deliberate policy of confiscating grain and food from peasants, Ukrainian organizations based in the US also called on the government to assist their starving compatriots. They also cautioned American leaders against recognizing the USSR as the country that had organized the famine which resulted in the deaths of millions of people in Ukraine.

A Ukrainian-American appeal dated September 12, 1933 reads as follows: "And as the acknowledgment of the Soviet Union by the U.S. of A. is now on the order of the day we are, as American citizens, addressing the Government with the request of sending before a special American mission to Ukraine in order to study the conditions of Soviet policy towards all the separate states entering into the Soviet Union. Most particularly we are applying for a close examination of Soviet policy against Ukraine—a country representing the greatest part of the Union, this land which is said to be the richest in natural resources of all Europe and where now, according to bolshevistic information, though no dryness nor riots have ravaged the fields, such a terrible famine is starving people that it comes even to cases of cannibalism."[25]

On October 30, 1933 Emil Revyuk, president of the United Ukrainian Organizations of the United States, with its center in Jersey City, and its secretary, Dr. Luka Myshuha, sent a memorandum to the American president. In it they proposed that a special governmental commission be sent to Ukraine in order to conduct an objective study of local conditions, and only in the event of a positive finding about Soviet policies should diplomatic relations be established with the USSR:

---

[24] April 6, 1933. [To] Mr. P. C. Hiebert, Chairman, Mennonite Central Committee, Hillsboro, Kansas. For the Secretary of State: Robert F. Kelley, Chief, Division of Eastern European Affairs, in US NARA, T-1249, roll 31, fr. 0149.

[25] This appeal is also cited in another document. See Committee of Salvation for Ukraine in Czechoslovakia. Prague XII, Slezska 7. Prague, 6.XI.1933. To His Excellency, President of United States of North America, Washington D.C. For the Committee of Salvation for Ukraine in Czechoslovakia. Chairman G. H. Botshkowsky General Secretary I. Palywoda, in US NARA, T-1249, roll 31, fr. 0271.

> During the past year, several million inhabitants of Soviet Ukraine, the land of our ancestors, have died from starvation. The existence of this horrific famine in Ukraine has been repeatedly confirmed by the leading European and American press. It is impossible to give the exact figure as to the total number of deaths from the great famine, principally because of the rigid censorship in Soviet Russia.[...] It will be sufficient for us, however, to affirm the well-authenticated reports of impartial American and European newspaper correspondents that during the past year several million inhabitants of Ukraine have died a terrible death from starvation, and even cannibalism was discovered in several sectors of the country, all of this in a land which is regarded as one of the most fertile in the world.[...] And because of the reasons already cited, we respectfully recommend to the President to conduct any further necessary negotiations with the Soviets on the subject of the recognition only on the condition that the Soviet Republic permits the sending of an impartial Special American Mission to Soviet Russia, particularly to Ukraine, for the purpose of investigating the conditions therein, and to ascertain the direct cause of this terrible famine which during the past year mowed down millions of victims in Ukraine.[26]

In addition to its practical focus, the memorandum contained analytical explanations of the root causes of deaths from malnutrition. The authors of this document opine that there were political reasons for the artificial engineering of the famine by the Kremlin as a method of weakening Ukrainians in the context of the war that Bolshevik Russia was waging against the Ukrainians' struggle for national and state independence, which in various forms and manifestations had lasted since 1918: "We are firmly convinced that the famine in Ukraine is not a result of poor crops or drought, but on the contrary, is a result of the political and cultural conflict between Ukrainian nationalistic aspirations and Moscow's imperialistic and centralizing designs; and also because of the Ukrainian peasants' opposition to Moscow's economic exploitation of Ukraine and to its forcibly imposed collectivization and other Communistic experiments practiced upon the Ukrainian people. The famine is the culmination of that unremitting and ferocious persecution of the Ukrainian people by the Moscow dictatorship, which beginning back in 1918—when the Bolsheviks forcibly seized Ukraine, which in accordance with the will of its inhabitants and their desire for self-determination had been formed into the Ukrainian National Republic—has continued with unabated force to this day."[27]

---

[26] *The Holodomor Reader: A Sourcebook on the Famine of 1932–1933 in Ukraine*, comp. and ed. Bohdan Klid and Alexander J. Motyl (Edmonton: CIUS Press, 2012), 298–99.
[27] Ibid., 299–300.

The lack of response to this appeal did not stop Ukrainian activists from directing their protests to leading US officials against the planned official recognition of the Soviet Union and the establishment of official diplomatic relations. On November 16, 1933 Revyuk and Myshuha sent a new protest to the US State Department, urging the government not to recognize the Soviet Union.[28]

Other Ukrainian diaspora organizations also sent letters to the US president with information about the famine in Ukraine. On November 6, 1933, for example, the Committee of Salvation for Ukraine in Czechoslovakia sent a letter to the American leader. Because of its importance, I quote from it at length:

> In Soviet Ukraine people are dying out from starvation. This famine is no casual phenomenon, nor is it a calamity due to natural causes. The system of Bolshevistic dictature with its anti-Ukrainian policy is responsible for it. Forcible collectivization of the entire land-industry in Ukraine ruined completely the Ukrainian agricultural population and called about the actual disaster. The horrible famine which already caused the death of hundreds of thousands or perhaps even millions of people—for accurate figures can, of course, not be established—is attested not only by heartbreaking letters from Ukraine, but also by reports of foreign—chiefly American and English journalists who, in spite of all bolshevistic restrictions succeeded in visiting the most hunger stricken territories.
>
> The existence of an extremely acute famine in Soviet-Ukraine and Kuban cannot be denied recently even by the Sovietic authorities themselves, though as recently as in last summer, when the calamity already ravaged the country they were categorically refuting it by their Press-office (Tass).
>
> Referring to abundant crops of this year in Ukraine, Sovietic authorities are excluding every possibility of this disaster being repeated anew. Still, competent experts well acquainted with the situation in Ukraine, are convinced of the inevitability of a new hunger-calamity in 1934, especially towards the end of winter and the beginning of spring. The same is stated in the known memorandum, from 19.VIII.1933 issued by D-r Ammende who was the first to move a project and international relief-action on behalf of the famished population under the Soviets.
>
> The fact of a tremendously dangerous famine particularly in Ukraine, has been acknowledged in a special meeting of the Council of the League of Nations of September the 29th. It has been adopted there to pass the matter over for close study to the International Red Cross, as an institution

[28] Telegram. Jersey City, November 16, 1933. Department of State, Washington. United Ukrainian Organization of the United States. Emil Revyuk, President. Dr. Luka Myshuha, Secretary, in US NARA, T-1241, roll 2, fr. 0131–0133.

most of all able to carry out on a large scale a universal relief-action behalf of the victims of the famine to came.

In Austria, on personal initiative of the Archbishop of Vienna, Cardinal Dr Innitzer, there was founded in October of this year an inter-confessional Committee of welfare of the perishing population under the Soviets.

Ukrainians of Western Ukrainian lands, who live beyond the boundaries of Soviet Ukraine, were, of course, eager to raise their voices in defense of their brethren.

As early as in July 1933 an "Ukrainian Central Relief-Committee on behalf of Soviet Ukraine" having been formed at Lviv began to alarm the public opinion in order to organize a planned work of assistance for Ukraine. Similar committees have been since instituted in all countries where there are Ukrainians, whether autochthons or immigrants. [...]

The Committee of Salvation for Ukraine of Prague, consisting of representants of the various Ukrainian institutions in Czechoslovakia, being the centre of the most numerous Ukrainian emigration in Europe, are joining the appeal of our American kinsmen and supporting their petition to the Government of the United States.

We are certain that the country of traditional democracy, the fatherland of Washington and Lincoln, a state that has given to the world the Independence declaration of 4.VII.1776, that has conquered its freedom by way of revolution against alien occupation, the country that so generously came to the rescue of the Sovietic population during the terrible famine of 1921–22, the great American nation would now again answer this appeal of Ukrainians, who are not giving up their strenuous efforts to conquer freedom and who paid for their right to independent life by going into death for the national cause.[29]

However, like many other Ukrainian appeals, including from Ukrainian Americans, this one was ignored. On November 16, 1933 President Roosevelt sent a letter to the People's Commissar of Foreign Affairs of the USSR Maxim Litvinov announcing Washington's decision to establish full diplomatic relations. American leaders continued to turn a blind eye to the deaths of millions in Ukraine, the Kuban, and other areas in the Soviet Union.

Since the US leadership did not respond to the written appeals of Ukrainian Americans, activists decided to stage a large protest meeting to attract the attention of the US through the press and political parties, and to call on the political leadership to help in one way or another because their compatriots were dying from the "Red famine." Learning of the preparations for this protest, planned for New York City, American communists attempted to thwart the peaceful gathering, and only police

---

[29] Committee of Salvation for Ukraine in Czechoslovakia. Prague, 6.XI.1933. To His Excellency, President of United States..., in US NARA, roll 31, fr. 0271–0274.

intervention ensured that the event took place in a relatively calm fashion on November 18, 1933. The demonstration was attended by 8,000 Ukrainians, who marched from George Washington Square to the Central Opera House between 67th Street and Third Avenue. The protest meeting was guarded by 300 police officers, including an armed unit, to ensure the safety of the protesters. A report in *The New York Times* said that a group of communists was arrested among some 500 protesters who had not been authorized to hold an alternative protest meeting and who were intent on disrupting the Ukrainian demonstration.

The newspaper report also mentions the reasons why the protest meeting was held. Shortly afterwards, a report to the US State Department described the reasons for the clash between American communists and the Ukrainians who were protesting against the Bolshevik famine in Ukraine: "Communist sympathizers tried to break up the meeting convened for the purpose of a peaceful protest against the Communist Government failure to help the starving population of Soviet Ukraine. Nineteen Communist hecklers were arrested before the meeting could proceed in order."[30]

Ukrainian organizations in the US did not lose hope that the country's leadership would accept their protests and send help to their compatriots in Ukraine. On November 13, 1933 the Ukrainian National Women's League of America (UNWLA), at a meeting of its departments in New York and the surrounding area, decided to set up an Emergency Relief Committee. The newly formed body was headed by Neonila (Nellie) Pelecovych and included Pavlyna Avramenko, Petrunela Kostetska, Olha Petrenko, and Julia Yarema. On October 2, they wrote a memorandum calling for assistance to Ukraine, which they sent to President Roosevelt and later to his wife, Eleanor, congressmen, senators, members of government, various organizations, and the press. The memo was also sent to humanitarian organizations, such as the American Red Cross and the International Committee of the Red Cross in Geneva.[31]

On November 21, 1933 a copy of the memorandum was sent to Secretary of State Cordell Hull. After briefly describing the history of Ukrainians, the authors make an emotional plea for help:

> The famine in Ukraine is the culmination of that unremitting and ferocious persecution of the Ukrainian people by Moscow dictatorship, which beginning back in 1918—when the Bolsheviks forcibly seized Ukraine which in accordance with the will of its inhabitants and their

---

[30] Telegram. Jersey City, November 16, 1933. Department of State... United Ukrainian Organization of the United States... in US NARA, T-1241, roll 2, fr. 0132.

[31] *Nashe zhyttia* (New York) 60, November 2003, no. 11, 1.

desire for self-determination had been formed into the Ukrainian National Republic, and which subsequently was overthrown by the Reds—has continued with unabated force to this day.

The memorandum included a special request to help homeless children as the most vulnerable victims of the Soviet man-made famine:

> Immediately following the World War, Ukraine became the hot-bed of even a more destructive civil war, which was in turn followed by the dark years of Bolshevik barbaric terrorism, reminiscent of the darkest ages of mankind, and which has continued to this very day, culminating in the present famine. Throughout these long years of wars, uprisings and cruel suppressions, the Ukrainian children have been the innocent victims of human strife and greed. Today, with the approach of the severe Ukrainian winter the position of these poor children, starving and homeless, seems even more desperate than ever before. And therefore, in view of all of these circumstances, so briefly outlined herein, we, American women of Ukrainian descent, on behalf of these children and starving [population] appeal to your sense of justice and humanity on behalf of millions of starving Ukrainians; and furthermore, in view of the facts that the Bolshevik authorities in their efforts to screen this terrible famine do not permit the sending of any aid whatsoever to the famine-striken [*sic*] Ukraine, we appeal to you to prevail upon the American Red Cross to establish a Red Cross base in Ukraine which shall serve as a medium of help sent by the Ukrainians and other peoples throughout the world.[32]

Despite all these appeals, the highest political leadership of the United States continued to adhere to a policy of silence, used euphemisms to disguise the fact that a humanitarian catastrophe was unfolding in Ukraine, and ignored the calls of Ukrainian organizations to help the starving and try to put a stop to the mass starvation. President Roosevelt and the head of the US Department of State generally refused to respond to the letters. On December 15, when Kelley replied to the above-cited letter, he did not even mention the word "famine" in relation to Ukraine, and clearly articulated the indifferent position of his country's leadership in the following brief statement: "In reply to your letter of 11 November 1933, addressed to the President, which was referred to this Department for attention, concerning

---

[32] Memorandum of the Ukrainian National Women's League of America, to the Secretary of State concerning the Famine of the Ukrainians in Soviet Russia. [To] Mr. Cordell Hull, Secretary of State, Washington, D.C. Ukrainian National Women's League of America. [Signed — Helen D. Lototsky] (Mrs.) Helen D. Lototsky, President. Emergency Relief Committee [Signed — Nellie Pelecovich] (Miss) Nellie Pelecovich, Chairman [Signed— Kostetski,] (Mrs.) Petrunella Kostetski, Secretary, in US NARA, T-1249, roll 31, fr. 0255–0256.

conditions in the Ukraine, you are informed that there does not appear to be any measure which this Government can appropriately take at the present time in this matter."[33]

On October 2, 1933 Stephen Skoblak, president of the Ukrainian National Council in Canada, sent a letter to President Roosevelt asking for help for the millions of starving people in Ukraine:

> We are taking the liberty of directing your attention to the deplorable fact that for a considerable time the population of Eastern Ukraine (now under a military Bolshevik occupation) are being systematically starved by the Moscow authorities. The tragedy of the great famine of 1921–22, when nearly ten million people died from hunger, is being repeated, but in all probability on a still larger scale. Thousands of letters are being received in Canada continuously, containing gruesome details of the vast number dying; there are settlements in Ukraine where only one-third—sometimes only one-fourth—of the original population are still alive. Crop failure is not the reason for this famine, but the brutal policy of the Moscow rulers who, needing grain for export to balance their budget, pitilessly take everything from the farmers, already proletarized. Especially in Ukraine, where the peasants are opposed to the foreign Russian rule, are they being deprived of literally everything, being left without even the smallest ration for daily meals, under the excuse that they are hiding food. With such tactics, even a bumper crop, of huge yield, could not save these people from starvation. Having in mind the tragic plight of their compatriots, and realising their moral duty in the matter, the Ukrainian National Council in Canada turn to you, as to a leader of a great civilized nation, with an urgent request to take the necessary steps to arrange for an immediate neutral investigation of the famine situation in Ukraine, with a view to organizing international relief action for the stricken population. Any private action, even on the largest scale, would prove inadequate owing to the magnitude of the calamity. We are prepared to supply you, if necessary, with original documents and information giving details of the famine conditions.[34]

The letter was delivered to the US Consul General in Winnipeg and included a bulletin describing the famine in Ukraine:

[33] December 15, 1933. [To] Mrs. Nellie Pelecovich, Chairman, Ukrainian National Woman's League of America, 307 East 10th Street, New York, New York. Robert F. Kelley, Chief, Division of Eastern European Affairs, in US NARA, T-1249, roll 31, fr. 0257.

[34] The Ukrainian National Council of Canada. October 2nd, 1933. President Franklin D. Roosevelt, President of the United States of America, Washington, D.C. Chairman of Advisory Board. President [Signed:] S. Skoblak. Chairman of Advisory Board [Signed:] L. Biberovich. Secretary [Signed:] J. M. Bajdack, in US NARA, T-1249, roll 31, fr. 0246.

There were several cases [...] where parents have eaten their own children in a state of insanity caused by extended starvation. [...] The conditions in Ukraine were bad enough in 1930, but in 1931 they became really critical. The present situation is as follows. There is literally no broad there; no potatoes [...]; no meat, no sugar; in a word, nothing of the basic necessities of life. Last year some food was obtainable occasionally for money, but this year most of the bazaars (markets) are closed and empty. All cats and dogs disappeared, having perished or been eaten by the hungry farmers. [...] There are many cases of suicide, mostly by hanging, among the village population, and also many mental alienations. The famine in Soviet Ukraine in 1921 was undoubtedly a terrible one, but it appears like child's play in comparison with the present situation. [...] First of all, there is no escape from this hell on earth, as no one can obtain permission to leave the boundaries of Ukraine, once the granary of Europe, and now a valley of tears and hunger.[35]

Unfortunately, this appeal to President Roosevelt was also ignored. On November 20, 1933 the State Department wrote to the US Consul General in Winnipeg: "The Acting Secretary of State has received, by reference from the White House, a letter of October 2, 1933, addressed to the President by Mr. S. Skoblak, President of the Ukrainian National Council in Canada, corner Florida Avenue and McKenzie Street, Winnipeg. In his letter, Mr. Skoblak describes the sufferings for lack of food of persons in the Ukraine, and, on behalf of the Ukrainian National Council in Canada, urges the President 'to take the necessary steps to arrange for an immediate neutral investigation of the famine situation in Ukraine, with a view to organizing international relief action for the stricken population.'" The reply from the State Department rather cynically directed the US Consul General in Winnipeg "to inform Mr. Skoblak that, as the conditions to which he refers do not appear directly to affect American citizens or interests, the Department is not in a position to take any action."[36]

The catastrophic famine in Ukraine was also known to representatives of the Jewish community in the US. In December 1933 Rabbi Manuel Laderman of Denver (Colorado) sent a telegram to the White House: "[Agency] Associated Press [on] December 17 [from] Vienna reports: Cardinal Innitzer heads movement [aiming] to ship surplus wheat [and] other foodstuffs to famine centers [in] Ukraine and North Caucasus [for the purpose] to save millions lives. I know of many letters telling frightful starvation there. People

---

[35] Ukrainian National Council of Canada. Bulletin No. I. Winnipeg, Sept. 15, 1933, in US NARA, T-1249, roll 31, fr. 0247–0249.

[36] November 20, 1933. To the American Consul General, Winnipeg, Manitoba, Canada, in US NARA, T-1249, roll 31, fr. 0250.

write highest hope is to taste bread again. Cannot Red Cross or other American agency do something to help [?]"[37]

On January 22, 1934 the US State Department responded negatively to this latest request for assistance:

> The receipt is acknowledged, by reference from the White House, of your telegram of December 28, 1933, addressed to the President, concerning conditions in the Ukraine, and suggesting that the American Red Cross or some other American agency take some action to help persons living there. In reply, you are informed that, according to the Department's information, the American Red Cross does not undertake to carry on relief operations abroad except upon the request, or by the consent, of the Government of the country in question; and that the Department is not in a position to suggest the name of any other American agency which might be interested in this matter. It may be added that, since the conditions to which you refer do not appear directly to affect American citizens or interests, this Government is not in a position to take any action in the matter.[38]

Among the American politicians who received the aforementioned memorandum from the Ukrainian National Women's League of America was Congressman Herman Kopplemann, who was of Jewish-Ukrainian origin. He obtained this document from Olena Horbal, head of the League's Ansonia (Connecticut) branch. On December 14, 1933 Kopplemann sent a request to Maxim Litvinov, the People's Commissar for Foreign Affairs of the USSR, asking him to comment on this document, a copy of which was appended to his letter. Litvinov cynically replied to the congressman that the memorandum was part and parcel of "such pamphlets full of lies circulated by counter-revolutionary organizations abroad, who specialize in the work of this kind" in order to "spread false information."[39]

Litvinov, who had no intentions of making any official pronouncements on the subject of the mass deaths of Ukrainians in the USSR as a result of the famine, instructed Boris Skvirsky, the press attaché (and future ambassador) of the USSR in Washington to write a reply to Kopplemann. In accordance with this directive, on February 3, 1934 Skvirsky informed the congressman that the information provided by the Ukrainian National Women's League of America was "wholly grotesque." He denied the mass

---

[37] Western Union. 1933, Dec 28, am 12 19. [To] The President, White House, Washington D.C. Rabbi Manuel, in US NARA, T-1249, roll 31, fr. 0281.

[38] Jan 22, 1934. [To] Rabbi Manuel Laderman, Denwer, Colorado. Robert F. Kelley, Chief, Division of Eastern European Affairs, in US NARA, T-1249, roll 31, fr. 0282–0283.

[39] *Holodomor Reader*, 301.

deaths in Ukraine resulting from the lack of food: "The death rate was the lowest of that of any of the seven constituent republics composing the Soviet Union, and was about 35 per cent lower than the pre-war death rate of Tsarist days."[40]

As was the case in many other countries, the US government did not protest against the genocidal policy of the Soviet leadership when diplomatic relations were being established with the USSR in November 1933. The possibility of helping the starving population or at least protesting the mass destruction of millions of people by famine was sacrificed or ignored to achieve other diplomatic goals. In the same way, the world remained generally silent during the Holocaust. Only a few congressmen heeded the appeals and protests of the Ukrainian diaspora in the United States. On May 29, 1934, during the Second Session of the 73rd Congress, Congressman Hamilton Fish signed House Resolution 399 in the House of Representatives, which he forwarded to the Committee on Foreign Affairs. It states:

> Whereas several millions of the population of the Ukrainian Soviet Socialist Republic, the constituent part of the Union of Soviet Socialist Republics, died of starvation during the years of 1932 and 1933; and
>
> Whereas the Government of the Union of Soviet Socialist Republics, although being fully aware of the famine in Ukraine and although having full and complete control of the entire food supplies within its borders, nevertheless failed to take relief measure designed to check the famine or to alleviate the terrible conditions arising from it, but on the contrary used the famine as a means of reducing the Ukrainian population and destroying the Ukrainian political, cultural, and national rights; and
>
> Whereas intercessions have been made at various times by the United States during the course of its history on behalf of citizens of states other than the United States, oppressed or persecuted by their own governments, indicating that it has been the traditional policy of the United States to take cognizance of such invasions of human rights and liberties: Therefore be it
>
> RESOLVED, That the House of Representatives express its sympathy for all those who have suffered from the great famine in Ukraine which has brought misery, affliction, and death to millions of peaceful and law-abiding Ukrainians; be it further
>
> RESOLVED, That the House of Representatives express its earnest hope that the Government of the Union of Soviet Socialist Republics will speedily alter its policy in respect to the famine in Ukraine, take active steps to alleviate the terrible consequences arising from this famine, and undo so far as may be possible the injustices to the Ukrainian people; and be it further

[40] Ibid., 301–2.

> RESOLVED, That the House of Representatives express its sincerest hope that the Union of Soviet Socialist Republics Government will place no obstacles in the way of American citizens seeking to send aid in [the] form of money, foodstuffs, and necessities to the famine-stricken regions of Ukraine.[41]

It is noteworthy that the United States continued to be interested in the famine after 1933. In May 1935 the State Department requested the US Embassy in Moscow to provide information on whether there had been a famine in the USSR in 1934 and 1935. In October 1935 the US Ambassador prepared a report to this effect, stating that "over the last twelve months, there has been a severe shortage of food in various regions of the country, including in some peripheral regions, and many people's health has deteriorated often as a result of failure to obtain adequate and sufficient food." The author of the note concludes sharply: "The information obtained by the Embassy gives grounds to claim that a significant number of people have died of starvation in the last twelve months in the Soviet Union."[42]

Half a century after the genocide, the Ukrainian diaspora appealed to the US government to set up a commission to study the circumstances surrounding the famine in Ukraine in 1932–33. Congress supported this initiative, which was largely facilitated by the Reagan administration.

The facts presented in American archival documents and various publications demonstrate that the US Department of State was certainly well informed about the reality of the Great Famine in Ukraine. The president, members of his cabinet, and congressmen also knew about it but, like the governments of other countries, they did not consider it necessary to make the necessary efforts to save millions of people from starving to death.

More research is needed to bring to light documents containing information about collectivization, the so-called "liquidation of kulaks as a class" and the famines in Ukraine, the Kuban, and other areas of the former Soviet Union. Particular attention is required to determine what officials of the US Department of State and other departments knew about the causes, course, scale, and consequences of collectivization and the Holodomor. Equally important are documents on related issues, such as the USSR's nationality policy, repressive measures instituted by the GPU, and living conditions in Ukraine and elsewhere during the famine period.

---

[41] Ibid., 300–1.

[42] Carynnyk, "Blind Eye to Murder," 122–23.

Archives

Informatsiino-dovidkovyi zal Haluzevoho derzhavnoho arkhivu Sluzhby bezpeky Ukraïny u Kyievi (HDA SBU). Kolektsiia dokumentiv 01.02, Dokumenty karal'no-represyvnoï systemy SRSR, 01.02.03 — Holodomory, 01.02.03.01. 1921–1923 rokiv, 01.02.03.01.02. Dokumenty taiemnoho dilovodstva, fol. 84 (22.11.2011).

National Archives and Records Administration in Washington [NARA]. Record Group No. 0220, no. A1 40325 A; A1 40325 B; A1 40325 C

NARA, RG 59, Stack area 250, Row 30, CDF, 1930–1939, Box 6612, Doc. No 860E.01/141–175; 860E.01BII/14–860E.652/I.

NARA, T-1241, roll 2.

NARA, T-1249, roll 31, 34, 35, 36, 40.

Rossiiskii gosudarstvennyi arkhiv ekonimiki (Russian State Archive of the Economy, RGAE), f. 413, op. 13, d. 645

RGAE, f. 8043, op. 11, d. 29, l.

Bibliography

Carynnyk, M. "Blind Eye to Murder: Britain, the United States and the Ukrainian Famine of 1933." In *Famine in Ukraine, 1932–1933*, edited by Roman Serbyn and Bohdan Krawchenko, 109–38. Edmonton: Canadian Institute of Ukrainian Studies, 1986.

Fisher, H. H. *The Famine in Soviet Russia, 1919–1923: The Operations of the American Relief Administration*. New York: Macmillan, 1927.

Investigation of the Ukrainian Famine, 1932–1933: Oral History Project of the Commission on the Ukraine Famine, edited by James E. Mace and Leonid Heretz. vols. 1–3. Washington: U.S. G.P.O., 1990.

Leshuk, L. *US Intelligence Perceptions of Soviet Power, 1921–1946*. London and Portland, Ore.: Frank Cass, 2003.

Morris, W. M. *Stalin's Famine and Roosevelt's Recognition of Russia*. Lanham, Md.: University Press of America, 1994.

Nashe zhyttia. (*Our life)*, edited by Irena Chaban, Tamara Stadnychenko, Lev Chaban, no. 11 (November 2003).

The Holodomor Reader: A Sourcebook on the Famine of 1932–1933 in Ukraine, comp. and ed. Bohdan Klid and Alexander J. Motyl. Edmonton and Toronto: CIUS Press, 2012.

Representations of the 1932–33 Ukrainian Famine in the USC Shoah Foundation's Visual History Archive

Inna Gogina

Eighty-eight years ago, millions of Ukraine's inhabitants were starved to death as a result of policies implemented by Joseph Stalin's totalitarian regime. The man-made famine of 1932–33, also known as the Holodomor, was a catastrophe that occurred not in a time of war but in peacetime. Today, almost nine decades later, there is no consensus among scholars on how to define the Holodomor. Ukraine and many other countries have recognized it as a genocide of the Ukrainian people carried out by the Soviet Union. Other countries have recognized it as a deliberate act of terror and mass murder against the Ukrainian people. Finally, some governments continue to deny that the famine was manmade, attributing it to natural causes. This paper does not tackle the issue of definition, but instead draws attention to the value of personal memories as recorded in oral history interviews.

As time passes, the details of historic events that occurred in the past begin to fade; so does individual and collective memory. How do we ensure that tragic events resulting in millions of lives lost are never forgotten? Personal eyewitness accounts allow us to gain an understanding of the full scale of the tragedy by learning about the impact of the tragic events on individuals. How do we make the voices of eyewitnesses heard in the twenty-first century and beyond? To address these challenges, in the past thirty years many institutions across the globe have leveraged evolving preservation and information technologies and engaged in developing digital collections aimed at heritage preservation, including documents, images, and audiovisual digital records. Memory preservation projects have gained momentum. This paper explores the Holodomor oral history testimonies that are preserved in one of the largest digital archives of individual memory in the world—the USC Shoah Foundation Visual History Archive (VHA).

Background

When researching Holodomor archival collections outside the former Soviet Union, one does not make an immediate connection with the USC Shoah Foundation's Visual History Archive—for an obvious reason: the difference in the collection's archival provenance and scope. The Survivors of the

Shoah Visual History Foundation—the USC Shoah Foundation's predecessor—was established by Steven Spielberg in 1994 in order to collect and preserve video testimonies from survivors and other witnesses to the Holocaust. Originally a repository of Holocaust testimony, the VHA has since expanded to include testimonies of survivors of the Armenian Genocide, the 1937 Nanjing Massacre in China, the 1975–79 Cambodian Genocide, the 1978–83 Guatemalan Genocide, the 1994 Genocide against the Tutsi in Rwanda, the ongoing conflicts in the Central African Republic and South Sudan, and the 2017 anti-Rohingya mass violence. Today, the USC Shoah Foundation Visual History Archive is considered one of the largest digital audiovisual archives of its kind in the world. Housed at the University of Southern California, it preserves and provides access to nearly 55,000 oral history interviews recorded in 65 countries, in 43 languages—a total of 115,000 hours of testimony footage.[1]

While the scope of the VHA interviews is dedicated to the Holocaust and other genocides and crimes against humanity and even though the Holodomor was not envisioned as a distinct collection in the VHA at its inception, the interviews in its main, Holocaust collection were structured so as to encompass the entire life of the interviewees, from childhood to the genocide events, then on to their post-genocide lives. It is during the preWorld War II discussions that the Holocaust survivors and witnesses recall their life in 1932–33, the period of the Ukrainian famine.

Holodomor accounts in the VHA

The Visual History Archive content related to Ukraine is very diverse. Approximately 10,000 interviewees were born within Ukraine's current borders. Every fourth interviewee in the archive speaks about the events he or she experienced while living there before, during, or after the World War II. Among them are 3,433 interviews conducted in Ukraine, with 348 interviews conducted in the Ukrainian language and 44 in a combination of Russian and Ukrainian.

Today, 789 testimonies in the VHA's Holocaust collection discuss the 1932–33 Ukrainian Famine. They include 775 testimonies collected by the USC Shoah Foundation, as well as some provided by partners: Jewish Family and Children's Services (JFCS) Holocaust Center (10), the Calgary Jewish Federation (2), the Blavatnik Archive Foundation (1), and the Montreal Holocaust Museum (1).

[1] Data shown in this paper reflect the VHA holdings as of November 1, 2019.

VHA experience groups

The two largest Visual History Archive experience groups discussing the Holodomor include *Jewish Survivor* testimonies (622) and *Holocaust Rescuer and Aid Provider* testimonies (132). Additional experience groups include Jehovah's Witness Survivor (4), Liberator (11), Miscellaneous (Second World War) (5), Non-Jewish Forced Laborer (1), Political Prisoner (4), Sinti and Roma Survivor (9), and War Crimes Trial Participant (1).

Interviewee age and gender

The interviewee's age, as it relates to human memory, is an important factor in the oral history testimony historical accuracy assessment. The VHA interviewees discussing the Holodomor were born within a 49-year time frame, 1893–1942. The oldest interviewee, Mikhail Rakov (interview 45895), was born in 1893 in Yampil (Vinnytsia, Ukraine), which was part of the Russian Empire at the time. The youngest, Riva Kats (interview 40691), was born in 1942 in the same town, which was part of the Soviet Union at the time. Both were interviewed in Mohyliv-Podilskyi, Ukraine, in 1998.

That the historical accuracy of the accounts of those interviewees who were born during or after the events of 1932–33 can be questioned is beyond dispute. They speak about events not from first-hand experience; instead, their memories are based on stories they heard while growing up or on what they learned afterwards. Those who were four to six years old or older when the Holodomor took place, however, can speak about their experience first-hand. Born during the 1923–27 time frame, the five most representative age groups of VHA interviewees were six to ten years old at the time of the Great Famine: b. 1926 (86 interviewees, 10.9%), b. 1925 (84, 10.6%), b. 1923 (62, 7.9%), b. 1925 (60, 7.6%), and b. 1927 (60, 7.6%).

Three hundred and twelve of the interviewees discussing the Holodomor of 1932–33 are male (40%), and 477 interviewees are female (60%).

Interview language and country

The interviews were conducted in the interviewee's language of choice. The majority (712) provided their testimonies in Russian. Additional interview languages include Ukrainian (63), a combination of Russian and Ukrainian (9), English (3), and a combination of English and Russian (2).

The interviews discussing the Holodomor were recorded in 13 countries. Ukraine is the country with the largest number of famine-related testimonies (535, 67.8%), followed by Israel (109 testimonies, 13.8%), and USA (81 testimonies, 10.3%). Other countries include Russia (28), Moldova (9), Belarus (6), Canada (5), Germany (5), Latvia (4), Australia (3), Estonia (2), Georgia (1), and Uzbekistan (1).

Archival Discovery System

In order to facilitate archival discovery of the preserved interviews, the USC Shoah Foundation developed an indexing methodology[2] and designed an online discovery system (Visual History Archive), allowing users to search the indexed testimonies with a free-text search tool and four structured query types: Experience Groups search, Index search, People search, and Google Maps-based Places search.

Index Search and USC Shoah Foundation Thesaurus

The Index search is the VHA discovery tool that yields the highest precision rate of search results. It allows finding segments of testimonies by searching for pre-coordinated controlled vocabulary terms in the USC Shoah Foundation Thesaurus, which currently has nearly 70,000 indexing terms. The main indexing term related to the subject of this paper, *Ukrainian Famine (1932–1933)*, was introduced in the USCSF Thesaurus in 2004. Conducting an Index search for this term yields 789 testimonies and 854 testimony segments in the search results. Additional indexing terms related to the Ukrainian Famine of 1932–33 and its historic precursors include:

— *collectivization* (used in 75 testimonies)
— *kolkhoz* (used in 1,396 testimonies)
— *"dekulakization" (USSR, 1928–1933)* (used in 74 testimonies)
— *New Economic Policy (USSR, 1921–1927)* (used in 17 testimonies)
— *nationalization* (used in 630 testimonies)
— *USSR 1929 (December 27)–1939 (August 31)* (used in 3,608 testimonies)

The structure of the USC Shoah Foundation's Thesaurus is based on the ANSI/NISO Z39.19 Guidelines for the Construction, Format, and Management of Monolingual Thesauri, which employ a hierarchical arrangement to define the relationships between indexing terms. In the Thesaurus, time is associated with specific countries and with a single year or time frame, enabling the archive's users to search for a place and a time using a single keyword. The pre-coordinated indexing terms signifying place and time were designed to index single years and time frames to reflect the main scope of the archive's collections: the Holocaust and other genocides, such as *Germany 1933 (January 31)–1939 (August 31)*, *USSR 1941 (June 22)–1945 (May 7)*, etc. Owing to the scope limitations, the indexing term *USSR 1932–33* was not available in the Thesaurus, and the broader term *USSR 1929 (December 27)–1939 (August 31)* was used instead to index

[2] USC Shoah Foundation, University of Southern California (2006). *Indexing Guidelines*: http://sfi.usc.edu/sites/default/files/docfiles/Indexing_Guidelines_0.pdf

discussions of the period in Soviet history that preceded the World War II, including collectivization, dekulakization, and the Great Famine:

USSR 1929 (December 27)–1939 (August 31) (used in 3,608 testimonies)

On December 27, 1929 collectivization begins. The purge of the Communist Party begins on January 12, 1933. The Jewish Autonomous district is established on May 7, 1934. Mass repressions begin on December 1, 1934. On August 23, 1939 the Soviet Union signs the non-aggression pact with Germany. In a secret protocol the two countries carve out German and Soviet spheres of influence in Eastern Europe. Germany invades Poland on September 1, 1939; World War II then begins.[3]

The USCSF Thesaurus contains many additional indexing terms that can be used to discover related content. The VHA discovery system allows building compound, post-coordinated queries by combining several indexing terms in a single, Boolean search using Boolean AND/OR operators. Using such queries allows aggregating testimony content related to all indexing terms included in the search. Two examples below demonstrate Boolean searches discovering content related to terms that are not Holodomor-specific but which can be helpful in research on the topic: *cannibalism* and *death of loved ones* during the Great Famine, respectively:

— *cannibalism* AND *Ukrainian Famine (1932–1933)* (fuzzy/narrow search: 23 testimonies)

— *loved ones' deaths* AND *Ukrainian Famine (1932–1933)* (fuzzy/narrow search: 45 testimonies)

Eyewitness accounts of the 1932–33 Ukrainian Famine in the Visual History Archive

The eyewitness accounts derived from the VHA testimonies exemplify the following aspects of the Great Famine in Ukraine: collectivization, dekulakization, deportations, border patrols, export of grain, arrests, famine, deaths of loved ones, and resistance. Testimony excerpts are provided in English translation. The Soviet legislation that resulted in the humanitarian catastrophe is also discussed here, in order to provide historical context.

Collectivization

On January 5, 1930 the Central Committee of the All-Union Communist Party (Bolshevik) adopted a decree calling for the complete collectivization

[3] This indexing term was introduced on November 26, 1996.

of all grain-producing regions by the fall of 1931 or spring of 1932 at the latest, and for the elimination of the kulaks as a class.[4] Nykyfir Iakhnenko (b. 1914) and Anna Kakhno (b. 1924) remember the implementation of the Soviet collectivization measures in their hometowns.

Nykyfir Iakhnenko, born in Kirovo (Nemyriv, Vinnytsia oblast)

Int.: Do you remember the year 1933 in any particular way?

NI: Of course I do; it was the famine then. They were taking people away while they were still alive, you know? Children, men—they were not dead yet, still alive, but they drove them out to the cemetery—clearly, to save an extra trip. That's it. It was a very difficult—how should I put it—story, the barbarism of Stalin's foul henchmen, you know?

Int.: How did it happen? What was the reason for the famine in Ukraine?

NI: What do you mean, 'how'? They cleaned everything out, you understand? Cleaned everything out. And because they were barbarians. Had there been no barbarians then… Well, let's say I was ordered to search, would I have searched for the bowl of millet in the compost pit? Even if I had found it, I would never have taken it out! But those people, they were narrow-minded pillagers, they shook out the grain with a broom. And they divided this grain among themselves, and that's why peasants had nothing left to eat.

Int.: Nykyfir Hryhorovych, did they shake down your house for grain, too?

NI: But of course! My younger brother, Grisha, starved to death.

Int.: How did it happen? Who swept the grain out?

NI: Who? Well, the Communists. Organized brigades were formed at that time. They were called the Red Broom. They came to every hoouse and swept everything out, you understand?

Int.: Were these Communists local?

NI: Local Communists.

Int.: From your village?

NI: Yes, from my village.

IN. Do you remember these people?

NI: Why wouldn't I remember them? Iosyp Lazarovych Iakhnenko…

Int.: Was he related to you?

---

[4] Decree of the Central Committee of the All-Union Communist Party (Bolsheviks) on the rate of collectivization and measures of state assistance to collective farm construction, January 5, 1930, in *Tragediia sovetskoi derevni: Kollektivizatsiia i raskulachivanie: Dokumenty i materialy*, vol. 2: November 1929–December 1930 (Moscow: ROSSPEN, 2000), 85–86.

NI: No, just the same last name. What's his name...the head of the village council was Pavlov. Then, Iulik Mudrak... Then, who else, uh, besides those shakers—Taras Smychok. Well, it was a large brigade, about 20 people.

Int.: Did they use violence or persuade people?

NI: But who cared about persuading at the time? Who needed to persuade anybody if they did not have a single kernel left?! So, people would hide it under the oven, in the compost pit, everywhere. But they would search for this grain, sweep it out, and the peasants did not have a single kernel left to feed themselves.[5]

Anna Kakhno, born in Kovalivka (Nemyriv, Vinnytsia oblast)

AK: Those were difficult years. The Soviet rule came down. Life was hard. Life under Stalin was tough all over because everything had been taken away from people, including my father. We were starving. The year 1930 began, collectivization started. My father did not want to join the kolkhoz. They took all of our household things away: the cow, the horses, all the tools, everything from our house, everything from our cellar. The clothes that we had on were all that remained. That's it. Bare walls in our house and nothing else. That's it. And that's how we had to live in 1930, 1931, 1932, and 1933—[there was a] terrible famine, because there was nothing left for anyone. They took everything away. There was nothing left.[6]

Int.: How did collectivization take place?

AK: How did it happen? At that time, they did not invite us, as in 'please, would you like to join or not', or 'if you'd like, please join, if not, you don't have to.' You HAD TO go. Go! Well, my dad—I don't know why he resisted, why he did not want to join the collective farm. He must have wanted to remain independent. So they took everything away. My father had five desiatinas. At that time there were desiatinas, not hectares. A total of five desiatinas of land. A pair of horses, a cow. Well, there were about five sheep. That's all. Two or three pigs. Well, chickens and geese—that was entire our farmstead. That's it. My father was not rich, but he worked very hard, because he had to provide for the family—to feed and clothe us all. So, he did not go to the kolkhoz then, and as a result they took away everything that we owned—everything. They pulled down our barns, took away

---

[5] Iakhnenko, Nykyfir. Interview 36663. Experience group: Rescue and Aid. Language: Ukrainian. Segments 14–17. Visual History Archive, USC Shoah Foundation, 1997. Accessed October 20, 2019.

[6] Kakhno, Anna. Interview 38045. Experience group: Rescue and Aid. Language: Ukrainian. Segments 4–5. Visual History Archive, USC Shoah Foundation, 1997. Accessed October 20, 2019.

everything, our cattle, everything from the house. We had only bare walls left; no table, no bench, no chair—nothing was left.

Int.: Who took your belongings?

AK: Who took [them]... There was the head of the kolkhoz, the head of the village council—that was a so-called 'brigade.' There, well... I don't recall all the details, but I remember well that they came to us every day. And every day they searched everywhere, because they thought that father had buried the grain somewhere. But we never had any extra grain to bury. There was never enough. That's it. Then later, after all of that, my father joined the kolkhoz anyway, because he had no choice, we had to live somehow. So, we all started working in the kolkhoz then, the entire family: father, mother, and I started working in the kolkhoz, too. That's it. And we lived that way until the war began.[7]

Dekulakization

Stalin's totalitarian machine was working full throttle. In order to enforce the January 5, 1930 decree of continuous collectivization, the Soviet government followed up with two additional directives within a matter of days. On January 30, 1930 the Politburo of the Central Committee of the All-Union Communist Party (Bolshevik) adopted a decree calling for the confiscation of the means of production, livestock, farm and residential buildings, processing plants, and feed and seed stocks from kulaks in these regions.[8] Three days later, on February 2, 1930, the Joint State Political Directorate (OGPU) adopted the Order on Measures for the Liquidation of the Kulak as a Class. It called for the "immediate liquidation of the counterrevolutionary kulak core, especially the cadres of existing counterrevolutionary and rebel organizations and groups, and the most malicious individual terrorists (first category)," and for the "mass expulsion (primarily from areas of complete collectivization and the borderland) of the richest kulaks (former landowners, sublandlords, local kulak authorities, and the entire kulak cadre from which the counterrevolutionary core, the kulak anti-Soviet core of churchmen and

[7] Kakhno, Anna. Interview 38045. Experience group: Rescue and Aid. Language: Ukrainian. Segments 16–19. Visual History Archive, USC Shoah Foundation, 1997. Accessed October 20, 2019.

[8] "On Measures to Eliminate Kulak Farms in Areas of Continuous Collectivization," Politburo of the Central Committee of the All-Union Communist Party (Bolsheviks), January 30, 1930 (Moscow: Russian Historic Society, Electronic Library), http://docs.historyrussia.org/ru/nodes/78140-postanovlenie-tsk-vkp-b-o-meropriyatiyah-po-likvidatsii-kulatskih-hozyaystv-v-rayonah-sploshnoy-kollektivizatsii-30-yanvarya-1930-g

sectarians are formed) and their families to remote northern regions of the USSR and confiscation of their property (second category)."[9]

Here is how two VHA interviewees, Ivan Honchar (b. 1926) and Anatolii Gelman (b. 1912), remember the Soviet dekulakization process.

Ivan Honchar, born in Osypenky (Vinnytsia oblast)

IH: We were a family of ordinary peasants, farmers. What did we have? My father... we had a house thatched with straw, divided into two parts. My father's parents lived in one half, and my family occupied the other half. This was one large room, a dirt floor, no floor covering, no division into rooms. Everything was in that room; we all lived there together. Well... Here is what my father owned: There was a cow, and there was a horse, co-owned with the neighbor, and there was a small plow. I know that. That was all. But for some reason, our family was placed on the dekulakization list.

Int.: What is 'dekulakization'?

IH: What is it, you say? 'Kulaks' was a term coined for the rich peasants who, say, exploited others, were rich, so they were supposed to join collective farms, the kolkhozes, first. When collectivization began in the early 1930s, it was proposed to my parents that they also join the kolkhoz. Well, people did not really go there of their own free will, because they had to turn everything they owned over to the collective farm: cows, horses, and the same plow, and everything else; turn it to the kolkhoz. So, people joined but not really willingly. And those who resisted, who did not want to join, were subject to certain measures—dekulakization. This is what dekulakization meant.

Int.: What kind of measures were they?

IH: What kind? First they approached my father: come join the kolkhoz. He declined for the time being. Not that he rejected it altogether; he must have decided to try wait it out. Then they started to come and threaten him with arrest. Father ran away and hid.

Int.: Who came for him then?

IH: Members of the Komnezam [Committee of Poor Peasants]. They were armed with guns, those Komnezam people. Father ran away and hid with distant relatives for several months.[10]

---

[9] OGPU Order on Measures for the Liquidation of the Kulak as a Class, February 2, 1930, #44/21 (Moscow: Russian Historic Society, Electronic Library), http://docs.historyrussia.org/ru/nodes/49508-iz-prikaza-ogpu-44-21-o-meropriyatiyah-po-likvidatsii-kulachestva-kak-klassa-2-fevralya-1930-g

[10] Honchar, Ivan. Interview 29137. Experience group: Rescue and Aid. Language: Ukrainian. Segments 12–14. Visual History Archive, USC Shoah Foundation, 1997. Accessed October 20, 2019.

Int.: Ivan Denysovych, why do you think people were starving to death at that time?

IH: Well, why starving to death? Because many were subject to the same treatment as we were. What was there to dekulakize in a family like ours? We really were not rich. Our family had nothing special, nothing that would merit special attention. Father paid taxes on time, worked really hard; both father and mother worked hard. So did other people. But when they cleaned everything out, took everything away... In our family, they literally cleaned out everything we had, even pots and pans, and took all of it away. And where else could we get anything?[11]

Anatolii Gelman, born in Kamianets-Podilskyi (Khmelnytskyi oblast)

AG: After the NEP [New Economic Policy], the dekulakization period began. They formed... I was an activist. They formed a brigade. The head of the brigade was the Communist Kolia Chaikovsky, and a Young Communist, Polia Metnik, was his assistant. And five or six others, I think, including me—all Komsomol members and Young Communists. We went to the village of Zelencha, in Dunaivtsi raion. It was the richest village in the area at the time. We were supposed to get dekulakization going there. A Jew named Shvidler lived in that village. He was the chairman of the consumer cooperative [*Potrebkooperatsiia*]. I knew him personally, so I stayed at his home. One night—this village is on the Trnava River, near the Polish border—somehow the Poles found out about the arrival of the dekulakization brigade. They broke into the village at night and killed everyone except me. Why not me? I was staying at Shvidler's, and when Shvidler heard the shooting—he lived near a forest—he said, 'Jump out of the window and run to the woods!' That is how I survived. I kept running for almost two hours straight. I was not myself when I reached home. This was my experience of the voluntary—so-called "voluntary"—collectivization that was carried out at that time.[12]

Arrests

Arrests aimed at suppressing local resistance during the mass collectivization shaped the early childhood memories of the VHA interviewees Boris Rekhtman (b. 1928) and Ivan Honchar (b. 1926).

[11] Honchar, Ivan. Interview 29137. Experience group: Rescue and Aid. Language: Ukrainian. Segments 19–20. Visual History Archive, USC Shoah Foundation, 1997. Accessed October 20, 2019.

[12] Gel'man, Anatolii. Interview 47344. Experience group: Jewish survivor. Language: Russian. Segments 66–68. Visual History Archive, USC Shoah Foundation, 1998. Accessed October 20, 2019.

Boris Rekhtman, born in Ternivka (Dzhulynka, Vinnytsia oblast)

BR: My first memories go back to around 1932. I was four years old then. I remember people dressed in police uniforms coming to search our home, searching for a long time, and then taking my father away. It was the time when they began building socialism, and they needed money. So they took my father away in order to beat some gold, money out of him. They took him to Dzhulynka and put him in jail. They beat him many times there, placed him in sewage, with feces up to his neck, and even swore to drown him in there. But since we had no money at the time and we were not wealthy, it was obvious that the accusation was false; they kept him there for six weeks and let him go home.[13]

Ivan Honchar, born in Osypenky (Vinnytsia oblast)

IH: Then they arrested my mother, took her to the jail in Bratslav. She was imprisoned there for several months. There were three of us children; they kicked us out of our house. Our grandfather lived in the other half of the house. He had no one else; our grandmother had died, and he was alone. They re-housed us with him. Another family was housed in our home, dekulakized like us. Their house was in the center of the village, and it had been taken over by the new kolkhoz administration. The dekulakized family was re-assigned to our home, and they lived there. And we lived with my grandfather then.

Int.: Ivan Denysovych, you said that your mother was in prison. Was there a trial?

IH: There was no trial whatsoever.

Int.: So how did she end up in jail?

IH: How? With nobody conducting trials at that time? They took her away, brought her to Bratslav to the prison and left her there. In any case, there was no trial in the village. Well, when my parents returned, they realized that you couldn't do anything against the authorities. And they did join the collective farm, after all. And from then on they became kolkhoz members, just like all the other villagers.[14]

---

[13] Rekhtman, Boris. Interview 25086. Experience group: Jewish survivor. Language: Russian. Segments 6–7. Visual History Archive, USC Shoah Foundation, 1996. Accessed October 20, 2019.

[14] Honchar, Ivan. Interview 29137. Experience group: Rescue and Aid. Language: Ukrainian. Segments 14–15. Visual History Archive, USC Shoah Foundation, 1997. Accessed October 20, 2019.

Law of the Spikelets

When the spring 1932 collectivization target failed, the Central Executive Committee and the Council of People's Commissars of the USSR issued a punitive decree on August 7, 1932 titled "On Protection of the Property of State Enterprises, Collective Farms, and Cooperatives and Strengthening Public (Socialist) Property" and an instruction concerning its enforcement, known as the Law of the Spikelets, or Law of the Three Spikelets. According to the decree, the maximum penalty for theft was execution by shooting, and if there were extenuating circumstances the punishement was ten years' imprisonment.[15]

Boris Khalfin (b. 1926) remembers his father being arrested and sentenced to death for stealing one and a half kilograms of flour from a local mill in 1933.

Boris Khalfin, born in Dnipropetrovsk (today Dnipro)

BK: My father was a laborer, that is, he worked as a loader at a local mill, moonlighting at the market there. Then grandfather and grandmother helped him buy a horse and buggy, a *brychka* they used to call them. When he was working as a loader at the mill in 1933, during the famine, he was arrested for smuggling one and a half kilograms of flour. There was a trial, he was sentenced to death. Well, my mother went, she wrote to every place. He sat on death row for two months. Then they commuted—I don't remember, I was little—but I do remember that they commuted his sentence, the death penalty, and released him in 1938, after which he could no longer get a job. Relatives chipped in bought him a horse and buggy, and he worked at the market to feed our family.[16]

Deportations

Calling for expulsion of the remaining elements of the "kulak activists," especially those among the richest kulaks and sublandlords, to remote areas of the USSR, the Politburo set the highest deportation quotas for Ukraine

---

15 Instruction to August 7, 1932 Order "On Protection of the Property of State Enterprises, Collective Farms, and Cooperatives and Strengthening of Public (Socialist) Property," September 16, 1932 (Moscow. Russian Historic Society, Electronic Library), http://docs.historyrussia.org/ru/nodes/63798-instruktsiya-po-primeneniyu-postanovleniya-tsik-i-snk-sssr-ot-7-avgusta-1932-g-ob-ohrane-imuschestva-gosudarstvennyh-predpriyatiy-kolhozov-i-kooperatsii-i-ukreplenii-obschestvennoy-sotsialisticheskoy-sobstvennosti-16-sentyabrya-1932-g

16 Khalfin, Boris. Interview 26727. Experience group: Jewish survivor. Language: Russian. Segment 7. Visual History Archive, USC Shoah Foundation, 1997. Accessed October 25, 2019.

compared to other Soviet republics: 15,000 to concentration camps and 30,000–35,000 into exile.[17]

Polina Bondar (b. 1923) remembers the eviction of her sister's husband and in-laws. Her sister, who was pregnant at the time, had to obtain a fictitious divorce from her husband in order to avoid deportation. Anastasiia Kovalchuk (b. 1927) explains that her father was forced to join the kolkhoz in Derebchynka (Vinnytsia oblast) under threat of deportation to Siberia.

Polina Bondar, born in Hulsk (prewar Kyiv oblast, now Zhytomyr oblast)

PB: In my family, before 1930 my sister, the one I said was older, took a liking to a guy, and he was from a family considered to be kulaks because they were rich. So people said that we should not let her marry him, but she didn't listen to us, fell in love with the guy, and it was decided to have a wedding. I remember it, my sister's wedding; my father even hired a brass band. The very handsome groom arrived on beautiful horses. His family, the kulaks, had several pairs of horses, and very beautiful gray horses arrived. They went to the church wedding ceremony.

Int.: Where was the church ceremony?

PB: Here, in Hulsk.

Int.: Was there a church here?

PB: Yes, there was a church here.

Int.: What happened next?

PB: They got married, came home, had the wedding, the groom took the bride home, and they lived there for a year. And after that, because he refused to turn over his property to the kolkhoz, they were dekulakized. Everything was taken away from them; the husband's father was arrested, the mother too, and they were sent to Siberia. The husband was left alone then. He had two brothers; at first they left them alone, but then those fellows were deported too.

Int.: What about your sister?

PB: My sister got a fake divorce.

Int.: How did this happen?

PB: Well, my father went to the village council to put in a request, [saying that] she no longer wants [to be married]. She had wanted to marry,

---

[17] "On Measures to Eliminate Kulak Farms in Areas of Continuous Collectivization," Politburo of the Central Committee of the All-Union Communist Party (Bolshevik), January 30, 1930 Russian Historic Society, Electronic Library), http://docs.historyrussia.org/ru/nodes/78140-postanovlenie-tsk-vkp-b-o-meropriyatiyah-po-likvidatsii-kulatskih-hozyaystv-v-rayonah-sploshnoy-kollektivizatsii-30-yanvarya-1930-g

she no longer wants it, she wants to go back. We saw that she was pregnant and was about to have a baby. They advised us in the village council that they did not mind giving her the divorce because otherwise the newborn would perish if they were deported to Siberia and the child was born en route. So we brought my sister back home, got them divorced. My sister's husband, his two brothers, father, and mother—my sister's in-laws—were all deported to Siberia.[18]

Anastasiia Kovalchuk, born in Derebchynka (Vinnytsia oblast)

AK: When the collective farms began, my father joined the kolkhoz. He was not deported because he was on good terms with the head of the local village council. He said, 'Stepan, here is what I will tell you: Hurry up and join the kolkhoz, otherwise they will deport you. I will tell you when.' So father joined the kolkhoz. In the kolkhoz, He lived a decent life there too, because he was on good terms with everyone: with the head of the kolkhoz, with the storekeepers. And no one oppressed him.

Int.: Did people want to join the kolkhoz, or not so much?

AK: Well, how can I say whether they wanted it? I remember when the famine broke out in 1933 and there were Komsomol brigades; they walked from house to house and cleaned everything out. I know that my father had a tub of wheat buried under his bed. He dug some dirt out, made a pit, and put this tub of wheat in it. It was covered as well, and there was a floor on top. The Komsomol brigades searched by knocking with a stick, and they heard the hollow sound there. They discovered it right away. That was the situation in the kolkhozes at the time. It was not that people did not want to join the kolkhoz. They were simply afraid: What does it mean to hand over the horses, hand over the plow, hand over the cart, hand over the sleigh, hand over the oxen and horses, and be left with nothing? We would feel the same now. But we are more aware, because all of us already learned our lesson; we get it. It was different then. They just threatened: 'we will deport you to Siberia.' All they had to do was select two or three families and deport them; that's how we got it. Our current government understands it that way as well. Because they did return that house later, when my late husband returned from the front; they gave that house back to him, as the older son, and he stayed there.

Int.: Do you think the government did the right thing by deporting people?

---

[18] Bondar, Polina. Interview 49440. Experience group: Rescue and Aid. Language: Ukrainian. Segments 19–22. Visual History Archive, USC Shoah Foundation, 1998. Accessed October 25, 2019.

AK: No, it wasn't right. Why create the famine in 1933? The way I understand it now, they should have found a different approach to people, rather than depriving them of everything immediately. Taking everything away. There were families then with 12 children, 16 children. There were no families with just one child, or two or three. People had large families back then. It was not that they simply did not want to join; they were afraid that tomorrow they would have no land, no horses, no wagon—nothing. How would they survive? They took everything away then, down to the last two–three kilos. I remember: My brother and I were sitting on top of the oven, well, a Ukrainian oven. They came in, woke us up, and cleaned everything out, including bits [of food] in tiny bags. How were we supposed to survive then?[19]

Border Patrols

In order to survive, the starving residents of the Ukrainian Soviet Socialist Republic fled across the border in search of food. The Soviet government's response was swift: On January 22, 1933 the USSR Sovnarkom (Council of People's Commissars) and the CC AUCP(B) (All-Union Communist Party [Bolshevik]) issued Order no. 50 preventing the mass flight of starving villagers in search of food, mandating the CC CP(B)U, Ukrainian SSR Radnarkom, People's Commissar of Internal Affairs of Ukraine (NKVD) Vsevolod Balitsky, and the head of the OGPU of the Ukrainian SSR Stanislav Redens to prevent the mass departure of peasants from Ukraine to other regions, as well as entry into Ukraine from the Northern Caucasus.[20]

In his testimony, Nikolai Verkhoglyadov (b. 1908) recalls turning back starving refugees attempting to flee Ukraine while he was serving in the border patrol stationed near Dzhankoi, in the northern part of Crimea [then part of the RSFSR].

Nikolai Verkhoglyadov, born in Kyiv

NV: In 1933 I was serving in the Navy. I had no idea that this was going on. Unfortunately, I too took part in it. Border patrols were set up to contain those fleeing from starving Ukraine to Crimea. And we served in those border patrols; I was there as well, I participated. Well, you know that a

---

[19] Kovalchuk, Anastasiia. Interview 49719. Experience group: Rescue and Aid. Language: Ukrainian. Segments 21–24. Visual History Archive, USC Shoah Foundation, 1998. Accessed October 25, 2019.

[20] USSR SNK and CC AUCP(b), "Directive on Preventing the Mass Exodus of Starving Villagers," January 22, 1933 (Moscow: Russian Historic Society, Electronic Library), http://docs.historyrussia.org/ru/nodes/77571-direktiva-tsk-vkp-b-i-snk-sssr-o-predotvraschenii-massovogo-vyezda-golodayuschih-krestyan-22-yanvarya-1933-g

starving person is sometimes swollen, but it seems that he is otherwise healthy. Food was delivered to us from our unit. And we shared it with them. But they should not have had that food, especially fatty borshch, especially buckwheat porridge, noodles with meat. We gave them as much as they wanted to eat, and they died. You understand?

Int.: Was this in Kerch?

NV: It was in Dzhankoi, the isthmus.

Int.: Where was the border patrol?

NV: We served in the border patrol there and did not let anyone through. Well, we didn't know anything about it. They told us: They are subkulaks who refused to work on collective farms. And we believed it all.[21]

Export of grain

The Soviet government directives did not stop at collectivization. The industrialization of Soviet cities was underway, and money was needed to support it, with export of grain designed as one of the funding sources. The Soviet government's plan for exporting goods in the third quarter of 1932 established quotas to export grain from the ports of Ukraine. Fulfilling these orders, the Odesa-based export corporation *Eksportkhleb* maintained 15 grain cargo ships in the Odesa region. From November 16 to 21, 1932, 25,000 tons of grain were dispatched to Odesa, 32,000 tons to Mykolaiv, and 12,000 tons to Kherson.[22] From the Port of Kherson alone during the third quarter of 1932 the plan set the grain export quota at 90,000 tons, destined for the ports of France, Italy, Egypt, and Greece.[23]

Iosif Raykin (b. 1923) remembers witnessing the loading of grain onto a Greek cargo ship docked in the Port of Kherson.

Iosif Raykin, born in Kherson

IR: I remember dead, swollen bodies lying on the streets, and I remember the following episode. There was a well-known grain elevator in Kherson, one of the largest in Ukraine; it was in the port. Foreign ships arrived. We young boys came to the port... A Greek steamboat was moored, loading bread, grain. And the sailors threw bread crusts to us. We jumped from the pier into the

[21] Verkhoglyadov, Nikolai. Interview 39218. Experience group: Rescue and Aid. Language: Russian. Segments 88–89. Visual History Archive, USC Shoah Foundation, 1997. Accessed October 30, 2019.

[22] City of Kyiv Appellate Court Statement on the case of the genocide in Ukraine in 1932–1933, February 22, 2010, vol. 214, l.d. 43–47. Human Rights in Ukraine. Website of the Kharkiv Human Rights Protection Group, http://khpg.org/en/index.php?id=1266828078

[23] City of Kyiv Appellate Court Statement on the Case of the Genocide in Ukraine in 1932–1933, February 22, 2010, vol. 211, l.d. 199. Human Rights in Ukraine. Website of the Kharkiv Human Rights Protection Group, http://khpg.org/en/index.php?id=1266828078

water to catch the pieces of bread crust. But what struck me was—I was a child and I could not… meaning, why was this happening when people were starving to death here? I remember another incident where people were lining up for bread. A man tore a piece of bread out [of a loaf], and people began to beat him. He fell to the ground, they beat him, and he continued to eat this bread. I remember that. At the same time, the Greeks were exporting grain from the elevator. I did not understand anything, and I asked my father about this. Dad didn't answer me. He said that when you grow up, you will understand all this. And soon dad was arrested.[24]

Famine

The VHA interviewees remember starvation that ensued during the Holodomor and the efforts to procure food in the struggle to survive.

Elizaveta Gaidenko, born in 1924 in Khodorkiv (prewar Kyiv oblast, now Zhytomyr oblast)

EG: Every day it got worse and worse. It got to the point that we were dying, starving to death. I turned into a mummy, so to speak. I looked like—if you know what Ethiopian children look like today, bare skin and bones—I was like that. Hair started growing on my face. Cannibalism began in our village. My mother hid me inside the oven's anterior chamber and locked me in with an iron gate, saying: 'Sit quietly, otherwise you will be eaten.' And she left for work. We survived this period somehow. Spring arrived. Leaves started growing on the trees. She picked these leaves, cooked these leaves, and mixed them with dust from rotting wood. And she baked—that is, heated—all of that in the oven, and we ate it. Then an old horse died in the commune where she fulfilled her work day obligations. The women who worked there dug up the carcass of that horse and took it out at night, cut it into pieces, and cooked it. I only remember the foam that came from the horse meat. And we ate it.[25]

Deaths of loved ones

The death toll resulting from unrealistic grain procurement quotas enforced by the Soviet authorities rose rapidly. Vasilina Sitko (b. 1926), remembers losing her entire family to the Great Famine.

---

[24] Raykin, Iosif. Interview 51042. Experience group: Jewish survivor. Language: Russian. Segments 24–26. Visual History Archive, USC Shoah Foundation, 1998. Accessed October 30, 2019.

[25] Gaidenko, Elizaveta. Interview 37375. Experience group: Rescue and Aid. Language: Russian. Segments 23–25. Visual History Archive, USC Shoah Foundation, 1997. Accessed October 30, 2019.

Vasilina Sitko, born in Zhytni Hory (Kyiv oblast)

VS: They dekulakized everything, took everything away—everything. They locked my father up in a prison cell, beat him up, and didn't let him come home. My mother was pregnant at the time.

Int.: What year was this?

VS: It was 1932, I remember exactly. They did not let Dad go, and meanwhile they confiscated everything that we owned: the house, grain, potatoes, fatback, clothes. They began taking all of that away. My mother was pregnant.[26]

They invaded the house, took the roof sheets off, took everything away. There were only two of us children left, Lena and me. And my mom would get up early in the morning, and all we had was a pail of water. Mom fell ill with malaria, and she was pregnant. A girl was born and died right away, unbaptised. My grandma said, 'Bury her in the garden.' We put the baby in the basket in which we had our Easter bread blessed and buried her in it, that baby girl. My mom was still sick, and our neighbor said we should look after her because she was about to die.[27]

Grandma died first, Maria; she starved to death. Then Mom's brother, Andrei, died. Then Aunt Tosia died. We buried them here at the cemetery; it is still there.

Int.: What about your mother?

VS: She died here; we buried her here, in a mass grave. There is a large grave. People are there.

Int.: Was it during the Holodomor?

VS: Yes, they buried all the people there, and they put my mom there, too. I take care of this grave now. They erected a cross on Grandpa's grave and wrote, 'Myronovsky, 57 years old.' He was young. He was a big, handsome man. After that my dad died, grandma, grandpa, brother, and sister all died. They took them all out of the same house.[28]

Resistance during the Great Famine

Peasant uprisings and individual resistance were not uncommon during the Holodomor. Nykyfir Iakhnenko (b. 1914) and Anna Kakhno (b. 1924)

---

[26] Sitko, Vasilina. Interview 47331. Experience group: Rescue and Aid. Language: Ukrainian. Segment 7. Visual History Archive, USC Shoah Foundation, 1998. Accessed October 30, 2019.

[27] Sitko, Vasilina. Interview 47331. Experience group: Rescue and Aid. Language: Ukrainian. Segments 9–10. Visual History Archive, USC Shoah Foundation, 1998. Accessed October 30, 2019.

[28] Sitko, Vasilina. Interview 47331. Experience group: Rescue and Aid. Language: Ukrainian. Segments 12–13. Visual History Archive, USC Shoah Foundation, 1998. Accessed October 30, 2019.

reflected on the opportunities to resist the state agricultural policy during Soviet totalitarian rule and on the persecution of political opponents during the famine.

Nykyfir Iakhnenko, born in Kirovo (Nemyriv, Vinnytsia oblast)

Int.: Please tell me: Did people mount any kind of resistance or protest during the Holodomor?

NI: What kind of protest could there have been when people could no longer walk, you understand? People were already so malnourished that they were unable to care for themselves, let alone protest. In order to protest, one needs to be physically strong. And they had reduced people to such a state that people were dropping dead on the go, like flies.

Int.: Please tell us: That same year, in 1933, in Vinnytsia, where you were, what were the city residents saying about what was going on in the countryside? How did they feel about it?

NI: How did they feel? They were horrified. Everyone was afraid to speak up. No one... If they had even mentioned the famine, they would have been grabbed by the KGB [*sic*] and executed on the spot.[29]

Anna Kakhno, born in Kovalivka (Vinnytsia oblast)

Int.: Anna Ivanivna, please tell me, when your father resisted joining the kolkhoz, was he the only one in the village, or were there more people like him?

AK: No, there were more people like him. They were all... Of course, there were others who had no cattle of their own, no horses of their own... some didn't even have cows. Well, there were all kinds of people then. That's it. So no one bothered with those people because they had nothing to bring to the kolkhoz. But those who were on the planned confiscation list, those ones had to turn everything in. They had to hand over their wagon, horses, plow, harrows, things that are needed to cultivate the soil. That's it. My father had all that. And from all those who had horses and who did not join the kolkhoz, all of that was taken away, like from my father. But eventually everyone joined the kolkhoz anyway, because where else would you go then? What could you do? The kolkhoz took the land from everyone, but you had to live somehow.[30]

---

[29] Iakhnenko, Nykyfir. Interview 36663. Experience group: Rescue and Aid. Language: Ukrainian. Segments 19–21. Visual History Archive, USC Shoah Foundation, 1997. Accessed October 30, 2019.

[30] Kakhno, Anna. Interview 38045. Experience group: Rescue and Aid. Language: Ukrainian. Segments 19–20. Visual History Archive, USC Shoah Foundation, 1997. Accessed October 30, 2019.

Int.: Please tell us more about the year 1933. How did the famine begin and why did it break out?

AK: When collectivization began, they demanded enormous grain procurement quotas.

Well, my father turned in everything we had; everything he could hand over, he did. And then, after all this, there was mistrust toward the people who didn't join the kolkhoz. Whatever was left by them, they came and took everything away, on their own. My mother managed to hide some clay pots in which we used to bring water to the field, to keep the water cool. Mom put millet in a pot and hid it in the attic under the rafters—the house had a straw roof. She disguised it, so as to hide at least something. The head of our kolkhoz was Kucherenko. He found that pot and took it away, and poured the millet out of it. And we had absolutely nothing left! Nothing was left! They took away the cow, the sheep, the pigs, the horses, even the chickens—absolutely everything. There was nothing left at all.[31]

The role of women in the organized resistance is a topic of rising importance in Holodomor scholarship and research.[32] Vladimir Svitko (b. 1922), remembers witnessing a women's revolt in his native village of Mshanets (Vinnytsia oblast).

Vladimir Svitko, born in Mshanets (Vinnytsia oblast)

VS: And there was a women's revolt.

Int.: Yes, please describe it.

VS: One time I was sitting by the window, and saw...

Int.: What year was that women's revolt?

VS: I don't remember either. But I remember that...

Int.: Well, was it after the Holodomor?

VS: Yes, it was after the Holodomor. And... I remember that I was surprised to see our schoolyard suddenly filled with women from everywhere—instantly filled. I thought: How could it be that they had run in from all sides, dressed like that, in all kinds of short winter coats, with pitchforks, with axes, with all kinds of women's tools. And they began to shout, calling out to my father. Father came outside. They began shouting

[31] Kakhno, Anna. Interview 38045. Experience group: Rescue and Aid. Language: Ukrainian. Segments 27–29. Visual History Archive, USC Shoah Foundation, 1997. Accessed October 30, 2019.

[32] See, e.g., Lynne Viola, "Bab'i bunty and Peasant Women's Protest during Collectivization," in *The Stalinist Dictatorship*, ed. Chris Ward (London and New York: Arnold, 1998), 218–19; Oksana Kis, "Defying Death: Women's Experience of the Holodomor, 1932–1933," *Aspasia* 7, no. 1 (2013): 42–67; Elissa Bemporad and Joyce W. Warren, *Women and Genocide: Survivors, Victims, Perpetrators* (Bloomington, Ind.: Indiana University Press, 2018).

that 'the chairman of either the collective farm or the chairman of the village council is hiding with you.' Father said: 'There's no one here. There's no one here. That's all.' They said: 'We'll come in to check.' And father said: 'How can I let you in? The entire crowd?! You will turn my home upside down! Go ahead and select three trustees. Let them come in, check, search, and that's it.' They dispatched six people. I saw some big women come in, wrapped in ropes, one with an axe sticking out, another with a big pestle in her hand... They searched the whole house; they didn't find anyone. Then they said: 'He's not here, he's not here! He probably ran there', to such-and-such an activist,' and they all ran over there. And after that, father... no, not that afternoon but in the evening, father knocked on the ceiling, and out came the village council chairman from the attic and went down the stairs. He was armed with a gun, but they would have killed him. He might have killed six people there, but they would have torn him to pieces. They would have killed my father, too, for hiding him. And so, he saved this man.

Int.: And what was the cause of the riot?

VS: Because people were starving, because everything was not done in a humane way. But the main thing is that there wasn't a single man there—only women. But this chairman of the village council or the collective farm, I don't know who he was, he fled to the county seat that night, and in the morning, the very next day, a police group arrived, a police unit. The women activists were arrested; they stayed in classrooms here, drank tea, just like that, and these activists were taken away. I don't know what happened next... It was such a turbulent time.[33]

Holodomor testimonies in the Institute's educational work

The Visual History Archive's rich content related to the Holodomor became the driving force behind an important educational project. In 2009–10 the USC Shoah Foundation produced a groundbreaking multimedia resource based on the VHA content for Ukrainian teachers—*The Ukrainian Famine of 1932–1933: The Human Dimension of the Tragedy*[34]—and held a national teacher-training seminar in Kyiv on its use. The prominent historians Timothy D. Snyder, Samuel Totten, and Stanislav Kulchytsky reviewed the teacher's guide before it was published, providing their historical expertise. The Kyiv seminar participants went on to train fellow educators in their home regions. As a result, 680 teachers from 19 regions of Ukraine received

---

[33] Svitko, Vladimir. Interview 41813. Experience group: Rescue and Aid. Language: Russian. Segments 22–25. Visual History Archive, USC Shoah Foundation, 1998. Accessed October 30, 2019.

[34] Oleksandr Voitenko, *Holodomor v Ukraïni 1932–1933 rokiv: Liuds'kyi vymir trahediï* (Kyiv, 2010).

training on the use of Holodomor eyewitness accounts in the classroom. Through the USC Shoah Foundation's work in Ukraine, teachers and students had an opportunity to learn from eyewitness testimony about the human dimension of their local history and the totalitarian policies that resulted in the humanitarian catastrophe.

I Witness, an educational website developed by the USC Shoah Foundation, brings the human stories of the Institute's Visual History Archive to secondary school teachers and their students through engaging, multimedia-learning activities. The site features a multimedia activity in the Ukrainian language, *The Holodomor in Children's Fates*.[35] This activity reveals the tragedy of the Holodomor from two perspectives: personal recollections of witnesses and official documents plotting the artificial famine in response to the peasants' resistance. Working with testimonies and analyzing documents, students will be able to explore the tragedy of the Holodomor through the prism of humanism, human dignity, and human rights. IWitness currently provides access to 3,183 complete life histories, testimonies of survivors and witnesses to the Holocaust and other genocides for guided exploration.

VHA access sites

The Institute offers access to the Visual History Archive to subscribing institutions, including universities, museums, libraries, centers, and memorial sites. Subscriptions come in two forms: full access and partial access. Full access to the nearly 55,000 testimonies in the Visual History Archive is provided to 138 subscribing institutions[36] in 15 countries around the world. Partial access is granted to 232 institutions in 36 countries. These smaller collections vary in size, generally ranging between a handful and several thousand copies of testimonies in the Visual History Archive.

In order to accommodate the demand from outside of the subscribing institutions, the Institute has established the Visual History Archive Online, which enables any user with an Internet connection to access indexing data on the nearly 55,000 interviewees and provides access to 3,108 full-length video testimonies.[37] The names of the 1.95 million individuals mentioned in the Archive are also indexed and searchable.

---

[35] USC Shoah Foundation, *Holodomor u dytiachykh doliakh* (Holodomor in Children's Fates: Lesson Plan),
https://iwitness.usc.edu/sfi/Activity/Detail.aspx?activityID=3061&retainFilter=true

[36] VHA Site Locator – Full Access Sites: http://sfi.usc.edu/locator/full_access_sites

[37] Visual History Archive Online: http://vhaonline.usc.edu/login

Acknowledgements

The author gratefully acknowledges the USC Shoah Foundation for permission to use the transcripts of the following testimonies: Bondar, Polina (1998), Gaidenko, Elizaveta (1997), Gelman, Anatolii (1998), Honchar, Ivan (1997), Iakhnenko, Nykyfir (1997), Kakhno, Anna (1997), Khalfin, Boris (1997), Kovalchuk, Anastasiia (1998), Raykin, Iosif (1998), Rekhtman, Boris (1996), Sitko, Vasilina (1998), Svitko, Vladimir (1998), and Verkhoglyadov, Nikolai (1997). English translations emendated by Ksenia Maryniak (CIUS). For more information, visit http://sfi.usc.edu/

Archives

Russian Historical Society, Electronic library of historical documents. http://docs.historyrussia.org/ru/nodes/1-glavnaya

USC Shoah Foundation, Holodomor in Children's Fates: Lesson Plan "Holodomor u dytiachykh doliakh". https://iwitness.usc.edu/sfi/Activity/Detail.aspx?activityID=3061&retainFilter=true

VHA Site Locator – Full Access Sites. http://sfi.usc.edu/locator/full_access_sites

Visual History Archive Online. http://vhaonline.usc.edu/login

Bibliography

Bemporad, Elissa, and Joyce W. Warren *Women and Genocide: Survivors, Victims, Perpetrators*. Bloomington, Ind.: Indiana University Press, 2018.

Indexing Guidelines. USC Shoah Foundation, University of Southern California, 2006. http://sfi.usc.edu/sites/default/files/docfiles/Indexing_Guidelines_0.pdf

Kharkiv Human Rights Protection Group. "City of Kyiv Appellate Court Statement on the case of the genocide in Ukraine in 1932–1933". http://khpg.org/en/index.php?id=1266828078

Kis, Oksana. "Defying Death: Women's Experience of the Holodomor, 1932–1933." *Aspasia* 7, no. 1 (2013): 42–67

Viola, Lynne. "Bab'i bunty and Peasant Women's Protest during Collectivization." In *The Stalinist Dictatorship*, edited by Chris Ward. London and New York: Arnold, 1998

Tragediia sovetskoi derevni: Kollektivizatsiia i raskulachivanie: Dokumenty i materialy, vol. 2: November 1929–December 1930. Moscow: ROSSPEN, 2000.

Voitenko, Oleksandr, ed. *Holodomor v Ukraïni 1932–1933 rokiv: Liuds'kyi vymir trahediï.* Kyiv: Maisternia knyhy, 2010.

Toward a Social History of the Holodomor and its Aftermath: Famine Survivor Testimonies in the Archive of the US Commission on the Ukraine Famine

John Vsetecka

Studies of the Holodomor have come a long way since the publication of Robert Conquest's *The Harvest of Sorrow: Soviet Collectivization and the Terror-Famine* in 1986, the first English-language scholarly text to address the 1932–33 famine. The book was published toward the end of the Cold War, a time when Soviet archives were still relatively off limits to Western scholars. Those who attempted to study the man-made famine in Soviet Ukraine at that time could only guess about what documents might be hiding in the archives in Moscow or Kyiv. However, as other scholars in this volume have made clear, an abundance of information related to the 1932–33 famine found its way into archives outside of the former Soviet Union. The availability of such information indicates that several countries, groups, and individuals—beyond Soviet borders—produced and kept sources related to the famine. Although many of these collections are still being discovered, they are integral for developing more comprehensive understandings of the famine's role not only in Soviet history, but in European, global, and world histories as well. One of these collections is the archive of the U.S. Commission on the Ukraine Famine (also referred to as CUF), a congressionally approved body that was established in 1984 to investigate the 1932–33 famine in Soviet Ukraine. This article details the work of the Commission and its archival holdings to highlight the important sources that the CUF collected on the Holodomor. Most prominent among this collection, however, are the Holodomor survivor testimonies that were collected as part of the Commission's public hearings and oral history project.

This article is broken up into two parts: the first part examines the CUF archive, its background, and the sources available in the collection. The second part of the article offers new research that is based on the testimonies collected by the Commission, and the insights offered from famine survivors demonstrate that the testimonies and documents in the CUF archive are key to understanding, in more complex ways, the social histories of the Holodomor as well as the famine's aftermath. Current research tends to examine the events *leading up to* the famine as well as the *unfolding* of the famine itself, but few works have paid attention to the period *after the famine*. While mass starvation largely stopped by the end of

1933 (although acute hunger and starvation still continued well into 1934 and beyond), the side effects of famine did not. Just some of the issues that continued to prevail were disease, displacement, homelessness, grief, and trauma. Simply put, the famine produced a number of reverberations that continued to affect many. A turn toward the famine's aftermath requires of us, then, to ask new questions: What were the famine's lasting effects? In what ways did the famine continue to have an impact on survivors after actual starvation ended? What were the problems left in the famine's wake? How did survivors attempt to come to terms with what happened? How did they grapple with the death of some three to five million Ukrainians? What do survivor testimonies tell us about the barriers they faced as they attempted to "move on"?

The testimonies in the CUF collection offer insight into several of the problems that survivors faced after the famine. The second part of this essay will examine one issue that was of immediate concern to survivors in the aftermath of hunger: dead bodies. The theme of corpses is one that emerges across hundreds of testimonies collected by the CUF. The detailed histories of body collection, removal, and burial speak to the way that the famine continued to be felt by survivors after starvation ended. Millions died within just a two-year span, and many famine victims succumbed to death on roads, in buildings, on sidewalks, inside houses, and in public squares. While starvation may have subsided, the famine's toll was visible in the form of dead bodies in public and private spaces in both urban and rural settings. Survivors' interactions with the dead, as detailed in the latter half of this article, tell us much about the way that the famine continued to be present in everyday life as starvation came to an end. As such, corpses were physical representations of the famine's lingering effects that survivors were forced to confront on a daily basis.

The U.S. Commission on the Ukraine Famine collection and its background

One reason why the CUF archive is not utilized often, I believe, is due to researchers' unfamiliarity with the collection's contents. Those who have worked on the 1932–33 famine for some time will no doubt be familiar with the Commission's work, but others may not even know of its existence. References to the Commission and its work appear sporadically in research on the Holodomor, and most recently, some of the testimonies collected by the Commission were used in Anne Applebaum's *Red Famine: Stalin's War on Ukraine.*[1] Applebaum's analysis of the Commission in the Cold War years offers some insight into why the CUF, and its work, was overlooked. One reason, she notes, is the Chornobyl disaster of 1986. This event quickly demanded the world's attention at exactly the same time that the Commission was conducting its investigation. However, the topic of the famine did not stray far from the minds of Soviet leaders during the late 1980s, as Applebaum highlights.

Year of birth:
1898 1
1899 4
1900 3
1901 1
1902 3
1903 3
1904 1
1905 4
1906 7
1907
1908 2
1909 1
1910 5
1911
1912
1913 1
1914 3
1915
1916 1
1917 3
1918 1
1919 2
1920 2
1921
1922 1
1923 2
1924 2
1925 2
1926 1
1927 1

Place of birth (oblast'):

Poltava 18	Chernihiv 2
Kharkiv 9	Kuban' (Krasnodarskii krai) 2
Kiev 6	Kherson 1
Zhytomyr 5	Donets'k 1
Khmel'nyts'kyi 4	Zaporizhzhia 1
Dnipropetrovs'k 3	Kirovohrad 1
Sumy 2	Cherkasy 1

Occupation 1932

Peasants (including children) 35
Teachers 7
Students (university, polytechnic) 5
White-collar workers 4
Workers (excluding dekulakized recently arrived in city) 4
Priests or dependents 2

Economic status of peasants before collectivization:

rich (40 or more acres) 12
middle (10-40 acres) 18
poor (less than 10 acres) 5

(13 of these peasants were dekulakized)

sex:
28 men
28 women

urban/rural origin:
49 rural
7 urban

Some of the demographic information collected by the CUF in 1984."Preliminary Statistics on Famine Survivors Interviewed Summer 1984," RG 220, Box 7, National Archives at College Park, College Park, MD

[1] Although Applebaum includes some of the testimonies in her book, they are selective and do not reflect the larger collection of testimonies that exist.

While the Commission continued with its investigation, it faced fierce opposition from officials in Moscow and Kyiv. Volodymyr Shcherbytsky, the Ukrainian Communist Party leader, ordered a group of scholars to refute the Commission's findings. Applebaum notes: "Shcherbytsky tasked scholars at the Ukrainian Academy of Sciences and the Institute of Party History—the organizations behind the publication of *Fraud, Famine, and Fascism*—with refuting the general accusations and in particular with countering the conclusions drawn by the U.S. Congressional Report" (Applebaum 343). Such efforts limited the spread of the CUF's work and propelled them into a competition of Cold War memory politics. Other works, including *The Holodomor Reader: A Sourcebook on the Famine of 1932–1933*, also make use of materials related to the U.S. Commission on the Ukraine Famine, but in a limited capacity (Klid and Motyl 67–68).

Beyond the work of scholars, states have also turned to the output of the CUF to promote recent resolutions and proclamations recognizing the 1932–33 Holodomor. In 2018, several American states referenced the Commission's work during the 85th anniversary of the Holodomor. A number of states issued documents marking the Holodomor as genocide based on the findings of the CUF in the late 1980s. In their final *Report to Congress*, the CUF made nineteen key findings. Number sixteen states that "Joseph Stalin and those around him committed genocide against Ukrainians in 1932–1933" (U.S. Commission on the Ukraine Famine, *Report to Congress* vii).[2] Nevertheless, while the CUF's findings have been used to promote public information campaigns about the Holodomor, especially by state governments, the content of the CUF archive still remains little used, particularly the survivor testimonies. However, as this article will discuss, the Commission's collection is rich in testimony and oral histories, documents related to American foreign policy during the Cold War, as well as education material related to the promotion of the Holodomor in school curricula. Such evidence tells us a great deal not only about the famine itself, but also about the way the memory of the famine was understood and articulated in the United States.

---

[2] For a complete list of states that recognize the Holodomor, see John Vsetecka, "Map of Holodomor Resolutions and Proclamations in the United States and Canada" on the HREC Education website. Link: https://education.holodomor.ca/resolutions/ (accessed February 26, 2020).

Another reason why the CUF archive has not been fully utilized, particularly the survivor testimonies, is due to researchers' distrust of memory as a source. Some scholars think the testimonies are biased and unreliable and cannot be used because they were collected so late after the famine occurred—approximately fifty years after the famine ended. Dominick LaCapra addresses this issue directly in his book, *History and Memory after Auschwitz*. He argues, "Memory—along with its lapses and tricks—poses questions to history in that it points to problems that are still

24. Чи Ви були репресовані?

25. Чи Ви тимчасово залишали своє село підчас голоду?

26. Чи Ви знаєте, де була найгірша голодівка?

27. Чи в Россії був голод? Як Ви це знаєте?

28. Чому був голод на Україні?

<u>Питання для осіб які жили в місті</u>

29. Коли Ви перший раз побачили голодних селян?

30. Як влада справлялась з голодними селянами?

31. Чи Вам бракувало хліба в місті?

32. Скільки хліба давали робітникам?

33. Що Ви знали про величену голода? Як Ви це знали? Чи влада визнавала, що був голод? Що влада говорила?

34. Коли та як скінчився голод? Що Ви робили після голоду? Як інші люди перебудували своє життя?

Some of the questions that Commission interviewers asked survivors. In the bottom half of the document are the six questions that were posed to those who lived in cities. "Pytannia do svidkiv," in RG 220, Box 7, National Archives at College Park, College Park, MD

alive or invested with emotion and value. Ideally, history critically tests memory and prepares for more extensive attempts to work through a past that has not passed away" (LaCapra 8).

The U.S. Commission on the Ukraine Famine also understood that some might be critical of memory as a source. In the introduction to their Oral History Project, the Commission wrote: "Memory is, of course, not always accurate, but neither is any other type of source which historians use. It is, however, a source which can contribute to future knowledge of the past in important ways. If we wish to understand that past, this, then, is a source we can ill afford to ignore" (*Investigation of the Ukrainian Famine*, Oral History Project of the Commission on the Ukraine Famine vol. 1, vii). While the testimonies are not without issues, they are an important source that highlight survivor narratives. These testimonies, when read against each other and put into context with other pertinent archival and documentary evidence, help to provide a much more robust and complex picture of events surrounding the Holodomor. They also present a much-needed social history that provides insight into the experiences of ordinary Ukrainians and speaks to topics that other archival evidence cannot.

The documents of the U.S. Commission on the Ukraine Famine are located in the National Archives and Records Administration building in College Park, Maryland. The collection, which is housed under "Records of Temporary Committees, Commissions, and Boards," consists of several boxes of files that are divided among seven groups. The files and documents range from the CUF working papers and reports to the collection of historical documents related to the famine. The archive also houses original sound recordings of oral histories collected from survivors. These are preserved on more than one hundred audio cassettes. Other important files include budget material, staff profiles, newspaper clippings, unpublished survivor testimony, educational materials, academic correspondences, and photos related to the investigation. All of this is in addition to the first and second interim reports, the Commission's final report to congress, and their three-volume oral history project. The interim reports, final report, and oral history volumes all contain valuable famine survivor testimony. The interim and final reports contain testimony in English, while the oral history volumes hold over two hundred survivor accounts in Ukrainian with short introductions in English. The reports, along with the oral history collection, are now freely accessible online.

The collection is also rich in other primary source material. It includes both American and Soviet newspaper articles, academic work that address the 1932–33 famine, fictional works about the Holodomor, and educational material that was prepared for school districts across the United States. There are pamphlets, genocide curriculums, and promotional materials that were designed by Dr. Myron Kuropas, the architect of the education campaign for the CUF. While it is widely known that one of the main tasks of the Commission was to collect survivor testimony, it may surprise readers to learn that the CUF spent much of its time and money promoting the study of the Holodomor in schools across the United States. The CUF held several conferences at universities and colleges with seminars to instruct teachers on how to incorporate the famine into their lesson plans. The CUF staff also attended curriculum design meetings at various school districts across the country.

Dr. James Mace, the early staff director of the CUF, made clear in his first year of work that a primary function of the Commission's job was to design and implement a school curriculum. Dr. Kuropas' main role in the Commission was to utilize the testimonies, oral histories, collected historiographies, and other materials to promote adding the famine into school programs. As early as November 1986, Mace began to push hard for the topic to be studied in schools. In a letter to John O. Flis, Supreme President of the Ukrainian National Association, he wrote of his desire to see "the Great Man-Made Famine in Ukraine" become "part of the historical knowledge of high school graduates" (Letter to John O. Flis, November 25, 1986, RG 220, Box 1, NARA).

Even though educational content was a fundamental part of the CUF's agenda from its inception, close examination of the CUF's files indicates that Mace may have intensified his educational lobbying efforts in November 1986 after experiencing setbacks from the California Board of Education in May of that year. Some members expressed reservations about including the famine in the school curriculum ("Commission Update (May 21, 1986)," RG 220, Box 2, NARA). The reasons for such hesitation by the California School Board are unclear, but one can guess that the uncertainty of whether the famine met the criteria of genocide was a key factor in the board's thinking ("Model Curriculum for Human Rights and Genocide," RG 220, Box 1, NARA).[3] Despite these uncertainties, the Ukrainian famine did make it into the model curriculum used by California schools. In a copy of the California draft curriculum booklet, the famine is given a mere three and a half pages. These pages briefly address the history of Ukraine, its role in the Soviet Union, and the reasons why the famine should be considered a genocide. These documents reveal a great deal about how the CUF attempted to integrate knowledge of the famine, based on survivor

[3] The draft curriculum booklet gives four reasons why the famine should be considered a genocide. These include destruction of the "Ukrainian national cultural leadership" and "nationally-minded Communist elite," the "abandonment of Ukrainization," and "a body blow to the traditional mass constituency of Ukrainian national self-assertion." (Model Curriculum for Human Rights and Genocide, RG 220, Box 1, NARA).

testimonies, into student textbooks across the United States. The CUF collection has many documents on this subject that will be of particular interest to those studying how information about the Holodomor was used in pedagogical settings.

The archive also holds a small amount of demographic information related to Holodomor survivors. The CUF compiled a chart (shown below) that indicates where the survivors lived in Ukraine. This enables researchers to compare the experiences of eyewitnesses from different regions of the country. Recent work by demographers, including a team composed of American and Ukrainian scholars, attempted to document more precisely the number of people who died in the famine based on location (Wolowyna, Kovbasiuk, Levchuk, Plokhy, Rudnytskyi, and Shevchuk, 2016). Further research into geographic variances of famine experience is still generally lacking in famine historiography. Statistics, such as those shown below, may help to provide further evidence of lived experience based on age, employment, gender, and location.

One will also find in this collection the question sheets that interviewers used when collecting survivor testimonies. The Commission's interview sheet consisted of thirty-four questions to ask survivors, with only six of those questions pertaining to individuals who lived in cities (see document below); thus, it is no surprise that the CUF's interview process garnered more information on rural populations than urban ones. The Commission hired staff to conduct interviews with survivors in their native language. Specific questions were asked depending on the survivor's location in Soviet Ukraine during the famine. If they were farmers and lived in a rural part of the country, they answered one set of questions. If they lived in a more urban setting, they answered another set of questions. The questions were based on what the Commission wished to learn from survivors, and they were designed with certain parameters in mind, which did not always let survivors tell their full story. However, the testimonies included in the Oral History Project were much fuller in content, which indicates that survivors had more of an opportunity to narrate their story, rather than being limited to answering specific questions. The collection of testimonies received high praise from one of the leading scholars of Soviet history. In his review of the Commission's work, Hiroaki Kuromiya wrote, "Best of all are the oral testimonies quoted in the full transcripts" (Kuromiya 231).

The CUF was officially established in 1984 after years of pressure on the Ameri-can government by the Ukrainian diaspora and academic community, who wished to bring greater awareness of the famine to the general public. The United States Congress originally funded the Commission's project with an allotted budget of $400,000, but that budget proved insufficient to fund the entirety of the Commission's work, and the organization's files show that it took on a substantial fundraising campaign in order to raise enough funds to complete the project.

CUF staff director Dr. James Mace received his PhD from the University of Michigan in 1981 and worked at the Harvard Ukrainian Research Institute shortly after completing his studies. While there, he assisted Robert Conquest with the publication of *Harvest of Sorrow*. Mace would serve as director of the U.S. Commission on the Ukraine Famine from its official start date in 1985 until the Commission concluded its work in 1988, although Mace continued to work on the Oral History Project after the CUF wrapped up its investigation. The bipartisan commission was made up of senators, ambassadors, public members from the Ukrainian diaspora, and even the Surgeon General of the United States. There were also two staff assistants aided with the steering of the commission, Dr. Olga Samilenko and Mr. Walter Pechenuk. Interviewers, transcribers, and other needed staff were hired when necessary to assist the CUF at various points during the project.

One of the advantages of working with the CUF's collection is the possibility of writing several different types of histories. The amount of material is vast and mostly unexplored, which gives researchers unique access to sources that will inevitably expand current ideas of how the Holodomor unfolded. Some of the topics and themes for which this collection holds great relevance include gender, education, children, cannibalism, resistance, collectivization, deportation, and the little-studied famine of 1946–47. No doubt, others will find even more topics to write about after working with the collection. The next section provides new research, based on work with the CUF testimony collection, to demonstrate how these sources can be used to help us understand the social history of the Holodomor and its aftermath.

The aftermath of famine

The literature on the 1932–33 famine is continually growing, but the period after the famine—what is here referred to as the "aftermath"—is still largely absent in the historiography.[4] There are many elements to the term "aftermath," and such a conceptualization needs further definition. In one sense, the aftermath of the famine can include the work of the CUF in the late Cold War period, when they collected the testimonies that make up the

[4] A collection of essays in an edited volume exploring some aspects of the Holodomor's lasting effects, which resulted from a conference titled, "The Great Famine in Ukraine: The Holodomor and Its Consequences, 1933 to the Present." See, Andrea Graziosi, Lubomyr A. Hajda, and Halyna Hryn, *After the Holodomor: The Enduring Impact of the Great Famine on Ukraine* (Cambridge, MA: Harvard Ukrainian Research Institute, 2014).

bulk of their collection. At the time famine survivors came forth to give testimony, victims of other twentieth-century tragedies began to share their experiences of mass violence with governments, commissions, and human rights groups. In many ways, the 1970s and 1980s were what Carolyn Dean refers to as an age of "moral witnesses." Dean contends that the *emergence of the witness* really began in the early twentieth century. She states, "The witness to genocide emerged in the interwar period (1919–39) and made the crime of genocide legible" (Dean 2). The "moral witness" was a category that embodied survivors and allowed them to become a living piece of historical evidence.

One example of this included David Rousset, a survivor of Auschwitz, who became one of the most vocal witnesses to speak out against the Soviet Union and the Gulag system. Rousset saw the Gulag as a continuation of the concentration camps he survived under Nazi rule, and he made it his mission during the Cold War to bring attention to the Soviet Union's labor camps. Emma Kuby states that this project of bearing witness to the camps "became enmeshed in the era's *cultural Cold War*, pitting pro-American actors against pro-Soviet ones in a contest for the hearts and minds of the world's peoples" (Kuby 3). Thus, the work of the CUF took place in a larger Cold War context that encouraged survivors of the twentieth century's most tragic events to share their stories. As such, there was some interest in understanding the horrors of Communism through the prism of the famine as a way to discredit the Soviet Union. Dean contends that "Moral witnesses expressed the public's initial horror of mass atrocities, its struggle to comprehend genocidal crimes and, more recently, its obligation to care for victims of such violence" (Dean 171). For many, an investigation of the Holodomor by a US-sponsored investigative commission represented an official rebuke of Soviet crimes while also serving as a first step toward transitional justice for survivors. Although different from more traditional forms of truth commissions, which generally occur in the country where the tragedy took place, the CUF was a tangible step toward acknowledging the famine publicly and letting survivors have a chance to narrate their version of events, many of whom were doing so for the first time.

Beyond providing unparalleled insight into the years during the famine, the survivors who shared their memories also relayed important information about how Ukrainians started to make sense of what happened to them in the immediate aftermath period. The immediate aftermath, or what I consider the days, months, and years that followed the famine's slow conclusion, was a time when Ukrainians began to confront the reality of what took place while also attempting to resume their lives. The Commission, too, had thought along these lines. One of the questions posed to those who lived in an urban setting was "What did you do after the famine?" ("Pytannia do svidkiv," RG 220, Box 7, National Archives at College Park, College Park, MD). This sparked a range of answers from survivors, but one topic that consistently appeared in almost all of the testimonies was the theme of death, bodies, and burial. Of course, it was hard not to notice the millions who died. The piles of corpses that littered the streets, the half-dead lying in front yards, and the mass graves on the outskirts of towns and villages were images permanently imprinted on the minds of survivors. The sheer numbers of corpses that remained unburied and in public view were reminders of the famine's lingering effects. The immediate aftermath period of the famine was marked by confrontations with dead had succumbed to hunger, murder, and other forms of violence. The testimonies in the CUF collection are particularly useful for understanding this topic, and they help to elucidate a social history of the famine, albeit a very dark one. The testimonies are significant because they speak to the silences in other types of sources and elaborate on the famine's lasting effects.

The literature on dead bodies and their political and social meanings in the aftermath of crisis is well documented. What is surprising, however, is the fact that little has been written about dead bodies and the Holodomor. Two authors have written extensively about dead bodies in the postsocialist and postwar contexts, and their insights offer valuable perspectives of necropolitics that can be built upon to offer new perspectives of the famine and its effects. Katherine Verdery, who has written about "the political lives of dead bodies" in the postsocialist sense, notes that dead bodies are significant because they "mark a change in social visibilities and values" (Verdery 19). Dead bodies, according to Verdery, provide a useful lens for understanding larger shifts and changes in personal and national values as they relate to their socialist pasts. In addition to highlighting change, however, bodies can also be markers of continuity. Verdery also contends that "Bodies have the advantage of concreteness that nonetheless transcends time, making past immediately present" (Verdery 27). In the case of the Holodomor, the presence of dead bodies in everyday life after the famine served as corporeal reminders of the famine's lingering presence. Famine survivor testimonies, which are detailed below, speak to the ways that dead bodies continued to represent the famine's continual influence on everyday life.

Christopher Mauriello, who detailed German civilians' "forced confrontations" with dead bodies after the Holocaust, also provides a useful analysis of how to think about the role of dead bodies after conflict. In his book, *Forced Confrontation: The Politics of Dead Bodies in Germany at the End of World War II*, Mauriello contends that "Postwar conflict politics was being inscribed on the bodies of the dead" and that "In the highly charged atmosphere of the last weeks of the war, mass graves and reburials were sites for some of the first encounters between multiple groups in a defeated and destroyed Germany" (Mauriello xxviii). In Ukraine, too, encounters with the dead had resounding effects. Although different from the "forced confrontations" that Mauriello writes about in his book, where American soldiers forced German citizens to look at dead bodies, dig graves, and help bury them as a way to make everyday Germans experience war-time horrors, Ukrainians also confronted the dead on a daily basis. They walked past them on their way to work and stepped over and around them in public areas such as train stations and markets. Others had even more physical encounters with the dead. This included physically picking up and hauling corpses away on carts and in trucks, stacking bodies at morgues, hospitals, and churches, and digging mass graves to dispose of the bodies they collected. In other instances, children sometimes stumbled across corpses while playing outside. Such encounters with the dead, as detailed in the following testimonies, indicate that the famine continued to be present in everyday life even after it was considered officially over. The next section uses selected testimony from Holodomor survivors to understand further the role that corpses played in the immediate aftermath of the famine.

Corporeal confrontations

There was a collective silence around the deaths. Ms. Maria N., a survivor who provided testimony to the CUF, stated that "bells did not toll for the dead" (U.S. Commission on the Ukraine Famine, *First Interim Report* 153). Those responsible for the removal of bodies are often referred to in testimonies as the "burial brigades." Those who were part of these brigades were conscripted into collecting bodies from the street and taking them to graves on the outskirts of cities and villages. This job, which was usually done by men (but not always), came with a vow of silence. They were not allowed to discuss their job, although it seems clear that everyone knew exactly what they were doing.[5] Several testimonies remark on the fact that

[5] One image, captured by Alexander Wienerberger in 1933, shows a cart of corpses being pulled by horses down a road as several people observe. This type of photo evidence highlights the complicated act of cleaning up the dead while people attempted to go about their everyday duties. Wienerberger titled this photo "Ein alltägliches Bild: Primitiver Leichentransport" (An everyday scene: primitive transport of the dead). Holodomor Photo Directory: http://vitacollections.ca/HREC-holodomorphotodirectory/3636285/data?n=40 (Accessed August 10, 2020).

they knew the people who collected the dead, although the nationality of such men depended on location; some were Ukrainian, some were not.[6]

Depending on where one lived, body collection was done by the local authorities, collective farm workers, village and city residents, or medical personnel. The so-called "burial brigades" would remove bodies using a variety of techniques and equipment, but the use of trucks and simple peasant carts was most common. The bodies were usually picked up once or twice a day and taken away from public view and usually thrown into mass graves outside of town. Mykola Kostyrko remembers that "On the streets, especially on the outskirts of town, lay the bodies of those who died of starvation" (U.S. Commission on the Ukraine Famine, *Second Interim Report* 6). Other survivors state that the bodies were piled near the woods and burned as a way to erase any indication of their existence. An anonymous male from the Zhytomyr region recalled that brigades often made use of the area's vast quarries to dispose of bodies in remote locations (Case History LH02, *Investigation of the Ukrainian Famine*, Oral History Project of the Commission on the Ukraine Famine, vol. 1, 21). Other survivors noted the presence of bodies in public spaces. Illia Mykytovych Demydenko recalled seeing corpses being piled up on a platform of a train station that ran routes between Kharkiv and Poltava (Case History LH59, *Investigation of the Ukrainian Famine*, Oral History Project of the Commission on the Ukraine Famine, vol. 2, 64).

The mass graves that were dug for the dead were purposely located on the outskirts of towns as a way to remove them from sight. The reasons for doing this were numerous. For one, there were issues of space, health, and sanitation that necessitated mass graves being away from living quarters. However, there were more dubious reasons as well. Mass graves in distant locations specifically helped authorities to make invisible, at least temporarily, any wrongdoing on their behalf. Fedir Kapusta remembered this well. Kapusta, who lived in the village of Horby in Poltava raion, noted in his testimony that authorities in his area would try to hide and conceal the hungry and exhausted (Case History LH08, *Investigation of the Ukrainian Famine*, Oral History Project of the Commission on the Ukraine Famine, vol. 1, 85). Those who helped collect the bodies were rewarded with bread, a cruel irony considering the presence of mass hunger. An eyewitness to one instance of body collection recalls the disregard the collectors had for the dead. Olek-sander Merkelo, whose testimony is found in the CUF's *Second Interim Report*, stated: "I saw how special brigades

[6] For more on the role of Holodomor perpetrators, see Daria Mattingly, "Idle, Drunk and Good-for-nothing: The Rank-and-File Perpetrators of 1932–1933 Famine in Ukraine and Their Representation in Cultural Memory," (PhD Dissertation, University of Cambridge, 2018).

gathered the corpses from the streets and the houses and carted them to common graves, or simply threw them in ravines. Even the 'undertakers' themselves were half-dead" (U.S. Commission on the Ukraine Famine, *Second Interim Report* 6). The disrespect for dead bodies can also be understood from post-mortem documentation. For example, we know that death certificates could never officially indicate that hunger was the real cause of death, although some do explicitly state this.[7] Most death certificates listed sickness or disease as the cause of death, as a way of denying culpability. For example, one death certificate belonging to an individual who died when they were just twenty-six years old lists the cause of death as cachexia.[8] One survivor, Oleksiy Keis, claimed that officials were never to write *holod* (famine) on death certificates, and instead they invented all kinds of causes of death to account for the mass deaths (Case History SW52, *Investigation of the Ukrainian Famine*, Oral History Project of the Commission on the Ukraine Famine, vol. 2, 1101).

Not everyone, however, had such contempt for the dead. For some Ukrainians who were responsible for collecting corpses in their villages, towns, and cities, the proper treatment of bodies offered a chance for small acts of honorability. Some burial brigades did their job properly and went house to house to collect the dead each morning from their neighbors and friends. Maria S., who was from Kyiv, remembered that two men went to homes every day to collect the bodies of those that died the previous evening. Maria recalled in her testimony that the two men who collected bodies treated the bodies with respect. She stated, "People in Ukraine were pious, who treated corpses with compassion and dignity" (Case History SW42, *Investigation of the Ukrainian Famine*, Oral History Project of the Commission on the Ukraine Famine, vol. 2, 987). The respectful treatment of the dead was a way for survivors to mark their humanness in a time when little regard for human life seemed to matter to those responsible for the man-made famine.

---

[7] A number of death certificates state that hunger/famine was the cause of death. Three death certificates from 1933 that are preserved in an archive in Cherkasy reflect this. The deaths of Ustym Linchevsky, Anna Trokhimchak, and Vasyl Tabanets all state that cause of death was due to *holod* (famine). All three death certificates can be found at the State Archives of Cherkasy Oblast. For Ustym Linchevskyi, see f. R-5899, op. 10, file no. 42, pg. 12. For Anna Trokhimchak, see f. R-5899, op. 17, file no. 9, sheet 21. And for Vasyl Tabanets, see f. R-5899, op. 17, file 9, sheet 10. Link: https://www.ck.archives.gov.ua/?type=vystavka&id=3 (Accessed July 28, 2020).

[8] See State Archives of Mykolaivs'koi Oblast, f. R-5950, op. 11, file no. 63, pg. 130. Link: http://mk.archives.gov.ua/onlinepresent/137-onlinegolodomor3233.html (accessed July 28, 2020).

The removal of bodies took place in both rural and urban settings, and the cities of Kyiv and Kharkiv are mentioned repeatedly in survivor testimony. One advantage of the CUF's interview questions was that they highlighted differences between removal practices in rural and urban settings. This tells us something about the way that geography played a role during the famine. According to witnesses, cities seemed to be of more importance to officials than rural villages. Removing bodies from cities was considered a priority, as the presence of the dead could further alert urban residents to the seriousness of the famine in the countryside and threatened to provide counterevidence to the official Soviet line that there was no starvation in Ukraine. One example is provided by Édouard Herriot's visit to Ukraine in 1933. Soviet officials notoriously cleared the streets in Kyiv, Odesa, and other cities of any sign of hunger and starvation in an effort to prove to the visitor that there was no famine. Satisfied with his visit, Herriot proclaimed that any notion of starvation in Ukraine was false. The Committee on Communist Aggression noted in their report that Herriot "made many public statements to the effect that he saw no famine in the Ukraine and that life there seemed to be quite normal" (Committee on Communist Aggression, *Second Interim Report* 14).

The city of Odesa was of particular concern to authorities due to its location on the Black Sea. Odesa, which was home to several ports, was a regular stop for many ships. Sailors often departed their ships to go into the city for eating, drinking, and entertainment. As such, any sign of dead bodies would pose issues. Mykola Kostyrko remembered this problem well. In his oral history account, he remembered that special brigades would come and remove the bodies from the streets so that foreign sailors who docked in Odesa would not see what was happening (Case History SW50, *Investigation of the Ukrainian Famine*, Oral History Project of the Commission on the Ukraine Famine, vol. 2, 1074).

Urban workers were recruited to help with harvests during the famine when collective farmers were unable to do the job, often because they were weakened by hunger or because entire villages had died out. This brought in a wide range of workers, many from outside Ukraine. This was another reason for the authorities to dispose of the millions of bodies. According to Ivan Oransky, a survivor from the Kharkiv region, bodies were "loaded into an ordinary peasant cart hitched to a horse, as though to cover it completely. They were thrown into one common pit. There was not even a proper grave. The earth was thinly spread out above the [corpses] (U.S. Commission on the Ukraine Famine, *Second Interim Report* 130). Larysa Donchuk remembered the process in Kharkiv as well. She stated: "In Kharkiv, which was Ukraine's so-called capital, trucks drove around at night and picked up those poor people, the dead and the near-dead, and took them who knows where" (U.S. Commission on the Ukraine Famine, *Second Interim Report* 138). Mykola Kovalovsky, who was also in Kharkiv, remembered witnessing the collection and disposal of bodies:

> And I saw with my own eyes how in the early morning the NKVD—it was still the NKVD (actually it was still the GPU)—went out and gathered up those bodies, and there were volunteers who helped them. And they loaded the bodies on trucks and carried them outside the city, where they left them. They put them in common graves and covered them with earth. I myself saw this with my own eyes.[9]

These testimonies reveal another aspect of the secrecy around disposal of bodies. According to them, trucks came at night to take away the bodies, which indicates that the process was meant to be conducted in private and away from prying eyes in order to hide what had happened. Despite such secrecy, it is clear from this evidence that many individuals witnessed the collection and disposal of bodies. It was an open secret.

The accounts of body collection and burial that are discussed in the testimonies collected by the CUF are corroborated by other sources. In Fedir Pigido-Pravoberezhny's *The Stalin Famine: Ukraine in the Year 1933*, several references are made to the secretive nature of burying the dead. In the book, one survivor remembers that bodies were removed at night to a special site that was both fenced and guarded. There was a sign on the outside of the fence that read "Prombud" (short for the vaguely neutral *promyslove budivnytstvo*, or industrial construction) (Pigido-Pravoberezhny 61). Once these sites were full of bodies, the mass grave would be covered with soil and the ground leveled. After this, the authorities would commission the building of parks and recreation areas on top of the mass graves, which further hid evidence of the dead. One of these sites became an exercise field that was used for training by the Red Army (Pigido-Pravoberzhny 61).

At the end of the famine, mass graves held anywhere from a few people to hundreds. By that time, cemeteries were completely full and mass graves were the quickest way to bury the millions who had died. It should also be said that Ukrainians were often prohibited by the Bolsheviks from burying their dead in cemeteries, so options for proper burials were limited. While some of the mass graves have been discovered, others have not. In 1939, while building an electrical transformer substation, builders found the earth below the planned construction site to be unstable (Pigido-

[9] Case History LH24, *Investigation of the Ukrainian Famine*, Oral History Project of the Commission on the Ukraine Famine, vol. 1, 279.

Pravoberezhnyi 61–62). Upon further investigation, it was found that the ground was filled with bodies, a mass grave from the time of the famine. Researchers have recently uncovered more mass grave sites, and it is possible that they may find more if they are willing to consult survivor testimonies. Recently, Yuri Dudnyk, a local historian in Cherkasy, found mass grave sites from the Holodomor in Dzenzelivka, Cherkasy region, that held over five hundred people ("Where Apples Grow on Mass Graves: 4 Stories about Realities of Holodomor," Hromadske International). It is likely that even more graves will be uncovered with the help of local populations and researchers.[10]

Direct encounters with the dead went beyond just witnessing the collection and disposal of bodies. While many survivors saw the dead and witnessed the burial brigades remove and dispose of bodies, others had even closer contact with the dead. One survivor, whose account was read to the Commission via another survivor, Varvara Dilbert, detailed her experience of being thrown into a mass grave by an angry worker. The anonymous female who shared her experience remembered that her stepmother was punished for refusing to turn over her livestock. As punishment for this offense, she was assigned to collect corpses. The narrator, who was the oldest child, was forced to accompany her stepmother as they collected the dead and transported them to mass graves. One day, several people thrown into a mass grave who were still alive began to moan.[11] In an attempt to help them, the narrator ran to a local priest's house and fetched some water to give to the individuals. However, the man in charge of the mass grave was angered by this and threw the narrator herself into the pit on top of the dead bodies. Fortunately, her stepmother was able to pull her out of the grave and save

---

[10] Researchers in Ukraine have made tremendous progress in recovering mass graves from the 1932–33 famine, and they are also starting to find mass graves from the 1946–47 famine. In 2005, the remains of over six hundred people were found near the Pidzamche train station in Lviv. The remains belonged to those who were fleeing famine in the eastern part of Ukraine. They were shot and killed by the Soviet secret police as they attempted to flee. See "Human remains in Lviv confirmed to be those of 1947 famine victims," *The Ukrainian Weekly* (January 13, 2008). Practices of burying famine victims that occurred during the 1932–1933 famine were mimicked during the 1946–47 famine as well. A new online resource, from the Holodomor Museum in Kyiv, provides an interactive map where users can find the location of mass graves by region or district. The map can be found here: https://map.memorialholodomor.org.ua/en/map-2/ (accessed February 27, 2020).

[11] At this time, it was common practice for brigades to throw people who were still alive into mass graves before they were dead. Those who looked like they were near death were considered dead and thrown in. The common test for whether someone would be collected by the burial brigades was their ability to stand up. If an individual could stand up, then they were spared from the death cart. If they could not stand up, they were loaded on with the dead and transported to their grave.

her life before she was buried alive (Case History SW1, *Investigation of the Ukrainian Famine*, Oral History Project of the Commission on the Ukraine Famine, vol 2., 722). As this testimony admits, punishment for a transgression was sometimes a forced encounter with the dead.

Another anonymous female survivor shared an account of a woman who lived in her village. The woman, whom the narrator describes in her story, was a mother to three children during the famine. Two of the children succumbed to hunger and died. Unable to bury the children herself, the mother put the two deceased children in a cellar. For a time, the survivors lived with the dead. Eventually the mother faced death, and she resorted to cutting up pieces of her dead children to feed herself and her remaining eight-year-old son. The mother soon died, but the son lived. The young boy was forced to admit how he survived when other members of his village asked about his mother and siblings, which is how the narrator learned about what happened. The reaction to the young boy's account was disgust, and some villagers even ran away in horror (Case History SW2, *Investigation of the Ukrainian Famine*, Oral History Project of the Commission on the Ukraine Famine, vol. 2, 720). Although graphic, narratives such as this one are important for understanding the dark realities that survivors faced after losing loved ones during the famine. Not only were survivors sometimes unable to bury their dead, they were also forced to *live with corpses and consume them* when completely desperate. Furthermore, the above two testimonies indicate that children regularly encountered dead bodies along with adults. Of course, not all children had the same experiences as the young boy mentioned above, but other testimonies indicate that children often found themselves coming face-to-face with dead bodies while doing everyday things.

Testimony from an anonymous male who was living in Kyiv during the famine provides a vivid account of a time when he and his young friends came across a corpse while playing together. The narrator claimed that one day he and his friends were playing a "cops and robbers" game outside. The narrator remembers that while playing this game, one of the kids jumped into some weeds to hide from the others, landing on top of a decomposing corpse. The smell of the rotting flesh soon attracted a crowd, so he phoned the local militia to come and pick up the body. (Case History LH28, *Investigation of the Ukrainian Famine*, Oral History Project of the Commission on the Ukraine Famine vol. 1, 347). This particular testimony is remarkable because it speaks to how commonplace corpses were in everyday life after the famine. Not only could children unexpectedly land on a corpse while playing games with their friends, they also knew exactly what to do when they encountered a dead individual. The narrator notes immediately after the story that he called the local militia to pick up the body, indicating that established processes for collecting dead famine victims were an integrated part of society that people came to include in their lifeways. Seemingly innocent games of "cops and robbers" took dark turns in 1930s Ukraine.

Conclusion

The topic of dead bodies, and their presence in everyday life during and after the famine, is just one of the major themes to appear in survivor testimonies collected by the U.S. Commission on the Ukraine Famine. Encounters with the dead, which came in many forms, served as regular reminders of the famine's lasting consequences. A turn toward the aftermath of famine, therefore, prompts us to push further into the famine's wake to consider how events like the Holodomor continued to reverberate in survivors' lives after the supposed conclusion of the event. One might push this query even further by asking whether the Holodomor—along with other famines, genocides, and crimes against humanity—really came to an end.

The research presented here is just one example of the type of work that can be done with the survivor and witness testimonies; many other histories are waiting to be written based on these sources. The CUF archive is one of the largest collections of survivor testimony outside Ukraine. All of the testimonies in the CUF's two interim reports and final report to Congress are in English, which makes them accessible to a wide range of researchers. The collection of testimonies in the Oral History Project, which are in Ukrainian, remain largely unused and will be of immense benefit to future famine scholars of famine in Ukraine. For researchers who write regularly on the Holodomor, the CUF may offer new insights into established topics. The testimonies challenge common understandings of the famine and draw attention to the people who lived through it. The more these testimonies are integrated into famine research, the more we will develop sophisticated and nuanced narratives of the Holodomor. Further use of these sources will promote what I believe is a much-needed turn toward the people and individuals who lived through 1932–33. The narratives in these testimonies force us to focus on the lived experience, however dire or grim, to broaden our understanding of famine and its effects. I hope the evidence presented here inspires others to visit the CUF archive and study the rich collection of sources that it houses.

Archives

State Archive of Cherkasy Oblast
State Archive of Mykolaiv Oblast
National Archives and Record Administration (NARA), College Park, College Park, MD

Government Publications

Select Committee on Communist Aggression. House of Representatives. Eighty-third Congress, Second Session. *Second Interim Report.* Washington, D.C.: U.S. Government Printing Office, 1954.

U.S. Commission on the Ukraine Famine. *Investigation of the Ukrainian Famine, 1932–1933. First Interim Report.* Washington, D.C.: U.S. Government Printing Office, 1987.

U.S. Commission on the Ukraine Famine. *Investigation of the Ukrainian Famine, 1932–1933.* Oral History Project of the Commission of the Ukraine Famine, edited by James E. Mace and Leonid Heretz. Washington, D.C.: U.S. Government Printing Office, 1990.

U.S. Commission on the Ukraine Famine. *Investigation of the Ukrainian Famine, 1932–1933. Report to Congress*, edited by James E. Mace and Leonid Heretz. Washington, D.C.: U.S. Government Printing Office, 1988.

U.S. Commission on the Ukraine Famine. *Investigation of the Ukrainian Famine, 1932–1933. Second Interim Report.* Washington, D.C.: U.S. Government Printing Office, 1988.

Bibliography

Applebaum, Anne. *Red Famine: Stalin's War on Ukraine.* New York: Doubleday, 2017.

Bida, Olesya and Anastasia Vlasova, trans. Vladyslav Kudryk. "Where Apples Grow on Mass Graves: 4 Stories About Realities of Holodomor." *Hromadske International,* November 23, 2019. https://en.hromadske.ua/posts/where-apples-grow-on-mass-graves-4-stories-about-realitie s-of-holodomor. Accessed July 29, 2020.

Conquest, Robert. *The Harvest of Sorrow: Soviet Collectivization and the Terror Famine.* Oxford: Oxford University Press, 1986.

Dean, Carolyn J. *The Moral Witness: Trials and Testimony after Genocide.* Ithaca, NY: Cornell University Press, 2019.

Graziosi, Andrea, Lubomyr A. Hajda, and Halyna Hryn, eds. *After the Holodomor: The Enduring Impact of the Great Famine on Ukraine.* Cambridge, MA: Harvard Ukrainian Research Institute, 2014.

Klid, Bohdan and Alexander Motyl, eds. *The Holodomor Reader: A Sourcebook on the Famine of 1932–1933 in Ukraine*. Alberta: Canadian Institute of Ukrainian Studies Press, 2012.

Kuby, Emma. *Political Survivors: The Resistance, the Cold War, and the Fight against Concentration Camps after 1945*. Ithaca, NY: Cornell University Press, 2019.

Kuromiya, Hiroaki. Review of U.S. Commission on the Ukraine Famine, *First Interim Report, Second Interim Report, and Report to Congress, Harvard Ukrainian Studies* 15, no. 1–2 (1991): 230–32.

LaCapra, Dominick. *History and Memory after Auschwitz*. Ithaca, NY: Cornell University Press, 1998.

Marchuk, Larysa. "Human remains in Lviv confirmed to be those of 1947 famine victims." *The Ukrainian Weekly*, January 13, 2008.

Mattingly, Daria. "Idle, Drunk and Good-for-Nothing: The Rank-and-File Perpetrators of 1932–1933 Famine and Their Representation in Cultural Memory." PhD Dissertation, University of Cambridge, 2018.

Mauriello, Christopher. *Forced Confrontation: The Politics of Dead Bodies in Germany at the End of World War II*. Lanham, MD: Lexington Books, 2017.

Pigido-Pravoberezhny, F. *The Stalin Famine: Ukraine in the Year 1933*. London: Ukrainian Publishers Ltd., 1953.

The Places of Mass Burials of Holodomor-Genocide Victims." National Museum "Holodomor Victims Memorial." https://map.memorialholodomor.org.ua/en/map-2/. Accessed February 27, 2020.

Verdery, Katherine. *The Political Lives of Dead Bodies: Reburial and Postsocialist Change*. New York: Columbia University Press, 2000.

Vsetecka, John. "Map of Holodomor Resolutions and Proclamations in the United States and Canada." HREC Education website. https://education.holodomor.ca/resolutions/. Accessed February 26, 2020.

Wienerberger, Alexander. "Ein alltägliches Bild: Primitiver Leichentransport" (An everyday scene: primitive transport of the dead), 1933. Holodomor Photo Directory, Holodomor Research and Education Consortium. http://vitacollections.ca/HREC-holodomorphotodirectory/3636285/data?n=40. Accessed August 10, 2020.

Wolowyna, Oleh et al. "Regional Variations of the 1932–34 Famine Losses in Ukraine." *Canadian Studies in Population* 43, no. 3–4 (2016): 175–202.

History as a Narrative of the People: The Maniak Collection as a Source for the Social and Cultural History of the Holodomor

Olga Klymenko

> I think that what I have written about the past will hardly be illuminated in history, yet while I have not described everything in the disturbing past, what I've written is how it was, for I was a witness and a martyr of that time. I urge you to forgive me for the extensiveness of what is written and not to leave me without an answer.
>
> *Hryhorii Kuchmii*[1]

The Maniak Collection consists of written accounts about the 1932–33 famine, a topic which was taboo in the Soviet Union until the late 1980s. They were submitted by members of the general public in late 1988–89 in response to a public call in Ukraine to contribute personal recollections to a "people's memorial" to the 1932–33 famine.

These letters constitute an important primary source for the study of the Holodomor, its impact on the lives of individuals and villages and the transformation of the Ukrainian countryside as viewed through the eyes of the famine's living witnesses and survivors.

The collection is named after Volodymyr Maniak, who, along with his spouse and co-editor Lidiia Kovalenko-Maniak, was instrumental in gathering the accounts and spearheading the publication of the ground-breaking book *33-ii: Holod: Narodna Knyha-Memorial.*[2] The volume includes 1,000 accounts, while another set of letters[3] intended for publication in an additional volume of personal memoirs has never been published. Electronic copies (scans) of close to seven hundred letters, some of them unrelated to the Famine, were given by the Maniaks to their acquaintance Wolodymyr Bojczuk, a French-Ukrainian historian, and were subsequently passed on by Bojczuk to the

---

[1] Kuchmii Hryhorii (Grigorii) | HREC (holodomor.ca). Letters cited in this paper are posted in alphabetical order in the "Maniak Collection" section of the Holodomor Research and Education Consortium website located at https://holodomor.ca/resource/maniak-collection/ and referred to from now on as "HREC (holodomor.ca)".

[2] Volodymyr Maniak and Lidiia Kovalenko, eds. *33-ii: Holod: Narodna Knyha*-Memorial (Kyiv: Radianskyi pysmennyk, 1991).

[3] Close to 5,000, according to some estimates.

Holodomor Research and Education Consortium.[4] This paper concerns that part of the HREC Maniak Collection that is already transcribed, partially translated, indexed, and published on the HREC website.[5]

Recognition of the need for a memorial book that would acknowledge the man-made nature of the 1932–33 Famine and the extent of human suffering it caused in Ukraine was linked to the initially cautious debate about events that had long been taboo subjects in the Soviet Union. This debate emerged in the nascent Ukrainian public sphere at the beginning of democratization in the USSR, spearheaded by Mikhail Gorbachev.[6] In the latter part of 1988, a key event in establishing the Maniak Collection appeared to be two public calls soliciting written witness accounts about the famine.

Literaturna Ukraïna (1988, No. 45), the official weekly of the Writers' Union of Ukraine, published a full page titled "*Holod-33*" (The Famine of '33). On that page, an editorial note refers to publications about the 1932–33 Famine in *Pravda*[7] and letters from readers on the topic to *Literaturna Ukraïna* and *Sil's'ki visti* as reasons behind *Literaturna Ukraïna* taking up

---

[4] Bojczuk passed on scans of the letters, along with selected draft transcriptions performed by his associates. He also sent to HREC a selection of twelve original letters as partial proof of the authenticity of the letters in his possession.

[5] Maniak Collection | HREC (holodomor.ca). Ninety-seven letters were prepared for publishing by Andrij Makuch in 2017–18. The author prepared the rest and is currently working on cataloging and indexing the remaining letters in the collection in preparation for publishing them in a format that would allow for subject and keyword search. 133 copies of the original letters are housed at the Ukrainian Canadian Research and Documentation Centre (UCRDC) Archives. UCRDC archivist Iroida Wynnyckyj obtained the letters during a meeting with Volodymyr Maniak in Kyiv in November of 1990. http://www.ucrdc.org/Archive-Oral-History-Maniak_Collection.html. Editorial assistance with the text of this article was provided by Ksenia Maryniak.

[6] On the events that led to the recognition of the Holodomor by the then Communist Party of Ukraine leadership, academics, and the leading role of civil society actors such as the Writers' Union of Ukraine in the emergence of the first and only installment of *33ii-Holod*, see: Heorhii Kas'ianov, *Danse macabre: holod 1921–1933 rokiv u politytsi, masovii svidomosti ta istoriohrafiï (1980-ti — pochatok 2000-kh)* (Kyiv: Instytut istorii Ukrainy NAN Ukrainy; Nash chas, 2010), 11–33; Georgy Kasianov, "Revisiting the Great Famine of 1932–1933. Politics of Memory and Public Consciousness (Ukraine after 1991)," in Michal Kopecek, ed. *Past in the Making: Historical Revisionism in Central Europe after 1989* (Budapest-New York: CEU Press, 2008), 197–219; Liudmyla Hrynevych, "Vid zaperechuvannia do vymushenoho vyznannia. Pro mekhanizmy vkhodzhennia temy holodu 1932–1933 rr. v ofitsiinyi publichnyi prostir v SRSR ta URSR naprykintsi 1980-kh," *Problemy istoriï Ukraïny: fakty, sudzhennia, poshuky: mizhvidomchyi zbirnyk naukovykh prats'*, Vyp. 18 (Kyiv, 2008), 211–44. http://dspace.nbuv.gov.ua/bitstream/handle/123456789/13343/22-Hrynevych.pdf?sequence=1

[7] The official newspaper of the Central Committee of the Communist Party of the Soviet Union, based in Moscow; publications on August 29, September 16, September 30, and October 3.

the topic. The head of the Writers' Union, Yevhen Hutsalo,[8] reported that a discussion about the famine at a meeting of the Presidium of the Writers' Union in late June of 1988 led to the decision to create a book that would be a people's memorial to the 1932–33 Famine, made up of the testimonies of survivors. On behalf of the Writers' Union, Hutsalo informally appealed to readers of the newspaper to take an active part in the creation of a book that would supply some "hard truths" about the famine and commemorate the millions of victims of Stalinism. Such a "people's memorial" would "supplement" what was lacking in the official historical narrative still perpetuated at the time in Ukraine, which silence was lamented by a teacher named Vasyl Pakharenko on the bottom half of the page in an opinion piece.[9]

On December 9, 1988, an appeal to the public to submit their personal accounts of the Famine appeared in *Sil's'ki visti*, the newspaper with the highest circulation in Ukraine at that time, reaching more than two million readers.[10] The appeal was signed by the history professor Stanislav Kulchytsky[11] and informed readers of the proposed memorial book's editorial board, including Volodomyr Maniak as editor-in-chief. The purpose of the book was to investigate the causes of the 1933 famine "that took away the lives of millions of Ukrainians and to name those responsible for this tragedy." Eyewitness accounts were requested in view of the fact that official documents were not likely to contain full and truthful information about the Famine because of the taboo during the Soviet period on any mention of the famine, even in secret government documents. The appeal listed a number of specific questions of interest to the editorial board and asked for the letters to be sent to *Sil's'ki visti* or to Volodymyr Maniak's home address.[12] On January 3, 1989, *Sil's'ki visti* published a report on the book's progress along with

---

[8] Yevhen Hutsalo, "Stvorymo knyhu narodnoi pam'iatï," *Literaturna Ukraïna* no. 45 (1988).

[9] Vasyl Pakharenko, a teacher from Cherkasy oblast, criticizes the official "blameless" version of the Famine and poses a question: Why is it that even the scholars and writers are afraid to talk openly about the famine in Ukraine in 1988? Vasyl' Pakharenko, "Holod," *Literaturna Ukraïna* no. 45 (1988).

[10] It seems to signify that the efforts of the Writers' Union spearheaded by Maniak, being a member, came to fruition.

[11] S. Kul'chyts'kyi, ""33-ii: Holod," Zaproshuiemo do stvorennia knyhy-memorialu," *Sil's'ki visti*, December 9, 1988. The appeal is given more detailed consideration below.

[12] According to Kulchytsky, Maniak was the driving force behind the memorial book. With the Writers' Union's backing, Maniak turned to the historians at the Institute of History of Ukraine and Kulchytsky personally offered to join forces. The work on the book was conducted in two "independent" streams: Maniak working on the letters, and historians on finding the documents that were added to the volume. Stanislav Kul'chitskii, "Kak osmyslivali Golodomor," in *Kak on nas unichtozhal. Stalin i ukrainskii golodomor* (Kyiv, 2007), 8. https://royallib.com/read/kulchitskiy_stanislav/pochemu_on_nas_unichtogal_stalin_i_ukrainskiy_golodomor.html#0.

excerpts from more than a dozen letters.[13] Indeed, on July 11, 1989, Volodymyr Maniak reported that he and Lidiia Kovalenko had completed the manuscript.[14]

Maniak described *33ii: Holod* as both an ethical and historical endeavor: "a fulfillment of a debt to the memory of millions of compatriots killed by the Stalinists," "an all-Ukrainian lament, all-Ukrainian memory cemetery, and encyclopedia of grief and sadness," and "a farewell to fear" implanted by the Stalinist famine and total collectivization. The memorial book, Maniak claimed, would portray the "unembellished" past "as it was in real life" and as such was "a sign of the new age: history was returning to the people and truth to history." The past as it appeared in *33-ii: Holod*

> ... does not belong to anyone in particular. ... It is capable of being an active force in preventing new mistakes and crimes, new flare-ups of violence... it is necessary to name those who caused the tragedy and to memorialize those who perished. It is also necessary to track the roots of society's demoralization and the desensitization caused by the famine.[15]

It is hard to overestimate the scale and significance of Maniak and Kovalenko's pioneering civic and historical endeavour.[16] The collection of letters in *Holod: 33ii* is the earliest large-scale attempt in Ukraine to "give voice to the people." It was a notable achievement of the nascent Ukrainian civil society to raise the Holodomor as a public issue and an important early primary source of witness accounts about this tragedy.[17] The memorial book

---

13 Oleksandr Matiiko, "Bil' dushi liuds'koï: Tvoryt'sia knyha-memorial "33-ii: Holod"," *Sil's'ki visti*, January 3, 1989.

14 Volodymyr Maniak, "Holod: chomu i iak. Rozdumy na drukopysom knyhy-memorialu "33-ii: Holod," *Sil's'ki visti*, July 11, 1989. It also serves as an introduction to the memorial book: Volodymyr Maniak. "Holod: chomu i iak," in Maniak and Kovalenko, *33-ii: Holod*, 7–14.

15 "Spiritual devastation," spiritual losses, depeasantization (*rozselianiuvannia*) and the acquired aversion to [work on] the land, and Ukrainian demographic losses caused by the Famine, that she estimates at 7.5 million, are the main themes of Lidiia Kovalenko's introduction to the memorial book. Maniak and Kovalenko, *33-ii: Holod*, 15–24.

16 Close to 6,000 letters were submitted to the editorial boards of *Literaturna Ukraïna*, *Sil's'ki visti*, and the Maniaks' residence in late 1988–mid-1989. Selected abridged accounts and responses to them were published in both periodicals. One thousand accounts—edited for readability, accompanied by a short biographical note and sometimes a picture of the correspondent—were divided into five oblasts, accompanied with photo illustrations, excerpts from official documents, and academic and editorial commentary, and appeared in *33ii: Holod*, which was ready for publication in July 1989 but only published two years later, in 1991, after the declaration of Ukraine's sovereignty.

17 The fact that the letters were edited for readability and abridged is a limitation of *33-ii: Holod* as a primary source from an academic standpoint. A few letters in HREC's collection are the originals of the letters which were included in the memorial book. They show the edits that were supposed to improve the readability and sometimes exclude content that was deemed

"marked the first instance of turning to everyday national consciousness as an alternative to official history."[18] Maniak was killed in a road accident in June 1992, and Kovalenko passed away not long after, in January 1993. As a result, the intended subsequent volume of personal famine accounts never came to fruition. The letters acquired by HREC are now being transcribed, translated, and published on the organization's website.[19]

Overview of the Maniak Collection

Unlike the accounts published in the memorial book, the letters in the Maniak Collection are unabridged and unedited, preserving the authors' original language. These letters, their language and stories can be considered relatively "uncontaminated" by external scripts and established frameworks, given the nascent state of public and academic debates about the Holodomor at the time they were written (November 1988–October 1989).[20] An overwhelming majority of the letters are rather spontaneous and unscripted open-ended responses to the appeal. They often do not confine themselves to the theme of famine or the questions raised in the calls for submission. The letters

---

redundant or not related to the Holodomor. It is possible that priority was given to the letters that focus on the experiences of the victims, but that would only be logical given the purpose of the book: it was, after all, a memorial book meant to memorialize the victims.

[18] Georgy Kasianov, "Revisiting the Great Famine of 1932–1933: Politics of Memory and Public Consciousness (Ukraine after 1991)," 206. Kasianov acknowledges: "The appeal to "witnesses" through the newspaper created a precedent for commemorative practice that was unique in the Ukrainian experience. This was, in effect, a program of "remembrance" that not only influenced the direction and nature of the whole process but also largely determined the way in which the events of 1932–33 were subsequently imagined in the mass consciousness — indeed, the formation of collective memory." Ibid.

[19] Maniak Collection | HREC (holodomor.ca).

[20] Elsewhere, Georgy Kasianov criticizes *33-ii: Holod* for a "one-sided presentation of the famine" which, in his opinion, carries all the attributes of the "canonical version" created in the diaspora, in which only those accounts that depicted the horrors of people dying in their own dwellings and "accompanying excesses" were preselected. Nevertheless, he believes that the rest of the letters in the collection represent a valuable source that is under-utilized by scholars. Heorhii Kas'ianov, *Danse Macabre*, 32. Indeed, as the memorial book's editors, Maniak and Kovalenko can be viewed as "cultural brokers" who create paratexts that "embed the individual story in the larger story of a group" to "affirm the authenticity of the witness and the narrative, "the epitextual conditions" of a witness narrative's circulation and reception" (Gillian Whitlock, *Soft Weapons: Autobiography in Transit* (Chicago: University of Chicago Press, 2007): 61–62, cited in Sidonie Smith and Julia Watson, "Witness or False Witness?: Metrics of Authenticity, Collective Informations and the Ethic of Verification in First-Person Testimony," *Biography* 35, no. 4 (Fall 2012), 595.) However, despite an overarching framework created by the introduction, conclusion, and other textual intermissions, and based on the content of the letters that I review here, it appears that the content of the memorial book was largely influenced by the material and themes derived from the letters rather than following some pre-selected ideological guidelines.

represent most regions of Ukraine affected by the famine in 1932–33.[21] Two-thirds of the correspondents were born between 1917 and 1926, which means that they were children from six to sixteen years old at the time of the famine.[22] Close to 90 percent of the letters are written in Ukrainian.[23] The overwhelming majority of those who wrote the letters survived the famine in rural districts.

Many letters are written by semi-literate people using *surzhyk*[24] and colloquial language. They often lack punctuation, capitalization, and paragraph arrangement, and contain confusing spelling and structure. Poor handwriting is another challenge. The writers often apologize for these shortcomings. Some correspondents mention that this is their first opportunity to speak about their experiences during the famine. Quite a few of them acknowledge writing a letter for the first time in their lives,[25] perhaps a testimony to the urgency and enduring significance of the Holodomor for them. A few pledge to speak only of those things they

---

[21] 224 testimonies have been uploaded to the Maniak Collection on the HREC website so far (Maniak Collection. Holodomor Research and Education Consortium (HREC). HYPERLINK "https://holodomor.ca/resource/maniak-collection/" https://holodomor.ca/resource/maniak-collection/ — from here on referred to as Maniak Collection | HREC (holodomor.ca)). Most testimonies describe events in locales in what are now Poltava oblast (61) and Vinnytsia oblast (42), followed by Kyiv (25), Kirovohrad (20), Zhytomyr (17), Cherkasy (17), Sumy (10), Mykolaiv (7), Cherhiniv (5), Odesa (5), Dnipropetrovsk (5), Kharkiv (3), Kherson (1), Khmelnytsky (1), Luhansk (1), and Zaporizhzhia (1) oblasts. Out of 111 letters prepared by the author for publication in 2019, in terms of the administrative division of late 1932–early 1933, most letters describe events in Kharkiv oblast (51), followed by Kyiv (21), Odesa (16), Vinnytsia (12), AMSRR -1; the location was not indicated for 3 letters. This, however, is just a rough indication of the geographic scope of the events described by the letters. The author is currently preparing for publication on the HREC website a new series of letters, some of which, for instance, focus on events in what are now Kherson and Kharkiv oblasts.

[22] Estimates are based on 111 letters processed by the author in 2019. Correspondents whose age was indicated by the year of birth or age at the time of the famine were born between 1904 and 1939.

[23] It is tempting to suggest that Ukrainian language in the letters serves as a social marker of the peasantry or indicates the extent of Ukrainization for the generation of those who grew up in the 1920s–30s. However, this is rather a hypothesis that requires separate examination. Alternatively, such results can be explained by the fact that the appeals were published in Ukrainian-language newspapers, so their target-audience turned out to be primarily Ukrainian speaking.

[24] Here, *surzhyk* implies a creole version of Ukrainian, contaminated by Russian words.

[25] See, for example, Chuprun Mariia | HREC (holodomor.ca). The power of such testimonies as a form "derives more from a pledge of truthfulness and a performance of good faith than from a strict, conclusive evidentiary reliability," and "plain language conveying 'the truth' of horrific experience" appears to be one of their authenticating aspects. See: Sidonie Smith and Julia Watson, "Witness or False Witness? Metrics of Authenticity, Collective Information and the Ethic of Verification in First-Person Testimony," 596, 620.

witnessed with their own eyes and to tell only the truth.[26] Some wrote more than one letter and inquired whether their previous letters were received, or why they were not published. Some ask for instructions on how to better compose a letter to ensure publication so that their story is heard or at least their name is mentioned as a famine survivor.[27]

There is a significant variety in types of accounts in the collection. Some are general one-page notes with a few words about the author's relatives who died during the Holodomor (often for reasons that the authors find difficult to put into words or are unsure about what details to include). Others are multi-page descriptions of the author's personal experiences, rich in details about the famine in its many experiential aspects. While some correspondents decry a life of deprivation and suffering, a few supply stories of resourcefulness and ingenious survival of the seemingly unsurvivable.[28] There are letters that put the famine in a long-term perspective, starting with family genealogy from the time of World War I, discussing the effects of the famine on families and villages, and finding their echo in the period of Gorbachev's *perestroika.* There are letters from local civic activists who collected testimonies in their villages[29] (some sent more than one letter),[30] letters with local newspaper clippings enclosed that contain stories of surviving the famine;[31] letters with original poems;[32] fictionalized accounts based on someone else's experiences, and those that fictionalize the author's own lived experience.[33] A few accounts contain

---

[26] Many correspondents apologize profusely for the lack of literacy or the "inadequacy" of their stories. They admit that they were urged to write about their experiences when they heard that someone was interested in hearing them out or that they wanted to make sure that future generations know the truth about what happened in 1932–33 and will not let anything like it happen again.

[27] "I beg you, I am not a very literate person, and I would like to get your advice on how to write so that you could print at least my last name and one line about how I survived the '33 famine by a miracle. I very much beg you to advise me how to write. My letter may have many grammatical mistakes, but I am sorry, I had very little schooling, only five grades. Everything I have written is the pure truth and nothing but the truth." Khurdei Oleksii (Aleksei) | HREC (holodomor.ca).

[28] Hruby Denys | HREC (holodomor.ca); Yatsenko Olha | HREC (holodomor.ca).

[29] Neporozhnii A.A., Petrenko Olha, Shcherbak Dominika | HREC (holodomor.ca).

[30] Slavhorodsky P. | HREC (holodomor.ca); Slavhorodsky P.M. | HREC (holodomor.ca).

[31] Hlushchenko Danylo, Komar A.H. | HREC (holodomor.ca); Tkachenko P. | HREC (holodomor.ca).

[32] Chvora Melaniia | HREC (holodomor.ca).

[33] Ivan Kravchenko, a native of the village of Biliaky, submitted a fictionalized memoir of his co-villager Hryhorii Musiienko. He claims that the account is "documentary" and all the characters are real. An entry about Kravchenko can be found in Ukrainian Wiki https://uk.wikipedia.org/wiki/Кравченко_Іван_Іванович). The main character in this colourful and vivid account tried to avoid the famine and thanks to his skills as an accountant escapes the village and finds work at the Semenivka raion council, where he survives by receiving a double

information about living in the city during the famine[34] or being a member of a search brigade.[35] For many, writing the letter was a cathartic event, even if some correspondents ask that their accounts not be published or that their names not be revealed.[36] In most cases, however, the authors want to make sure that their personal stories and the names of the victims are known and will live in public memory. They also want to make public the names of the perpetrators for an entirely different reason: that they not only be known but also prosecuted.

Correspondents often write about their families, villages, hamlets, and their own lives before and after the Holodomor, conveying the sense that the 1932–33 famine was a life-altering event in their own lives and in the lives of many others. There are occasional letters in the collection that are apologetic towards the collectivization and blame the Ukrainian SSR's leadership for the famine,[37] letters whose authors are unsure whom to blame more—Stalin or the local enforcers of his regime[38]—and those that suggest that the atrocities of the famine years should be left in the past. Yet almost every letter offers evidence that requisitioning went far beyond grain procurement and that the famine was caused by almost universal and *total* grain and foodstuff seizure and accompanied by the breakdown of

---

ration (two meals a day in a cafeteria) but eventually returns to his village in time for harvesting. Kravchenko Ivan (for Musiienko Hryhorii) | HREC (holodomor.ca). Vasyl Yarmolenko supplied a 24-page fictionalized memoir of him as a child experiencing the famine with his extended family in the village of Yakubyntsi in Myrhorod raion. Yarmolenko Vasyl | HREC (holodomor.ca). Nadiia Dabizha (Domaratska) (b. 1925, native of Novopavlivka (Bashtanka raion, Odesa oblast at the time) provides a brief account of the fate of the members of her extended family who were affected by the famine and war (pp. 38–39). Her grandfather died of famine, as well as some of her aunts and uncles and cousins. The bulk of the testimony, pp. 2–37, comprises two stories written by her. One, "1933," is a story she recorded from her uncle, Stepan Shcherbyna, b. 1908, about him returning to his home village for a short stay from the Donbas, where he worked at a mine in 1933, and getting in trouble with the local authorities, being stuck and hiding in the village (unpublished).

[34] Olha Yatsenko describes surviving the famine as a technical college (*tekhnikum*) student in Poltava, Yatsenko Olha | HREC (holodomor.ca); Pavlo Mysak experiences famine as an 18-year-old student studying in his third year of *robfak* (worker's faculty; a special program of studies preparing working-class students for university studies) at Vinnytsia Pharmaceutical Institute in 1933. Mysak Pavlo | HREC (holodomor.ca).

[35] Melnyk Oleksii | HREC (holodomor.ca)

[36] "Please do not give my name." Thus concludes a letter from the village of Shkurupii, Reshetylivka raion, Kharkiv oblast (now in Poltava oblast), that documents the deaths of children whom the author knew and includes a poem about the Famine. Chvora Melaniia | HREC (holodomor.ca. Tetiana Komlichenko wants to believe that future generations will not know such tragedies as her generation lived through, apologizes if she has written something wrong, and requests that her letter not be published in the newspaper. Komlichenko Tetiana | HREC (holodomor.ca).

[37] Parasotka Stepan | HREC (holodomor.ca).

[38] Komlichenko Tetiana | HREC (holodomor.ca).

social order, abuses of power, violence, banditry, and extrajudicial killings.[39] Many of these written accounts are rich in recollections about both the perpetrators of atrocities and those who did what was in their power to help people survive.

The outlook of the writers is usually local: they describe events in their immediate locale or within a few neighboring villages. A few exceptions are accounts of those who managed to travel outside the village in search of food or work or had relatives elsewhere (in the Donbas or Caucasus) with whom some of the authors were placed as children to give them better chances of survival,[40] or students who lived in the cities but were sent to the villages as agitators or helpers and could observe events from a wider perspective.

At the same time, their perspective is usually also long-term. The writers place the events of the famine in the continuity of their own lives and lives of their families and locales to demonstrate how they were affected by the famine, and how what happened during the famine compares to other significant events—the Civil War, the 1921–22 famine, NEP, World War II (the "Great Patriotic War"), the 1946–47 famine, and post—World War II life, up to the time of writing. Thus, the letters in the Maniak Collection contain survivors' stories and myriad, details, subjects, and perspectives that might not have been illuminated through structured interviews only about the Holodomor.[41]

The Maniak Collection offers, on the one hand, a large volume of letters and a wide scope of recurrent themes that allow for generalizations and, on the other, an extraordinary richness of detail and description in living language. The individual stories of survival and personal reflections about experiences before, during, and after the Holodomor are an invaluable source on a variety of subjects directly related to the Holodomor and an important source of insights into various aspects of social and cultural history of the Ukrainian peasantry from the 1920s well into the middle of the twentieth century.

Next I will highlight some subjects that appear to have had an overarching importance for authors of many of the letters and that often reach beyond the questions suggested in the calls for submission and the subject of the Holodomor.

---

[39] Demydenko Yeva | HREC (holodomor.ca); Shevchyk Mykhailo | HREC (holodomor.ca); Ilchenko Ivan | HREC (holodomor.ca); Prokopchuk Mykhail | HREC (holodomor.ca).

[40] Mazepa Hanna | HREC (holodomor.ca); Kutsenko, Yakiv (Yakov) | HREC (holodomor.ca)

[41] Here I mean interviews of witnesses that are usually limited in scope by the type of questions posed by interviewers.

The call and the responses: Questions answered and unanswered

In the appeal published on December 9, 1988,[42] Kulchytsky, on behalf of the editorial board of the memorial book, asked the public to contribute to the creation of this "sad but badly needed historical document" by submitting written testimonies on topics of special interest to the editorial board, including: the so-called "sabotage" of grain procurement by party workers and economic functio-naries *(hospodarnyky)* (according to the published words of Stalin, most rural Communists sabotaged the grain requisitioning); repression of the leaders and rank-and-file members of collective farms for arrears in grain requisitioning; forms of decentralized help to the starving (at the republic, oblast, raion and local, collective farm levels); the fate of villages named on blacklists ("black board"); numbers of famine victims in villages; assistance from cities for spring sowing in 1933; and any other recollections of eyewitnesses.

Very few letters address all or even most of the questions in Kulchytsky's appeal.[43] The authors simply recall the most memorable aspects of their own experiences during the Holodomor, not necessarily in any structured manner. Only one author attempts to respond to the questions posed by Kulchytsky, but not before writing a few pages of his own reflections on the detrimental impact of the famine on the social fabric and morals of his native village.[44]

Moreover, I have not come across any responses to the question about blacklisted villages, and very few letters mention any help coming from outside the village to alleviate the famine in the spring of 1933. Yakiv Panov from the village of Soldatske, Velyka Pysarivka raion in Kharkiv oblast[45] claims that the peasants sowed the fields themselves with what they had. The horses were so exhausted that they fell in the furrows, and the drivers would lift them up. So, his answer to the question whether anyone helped the starving people is "No, they confiscated everything until people died of hunger. And those who were left alive were driven into the collective farm."[46] His account is seconded by Mykola Syvoborodko: "[As for] Forms of

---

[42] S. Kul'chyts'kyi, "33-ii: Holod". Zaproshuiemo do stvorennia knyhy-memorialu."

[43] Here I am referring to the set of 150 letters from the Maniak Collection that I read and indexed by November 2019.

[44] Mykola Syvoborodko recalls the events of the famine in the village of Semenivka, Arbuzynka raion, Odesa oblast (now in Mykolaiv oblast). He addresses questions about the sabotage of grain procurement by party and industrial institutions, repressions against the executive personnel in raions and oblasts as well as regular collective farm workers, decentralized aid to the starving, "helpers" from the city, and human losses. Syvoborodko Mykola | HREC (holodomor.ca).

[45] In 1933; now in Sumy oblast.

[46] Panov Yakiv (Yakov) | HREC (holodomor.ca).

decentralized aid for the hungry. In our area there was no such help." Only later, for hoeing, weeding, and harvesting crops, they sent students from schools in Odesa, although "this did not contribute noticeably" because as students/city dwellers they "had no understanding of rural husbandry and could not differentiate a cow from a bull, corn from wheat, or sunflowers from millet, barley or oats."[47]

Some letters mention visits by Ukrainian SSR officials. For instance, Yurii Kozlov, a student at the time, mentions that Pavlo Postyshev visited Pyriatyn and that Hryhorii Petrovsky did so in the summer of 1933, but their visits made no difference to the conditions of the starving.[48] According to Syvoborodko, officials in Kyiv knew about the famine and did nothing, either because they did not want to or because they could not.[49] Pavlo Mysak mentions that Petrovsky visited Kovalivka[50] in May 1933. Following his visit and by his order, one train car of flour was delivered to Kovalivka. Since "neither medical staff nor village leaders were in control," this giveaway led to catastrophic results. "The flour was apportioned to the people; they baked bread and ate it and even more began to die."[51]

Hardly any letter in the set mentions acts of sabotage of the grain procurement by the Communist Party, village councils, or collective farm leaders. Those respondents who discuss the issue suggest that accusations of sabotage usually were the result of some gesture of compassion toward the villagers or collective farmer workers. The perceived offenders were

---

[47] Syvoborodko mentions some "helpers" sent from the cities to help in the fields and describes them as inept, except for a group from one of the local German colonies that turned out to be relatively useful. Syvoborodko Mykola | HREC (holodomor.ca)

[48] "In 1933, H. I. Petrovsky [co-chairman of the USSR Central Executive Committee] came to Pyriatyn; he helped only a little bit, but he gave the order to sweep up all the flour dust in the mills and cook it with some nettles to make a soup. At the same time, the mills worked and processed the available grain that was there and that was brought from somewhere. Sometime in June-July, [Pavlo] Postyshev [Second Secretary of the Central Committee of the Communist Party (Bolshevik) of Ukraine] arrived. What issues he resolved, I do not know." Kozlov Yurii | HREC (holodomor.ca).

[49] "Did the leaders of the Soviet government, the Central Committee of the Communist Party of Ukraine (Bolshevik), know? Yes, they knew. This is corroborated by the visit of the secretary of the CC CPU Stanislav Vikentiiovych Kosior, who arrived at the state farm [*radhosp*] by car. I saw him myself. He was meeting the management of the state farm. We youngsters listened in on the adults from afar. S. V. Kosior was asking about the state of affairs in the area. A bit later at the Kavuny station in Arbuzynka raion, H. I. Petrovsky, head of the All-Ukrainian Central Executive Committee, arrived in a train with 2–3 cars and spoke in front of the people. The leaders of the oblast were in the raion frequently. We boys ran to look at them. Though for some reason nobody helped during the famine or did not have the ability to do so." Syvoborodko Mykola | HREC (holodomor.ca)

[50] A village of "more than ten thousand inhabitants" in Nemyriv raion, Vinnytsia oblast.

[51] Mysak Pavlo | HREC (holodomor.ca)

demoted, stripped of party membership,[52] put on trial, executed, deported, or sent to prison camps as "saboteurs."[53]

Mykola Syvoborodko denies that there was sabotage by local Communists, who were persecuted nonetheless.

> I can say with certainty that the rural Communists never sabotaged the grain procurement. On the contrary, they did everything they could to carry out the secondary and tertiary plans. And if they did not carry them out it was because there was nothing left from which to carry them out—everything had been taken. There were cases of certain villagers hiding grain, not because they did not want to give it up but because they needed it to save themselves from starvation. ...
>
> The repressions against executive personnel in raions and oblasts became incredible. We regular collective farm workers sometimes couldn't even remember their last names, as one after another they disappeared after being labelled "enemy of the people" or some other formulation.[54]

Maria Bilenko's father was stripped of his candidacy for membership in the Communist Party for refusing to take away all grain and food from the collective farm members, leaving some for children. Like Syvoborodko, she knows of "no sabotage as such in the village, because in almost everybody's case there was nothing left to eat. Still the raion leaders deported a lot of people to Siberia for allegedly sabotaging grain procurement."[55]

Attempts to distribute some flour, grain, or other food to make sure that the collective farm workers were capable of working were punished by the authorities. Yakiv Petrenko recalls that in the spring of 1933, when the sowing had to be done, people were too exhausted and swollen to work. The collective farm board decided to distribute some buckwheat intended for sowing so that the collective farmer workers could gain some strength and sow. For this, four members of the board, including the head of the

---

[52] Maria Bilenko, from an unnamed village in Berezan raion (unnamed oblast, likely Kyiv). She believes that her father was lucky because otherwise "he would not be left alive." Bilenko Mariia | HREC (holodomor.ca).

[53] Tetiana Komlichenko's father, village council head, along with eight collective farm managers, was "accused of having ties with kulaks and failing to fulfill the grain [delivery] quotas" and was sentenced by an NKVD extrajudiciary tribunal (*troika*) to eight years of "remote labour camps" in late 1932. One person in the group received a death sentence and seven others to 3–8 years hard labour. These events took place in the village of Zuivtsi in Myrhorod raion, Kharkiv oblast (now in Poltava oblast). Her father returned home in 1936 and was executed by the Nazis in 1942 for assistance to Soviet partisans. Komlichenko Tetiana | HREC (holodomor.ca).

[54] Syvoborodko Mykola | HREC (holodomor.ca).

[55] Bilenko Mariia | HREC (holodomor.ca).

collective farm, were sentenced to "different [prison] terms."[56] In another case, in the summer of 1933, at a meeting of the village activists (*aktyv*), a collective farm head proposed milling some of the spring grain crops and giving the collective farm workers flour to ensure that they would have enough strength to gather the harvest. He was "taken away before the next morning without trial or investigation," and from that time on other activists were afraid to sleep at home, hiding at the windmill or sawmill.[57]

Notable themes covered quite extensively in the letters are the repression of leaders and ordinary collective farm members for "arrears in grain requisitioning" and details of the process, more often than not the sweeping requisitioning of all grain, any food items, and seed.[58]

The majority of the letters provide information about mortality levels in the writers' immediate or extended family[59] and attempt to estimate the number of victims in their locale,[60] whether in terms of the average number of people who died in each family, households that lost family members, or actual numbers from their own memory, local records, or the recollections of survivors.[61] Recurring themes also include familial mortality (according to many correspondents, it was usually higher in larger families), mortality

---

[56] Yakov Petrenko, a child at the time of the famine, recalls the events in the village of Kalynivka in Narodychi raion, Kyiv oblast (now in Zhytomyr oblast). Petrenko Yakov | HREC (holodomor.ca).

[57] Yukhym Dibrova's memoir is about events in the village of Ivanhorod, Oleksandrivka raion, Dnipropetrovsk oblast (now in Kirovohrad oblast). Dibrova Yukhym | HREC (holodomor.ca.) When Mykhailo Shevchyk's father, an elected head of the collective farm, implemented a decision of the board to mill several centners of the grain to feed the farm workers in the summer of 1933, his *kum* Vasyl Kindratovych reported Shevchyk's father's "revolt" to the "appropriate agency," which arrested him. Shevchyk Mykhailo | HREC (holodomor.ca).

[58] "Rank-and-file collective farm workers who failed to submit the required grain quotas were sentenced in large numbers, and those sentenced were not coming back, dying in prison." Petrenko Yakov | HREC (holodomor.ca).

[59] "Families around us died out. The streets became deserted. The whole family of my father's older brother, Fedir Danylovych Panov, died out. My mother's sister had five small children. She and the children died. My uncle travelled around looking for food. He arrived at the Kyrykivka railroad station swollen from hunger and unable to walk. The people collecting corpses wanted to send him to the next world while they were at it. But he cried and persuaded them to leave him, and at night he crawled home. He lived there until the war, and then he was sent to the front, where he shouted: "For the Fatherland, for Stalin!" He returned from the war, lived for a while, and then died." Panov Yakiv (Yakov) | HREC (holodomor.ca).

[60] Hlushchenko and Komar compiled lists of people who died in villages belonging to Khvoshchivka village council in 1933: 111 people died in Khvoshchivka, 26 in Petrakiivka, and 2 people in Olimpiadivka, altogether 139 people. Hlushchenko Danylo, Komar A.H. | HREC (holodomor.ca).

[61] "In the village of Halaiok, according to incomplete data, 830 people perished from starvation during the 1932–33 famine, which constituted one-third of the population of about 2,300 people. This is imprinted vaguely in my memory and in the memory of older villagers who are still alive." Panov Yakiv (Yakov) | HREC (holodomor.ca)

estimates in their villages, farmsteads, and neighborhoods (*kutok*),[62] and explanations of why mortality in their village was higher or less staggering than that in neighboring villages.[63]

Two other prominent features are the suffering and names of those who perished during the famine—*the victims*—and those who, in the view of the correspondents, committed crimes against the victims, causing them physical and psychological suffering and death by taking away all their grain, food and often literally everything—*the perpetrators*. Other important subjects that were not specifically requested by the appeal but receive extensive coverage in the recollections of the correspondents are famine survival strategies—what people ate, what life choices they had to make, and the famine's impact on their lives and the life of the village—and how the famine and its effects compare to other events in their lives.

Victims, perpetrators, 'saviors,' and the famine's long shadow

Those who responded to the appeals for recollections of the 1932–33 famine cite two important motivations for writing the letters. One was to honor their dead—to name their family members, neighbors, friends, and members of their community who perished and to describe their struggle to survive and their physical deterioration and death. Often in the conclusion of their letters the authors request that the names of their family members be mentioned in the memorial book and not forgotten. These authors often express support for the publication of the memorial book and for the erection of monuments to memorialize the victims, and even offer donations from their pensions toward their truth the construction of such a

[62] According to Fedir Skrypnyk, in his native village of Tabanove, Pidvysoke raion, Kyiv oblast (now Holovanivka raion, Kirovohrad oblast), "Dozens died every day. Many of them were buried a few days after death at the place where they died (at their farmsteads), dragged into shallow graves ... On our corner (of the street) the houses were densely packed, and in each house there lived 6–8 people and only 2–3 people remained alive. At a nearby neighbour's house (two houses away), Osyp Sak's family ('Sachok' was his nickname in the village) had 12 people, but only one survived the famine—Darka. Some houses became completely abandoned." Skrypnyk Fedir | HREC (holodomor.ca). Ivan Petrenko writes that there were 360 households in the village, 4–5 people were dying daily, and approximately 1/4 of the houses were empty—people either died or left in search of food. Petrenko Yakov | HREC (holodomor.ca). "Our village Semenivka was large, composed of 7 neighborhoods [*kutkiv*], in which there were 200–250 households. In total more than 1,700 households. No more than half remained after the famine, if not less. To estimate, in each household there were no less than 5–7 people. Even assuming that the smaller number "3" [was left in each household], there would still be more than 5,000, although there were many more. In the aftermath of the famine, entire village areas became empty or half-empty. It was spooky to walk in this half-empty village." Syvoborodko Mykola | HREC (holodomor.ca).

[63] A number of accounts suggest that children and older people would be the first to die. See for instance Kozlov Yurii | HREC (holodomor.ca).

memorial. An equally important incentive for many contributors is to voice their "truth" about the famine. Writing serves as a symbolic act of justice, testimony about the crimes committed against their kin and neighbors that requires naming and judging the perpetrators.

The letters are filled with vivid descriptions of abuse and violence by local village and collective farm officials, search brigade members, and grain procurement commissars. Grain confiscation was carried out violently, accompanied by confiscation or destruction of all foods and many household items, humiliation, and use of torture.[64] Heads of households were often detained in village council premises and beaten, tortured "for arrears"; mock execution was practiced.[65]

> In fulfilling their task, some of the activists carried out terrible crimes. They harassed people, demanding the grain: burned their faces with cigarettes, poked needles beneath their fingernails, broke their fingers in doorways, ripped out beards, and there were even cases of murder. In this way, the grain was completely squeezed out of the village, there was not even anything left for sowing.[66]

Another frequent occurrence was punitive dispossession. Families were thrown out of their houses, everything in their possession was taken from them,[67] family members were arrested, imprisoned, and deported to labor camps. Respondents often use the expressions "for good," and "never returned," indicating that they never learned the fate of their relatives and neighbors who were taken away.[68]

Additionally, various forms of abuse of power were exercised to extract more money, grain, and even attractive houses and all the worldly possessions of the Ukrainian peasant families. Some of these mechanisms of extraction included charging for certificates about completed procurements

---

[64] "Whoever had two cows and two horses was considered a *kulak*, and during the January frosts, activists drove little children and nursing infants out of their homes into the severe frost, and they froze to death and no one cared." Khurdei Oleksii (Aleksei) | HREC (holodomor.ca).

[65] Mock executions were practiced to enforce collectivization or extract information about "hidden grain." See for instance Demydenko Yeva | HREC (holodomor.ca). Temstunik recalls a person afflicted with schizophrenia who died of shock during a mock execution session. Temtsunik Heorhii | HREC (holodomor.ca); See also Shevchyk Mykhailo | HREC (holodomor.ca). Prokopchuk Mykhail | HREC (holodomor.ca).

[66] Demydenko I. | HREC (holodomor.ca).

[67] See for instance Porshakov V.M. | HREC (holodomor.ca) and Tulynska Oleksandra | HREC (holodomor.ca).

[68] It is for the most part unclear why they never inquired about what happened to those who were "taken away," even years later. Was it fear, habit, or acceptance that kept them from ever inquiring about their fate?

norms, delaying the issue of certain certifi-cates, and demanding bribes or imposing monetary fines for failure to submit them on time.[69] Coveted cows were taken away by village or collective farm officials under the guise of collectivization; items were stolen during the searches by local activists and the search brigades, and grain was taken from families by deception.[70] The homes of people who had been forced out were often then occupied by local officials[71] instead of being sold to cover the alleged arrears.

No wonder that, for the bulk of respondents, what happened during the fami-ne is not recalled as a distant, forgotten past destined for a history book. It is something for which they demand atonement and punishment so that it never is repeated.

Those respondents who address the question of blame for the 1932–33 famine almost universally perceive the famine as artificial, inflicted on them by the actions of concrete individuals, a result of excessive confiscation of all grain, food, and even seed, for which they blame Stalin and/or the local officials (heads of the village council, heads of the collective farms), procurement commissars (*upovnovazheni*) and activists (enforcers (*buksyry*), the Red Broom, and brigades) who were in charge of the requisitioning.

Naming the perpetrators and calling for atonement

Most respondents name Stalin as the principal designer of the famine and call him for that reason many names, including "the Executioner" (*kat*), "the Devil" and "King Herod."[72] Nevertheless, it is the actions of those close to

---

[69] A caustic account of the methods used by the village council and collective farm officials to extort money via fines and certificates is given by A.I. Beliavsky. In particular he describes the events that took place in the village of Rudnia-Ososhnia, Narodychi raion, Zhytomyr oblast (now Shyshalivka village, Bazar raion, Kyiv oblast), which was depopulated after the Chornobyl nuclear disaster. Beliavsky A.I. | HREC (holodomor.ca).

[70] Khurdei recalls how a requisition commissar offered his mother the favor of threshing their harvest and then simply never gave them the grain. Khurdei Oleksii (Aleksei) | HREC (holodomor.ca).

[71] "Our neighbour was a much richer family than ours... this homestead was better-liked by one of the activists, P.P. Chorny. The owner of the homestead, Kh.M. Koval, and his entire family were forced out of the house, clothing and all, everything was ransacked, and soon after P.P. Chorny himself settled in this house." Demydenko I. | HREC (holodomor.ca).

[72] A rather unique account opposes laying the responsibility for the famine, "for all the evils" on Stalin and Stalin alone, calling such an interpretation one-sided and biased. "Stalin was to blame, and that is indisputable. But even more guilty were the former leaders of Ukraine—[Stanislav] Kosior, [Pavel] Postyshev, [Vlas] Chubar, [Panas] Liubchenko, and others. It is they who, in their struggle for power, to promote their careers, artificially created a famine in Ukraine and killed millions of people! All their merits are insignificant compared to the crime they organized in 1932, sweeping all of the grain not only from the collective farms but also from the collective farmers. It is they who fulfilled five-fold the grain procurement plans. After all, it is a fact that in the oblasts of other republics bordering with Ukraine... there was never a

home who carried out the procurement orders—local activists and officials—that left the lasting scars. Their actions are compared to "crimes against humanity," and the perpetrators are called "Nazis," "Hitlerites," "gangs," "sadists," "Stalinist Janissaries," "Maoists," "storm troopers"[73] and "Sonderkommandos."[74] These are just some of the epithets that the survivors use in writing about their tormentors.[75] They do not shy away from providing full names of the activists and officials whom they deem personally responsible for the actions that led to death by starvation of their family members and fellow villagers.[76]

The principal concerns for the authors whose families suffered the most during the famine is that the perpetrators, who were still alive and often living in the neighborhood, or whose addresses elsewhere they knew, might never be brought to justice. It was often the case that these people, and even their offspring, continued to poison the lives of survivors.

---

famine of this kind, and no one there died of hunger. Whereas Ukraine, under the leadership of these sycophants, careerists, and soulless individuals who did not care about their people, had to endure this terrible tragedy. They really were the enemies of our people!" The author worked in 1933 as assistant to the head of the political department of the Komsomol of the Novomoskovsk MTS [Machine-Tractor Station] in Dnipropetrovsk oblast. He believed that the famine was a temporary shortfall of collectivization and that the collective farms "helped our army defeat German fascism and end the war with a glorious victory". Parasotka Stepan | HREC (holodomor.ca). However, others had a different memory of what Stalin did and how the memory about it was suppressed. "When the Cultural Revolution was happening in the People's Republic of China, our newspapers wrote that the Chinese were doing it wrong, but they are silent about what was done in our country in the '30s, '40s, '50s, and you have to ask who they borrowed our experience from, but Mao Zedong did not do what Joseph Dzhugashvili [Stalin] did, he didn't starve them and didn't have such outrages in the prisons and labor camps like our "great leader of the peoples" did." Khurdei Oleksii (Aleksei) | HREC (holodomor.ca).

[73] Fedorenko Platon | HREC (holodomor.ca).

[74] Shevchyk Mykhailo | HREC (holodomor.ca).

[75] "As a mature adult I became interested in the moral profiles of people who joined such "sonderkommandos" and did not earn any respect or honour in other villages. I came to the conclusion that there were a lot of viciously envious individuals among them who were advancing their careers." Shevchyk Mykhailo | HREC (holodomor.ca).

[76] Stepan Vovk recalls: "On January 26, 1933, all we had left was 12 cups of peas, two bowls of wheat flour, and three buckets of fodder beets. On the aforementioned date, a group of "activists," Stalin's minions, entered our house [demanding that we] turn over our grain to the state. My sister asked, where are we to get this grain when we're already swollen [from hunger]. The first activist said, "And if we find it, what then?" ...They turned everything upside-down in the house, where three families lived—my older brother and his wife, my older sister, and the three of us. They began patting down our clothing, and Petro M. Yakubenko found the peas on my sister, pulled them off her head along with her hair, and dragged her all the way to the doorstep. They found the flour and the three buckets of beets, and left us hungry, naked, and cold. We sat and cried bitterly." Vovk Stepan | HREC (holodomor.ca).

In one of the most damning accounts of surviving the famine, V.M. Porshakov squarely puts the blame on local activists and officials.

> Father was deported, and as you can imagine we were gutted—like a live chicken by a dog. And do you think this was [done] by Stalin? No, by those beggars who did not want to work even then and envied someone who had a slice of black stale bread on the table.
>
> First they took away Father, then the livestock, and then even the children's hand-woven clothing was taken and sold at an auction. Then they searched with metal rods for a bucket of grain buried somewhere. Mother had hidden a half-litre bottle of grain, and they spilled it and took it away, and I remember well that Stalin was not among them.
>
> ... And then in 1933 the famine began, and we were on the street wandering. Because an order came—you think it was from Stalin? No! The village council ordered that no one was to let us into anybody's house, threatening to exile those who did. This order was issued by our fellow villagers, brothers, friends and humans, and not by donkeys or lions who might be forgiven. So let them now face fair judgment for their deeds.[77]

He hopes that "they know that there will be atonement for their deeds, they brought it upon themselves" and wishes that "their children would come to their senses and stop their evil deeds, though they still flutter at the prospect of profit."[78]

Heorhii Temtsunyk,[79] whose father perished in the Rybinsk camps, questions why the "cannibal" Kaganovich is alive, living in Moscow, and "the Party and Soviet government" allow it.[80] Mariia Chuprun shares a similar

---

[77] Porshakov V.M. | HREC (holodomor.ca).

[78] Ibid. Olha Andreieva and Stepan Vovk are also concerned by the evil deeds of the offspring of the famine-time perpetrators at whose hands they suffered. Andreieva Olha | HREC (holodomor.ca); Vovk Stepan | HREC (holodomor.ca). Antonina Dmytrenko suffers from the thought of "Stalin's voluntarism" and all those "servants and informants" on whose consciences lie hundreds of deaths from famine, and one perpetrator in particular, who is still alive and enjoys all privileges and still torments and insults her and others whose children survived the 1933 famine. (Dmytrenko writes about events in the village of Zelene in Petrivka raion, Dnipropetrovsk oblast (now in Kirovohrad oblast)). At the time of writing this follow-up letter, she had sent two letters to *Sil's'ki visti* for the "Pain of the Soul" section, but they had not been published. Her abridged and edited original letter sent to Maniak in December of 1988 was eventually published in the memorial book and made known the name of the activist who tormented their family—Petro Svyrydenko. (*33-ii: Holod,* 180–81). HREC has in its possession the unedited version of the letter, along with the edited version. Quoted here is her yet-unpublished follow-up letter dated 21.08.1989. Both will be published on the HREC website shortly.

[79] From the village of Holoskove, Kryve Ozero raion, Odesa oblast (now in Mykolaiv oblast). Temtsunyk Heorhii | HREC (holodomor.ca).

[80] "During the repressions in 1937, I was the only one in our family who survived. My father was awarded St. George's crosses and a sabre (a gift from Kotovski) for bravery. He perished in the Rybinsk labour camps. And the executioner Lazar Kaganovich lives in Moscow and receives

experience. Her father was deported with family to Siberia, where he was forced to work in mines. He survived, and even after the war, upon return to their native village, Chuprun and her father continued to be harassed by activists as "kulaks" (*kurkuli*) while many activists were "turncoats" collaborating with the Nazis who got away with it after the war.[81]

Perpetrators were far more numerous and their role was much more damaging than that of Nazi collaborators, opines Mykhail Shevchyk:

> Today it is no secret for anyone that the creator of the famine was Stalin. But what could he have done without reliable assistants of all ranks, those nonentities who strove for power? It seems to me that a not unimportant role was played by local leaders, and that's a fact.
>
> As we know, Hitler did not intend to do good on Nazi-occupied territory; on the contrary, he did his best to take everything from there to the last thread. But the thief failed to implement his plan because, fortunately for us, there were not many people locally who wanted to serve the führer, and Hitler's broom proved powerless to repeat 1933.[82]

Neither loyalty to the regime nor the status of Civil War hero, nor relative poverty and compliance with the increasing pressure to collectivize the household, or even family ties could protect one from total grain confiscation by the fervent search brigade activists. Mykhailo Leukha's father was among the first members of the Committee of Poor Peasants (*KNS*),[83] and his mother enrolled their household in a joint land cultivation collective (SOZ)[84] after her husband's death. When they failed to comply with a second grain quota, Leukha's uncle was among the search brigade members who took away all the remaining grain from the family.[85]

---

his personal pension. And he's living a long life—95 years. He is a cannibal. And the Soviet government and the party allow this." Ibid.

[81] Chuprun Mariia | HREC (holodomor.ca).

[82] Shevchyk Mykhailo | HREC (holodomor.ca).

[83] *KNS* — an abbreviation of Ukrainian *Komitet nezamozhnykh selian.*

[84] SOZ or TSOZ — an abbreviation of Ukrainian *Tovarystvo spilnoho obrobitku zemli* — an early organizational form of collectivization of agriculture in Ukraine in the 1920s–early 1930s.

[85] "They imposed on us the surrender of grain; the first time we complied, the second it was not possible. A son of our grandfather and his father came to our house with an official; in our attic there were two sacks of three *poods* of rye and wheat. They climbed up and took them away." Leukha's mother begged her brother-in-law to leave something for his own father and his three nephews, but in return she was threatened with a gun and he and other activists hauled away the sacks on a cart. Leukha's mother sent her 78-year-old father-in-law, the respondent's grandfather, to go after his son. Grandfather Yahor was apparently unsuccessful and soon died as result of the actions of his own son. Leukha Mykhailo | HREC (holodomor.ca). Motria Semko mentions how an activist-son interrogated his own mother in order to find some grain. Semko Motria | HREC (holodomor.ca). When the "red broom" in the guise of five strangers and two locals visited their household, it was Vasyl Kindratovych, whose child

The line between a former search brigade activist and a famine victim could become blurred as the famine progressed: those "very ardent activists who had de-kurkulized people" could themselves die a few weeks later when their subsistence ran out. The irony of it was not lost on a few respondents. "Some of those activists, after Stalin's article "Dizzy from Success,"[86] explained to their own bloated children that Soviet authority had been about to be established but something had gone wrong; and they determined this because there was no one left for them to rob, and they had to work on equal terms."[87]

P.M. Slavhorodsky, who sent to Maniak at least three letters, recorded the testimonies of famine survivors in the villages of Zhabianka, Buzhanka, and Yablunivka in Lysianka raion, Kyiv oblast (now in Cherkasy oblast). One of his respondents, Paraska Romanenko, reflects on the fate of those who took the last grain from her family: "While they were taking bread from the people, they themselves ate bread fit for a human being. But when there was nothing left to take, they themselves died. And all those robbers died before they were old."[88] Slavhorodsky explains: "When [search brigade activist] Myrin Poliarush was already emaciated from hunger, he went to the raion committee to ask for help. He was walking across the place where

---

Shevchyk's father had baptized (he thus happened to be his *kum)*, who literally swept the floor for every last grain of wheat in the house, and people "who one time opposed the Soviet government with weapons in their hands" were unceremoniously taking away goods "earned by honest and hard labour" from the family of a former machine gunner of the First Cavalry Army [of the Red Army]. Shevchyk Mykhailo | HREC (holodomor.ca).

86 Published on March 2, 1930, in *Pravda*, Stalin's article titled "Dizzy from Success: On Problems of the Collective-Farm Movement" called for a halt to the collectivization program, saying it had been carried out with excessive zeal and "excesses" needed to be corrected.

87 Hryhorii Kuchmii, born in 1919, recalls the events in the village of Yabluchne, Velyka Pysarivka raion, Kharkiv oblast (now in Sumy oblast). Demotion, however, did not diminish the ferocity of former search brigade activists. "The masses of dead bodies began to decompose, and a brigade was appointed by the local government and given extra rations to dig large pits at the cemetery, wearing gas masks. ...The former ardent activist Grigory Arestovich ("Aristonchik") Kovalenko landed in that burial brigade and loaded onto the carts not only the dead but the living who still felt alive and one woman who still physically felt well; he forcibly threw her into a trunk and closed it and she died in it, only because of his hatred for her. Many people learned about this, and those who were able began to hide from his eyes." Kuchmii Hryhorii (Grigorii) | HREC (holodomor.ca). Yet another self-acknowledged member of the often hated and feared burial brigade, Vladimir (Volodymyr) Yermoshenko, who was 17 at the time of the famine and whose family had died in it, writes that he worked in a burial brigade only to stay alive. He received a bowl of soup a day for interring 61 people "like animals." He admits that he did not do a very good job at it because he was too weak. To survive, he ate dead horses, frogs, etc. He blames the famine on those who wanted to make a career by taking from people their last bowl of soup. Yermoshenko Volodymyr (Vladimir) | HREC (holodomor.ca).

88 "Told on 27 May 1984 by Paraska Hryhorivna Romanenko (Kutsenko), resident of the village of Zhabianka, born in 1907." Slavhorodsky P.M. | HREC (holodomor.ca)

livestock was buried and fell down and died."[89] In another letter, Slavhorodsky encloses a picture of a man, the head of Yablunivka village council Mykhailo Andriichuk, whose life was cut short at twenty-five in 1932 by one of the villagers for "taking everything to the last grain."[90]

Events of the Holodomor cast a long shadow in more than one way. Numerous accounts draw parallels and establish continuity between the crimes committed during the famine, the events of the Nazi occupation, Stalinist crimes as a whole, and the present-day Gorbachev reforms.

Those who oppose *perestroika* are construed as the same people who committed crimes during the famine, and the lack of justice is viewed as something that might hinder society for years to come. Mykhailo Moskovchuk, responding to a letter published by *Sil's'ki visti*, suggests that "the activists of those as well as of subsequent years are still around, and there are a lot of them, in governmental administration." They "continue to hinder the reforms." "Wherever they may be located, they need to be handed over to the local authorities and expelled from administrative positions."[91]

Several accounts mention the activists who ended up collaborating with the Nazi occupation. Some of them were executed by the Nazis during the war, and others after the war.

A.I. Beliavsky recalls that one famine-era activist was trying to persuade a man in 1941 to avoid conscription and instead stay and wait for the Nazi troops to come. He was arrested and executed by the NKVD.[92] Fedir Skrypnyk recounts the deeds of two notorious local "proactive activists" who were "already working" while "the de-vils were still fist-fighting"—Vasyl Babenko (nicknamed *Pup* [Navel]) and Yakiv Kondratiuk (nicknamed *Barabolia* [Potato]). "Soon the activist Yakiv died from starvation and Vasyl once again became an activist during the Nazi occupation. He became an active [auxiliary] police officer in Perehonivka, where he tortured our Red Army prisoners of war and other citizens. For this he undoubtedly got what he deserved."[93] Some famine-era activists who in turn served the Nazis, delivering *Ostarbeiter*s and snitching on people who were hiding wounded Red Army servicemen, then got back their pre-war jobs after the war.[94] Nina Kvashuk cannot help but gloat that one of the activists who tormented her family during the famine, Melania Lutai, regained her position (head of either the village council or the

---

89 Ibid.
90 Ibid.
91 Moskovchuk Mykhailo | HREC (holodomor.ca).
92 Beliavsky A.I. | HREC (holodomor.ca).
93 Skrypnyk Fedir | HREC (holodomor.ca).
94 Chuprun Mariia | HREC (holodomor.ca).

collective farm) but was "put down like a dog" with a shot through a window during an evening meeting.[95]

One eyewitness summarizes:

> The hunger was created deliberately in order to destroy the recalcitrant peasant population, as well as to destroy the leadership of Ukraine. Not all of them were enemies of the people. But Molotov and [Secretary of the Central Committee of the Communist Party Lazar] Kaganovich were not the only ones who were guilty, the peasants themselves were also guilty. For example, in our village Nikita [Mykyta] Denysovych Poimanov and his wife went from house to house and took away even cucumber seeds from the farmers, thereby killing hundreds of people. When the Germans arrived, their policemen hanged the old man and his wife from a pillar in the center of the village. But for the hundreds of people who died in our village, for the millions of people who died in Ukraine, it was not enough to hang an old man and woman. Many were guilty.[96]

And while some letters end optimistically, noting that Gorbachev's reforms made it possible to speak about the famine and that maybe, by educating people about it, such tragedies can be prevented from happening again, Oleksii Khurdei, a child-survivor of the famine, is rather pessimistic:

> I am sure that if those times returned, it would all be exactly the same; it is even the same now, the blood of our children and grandchildren is being shed in Afghanistan for ten years now, and no one is to blame for it. Whoever started the war is gone; he died, and how can you go after dead people.[97]

Conscientious leaders and "saviors"

The famine had not only its victims and perpetrators but also local heroes-sa-viors whose actions helped people survive—there were those who went easy on procurement, provided food rations to schools, nurseries, and collective farms, gave people jobs, or distributed grain in advance of the upcoming harvest, whose role can be defined as that of "saviors," "conscientious leaders." They were usually persecuted and perished for these acts of caring, during the famine or in later rounds of repressions, but they were not forgotten.[98]

---

[95] Kvashuk Nina | HREC (holodomor.ca).

[96] Panov Yakiv (Yakov) | HREC (holodomor.ca).

[97] Khurdei Oleksii (Aleksei) | HREC (holodomor.ca).

[98] Some of the examples were mentioned above in the discussion about the alleged "acts of sabotage" and repressions against the local leaders who were distributing some flour, grain, or

Danylo Hlushchenko and A.H. Komar gratefully remember A.A. Zaturensky, who was prosecuted in the 1930s and perished.[99]

> Many dozens or maybe even several hundreds of lives from Khvoshchivka, Petrakiivka, and Olimpiadivka were saved thanks to the director of the Khvoshchivka peatland development site Arok Aazarovych Zaturensky. He employed many people there and organized two meals daily for those who worked there and members of their families. He lent two tons of flour to the collective farm, which was used to cook what they called *balanda* [a thin and lean broth] for those starving in the most critical days before the harvest was collected. This gave many fellow villagers a chance of survival.

Demydenko, describing the events of the famine in the village of Yalyntsi, Hradyzk raion, Kharkiv oblast,[100] gives credit for lower death rates compared to other villages to the various representatives who were sent to carry out bread procurement [*khlibovykachku*], and also "activists of the village,...members of the party who (in their heart) had a different position" on the grain procurements campaign. He recalls that when Ivan Ivanovych Pshenychny, a prudent and good person, whom my fellow villagers remember with great respect, was put in charge of the procurements, "the activists changed their behaviour considerably." The head of the village council Yakiv Petrovych Perepylytsia would come to visit Demydenko's father at night to warn of a possible "visit" by the activists to our street. Andriy Yosypovych Kirshko, who "for that time was a well-read and educated person," was also recruited as an activist "but quickly understood the essence of this activity" which was, as he put it, "against human nature." He wrote letters of protest to various institutions and was rumoured to have had a meeting with Chubar himself. After this incident, the grain procurement plan was reduced by one-third."[101]

---

buckwheat to prevent people from dying. See also Dibrova Yukhym | HREC (holodomor.ca) and Petrenko Yakov | HREC (holodomor.ca).

99 Hlushchenko Danylo, Komar A.H. | HREC (holodomor.ca).

100 Now village of Yalyntsi, Kremenchuk raion, Poltava oblast.

101 The fate of Kirshko was tragic. "The high death rate among the villagers left a depressing impression on Kirshko. He distributed all of the food that he had to beggars and eventually he ended up in their situation. ... every day he goes to the village council to say once more that things cannot go on like this, that the village is dying ... each time... he was thrown out of the building, under the fence. Eventually it was discovered that he had cut up his children, all three of them, and pickled them like pork in a barrel. Nonetheless he died there under the fence. Maybe this was the protest of a madman against the abuse of our people? It is hard to answer this question." Demydenko I. | HREC (holodomor.ca).

The actions of Mykhailo Shevchuk senior, an elected chairman of the collective farm, who implemented a decision of the board to grind some several centners of grain to feed the collective farmers in the summer of 1933, "constituted a formal violation of the first commandment of collective farming," and for that he was reported to the "appropriate agency," which arrested him. This act of courage, as well as the communal meals (broth with a dumpling per person) and a nursery where children were given some milk and bread, saved many lives on the Chapaiv collective farm in Zlodiivka.[102]

"It is obvious," reflects Shevchuk, "that among the people who held top positions in the raion and locally, there were moderate, prudent individuals who assessed the situation objectively and did not rush blindly to curry favor." And even if Stalinism was a "difficult period," "it would be wrong to portray it exclusively in shades of black, because, in addition to the 'leader,' there was the [Communist] party, the Soviet government, hundreds of thousands of honest Communists who ... really cared about the welfare of the people."

In the words of another survivor, one cannot help but admire the "courage, bravery and feelings of mercy one must have, in this terrifying time to dare sabotage the grain requisitioning and help people in their terrible misfortune."[103]

A remembrance of a kind deed could even save a former activist's life. In a lucky twist of fate, a member of the Komsomol from Khorol was sent to "pump out" the grain from a farm in the surrounding district. His search brigade removed several sacks of grain from one household, but the horse cart to collect them was delayed somewhere, and he was left to guard the sacks. A housewife asked him for permission to take a little grain from each of the confiscated sacks. He allowed her to do so. Later on, in 1941, as a Red Army commander hiding from the Nazis, he found himself in the same village and bumped into his "old acquaintance," who did not report him in appreciation for the compassion he had shown her in the past.[104]

Food substitutions, survival strategies, and stories of survival

Two related and vital subjects that receive extensive coverage in the letters are food substitution and survival strategies.

The Maniak Collection is undoubtedly a major source of information about food substitution during the famine and of individual stories of survival. Local circumstances that facilitated survival in a particular locale,

---

102 Shevchyk infers this from a lower death count in Zlodiivka compared to other villages. Shevchyk Mykhailo | HREC (holodomor.ca).

103 Demydenko I. | HREC (holodomor.ca).

104 Shevchyk Mykhailo | HREC (holodomor.ca).

such as environmental conditions or local leadership, are also an important component in a majority of accounts.

Almost every letter provides descriptions, some very detailed, of what peasants were forced to eat once food became scarce or was taken from them altogether— including weeds, tree bark, tree leaves, roots, pets, shellfish, bird eggs, and dead livestock. They also explain various methods of making edible seemingly inedible things and creatures: most notably, all kinds of variations of a watery broth (*boltushka*) and pancakes (*matorzhenyky*).

Ivan Vovk recounts:

> On the collective farm they cooked a sort of soup-water [*boltushka*] for all the starving people, which could not save us. People ate everything: the roots of the Tartar herb (sweet flag), which we dug up from the Molochna river, which made one's head hurt and foggy and led to bowel obstruction and people dying. People ate various weeds in the spring; they dug up rotten potatoes, marrow from sunflower stems, last year's beets that were rotten and frozen, whatever they managed to find in the ground. Such food was somehow, as they say, like a treat [*kalach*]. They ate turtles, mollusks, hazel buds, dogs, cats, and even humans.[105]

Heorhii Tsentsunik's family was "luckier" because of the relative variety of substitute foods on their "Stalin's menu," in part because they owned a rifle and beehives:

> We had a rifle, and our older brother went to the mill where he got lucky shooting rats, and this was our "meat dish." We even knew that a soup made with sparrows and orach was tastier than one with crows. Crow soup tasted like tar. When the weeds flowered, they covered the fields, then the bees saved us. Less than half of the people survived in our villages. I can tell you about the "Stalin menu" — horses, dogs, cats, rats, sparrows, crows, orach, bark, reed root, and so on.[106]

In carrying out my research it became apparent that certain objects that are mentioned recurrently in the famine survivors' memoirs could be considered as *survival markers*, i.e., objects in the possession of families or in the vicinity of villages that were likely to increase their chances of survival during the famine, in addition to the commonly used weeds, leaves, and tree bark. Examples of survival markers include enterprises that were

---

[105] Vovk Ivan | HREC (holodomor.ca).
[106] Temtsunik Heorhii | HREC (holodomor.ca).

likely to generate food waste, such as distilleries,[107] sugar refineries, oil presses, and mills that could serve as sources of spilled flour, pulp, or chaff, as well as fields with accidentally forgotten and frostbitten potatoes or sugar beets that could be found in winter.[108] Environmental factors such as proximity to a river or pond could provide starving villagers with fish, shellfish, and frogs.[109] Chickens produced a few eggs a day. Particularly important was the role of a cow, called the "mother of the family." Cow ownership significantly increased chances of survival for a family, especially for a family with young children. Cows were also highly desirable plunder for unprincipled officials and thieves alike, and for that reason were often kept inside the houses at night.[110] Horses, by contrast, were almost universally confiscated early on during collectivization, and many accounts report horses dying en masse in the collective farms because of the lack of feed. The local authorities would declare that the horses died of anthrax or were poisoned by saboteurs, and their corpses were dragged to designated burial places, often cut up, doused with gasoline, and set on fire. However, those willing to take the risk recount dragging horse carcasses or parts and using them to sustain themselves.[111]

---

[107] Vasyl Yarmolenko recalls many people from other raions (Shyshaky, Velyka Bahachka, and especially Reshetylivka) coming in search of food to his native village of Kybyntsi (in Myrhorod raion, Kharkiv oblast, now in Poltava oblast) because it had a distillery and livestock feeding facility, two state mills, and a railway station. Yarmolenko Vasyl | HREC (holodomor.ca).

[108] "For an unknown reason, at a state farm about 5–7 km from our village, some sugar beets remained in a large area, where everyone who was able went with sacks and axes and chopped them out of the ground and brought them home. A great number of people died there in the field in the winter, and their corpses were found only later, during harvesting of the wheat." Kuchmii Hryhorii (Grigorii) | HREC (holodomor.ca). See also Bilash Z. | HREC (holodomor.ca).

[109] "Among those who survived until the spring, some were saved by the blessed weeds and the blessed Syniukha River. People caught mussels and frogs, and ate all sorts of carrion." Chabanenko Feodosiia | HREC (holodomor.ca). "To the south of the village flowed the powerful Dnipro River with its numerous bays, channels and lakes, where fish and wildlife proliferated. At the onset of spring, all those who were still able to walk rushed to shallow waters to catch fish, frogs, mollusks and such. A good portion of the villagers spent their days and nights here, not returning to their homes. When the spring waters began flowing, it was possible to kill the water rats that were forced onto small islands by the flooding. Eggs of various aquatic birds were also gathered, this is how we survived." Demydenko I. | HREC (holodomor.ca).

[110] "It was more terrible for our family than for some other families because our good cow, under the pretext of collectivization, was taken away for the chairman of the village council and the chairman of the collective farm. My father wrote several times to the ODPU [OGPU, political police] to try to have the stolen cow returned legally. As the eldest child, I (with my mother and some of the younger ones) took our cow from the field several times, but each time they took it back from us. And the cow at that time was like a mother for the family, because whoever had a cow could survive on milk and weeds." Vovk Ivan | HREC (holodomor.ca).

[111] Hryhorii Kuchmii recalls an order issued that if anyone's livestock died for any reason on the collective farm, it was to be chopped up, kerosene poured on it, and reported as a die-off from Siberian anthrax so that people would not dig it up and eat it. He recalled how, swollen

I also place in the category of survival markers the daily rations—daily meals, usually a watery soup made from some inferior quality non-wheat flour, rarely with a dumpling per person—that were provided per workday to those who worked on the collective farms. Similar soup rations were provided to children in nurseries and schools in some villages (likely by the collective farms—it is not always clear in the letters). If the ration was more than just broth and included some bread or a dumpling or two, some parents would consume only the broth and bring the bread and dumpling home to their children.[112] Receiving such a ration was often a decisive factor in surviving and a powerful incentive for joining the collective farm.[113] Also, those who worked in dining halls or even on pig farms would bring home and cook potato peelings for their families to eat.

I also use the term *survival strategies* with regard to a single action or a combination of actions taken by an individual or a group in order to find food, work, or a safe place, or to pull resources to increase the likelihood of surviving the famine. In this category, I include attempts to travel outside their immediate locale, either locally or to Russia, Belarus, Crimea, and the North Caucasus to exchange valuables for food. These trips were hit and miss—more often than not, people went missing on such trips, got robbed and pushed off train cars, or returned empty-handed or with some food but too late, finding their family members already dead by the time of their return.[114]

---

and weak, he with great difficulty dug up from a pit the hindquarters of a horse that had been condemned as a die-off from Siberian anthrax, cut off the hind leg, dragged it home in a sack, boiled it and ate it. And not only did they did not get sick from Siberian anthrax, he wrote, but "on the contrary, we grew stronger, and I have lived already seventy years." Kuchmii Hryhorii (Grigorii) | HREC (holodomor.ca). See also Tulynska Oleksandra | HREC (holodomor.ca) and Panov Yakiv (Yakov) | HREC (holodomor.ca). In one case, people did get poisoned from eating dead horses. They reportedly "gave over their good horses to the collective, but enemies mixed rat poison into the chaff and molasses" and "the horses fell like flies." People found the horse bones, sucked on them and died. Leukha Mykhailo | HREC (holodomor.ca).

112 "They opened nurseries on the collective farm where there were many children. The collective farm board tried to save the children from starvation. My brother and I were also in the nursery. In the field, during the sowing and the harvesting of grain, they cooked something to eat once [a day], mostly dumplings, because my mother often brought them home for us." Komlichenko Tetiana | HREC (holodomor.ca). See also Tulynska Oleksandra | HREC (holodomor.ca).

113 "The majority who were on the collective farm survived because there they were provided at least something, and those who did not want to join the collective farm died," asserts one of the survivors, while another insists that their family survived because her grandfather worked on the collective farm and received a higher work day ration. Neporozhnii A.A., Petrenko Olha, Shcherbak Dominika | HREC (holodomor.ca).

114 "When it warmed up, my father packed into a bag some embroidered towels *[rushnyky]*, bleached home-woven cloth, tablecloths, woolen headscarves, colorful wide Cossack belts, necklaces, ducats—all of mother's dowry that was left from their wedding and was stored in a chest. My father took all this to Kursk oblast [in Russian SFSR] to exchange for grain and

Many desperate parents sent their children to relatives (often childless or working in cities) who were likely to provide for them[115] or abandoned their children at railway stations in cities like Poltava and Myrhorod, where they would be picked up and brought to the city orphanages. Some orphaned children ended up placed in *patronaty*[116] set up in villages, which seemed to provide better odds of survival.[117]

Examples of survival strategies pursued by children, aside from working on a collective farm and searching for food substitutes, include seeking food or work outside their native village, in a city or on a state farm (*radhosp*). Boys as young as nine years old left for the cities, where they struggled to survive by begging (a strategy for many adults and children),[118] helping with menial jobs in exchange for cafeteria leftovers, or walking dozens of miles to seek work at state farms. Similarly, teenage girls quit school to work on the local collective farm in order to support themselves and their families. Theft was another survival strategy for desperate persons

---

bread." Ilchenko Ivan | HREC (holodomor.ca). Ivan Vovk's father collected all the homewares of any value and went to Kaluga in Russia to exchange them for at least some food to save the family from starvation, but he returned with nothing. Vovk Ivan | HREC (holodomor.ca). "Those who had some things would take them to Russia [to trade] for foodstuffs. She [Petrenko] had a beautiful scarf, shoes, and a necklace, and she exchanged these in Russia for two *poods* of rye and two large loaves. ... They say one neighbour did not return; someone threw his sack from the train, and he fell off the train going after it." Neporozhnii A.A., Petrenko Olha, Shcherbak Dominika | HREC (holodomor.ca). Others travelled to Pervomaisk, Voznesensk, or Odesa to beg for alms or travelled with families to the Caucasus to trade for grain. Mykola Syvoborodko recalls that many residents of his native Semenivka were killed or crippled in a railroad accident on such a trip. Syvoborodko Mykola | HREC (holodomor.ca). See also a story about Musiienko's unsuccessful attempts to travel to Crimea and Belarus in his memoir, recorded by Ivan Kravchenko. Kravchenko Ivan (for Musiienko Hryhorii) | HREC (holodomor.ca). Possessing valuables which could be exchanged for food in the state-run hard-currency stores (*Torgsins*) in the cities or at some local markets can also be treated as a survival marker.

[115] Kutsenko, Yakiv (Yakov) | HREC (holodomor.ca)/

[116] A type of orphanage.

[117] "In the spring of 1933, a *patronat* was established on the collective farm. It housed the children-orphans who had been brought from Myrhorod after being abandoned at the [railway] station by their parents. They remained there until they reached adulthood, and then went on to study or work." Komlichenko Tetiana | HREC (holodomor.ca).

[118] Begging was a widespread phenomenon. Yeva Demydenko recalls: "Many beggars appeared in our village from neighbouring villages, who extended their hands like ghosts to beg for something to eat. Dirty, with deeply sunken eyes, they were terrifying. And some of them, when they drank a lot of water, swelled up, their legs became like logs, the water sloshed inside them like in a leather sack. And so they died, without any help, on the street." Demydenko Yeva | HREC (holodomor.ca. See also Ilchenko Ivan | HREC (holodomor.ca).

deprived of any other means.[119] Not only picking up grains at night in the fields[120] but also collecting flour dust from under a windmill was considered stealing.[121] In the best case, the thief was arrested, imprisoned, and fed in jail.[122] Many thieves caught in the act of attempting to steal some produce or even cows, however, were killed on the spot by peasants protecting their food supplies, and these extrajudicial killings were not investigated.

Controversially perhaps, cannibalism, which is often mentioned and witnessed first-hand by the respondents, can be considered a survival strategy. It also appears to be the only crime against persons that was investigated and adjudicated in court. While familial cannibalism is often portrayed as an act of desperation or even mercy, there were cannibals for whom it became an industry, and some accounts mention up to eighteen victims killed by a family of cannibals. If cases of cannibalism were uncovered, the perpetrators faced disgust, outrage, and street justice in their own villages,[123] while those who were incarcerated did not return to their villages after serving their sentences.[124]

These are just some examples of *survival markers* and *survival strategies* identifiable in the letters. None of the strategies themselves guaranteed survival,[125] and most were perilous. As demonstrated in the letters, it was often a combination of environmental factors, local

---

[119] "Some tried to steal something just to be sent to jail. They would be given rations there, and this was a guarantee of avoiding famine and death." Syvoborodko Mykola | HREC (holodomor.ca).

[120] Many recount guards in watchtowers protecting the fields, firing at people, and taking away "illegal" brew and throwing people in jails.

[121] Mazepa Hanna | HREC (holodomor.ca).

[122] Mykhailo Moskovchuk's family was branded "enemies of the people" and thrown out of their house by the enforcement brigade. "They barely survived. Moskovchuk's older brother and his friend asked to be accepted into the Red Army but were told that the army does not accept the sons of kulaks. They were not given any work either. So, because they were starving, they crawled into the collective farm pantry, took two loaves of bread each, and were then arrested and incarcerated. Moskovchuk's brother died in prison of starvation but his friend survived. Moskovchuk Mykhailo | HREC (holodomor.ca).

[123] "There was cannibalism: a mother (last name Postolenko) ate her own young children, and she fed a third child with this meat, but she was caught when she was cutting up the body of the third. They took her somewhere, and people beat her." Kozlov Yurii | HREC (holodomor.ca).

[124] "Parents died from hunger, and two brothers and a five-year-old sister remained; they stabbed her to death and ate her. A mother and daughter ate her six-year-old brother and son; they were taken to the police and their fate is unknown." Khurdei Oleksii (Aleksei) | HREC (holodomor.ca).

[125] Ivan ilchenko recalls Vyfaten Musii, a man in his village who was a skilled hunter with a large family. They ate mice, crows and sparrows but the whole family died anyway. Ilchenko Ivan | HREC (holodomor.ca).

leadership,[126] individual circumstances, and ingenuity that increased a person's chances of survival.

Platon Fedorenko, fourteen years old at the time of the famine, and his two younger sisters at first foraged for weeds to use as food and then went to work at a collective farm where they were given meals twice a day, morning and evening, which is how they survived.[127]

Yakiv Panov's family[128] was saved from starvation because his father buried a bag of millet under an apple tree. His father would dig it up at night, they would covertly grind some millet with the husks in a mortar, and by morning the mother would cook a gruel. His mother also sold a silver cross for one kilogram of millet. However, once there was nothing to plant in the gardens, his father was forced to join the collective farm. He received a kilogram of fodder bran for one hectare of mowed field and was fed a lunch that consisted of "just enough flour to cloud the water," while Yakiv, who was ten at the time, "crawled around the meadow, plucked the heads of the clover, and ate them." With such poor nutrition, Panov's father was soon too exhausted to work and hence received no more rations. Then the younger Panov went with his neighbor (a boy) to Kharkiv "in search of bread." In Kharkiv the police caught them and sent them home by train. Then he went looking for a state farm, and 35 km away he found the Parkhomivka State Farm, where they took him in, and he gathered spikelets in the field with other children like himself. They were led by a young Pioneer leader (*pionervozhataia*). And this is how he survived until the harvest.

Olha Yatsenko was seventeen and a technical college (*tekhnikum*) student in Poltava in 1933. She recounts in great detail how she and other students survived the famine by pooling their meager resources, how much and what they ate, how much it cost. Along with 7,000 students she received her meals in a student dining hall that smelled horribly "because they were cooking dinner with horse bones that came from the horses that we saw being led in herds through the city of Poltava to the meat-processing plant."

Students received a stipend[129] and a daily ration.[130] Some students somehow forged bread ration cards to get an extra piece of bread and

---

[126] Ivan Demydenko credits a favourable environment (the river) and conscientious representatives and activists, who were doing what was possible to reduce the requisition quotas or warn people about searches, for the higher survival rates in his village compared to some others. For details, see Demydenko I. | HREC (holodomor.ca).

[127] Fedorenko Platon | HREC (holodomor.ca).

[128] Panov had seven siblings, five brothers and two sisters.

[129] 35–40 *karbovantsi.* Yatsenko Olha | HREC (holodomor.ca).

"roamed the stores, finding cornmeal in one (brought in from Moldova), horse sausage in another." She and her girlfriends learned to sell one ration for 5 *karbovantsi*, which they spent to buy sugar, and would buy six glasses of boiling water for they believed that it was equal [in caloric value] to 100 grams of bread. "That is how we kept ourselves from starving. We knew how to share and save money."[131]

Obviously, the difference between the student Yatsenko and a peasant she witnessed in the city square "dead, a sack lying next to him, empty, not having found anything for his family" was that she had some money and a ration to manage. When she, along with ninety other third-year students, was sent to one of the collective farms not far from Poltava, they did not see anyone. "The houses were completely empty, their doors open."[132]

Yatsenko also appears relatively lucky compared to another student, Pavlo My-sak, whose family resettled to Vinnytsia, where the father obtained a job as a guard in an office.

In 1933, as a third-year student of the *robitfak* (workers' faculty) at the Vinnytsia Pharmaceutical Institute, Mysak received a ration of only 50 grams of bread, and the majority of students were dying. He became swollen and was saved from death by his mother, who cooked a "soup" of unripe currants and apples; divided his 50 grams of bread into three parts for Mytsak, his father and herself; and baked pancakes of dried and ground couch grass with unripe apples. He recalls that in the spring of 1933,

> The townspeople saw with their own eyes how peasants from all the villages of the area flooded into the city for a piece of bread with outstretched hands, and the starving filled all the streets of the city. The city was also starving and so could not help them. The starving died like flies that had been poisoned; city transportation could not manage to bring the dead bodies to the graveyard for burial.[133]

---

[130] Her daily ration consisted of 400 grams of bread when at the *tekhnikum* and of 200 grams of millet bread when they were sent on a *praktikum* in the raion (outside the city) in March 1933. Ibid.

[131] Ibid.

[132] Yatsenko's family consisted of eight people. Her grandmother starved to death, her brother was swollen from starvation. Her father was an office worker (*sluzhbovets*) and her friend, whose husband was in the NKVD and received a ration, would occasionally give Yatsenko leftover bread and soap. She compares the 1933 famine to the seige of Leningrad and, unsure whether her story is important for the memorial book, concludes: "I did live through it all, and people at the time did what they could to survive and save their families. Some succeeded, and others did not!" Yatsenko Olha | HREC (holodomor.ca).

[133] When assigned by the city Komsomol in May 1933 to the state farm at the village of Kovalivka, Nemyriv raion, as a representative carrying out mass political agitation, he observed, "The fields were poorly cultivated, the tractors and other agricultural machinery

Denys Hruby[134] and a classmate (they were nine and ten years old at the time of the famine) decided to improve their chances of survival by leaving home and venturing to a city. After search brigades took all the food, their cow, and even his mother's sheepskin coat and other clothing, only five chickens remained, laying two eggs a day. Their family of four was living each on half an egg per day. He would make ink and trade it for food. When he was unable to help bring in food, he was deprived of his half-egg. Denys' schoolmate Pavlo suggested that they take off to Odesa: "Let's run away from the village. Otherwise we'll croak." They snuck onto a train and found shelter in a shack near Pavlo's aunts' home.

They were in Odesa for around two and half months, surviving on cafeteria leftovers in exchange for helping an old man who chopped wood for the cafeteria kitchen, begging for bread near bread stores when cafeteria workers had no work for them and Pavlo's aunts had no food to share. Once they heard that things had improved in their village and harvesting had begun, they left Odesa, just as homeless children began to be rounded up into orphanages. On their way home, they were robbed of the bread they had in their sacks and kicked off the train but still made it home. Hruby's story is striking for the ingenuity and courage exhibited, particularly impressive for a minor.[135]

To whatever factors the witnesses, who were also the survivors, attributed their survival, many wondered why they were spared while so many others perished. Was it by chance that some activist "overlooked" hidden seeds or millet? Was it because the neighbor's house was bigger and had a tin roof that the neighbors' goods were confiscated and not the respondent's, or were they spared from dekulakization because the Stalin portrait cut out from a newspaper and glued under the house icons (using crumbs of rye bread moistened with saliva) had caught the eye of a district official? One could only wonder.

---

were more often idle than operating, there were no specialists." Mysak Pavlo | HREC (holodomor.ca).

[134] Born in 1924, a native of the village of Horodyshche, Pishchanka raion, Vinnytsia oblast, Hruby was retired at the time of writing, a CPSU member, and a veteran of World War II. Hruby Denys | HREC (holodomor.ca).

[135] This ingenuity seems to have helped him in his future life. He completed seven grades in the village, receiving top marks in each, and in 1940 was accepted at the Vinnytsia Pharmaceutical School without an entrance exam. After the war, Hruby worked on the collective farm at various jobs: inventory manager, accountant, foreman of a field brigade, chief agronomist of the collective farm (eleven years), head of the village council (thirteen years), and as agronomist for plant protection (nine years). Ibid.

The long view on famine: Rupture and continuity

There are two other categories of accounts in the Maniak Collection that merit a closer look: (1) individual stories of children who lost one or both parents and often were forced out of their homes and remained victimized for life, thus detailing their life long grievances, and (2) accounts that attempt to make sense of the events of the Holodomor and are usually not confined to the author's own stories or events of 1932–33 thematically or chronologically. These are rather eloquent letters by people who managed to receive some post-secondary education, get better jobs, and were attempting to look back and reflect on the lasting effect of the Holodomor on them personally, on the village, and even on the country. These accounts provide a more panoramic view of the Holodomor in the Ukrainian peasants' *longue durée* from their own perspective, in their own words.

A few respondents supply "prequels" and "sequels" to the Holodomor. In the former, World War I, the Civil War, the 1921–23 famine, NEP, dekulakization, and collectivization are often used as benchmarks for explaining why the author's family found themselves in certain circumstances when the famine struck. In the latter the authors demonstrate how the famine changed the situation for those who could not leave the village and were left with no choice but to join the collective farm to survive. Even as the mass deaths subsided, the dehumanization, the physical devastation and depopulation of the villages, the destruction of the social fabric and the mores, and excessive taxation constituted heavy weights on their lives. It was only just before World War II (the "Great Patriotic War") that things began to improve, but then that war devastated the villages and destroyed the agriculture once again, took away those remaining (predominantly male) relatives who had survived the famine, and left many disabled, living off miserly pensions. Famine, along with collectivization, is viewed as a rupture, a crucial event that altered life by driving peasants forcibly into the collective farms. At the same time, it is viewed as one, even if the most traumatic, in a chain of events and years filled with poverty, extortion, and hard labor.

Mykhailo Shevchyk,[136] a self-identified member of the Communist Party and believer in the Soviet system, calls 1933 "the devastating year," compared to which "past wars seem like child's play." While only ten villagers fell in the fields of World War I and the Civil War, and twenty-two villagers did not return home from the fronts of the Great Patriotic War, the famine took "nearly forty people" in less than a year. His account is not

[136] Born in 1926, the author lived until he was seventeen in Poltava oblast (village of Zlodiivka, Velyka Bahachka raion), served in the Red (later Soviet) Army from 1943 to 1950, graduated from the Kharkiv Law Institute, and subsequently was sent to work at a prosecutor's office in Ternopil oblast; he was retired at the time of sending his letter in April 1989.

typical in that no one was dekulakized or deported from his village.[137] However, the sentiment expressed by Shevchyk that surviving the Holodomor was worse than surviving World War II as a serviceman of the Soviet Army is echoed in other veterans' accounts, and the rough estimates placing the number of victims between one-third and one-half of the population are rather typical.[138]

Platon Fedorenko, another believer in the Soviet system, traces the roots of the peasants' suffering to the abandoning of the NEP and the introduction of collectivization.

> It was also difficult during the 1921 famine, but there was a drought and crop failure. And then after some time Vladimir Ilyich Lenin introduced the NEP,[139] which was intended to last 10–15 years. But after Lenin's death, Stalin tied it up and in 1928 started collectivization, which led to a disaster not only in industry, negligible and weak at the time, but also in agriculture, because it was carried out not to Lenin's plan but forcefully according to Stalin's insane ideas. May he be damned by all people who are still alive today for all the misery that our innocent, hard-working, and glorious Soviet people experienced in these terrible 1930s, 1933, 1936, 1937, and 1938.[140]

A letter written by Yurii Kozlov, a student in the Pyriatyn Industrial College (*tekhnikum*) in 1930–33, echoes Fedorenko's assessment in describing how the abandonment of the NEP affected Pyriatyn, as well as Kozlov's native village of Tarasivka in Pyriatyn raion.[141]

> Before collectivization, people lived very well. They were given land and they worked on it, some worse, others better, and they managed a living. Those who had enough adults in the family could produce all they needed.

---

[137] In total, according to Shevchyk's calculations, about one-fifth of the inhabitants of Zlodiivka perished during the famine. "[T]here were 16 households on our street accounting for 86 residents. Of those, 15 died. In other settlements, the number of casualties was much greater."

[138] According to Ivan Ilchenko's father, "the most frightening and unforgettable events in our lives were the 1933 year of the famine and the war with fascist Germany in 1941–45." Ilchenko's father, brother, and he himself fought on the fronts of the war, and his sister was sent to Germany as a forced laborer. Famine was almost twice as devastating to the population of his native hamlet as World War II: "In 1933, 52 people died of starvation; in 1941–45, 30 people died in the war. Thirty-two young people were sent as forced labor to Germany." Ilchenko Ivan | HREC (holodomor.ca). Ivan Benedysiuk, who was eight in 1933 and later fought in WWII, calls the war, where he faced death every day, terrifying but 1933 even more terrifying. (Unpublished letter).

[139] New Economic Policy.

[140] Fedorenko Platon | HREC (holodomor.ca).

[141] Village of Tarasivka, Pyriatyn raion, Kharkiv oblast (now in Hrebinka raion, Poltava oblast).

> ... In Pyriatyn, there was so much grain in the market that they bought and poured it into piles. In Pyriatyn itself there were three mills, which were also chock-full of grain.[142]

In Tarasivka, the Beetroot Society procured seeds, fertilizers, and other items for peasants, while a Machine Station would lend out a threshing and locomotive steam engine and horse-drawn seed drills for beet sowing and bought metal cultivators, harrows, and other equipment. "The peasants managed their own property and their land personally. In the villages you could hear sounds of joy and cheerfulness, though no one was very well dressed (clothing was mostly homespun and dyed with elderberries, oak bark, etc.)." By contrast, collectivization was conducted with a heavy emphasis on arresting those who did not wish to join or work on the collective farm and was marked "by low productivity, poor harvests, lack of education or understanding of new techniques or equipment." As a result, "people lost all hope," cattle starved, sowing in 1932 "was done very badly," and an invasive search of rural households for "old" grain all led to starvation by the winter of 1933.[143]

These and other respondents believe that forced collectivization, forced grain requisitioning, and the subsequent famine killed the peasants and agricultural specialists as well as agricultural entrepreneurship and the Ukrainian peasants' spirit.[144]

---

[142] Kozlov Yurii | HREC (holodomor.ca). Yukhym Dibrova mentions that after NEP, before collectivization peasants owned imported tractors and their own threshers; stables were not big enough to accommodate all the horses. Dibrova Yukhym | HREC (holodomor.ca).

[143] Kozlov Yurii | HREC (holodomor.ca).

[144] Dibrova Yukhym | HREC (holodomor.ca). Similar in tone and emphasis is the letter of Ivan Demydenko. "The village was big. Hardworking and friendly families of villagers, who had received land following the Revolution, lived well and aspired to be productive. In almost every homestead there were cows, oxen, horses, sheep, pigs, and various poultry. The villagers had bread and something to put on it. Along with the individual homesteads in the village, there were working cooperatives. The village enriched itself with each passing day; life was becoming better. Like a terrifying nightmare, mass collectivization befell the villagers like snow on one's head. The sounds, laughter, and songs of the village disappeared. People walked around gloomily, whispering to each other. Soon, seven collective farms were organized in the village, where carts and sleighs were confiscated, oxen and horses were taken away. At the centre of the collective farms were the homesteads of dekulakized villagers. But what kind of kulaks were they? They lived perhaps better than others, thanks to their labor and hardworking families. None of them exploited hired workers, but all of them were persecuted and many never returned to their native village from Stalin's camps. Demydenko I. | HREC (holodomor.ca). Stepan Vovk emphasizes the loss of agricultural expertise. "So many farmers we lost, who toiled and worked so hard on this sacred Ukrainian land. Mykhailo Stepanovych Kudyn, Semen Bahrii were born specialists, and they sent a threshing machine to help people thresh the grain that the peasants had on their own plots. Pavlo Hrabovsky, an avid farmer,

A few accounts compare the 1932–33 famine with those that occurred in 1921–23 and 1946–47.

For Nadiia Aksiuk of Zinkiv,[145] it was the 1921–23 famine that took the lives of her mother's father and sister; people died of typhus and dysentery as well as of starvation. The 1946–47 famine was caused by the post-war decline. In contrast to those two famines, which appeared to have had some natural causes, she declares that the 1933 famine was artificial, organized by Stalin.[146]

Yakov Petrenko counts the 1933 famine, along with the 1937–38 purges and 1946–47 famine, as "links in one chain" of Stalinist purges aimed at mass murder of the Ukrainian people.[147] Others also remember the 1932–33 famine as an event that changed the very fabric of rural life irrevocably. They describe it as crucial in a chain of events that led to a life full of hardship and lifelong victimization. Their living standard seemed to have improved briefly just before the war, in 1938–39, and then not for another decade, but even then, the sense of deprivation and moral decline persisted.

Hryhorii Kuchmii, who survived the famine as a fifteen-year-old living on weeds and dead livestock, comments sarcastically that once the famine was over, people seemed to accept their poor living conditions and went back to praising Stalin.[148]

> It is said that you must live your life so as not to be ashamed of how you lived, but no, this is not meant to be for our resentful people, since the entire journey of our lives was spent in fear and poverty, and in relentless

---

and a number of others were repressed, and none of them returned, dead or alive." Vovk Stepan | HREC (holodomor.ca).

145 Then in Kharkiv oblast, now in Poltava oblast.

146 Aksiuk Nadiia | HREC (holodomor.ca). According to Aksiuk, there were around 300 households and close to 800 people inhabiting the village by 1933. Dmytro Kovryha also compares the 1921 famine to the 1933 famine in the village of Hysune in Hradyzk raion, Kharkiv oblast (now in Poltava oblast), which is now under the waters of the Kremenchuk reservoir. In his opinion, the former was caused by drought, while the latter, which took the lives of 20–25 per cent of his village's residents, was caused by excessive requisitioning and the lack of payment of the collective farm workers for their labor. Kovryha Dmytro | HREC (holodomor.ca).

147 Petrenko Yakov | HREC (holodomor.ca).

148 "The time for grain-harvesting came, the soup began to be boiled thicker at the collective farm, and a kilogram of bread was given to each person per day. People began to have a human appearance, and by autumn 1933, although they were very poorly dressed and shod and in very poor living conditions, they began to dance with tears of joy, to sing and to praise the "father" and "teacher," the "beloved and wise leader of ours," Joseph Stalin, who by his decree had crushed many millions of people with famine in Ukraine, and in the short period from 1937 to 1938, murdered tens of millions of a great and glorious people." Kuchmii Hryhorii (Grigorii) | HREC (holodomor.ca).

> and unpaid labor. We cannot complain about life; God forbid that Stalinism returns.[149]

Stanislav Bondarenko's[150] memoir backs this portrayal of a life of hardship and abuse. He barely survived the famine by eating weeds and later fought and received crippling wounds in World War II. He recalls that the harvest was good but that grain procurement plans were excessive even after the famine was over, and peasants were unable to fulfill them. Once the peasants "started recovering" they were hit by excessive -taxes, while their pay in kind per workday was meager ("mere grams"), keeping them in poverty, "naked and barefoot." Then came World War II, but the 1933 famine was still considered worse than the war. After the war another famine struck in 1946–47, and people travelled up to 20 kilometers to sell items in exchange for food, and new taxes and involuntary government loans were imposed. Those who tried to glean corn cobs or beets in the fields, for example, were sentenced to 8–9 years in labour camps, and those who did not deliver enough workdays were sent "to Solovky"[151] for up to 25 years. "Those who did not live through this probably would not believe that this is the way it was and people lived that way," concludes Bondarenko.[152]

Mykola Syvoborodko,[153] another self-described communist and atheist whose father was a communist too, dedicates the lion's share of his long and detailed account to the moral decline and devastation of the village by the famine. He points to the declining number of children in peasant families, from three to six to one or two, as well as the destruction of the church, which traditionally had helped the poor and the hungry; once the priests were severely prosecuted and churches closed, "there was nobody left to be merciful." While there were women's protests (*babyni bunty*) against the closure of the churches in 1928–30, there was no one to protest the famine. "Even before 1933, the most spirited villagers had already been exiled to the Solovets islands, put on trial, exterminated, and rendered powerless. So we submissively waited for our end and saved ourselves as best we could."[154]

---

[149] Ibid.

[150] Bondarenko was born in 1926 into a poor family that had no house of their own and his father was among the first who joined the collective farm in 1929. He recalls the events in his native Denysivka in Orzhytsia raion, Kharkiv oblast (now in Poltava oblast).

[151] A notorious Soviet penal colony at Solovets Islands on the White Sea in Arkhangelsk oblast.

[152] Bondarenko Stanislav | HREC (holodomor.ca).

[153] Syvoborodko writes about the events in Semenivka, Arbuzynka raion, Odesa oblast (now in Mykolaiv oblast).

[154] Syvoborodko Mykola | HREC (holodomor.ca). Pavlo Mysak writes that the push for complete collectivization meant "to drive peasants in" like a herd of animals and led already in

Syvoborodko writes that the famine led to a "disgusting phenomenon that grew and captured the entire nation": thievery and such "moral deformations" as indifference to work and snitching.

> Never certain as to whether famine would occur again, villagers began stealing. What had previously been considered sinful lost its moral judgment. Without the ability to feed themselves, collective farm workers began stealing everything that passed into their hands: grain, vegetables, fruits, all other food. Later journalists began calling them thieves ("those who carry things"; *nesuny*). Their attitude towards work became indifferent; nobody was responsible for anything. The moral decay was accelerated by the Nazi occupation. Snitching became commonplace. Everyone realized that they should think one way, speak a second way, and act in a third way. I believe that all of these deformations began here. Previously people tried to work the land to their best ability, but now nobody can drag young people back to the village.

In 1934–46 the collective farm in Syvoborodko's village became a "frontrunner," and the collective farm workers began earning 2–3 kg, later 5–6 kg, and in 1938–39 as much as 8 kg of products in kind per workday. "An average collective farm-worker who did not have a permanent position could not earn for more than 120 working days, and women even less. In a permanent position (working with horses, pigs, or cows) they could earn for up to 200 working days."[155]

When Denys Hruby returned to his village during the harvest season in the summer of 1933, when widespread death had ceased, rye was being sown in the private plots, and people had grain to eat, he noticed that the homes were covered with straw. "Those with tin roofs had been stripped so as to cover the collective farm building, since the kolkhoz was only just being born." Two collective farms were established.

1931–32 to a "terrible" situation with food; there was none. The collective farm peasantry "worked for free, didn't receive grain or money," which was the case with his father, who left the collective farm and found paid work as a guard in a Vinnytsia office. High taxes were imposed on individual farmers to push them into the collective farms. In response, some individual farmers decided to let their horses go free, abandon their fields and seek work and a "better destiny" elsewhere. Collective farms and individual farmers' fields "for the most part were impoverished, left empty, unsown; there was no one to work them.

The peasants' resistance did not have much effect; they were dekulakized, even the ones who were going along were subjected to expulsion to Solovetsky Islands prison camp, Siberia, and other places.

The hastiness of the formation of the collective farms in Ukraine meant that they took the grain, took it all away. Such Stalinist methods of leadership led to grief and a tragic famine." The peasantry was reduced to "poverty and beggary". Mysak Pavlo | HREC (holodomor.ca).

155 Syvoborodko Mykola | HREC (holodomor.ca).

> Drunkards were in charge of the village. They stole and sold things at cheap prices and then drank away the proceeds. In the village they ransacked the church and sold the stone to a neighboring village, which used it to build a two-storey school. (It exists to this day.) A nobleman had once lived in our village; there were many fine buildings, a palace. They ransacked everything.[156]

As Mykhail Prokopchuk puts it, "those who could walk, who had a little bit of strength, went to the collective farm to work, where they were given a bowl of watery gruel and a piece of bread once a day." The activists "foolishly executed the instructions of the great leader [Stalin], destroying the rural workers, to whom Lenin had given land to make our Motherland rich. And then what happened? We still haven't managed to recover."

On an individual level, starvation created orphans and forced other vulnerable children to abandon their studies, sometimes irrevocably. Some were too weak to go to school or were bullied as children of kulaks or "enemies of the people" or had to forage for weeds to eat[157] or work as assistant shepherds or field laborers in order to receive food rations, and later a workday pay, to survive. Memoirs of this kind are often written poorly. Their language indicates that illiteracy was often a consequence of the Holodomor and led to a life of hard menial labor, which had a lasting debilitating effect, on the lives of women in particular.

Motria Semko, whose family of eleven was dispossessed, father deported, and most family members died, including both her mother and father, ended up working as a tractor driver for forty-one years and living in a dugout for decades after the war. Motria describes paying more taxes than "a man," including 41 kg of meat and 220 eggs, and being forced to buy bonds for a sum of 300 rubles because those who refused were not given any work. To offset those taxes, she raised rabbits and chickens. Only after "Malenkov reduced taxes to 8 rubles per *are* of land" did her situation ease somewhat.[158]

---

[156] Hruby Denys | HREC (holodomor.ca).

[157] Yelyzaveta Moskovchuk was orphaned at the age of five and was forced to forage for weeds to survive, which were hard to find because everybody else was also looking for them. She ruminates that she was forced to perform hard physical labor at a young age, which had lifelong health implications. Moskovchuk Yelizaveta | HREC (holodomor.ca).

[158] Semko Motria | HREC (holodomor.ca). In a similar account, Mariia Luzan writes that she lost a sibling and her father to famine. Her mother could barely make ends meet and walked 25 km every night to the house of her brother, who would give her some food in secret from his own family. After the famine was over, Luzan recalled that on the collective farms, workers were given 200 g of rye per workday but then taxes were added, so her mother would walk 18 km to sell 2 *poods* (almost 33 kg) of rye at the market in order to pay the tax. And so, "one trouble

Yevheniia Aleksieieva was abandoned by her mother and moved through a series of orphanages, witnessing the deaths of dozens of children at the height of the famine. A veteran of World War II who had joined the Red Army as a volunteer and a "labour veteran," she experienced nothing but hardship. "We worked almost for free, without weekends, vacations, or maternity leave, and we earned next to nothing for retirement..."[159]

Some boys who survived World War II managed to get an education and make a better life for themselves beyond the village. Others were not so lucky. Stepan Vovk, who was expelled from school and harassed by activists for reciting the ditty "No cow, no pig, only Stalin on the wall," writes that he "counted the days before being conscripted into the army" and swore never to return to his native village. However, because he was disabled during "the cursed war," he didn't have any choice but to return. "It would have been better if I had not been born, so that I wouldn't have had to suffer such pain," Vovk writes of his fate, adding, "What one's fate is in the morning, so it is to the last."[160]

One may consider these child-survivors "lucky" compared to those of their generation who perished during the famine or war—or, in another harrowing instance, the three schoolchildren who "disappeared for good" in 1935 after writing a letter to Molotov[161] asking why the famine happened.[162] Be that as it may, Tetiana Komlichenko expressed a sentiment shared in numerous accounts that provide rich material for a history of childhood during the Holodomor: "Childhood of our generation was no joy: there was a famine, there was a war."[163]

---

was chasing another" into the war, when Maria was taken to Germany as an *Ostarbeiter*. Luzan Mariia | HREC (holodomor.ca).

[159] Aleksieieva Yevhenia (Kolomiiets Ivha) | HREC (holodomor.ca).

[160] Born in 1915 into a ten-person family of landless peasants, Vovk lost both his parents to typhoid in 1918, and by January 26, 1933, the day when a search brigade came to take away all their remaining food, there were only three family members left: his older brother, sister, and himself. Vovk Stepan | HREC (holodomor.ca).

[161] Viacheslav Molotov was the Chairman of the USSR Council of People's Commissars at that time.

[162] The Chekists arrived and summoned them to the director's office more than once, after which they were "taken away and their fate is unknown." Panov Yakiv (Yakov) | HREC (holodomor.ca).

[163] Tetiana Komlichenko's father was sentenced to eight years in labor camps by a special *troika* in 1932, served his sentence, returned to his native village, and was executed by the Germans in 1942 for helping Soviet partisan fighters. Komlichenko Tetiana | HREC (holodomor.ca).

Conclusion

Olga Andriiewsky has argued that social memory was one of the hidden casualties of the Holodomor, because "after 1932–1933, the Ukrainian village lost much of its autonomous capacity to tell stories, to relate their own collective memory, to construct its own portrait of itself."[164] The written testimonies of Holodomor survivors in the Maniak Collection give a voice to ordinary people. Their stories about the struggle to survive and to make sense of the immense personal and collective trauma, told in their own words, are now rediscovered and available for research and interpretation by cultural and social historians.

These accounts may also pave the way for contributions to the field of historiography, in Dominick LaCapra's words, "making a difference in the present and future…that conjoins critically tested memory and comparably tested document-and-text-based knowledge in furthering collective projects seeking truth, compassion, and justice."[165]

Archives

Maniak Collection. Holodomor Research and Education Consortium (HREC). https://holodomor.ca/resource/maniak-collection/

Bibliography

Andriewsky, Olga. "Towards a Decentered History: The Study of the Holodomor and Ukrainian Historiography." In *Contextualizing the Holodomor: The Impact of Thirty Years of Ukrainian Famine Studies.* Toronto: Canadian Institute of Ukrainian Studies, 2015: 14–48.

Hrynevych, Liudmyla. "Vid zaperechuvannia do vymushenoho vyznannia. Pro mekhanizmy vkhodzhennia temy holodu 1932–1933 rr. v ofitsiinyi publichnyi prostir v SRSR ta URSR naprykintsi 1980-kh." *Problemy istoriï Ukrainy: fakty, sudzhennia, poshuky: mizhvidomchyi zbirnyk naukovykh prats'.* Vyp. 18. Kyiv, 2008: 211–44. http://dspace.nbuv.gov.ua/bitstream/handle/123456789/13343/22-Hrynevych.pdf

Hutsalo, Yevhen. "Stvorymo knyhu narodnoï pam'iati." *Literaturna Ukraïna,* no. 45 (1988).

[164] Olga Andriewsky, "Towards a Decentered History: The Study of the Holodomor and Ukrainian Historiography," in *Contextualizing the Holodomor: The Impact of Thirty Years of Ukrainian Famine Studies* (Toronto: Canadian Institute of Ukrainian Studies, 2015), 35.

[165] Dominick LaCapra, "Trauma, History, Memory, Identity: What Remains?," in *Understanding Others: Peoples, Animals, Pasts* (Ithaca-London: Cornell University Press, 2018), 114.

Kasianov, Georgy. "Revisiting the Great Famine of 1932–1933. Politics of Memory and Public Consciousness (Ukraine after 1991). In *Past in the Making: Historical Revisionism in Central Europe after 1989*, edited by Michal Kopecek, 197-219. Budapest-New York: CEU Press, 2008.

Kas'ianov, Heorhii. *Danse macabre: holod 1921–1933 u politytsi, masovii svidomosti ta istoriohrafiï (1980-ti — pochatok 2000-kh).* Kyiv: Instytut instorii Ukrainy NAN Ukrainy; Nash chas, 2010: 11–33

Kul'chyts'kyi, S. "'33-i: Holod". Zaproshuiemo do stvorennia knyhy-memorialu." *Sil's'ki visti*, December 9, 1988.

Kul'chitskii, Stanislav. "Kak osmyslivali Golodomor." In Stanislav Kul'chitskii. *Kak on nas unichtozhal. Stalin i ukrainskii golodomor,* 4–11. Kyiv, 2007. https://royallib.com/read/kulchitskiy_stanislav/pochemu_on_nas_unichtogal_stalin_i_ukrainskiy_golodomor.html

LaCapra, Dominick. "Trauma, History, Memory, Identity: What Remains?" In *Understanding Others: Peoples, Animals, Pasts*, 81–114. Ithaca-London: Cornell University Press, 2018. https://www.jstor.org/stable/10.7591/j.ctt21h4w4m

Maniak, Volodymyr. "Holod: chomu i iak. Rozdumy nad rukopysom knyhy-memorialu "33-ii: Holod"," *Sil's'ki visti*, July 11, 1989.

Maniak, Volodymyr, and Lidiia Kovalenko. eds. *33-ii: Holod: Narodna Knyha-Memorial.* Kyiv: Radian's'kyi pys'mennyk, 1991.

Matiiko, Oleksandr. "Bil'dushi liuds'koï: Tvoryt'sia knyha-memorial "33-ii: Holod"," *Sil's'ki visti*, January 3, 1989.

Pakharenko, Vasyl'. "Holod". *Literaturna Ukraïna*, no. 45 (1988).

Smith, Sidonie, and Julia Watson. "Witness or False Witness?: Metrics of Authenticity, Collective I-Formations and the Ethic of Verification in First-Person Testimony." *Biography* 35, no. 4 (Fall 2012): 590–626. https://www.jstor.org/stable/23540886. Accessed November 20, 2019.

The Holodomor in the Light of Japanese Documents

Hiroaki Kuromiya

Japan was one of the few nations that stationed diplomatic posts in Soviet Ukraine. Its consulate in Odesa had opened in 1902, apparently for the military purpose of watching the movements of the Imperial Russian Black Sea Fleet. The consulate was closed at the time of the Russo-Japanese War in 1904–05, reopened in 1906 and closed again in 1909.[1] With the resumption in 1925 of diplomatic relations between Moscow and Tokyo, the Odesa consulate was opened once more in 1926 for a period of eleven years, after which it was closed, along with many other foreign legations, in 1937—the year of the Great Terror. Given its location in Odesa during the Holodomor, the Japanese consulate might seem a source for a trove of documents on the Holodomor. Certainly, in view of potential military conflict, the consular officials closely observed the Ukrainian scene, even though they were followed by the Soviet secret police wherever they went. We know from Polish and Ukrainian archives that Japanese diplomats in Ukraine frequently exchanged information with other foreign diplomats, particularly the Poles.[2] Needless to say, such exchanges did take place during the Holodomor as well.[3] It is therefore a great pity that most of these Japanese diplomatic documents, which must have included much information on the Holodomor, were lost (mostly destroyed deliberately) in 1945 at the end of World War II.

Nevertheless, a few illuminating documents survive. Along with accounts and assessments by Japanese journalists active in the Soviet Union at that time, they are valuable for the study of the Holodomor. Although they do not change the overall picture as we know it today, they do open an interesting perspective into the Holodomor. The Japanese government knew well that people were dying en masse in 1932–33. However, as in

---

[1] *Gaimushō nenkan. Taishō jūgo nen ki. Ichi* (Annals of the Ministry of Foreign Affairs) (Tokyo: Gaimushō, 1926), 299.

[2] There are many cases of such information as related by Polish diplomats. See, for example, Centralne archiwum wojskowe, I.303.4 1982 (regarding 1933–34). More generally, see Hiroaki Kuromiya and Andrzej Pepłoński, *Między Warszawą a Tokio: Polsko-japońska współpraca wywiadowcza 1904–1944* (Toruń: Adam Marszałek, 2009).

[3] Jan Jacek Bruski, ed., *Hołodomor 1932–1933. Wielki Głód na Ukrainie w dokumentach polskiej dyplomacji i wywiadu* (Warsaw: Polski Instytut Spraw Międzynarodowych, 2008); *Pol'shcha ta Ukraïna u trydtsiatykh-sorokovykh rokakh XX stolittia. T. 7. Holodomor v Ukraïni 1932–1933* (Warsaw: Instytut Pamięci Narodowej–Komisja Ścigania Zbrodni przeciwko Narodowi Polskiemu; Kyiv: Haluzevyi derzhavnyi arkhiv Sluzhby bezpeky Ukrainy, 2008).

Poland and the United States, political considerations made it difficult to expose the horror of the Holodomor widely.

* * *

In the 1930s, Japan was in a potentially hostile relationship with the Soviet Union over hegemony in Asia, particularly in China. Moscow had long been agitating the Chinese against imperialist countries, notably China's neighbor, Japan, which, in turn, regarded the Soviet Union as hostile to its ambitions in Asia.

Japan's imperialist ambitions manifested themselves in the invasion of Manchuria in 1931 and the foundation of a puppet government, Manchukuo/Manzhouguo, in 1932. This led to a direct confrontation between Japan and the Soviet Union along the Manchu-Soviet, Mongol-Manchu borders, which were thousands of kilometers long. Japan sought to mobilize Ukrainians in the East and West as a potential force against Moscow.[4] The escalating tension in the Far East greatly contributed to the Holodomor. After signing a non-aggression pact with Poland in 1932, Moscow diverted resources to Siberia and the Far East. The grain Moscow purchased abroad secretly was sent not to Ukraine but to the Soviet East.[5] Moscow even diverted foods and other goods (35,000 tons of flour and 8,590 tons of millet, for example) to Mongolia (the Mongolian People's Republic), where massive popular rebellions were raging against the forced Sovietization of the country.[6]

The full scale of Japan's interest in Ukraine is difficult to gauge because of the loss of documents. What we have, however, does show that considerable effort was exerted to study Ukraine as a strategically important republic, even though it was separated from Japan by some eight thousand kilometers. From the famine period alone, one can find a 200-page report ("The Status of Ukraine in the Soviet Union") written by Consular Secretary Shizuo Mitani in September 1932,[7] another 170-page

---

[4] Hiroaki Kuromiya, "Ukraine and Eurasian History in the Twentieth Century," *Harvard Ukrainian Studies* 34, no. 1–4 (2015–16): 195–213.

[5] On the redistribution of precious resources to the Far East and Siberia, see *Tragediia sovetskoi derevni: kollektivizatsiia i raskulachivanie*, vol. 3 (Moscow: ROSSPEN, 2001), 365; and Oleg H. Ken, *Mobilizatsionnoe planirovanie i politicheskie resheniia (konets 1920-kh–seredina 1930-kh gg.)* (Moscow: OGI, 2008), 278. On Tokyo knowing about Moscow's import of grain from abroad at that time see Chūzō Yoshimura, *Nichiro no genzai oyobi shōrai* (The Present and Future of Japan-Russia) (Tokyo: Nihon Kōronsha, 1934), 136.

[6] *Mongolyn tukhaĭ BKhK(b)N-yn barimt bichigt, 1920–1952: barimtyn emkhtgel*, vol. 1 (Ulaanbaatar: Undesnii Arkhivyn Gazar, 2002), 422–27.

[7] Japan Center for Asian Historical Records (JACAR): https://www.jacar.go.jp, reference code, B10070247300. All the documents from JACAR cited hereafter were consulted over several years, most recently on July 1 and 2, 2019.

report on agriculture ("The Ukrainian National Economy: The Results of 1932 and the Plans for 1933") written by the same secretary (dated March 1933),[8] a report by the Consul Bunichirō Tanaka on the speech Pavel P. Postyshev gave in Kharkiv in June 1933 attacking the former Commissar of Education Mykola O. Skrypnyk and his "nationalist" policy,[9] a report by the new Consul Minoru Hirata on the changes to Ukrainian orthography (dated September 10, 1934),[10] and many other diplomatic notes.

Moscow's concern about Japanese interest in Ukraine in this period is evident in the following episode: when the Red Army conducted military manoeuvres in Ukraine from August 30 to September 4, 1934, the Polish Consul in Kyiv described them in a report to Warsaw as "a [show of force] against foreign countries, particularly Japan"![11]

These and other Japanese documents also provide interesting first-hand information on the Holodomor in Ukraine.

* * *

In March 1932, Consul Tanaka reported the conditions of workers in Odesa as dire. From January almost none of the necessities of daily life could be bought at factory stores. Nearly half the workers were ill, with many suffering from tuberculosis. Work had slowed down in many factories and in the port, resulting in numerous layoffs. Those made redundant lost both their right to eat at factory canteens and their bread rations. At one factory, thousands of hungry workers stormed the canteen, causing injuries to each other.[12]

Subsequent reports became more dire. On December 1, 1932, for example, Tanaka wrote to Tokyo that the food supply in Odesa had deteriorated to the extent that it was worse than it had been at the time of the "great famine" in 1921–22. Two weeks later, on December 16, he dispatched another report in which he noted that the situation had worsened.[13]

In the survey of agriculture in Ukraine mentioned above, Mitani wrote in March 1933 that the agricultural sector in Ukraine in 1932 had turned

---

[8] JACAR: https://www.jacar.go.jp, reference code: B08060688800 (consulted 1 July 2019). All the documents from JACAR cited hereafter were confirmed on this date).

[9] JACAR, C05022799500.

[10] JACAR, B04011371700. Hirata correctly noted that this change was part of Mos-cow's Russification of Ukraine.

[11] Rossiiskii gosudarstvennyi voennyi arkhiv (RGVA), f. 308k, op. 3, d. 314, l. 207. See also Wojciech Włodarkiewicz, *Przed 17 września 1939 roku: Radzieckie zagrożenie Rzeczypospolitej w ocenach polskich naczelnych władz wojskowych 1921–1939* (Warsaw: Wydawnictwo Neriton, 2002), 132.

[12] JACAR, B04012870700.

[13] JACAR, B08060701400.

out to be a "big failure," with both production and procurement far lower than in previous years. Everything in the countryside was in short supply, and the collective farm markets, legalized in 1932, were virtually non-existent. Oddly, however, Mitani did not comment on the ravages of the famine itself, which must have been obvious to everyone in Odesa.[14]

Tanaka's report on May 5, 1933 was explicit. From April, typhus had overwhelmed the hospitals. Many had died. Elementary schools were closed temporarily. The children's march for May Day, which normally took place April 30, had been canceled. Tanaka transmitted to Tokyo reports from Kharkiv that hospitals were so full that schools had to be used as temporary hospitals. Typhus had taken a large toll in the countryside, where medical care was limited. Trams had to be disinfected to prevent contagion. In response to the climbing death rate, bread rations were raised from 100 to 200 grams a day for some workers. Rations for other products such as sugar were raised in view of the approaching May Day celebration. Internal passports were introduced, and those without a passport were being deported, a train load each day, the young and strong to the Far East and the rest to the North for timber work.[15] Three weeks later Tanaka wrote that deaths from typhus and "malnutrition" continued at the same levels even after rations were raised. He noted further that the secret police were confiscating valuables (such as gold, silver, and old coins) from the population.

Trade in the port of Odesa was almost at a halt because both exports and imports had declined drastically, while seven boats purchased from Germany were used to transport military-related materials to the Far East.[16]

The most explicit documentation found in Japanese archives is highly revealing of the atmosphere of the time. Writing from Odesa on August 1, 1933, Tanaka reported that grain production had improved and that the extreme situation of the food supply was alleviated accordingly. However, Tanaka attached a contradictory report on cannibalism, which reveals a situation in July 1933 that was no better than a few months earlier. It reads:

> The urban residents are short of foods and lack means of procurement, while the rural residents have no freedom to consume their own produce unless they fulfill the government quota for delivery of new grain and other produce. So they can only steal. They suffer from lack of food.
>
> Recent cases of cannibalism in various locations are not accidental and appear to have become a kind of social phenomenon. The following cases have become known [to us] recently.

---

[14] JACAR, B08060688800, pp. 31, 34, 37, 41, 41, 47, 54, 55, and 166.
[15] JACAR, C05022789900.
[16] JACAR, C05022791000.

1. Around 20th of July a woman was detained for selling human meat at the market in the city of Odesa.

2. In a village near Nikolaev [city of Mykolaiv] an order was issued in mid-July prohibiting children outside their homes without supervision.

3. In late July in a village near Odesa, an old woman with no job ate two infants.

4. A female teacher from the capital of Moldova, Balta, told a story she heard that in the city there were instances in which new graves were excavated and human meat was cut from the bodies.

5. In late July a land surveyor was sent to Novoukrainka, a village in Odesa oblast with the "worst agricultural record" [either for production or delivery]. He was attacked and eaten by the peasants. Therefore the district head of agriculture had to request a replacement from Odesa.[17]

Another similar report from Japan's military intelligence in August 1933 warned that given the serious drought in "southern Russia" (including Ukraine), "serious famine seems inevitable."[18] Fortunately this prediction did not prove quite right in 1934.

These official documents seem oddly restrained given the circumstances, although it is difficult to fathom the overall extent of frank reporting owing to the loss of other documents. Some Japanese publications did include more explicit discussion of the famine. A book published in 1934 by the head of research of the "Good Neighbor" society (*Zenrin kyōkai*) in Tokyo raised the alarm that hungry people in Ukraine had eaten every dog and cat (and some humans as well). He added that the situation was extremely dire with crime rampant and that as many as ten million people were believed to have died. Unlike in the famine of 1921–22, this time no foreign aid was received.[19] A small pamphlet published in 1934 by the Japanese Army gives an accurate assessment. Traditionally, the peasants in the Northern Caucasus and Ukraine were the most discontented with the Soviet government. There was an ethnic reason for this fact. They sabotaged agriculture in 1932, leading to a very poor harvest. "It resulted in a great famine last spring." The situation improved somewhat the following spring (1934). All the same, the peasants were mistreated and their lives were so impoverished that "one could not overlook the fact that they entertained much discontent even though they might not speak out."[20] In an

---

[17] JACAR, C05022794200. The report is reproduced on p. 125. Balta was the capital of the Moldavian Autonomous SSR, within the Ukrainian SSR, from 1924 to 1928. In 1933 the capital was in Tyraspil'.

[18] JACAR, C14121174600.

[19] Yoshimura, *Nichiro no genzai oyobi shōrai,* 134–37.

[20] Rikugunshō gunji chōsabu, ed., *Kindai kokubō yori mitaru Sorenpō* (The Soviet Union as Seen from the Point of View of National Defense) (Tokyo: n.p.), 16–17.

English-language journal published in 1934, Japanese journalist Katsuji Fuse wrote: "As a result of the forcible export of products, the drain on resources within Soviet territory came to be felt keenly, and famines broke out in the Ukraine. The conditions, however, began to improve greatly about last autumn [of 1933], shortly before I left the Soviet capital."[21]

In his writings after World War II, Fuse analyzed the Ukrainian famine. In his biography of Stalin published in 1949, for instance, he observed that Moscow deliberately created an economic system whereby it could control the economy as it wished. Moscow, according to Fuse, forced Ukraine to grow hemp and beetroot. As a result, the Ukrainians went hungry unless they got grain from elsewhere. The reason why famine took place in the breadbasket of Europe—Ukraine—and why the Uzbek peasants were told to "eat cotton" is that they were victimized for the sake of creating a "controlled economy" meant to oppress national minorities.[22] Apart from the particulars, Fuse's observations are noteworthy, inasmuch as he was a veteran observer of the Soviet Union and had personally interviewed Lenin, Trotskii, Stalin, Radek, and many other Soviet luminaries.

* * *

In comparison with other foreign (Polish, German, British, and Italian) documents and reports with which I am familiar, Japanese archival documents are meager and far less explicit about human casualties. One might suppose that the documents destroyed in the war were more explicit and revealing. And yet, even the published reports in the press were restrained. It is not that there were no reports. They were published in many places. What is striking about the Japanese documents and publications is that they seem to take the Great Famine/Holodomor as no surprise: it was the logical conclusion of Stalin's brutal policy. Whatever their reading of the Soviet events in the 1930s, it is important to understand the reasons why the Japanese assumed the famine to be a "natural" development and apparently raised no particular alarm about the situation. Did they lack human compassion? There are two possible explanations for this seemingly odd reaction to the deaths of millions.

First, in fear of Soviet military actions against Japan in Manchuria, Tokyo made every effort not to provoke the Soviet Union. There may have been official censorship (as well as self-censorship by journalists) restricting the publication of sensitive and sensational information on the

[21] Katsuji Fusé, "Japan and Soviet Russia," *Contemporary Japan*, March 1934, 600–610.
[22] Katsuji Fuse, *Sutārin den* (A Biography of Stalin) (Tokyo: Tōka shobō, 1949), 222.

Soviet Union.[23] This is somewhat similar to the way Poland officially reacted to the Holodomor in Ukraine: Poland, believing that the relations formed by the ratification of a non-aggression treaty with the Soviet Union were most favorable for Poland, was consequently unwilling to use the Holodomor in Ukraine politically lest they damage relations with Moscow.[24]

Second, almost all Japanese visitors to the Soviet Union during the First Five-Year Plan (1928–32) were simply astonished by the level of poverty and human suffering and sacrifice in the country. This is significant because Japan at the time was not a wealthy country. Like many other countries, Japan had been hit hard by the Great Depression of 1929. In Japan, unemployment ran high, the standard of living had dropped, and poverty as well as localized hunger did exist.

Japan's hardships were further magnified by an increasing militarization of the country, with vast resources diverted from consumption to armament. Even so, Japanese visitors were deeply disturbed by what they saw in the Soviet Union. For example, Hikosaburō Hata, Japan's military attaché in Warsaw (1930–32) and Moscow (1934–36), who observed the Soviet scene intimately on the ground, noted that the Soviet people's suffering could not be compared with anything he had known in his life.[25] At the same time, the Japanese visitors were astonished that the Soviet people silently submitted, going on with their lives without so much as a complaint. One Japanese military officer who in spring 1931 traveled from Harbin, China, to Moscow by the Trans-Siberian Railway, described the utter poverty of people in the Soviet Union. He noted that he could not look at the children and women "without tears." They contrasted sharply with the well-dressed and seemingly well-fed Red Army soldiers. Forcing such sacrifice on the population for the sake of "national defense," he observed, was not something other countries could do.[26] True, the period of the First Five-Year Plan was one of deprivation but not one of famine, let alone of the Holodomor.

---

[23] Unfortunately, it is not known, at least to the author of the present essay, how much of the material the journalists had collected on the Holodomor and other events in the Soviet Union survived World War II. Further research may unearth valuable observations.

[24] Robert Kuśnierz, *Ukraina w latach kolektywizacji i Wielkiego Głodu (1929–1933)* (Toruń: Grado, 2005), 220–21.

[25] Hikosaburō Hata, "Saikin ni okeru Soren no genjō ni tsuite" (About the Current Situation in the Soviet Union), *Gaikō jihō*, no. 761 (August 15, 1936): 112.

[26] Tatsumi Kusaba, "Shasō yori rokoku o mite" (Russia Seen from Train Windows), Ms., Bōeishō bōeikenkyūjo toshokan (Tokyo), n.d., 4–5. Kusaba was interned in the Soviet Union after World War II. Moscow sought to force him to testify against his former colleagues at the Tokyo War Crimes Trial. Loath to testify, however, he committed suicide in Tokyo under Soviet detention.

Stalin's ironclad rule made a striking contrast to the contemporary political life of Japan, where most government cabinets barely lasted a year and assassinations of politicians by angry radical groups were rampant. Japanese observers were in fact frightened that any fight against such a formidable country as the Soviet Union, with its persevering population, would be extraordinarily difficult, far more so than the Russo-Japanese War of 1904–05 had been.

It was this sense of fright that dominated the Japanese documents and reports. While many saw the Holodomor as a sign of the failure of Stalin's Five-Year Plan, Fuse, who interviewed Stalin in 1925, reasoned otherwise. In November 1933 he reported on the conversation he had had with Radek a few months earlier, in which Radek, acknowledging the famine in Ukraine, bragged that Stalin's nerves were "like wire cables." In this Fuse saw the secret of Stalin's "success."[27] After returning to Japan, he gave a lecture on the Soviet Union in January 1934 in which he again emphasized his alarm that Moscow did not cringe in the face of the famine in Ukraine and on the contrary continued its military buildup "to great success."[28] Bogusław Miedziński, a Polish journalist and politician, reported a similar encounter with Radek: when asked how many people had died in the Ukrainian famine, Radek dismissed the question as unimportant by replying, "So what?" Even if the Poles were right that a famine existed in Soviet Ukraine and even if two million people had died in Ukraine, he reasoned, it just meant that the Soviet population would be 178 million instead of 180![29] Certainly this argument of the means justifying the goal was common among the Bolsheviks. G.V. Chicherin, a Bolshevik and "cultured" man who loved Wolfgang Amadeus Mozart, was no exception. In 1922, when he was asked about millions of deaths from hunger in "Southern Russia," he said: "In our country and in China people have starved to death all the time. Sometimes there were only thousands, sometimes hundreds of thousands, and sometimes 'millions.' All the same we have the right methods [of governing]."[30] Later, in 1937, at the time of the Great Terror, Fuse recalled

---

[27] Katsuji Fuse, "Ukuraina: kikin no shiren" (Ukraine: The Trial of Famine), *Tōkyō nichi nichi*, November 13, 1933, 2.

[28] *Zoku gendaishi shiryō. Kaigun, Katō Kanji nikki* (Modern History Sources 2. Vol. 5: The Navy. The Diary of Katō Kanji) (Tokyo: Misuzu, 1994), 518, 527.

[29] Bogusław Miedziński, "Droga do Moskwy," *Kultura* (Paris), no. 188 (1963): 82. The original Polish is: "Moi Panowie, nie rozumiem dlaczego przywiązujecie do tej sprawy taką wagę. No, przypuśćmy na chwilę, że macie rację i zginęło na Ukrainie 2 miliony ludzi i że odnośna cyfra ludności sowieckiej będzie, na przykład, nie 180 a 178 milionów. No to co?"

[30] Hans Adolf Jacobsen, *Karl Haushofer: Leben und Werk. Band 1. Lebensweg 1869–1946 und ansgewählte Texte zur Geopolitik* (Boppard am Rhein: Harald Boldt, 1979), 222. The original German quoted by Karl Haushofer is: "Bei uns und in China sind immer Menschen verhungert;

that while he was stationed in the Soviet Union during the famine he had been most struck by one thing: "in spite of the awful events of famine in Ukraine, the Kremlin did not cringe but continued to carry out the Five-Year Plan."[31] In an odd sense, the extreme Soviet brutality left the Japanese observers in awe. In hindsight, their analysis of Soviet policies was largely correct. Similarly, some Japanese observers assessed the Great Terror with startling accuracy. Unlike Hitler and the German Military High Command, Japanese military observers did not regard the Great Terror against the Red Army high command merely as its decapitation. They saw it as Stalin's preparation for war by promoting politically loyal commanders from the ranks.[32] The extant Japanese documents and reports on the Holodomor are limited in number and scope. Nevertheless, those that remain provide a remarkably astute analysis of Stalin's policies.

Bibliography

Bruski, Jan Jacek, ed. *Hołodomor 1932–1933. Wielki Głód na Ukrainie w dokumentach polskiej dyplomacji i wywiadu*. Warsaw: Polski Instytut Spraw Międzynarodowych, 2008.

Fuse, Katsuji. "Ukuraina: kikin no shiren" (Ukraine: The Trial of Famine). *Tōkyō nichi nichi*, November 13, 1933, 2.

- "Tai So ninshiki zesei no ki" (Time to Correct Our Views of the Soviet Union). *Gaikō jihō*, no. 776 (April 1, 1937): 102–14.

- *Sutārin den* (A Biography of Stalin). Tokyo: Tōka shobō, 1949.

- "Japan and Soviet Russia." *Contemporary Japan*, March 1934, 600–10.

Gaimushō nenkan. Taishō jūgo nen ki. Ichi (Annals of the Ministry of Foreign Affairs). Tokyo: Gaimushō, 1926.

Hata, Hikosaburō. "Saikin ni okeru Soren no genjō ni tsuite" (About the Current Situation in the Soviet Union). *Gaikō jihō*, no. 761 (August 15, 1936): 100–20.

Jacobsen, Hans Adolf. *Karl Haushofer: Leben und Werk. Band 1. Lebensweg 1869–1946 und ansgewählte Texte zur Geopolitik*. Boppard am Rhein: Harald Boldt, 1979.

Ken, Oleg H. *Mobilizatsionnoe planirovanie i politicheskie resheniia (konets 1920-kh–seredina 1930-kh gg.)*. Moscow: OGI, 2008.

---

manchmal waren es nur Tausende, und manchmal waren es Hunderttausende und manchmal 'Millionen'; aber wir haben doch die richtige Methode."

[31] Katsuji Fuse, "Tai So ninshiki zesei no ki" (Time to Correct Our Views of the Soviet Union), *Gaikō jihō*, no. 776 (April 1, 1937): 119.

[32] See the Japanese military attaché's lecture (transcribed and reported to Stalin himself by an unknown Soviet agent in Tokyo): *Lubianka. Stalin i Glavnoe upravlenie gosbezopasnosti NKVD 1937–1938* (Moscow: MFD, 2004), 440–51.

Kuromiya, Hiroaki. "Ukraine and Eurasian History in the Twentieth Century." *Harvard Ukrainian Studies* 34, no. 1–4 (2015–16): 195–213.

Kuromiya, Hiroaki and Andrzej, Pepłoński. *Między Warszawą a Tokio: Polsko-japońska współpraca wywiadowcza 1904–1944*. Toruń: Adam Marszałek, 2009.

Kusaba, Tatsumi, "Shasō yori rokoku o mite" (Russia Seen from Train Windows). Ms., Bōeishō bōeikenkyūjo toshokan (Tokyo), n.d.

Kuśnierz, Robert. *Ukraina w latach kolektywizacji i Wielkiego Głodu (1929–1933)*. Toruń: Grado, 2005.

Lubianka. Stalin i Glavnoe upravlenie gosbezopasnosti NKVD 1937–1938. Moscow: MFD, 2004.

Miedziński, Bogusław. "Droga do Moskwy." *Kultura* (Paris), no. 188 (1963): 74–86.

Mongolyn tukhaĭ BKhK(b)N-yn barimt bichigt, 1920–1952: barimtyn emkhtgel. Vol. 1. Ulaanbaatar: Undesnii Arkhivyn Gazar, 2002.

Pol'shcha ta Ukraïna u trydtsiatykh-sorokovykh rokakh XX stolittia. T. 7. Holodomor v Ukraïni 1932–1933. Warsaw: Instytut Pamięci Narodowej–Komisja Ścigania Zbrodni przeciwko Narodowi Polskiemu; Kyiv: Haluzevyi derzhavnyi arkhiv Sluzhby bezpeky Ukrainy, 2008.

Rikugunshō gunji chōsabu, ed. *Kindai kokubō yori mitaru Sorenpō* (The Soviet Union as Seen from the Point of View of National Defense). Tokyo: n.p.

Tragediia sovetskoi derevni: kollektivizatsiia i raskulachivanie. Vol. 3. Moscow: ROSSPEN, 2001.

Włodarkiewicz, Wojciech. *Przed 17 września 1939 roku: Radzieckie zagrożenie Rzeczypospolitej w ocenach polskich naczelnych władz wojskowych 1921–1939.* Warsaw: Wydawnictwo Neriton, 2002.

Yoshimura Chūzō, *Nichiro no genzai oyobi shōrai* (The Present and Future of Japan-Russia). Tokyo: Nihon Kōronsha, 1934.

Zoku gendaishi shiryō. Kaigun, Katō Kanji nikki (Modern History Sources 2. Vol. 5: The Navy. The Diary of Katō Kanji). Tokyo: Misuzu, 1994.

Perspectives on the Mennonite Experience during the Holodomor (1932–33): Resources in North American Archives and Libraries[1]

Colin P. Neufeldt

The Holodomor looms large in the current historical consciousness of Ukrainians. It has been the focus of numerous academic and non-academic articles and books, many of which have debated whether or not the Holodomor constitutes a genocide (see Bezo et al.; Stark; Klid; Moore; Himka; Dietsch; Comerford et al.; Kulchytskyi, "The Holodomor of 1932–33"; Kasianov; Kuryliw; Shapoval). Academics who focus on Soviet Mennonite history, however, have generated comparatively few academic publications analyzing the Mennonite experience during the 1932–33 famine in Ukraine (see Beznosov; Neufeldt, "The Public," 48–63; Neufeldt, "The Fate," 237–58). One of the reasons for this is that there are few historians who focus on the Mennonite community in Ukraine in the 1930s, and within this small cohort only a handful have worked in Ukrainian archives. Moreover, not all of these historians have a reading knowledge of the Russian, Ukrainian, and German languages, which presents a challenge when researching primary source documents.

More scholarly research of documents in Ukrainian archives is therefore required to develop a robust body of publications on the Soviet Mennonite experience during the Holodomor. At the same time, however, these future studies must also incorporate source material available in

[1] The author thanks the following individuals for their comments and suggestions in preparing this article: Lynette Toews-Neufeldt, Conrad Stoesz (Mennonite Heritage Archives), Aileen Friesen (University of Winnipeg), Jon Isaak (Centre for Mennonite Brethren Studies), Laureen Harder-Gissing (Mennonite Archives of Ontario / Milton Good Library, Conrad Grebel University College), Chantel Fehr (MCC Canada), Richard Thiessen (Mennonite Historical Society of British Columbia), Ted Regehr (Mennonite Historical Society of Alberta), Victor Wiebe (Mennonite Historical Society of Saskatchewan), Frank Peachey (Mennonite Central Committee), John Thiesen (Mennonite Library and Archives, Bethel College, North Newton, Kansas), Kevin Enns-Rempel (Hiebert Library, Fresno Pacific University), Olivia Neufeldt, Alexandra Neufeldt, Andrew Sorokowski and Myroslav Shkandrij. The author also appreciates the comments of the participants at the "Documenting the Famine of 1932–33 in Ukraine: Archival Collections on the Holodomor outside the Former Soviet Union" conference (sponsored by the Holodomor Research and Education Consortium, Canadian Institute of Ukrainian Studies) at the University of Alberta on 1–2 November 2019, when a first draft of this paper was presented.

European and North American archives.[2] This paper will explore important resources that focus on the Soviet Mennonite Holodomor experience currently available in archives in North America. Although these North American resources are limited, they do provide important perspectives on the Holodomor that are not available in Ukrainian archives.

In this analysis, reference will be made to specific North American archives. These archives include the following: Mennonite Historical Society of Canada Archives[3] (hereafter "MHSC"), online; Mennonite Brethren Historical Commission[4] (hereafter "MBHC"), online; Mennonite Heritage Archives[5] (hereafter "MHA") in Winnipeg, Manitoba; Centre for Mennonite Brethren Studies[6] (hereafter "CMBS") in Winnipeg, Manitoba; Mennonite Central Committee Canada Archives[7] (MCC Can) in Winnipeg, Manitoba; Mennonite Archives of Ontario / Milton Good Library[8] (hereafter "MAO") at Conrad Grebel University College in Waterloo, Ontario; Archives of the Mennonite Historical Society of British Columbia[9] (hereafter "MHSBC") in Abbotsford, British Columbia; Archives of the Mennonite Historical Society of Alberta[10] (hereafter "MHSA") in Calgary, Alberta; Archives of the Mennonite Historical Society of Saskatchewan[11] (hereafter "MHSS") in Saskatoon, Saskatchewan; Mennonite Archival Commons[12] (hereafter "MAC"); Mennonite Central Committee[13] (hereafter "MCC US") in Akron, Pennsylvania; Bethel College Mennonite Library and Archives[14] (hereafter "BCMLA") at Bethel College in North Newton, Kansas; Mennonite Historical Library / Goshen College Archives[15] (hereafter "MHL") in Goshen, Indiana;

---

[2] European archival resources include the Mennonitische Forschungsstelle in Bolanden-Weierhof, Germany; and Bibliothek der Mennonitengemeinde zu Hamburg und Altona, Hamburg, Germany. See https://www.mennoniten.de/werke/forschungsstelle/ ; https://www.mennonitischer-geschichtsverein.de/ ; https://mennoniten-hamburg.de/bibliothek/

[3] See http://www.mhsc.ca/

[4] See https://mbhistory.org/

[5] See https://www.mharchives.ca/ and https://www.thectms.org/wp/

[6] See http://cmbs.mennonitebrethren.ca/

[7] MCC Canada does not have any archival materials on Soviet collectivization or the Holodomor.

[8] See grebel.ca/mao, and grebel.ca/library

[9] See http://mhsbc.com/holdings.html

[10] See https://mennonitehistory.org/ and https://mennonitehistory.org/archives/

[11] See https://mhss.sk.ca/index.shtml

[12] See: http://mac.libraryhost.com/ and http://mac.libraryhost.com/?p=collections/collections&unsetrepositoryid

[13] See https://mcc.org/

[14] See https://mlabethelks.org/ http://mac.libraryhost.com/?p=collections/collections&setrepositoryid=1 and https://www.bethelks.edu/community/mennonite-library-and-archives

[15] See https://www.goshen.edu/mhl/

Hiebert Library and Archives[16] (hereafter "HLA") at Fresno Pacific University in Fresno, California; the Center for Mennonite Brethren Studies[17] (hereafter "CMBS Hi") at Tabor College, Hillsboro, Kansas; and Library and Archives Canada[18] (hereafter "LA") in Ottawa, Ontario.

I. Historical context

Mennonites have had a long historical connection with Russia, Ukraine, and the Soviet Union. Invited by Catherine the Great to establish colonies in "Novorossiya" (New Russia), Mennonites were granted special privileges to develop their own political, educational, and religious institutions in their own communities. The first colony was Khortytsia (Chortitza), with nineteen villages near Zaporizhzhia along the Dnipro River. The second was Molotschna, with sixty villages along the Molochna River northeast of Melitopol. By 1914, there were thirty-three Mennonite colonies in Ukraine with more than 180 villages. Of the approximately 120,000 Mennonites living in the former Russian Empire prior to World War I, around 75,000 lived in Ukraine. As a result of World War I, the Russian Civil War (1918–22), and Mennonite emigration efforts in the early 1920s, there were just over 56,800 Mennonites residing in Soviet Ukraine in 1925 (see Krahn; Marochko, 78).

The Mennonite community in Ukraine was a German-speaking, ethno-religious sect that did not fit easily into the Bolsheviks' class ideology. There were some Mennonites—*bedniaki* in Russian or *bidniaky* in Ukrainian [poor peasants], *batraki* in Russian or *batraky* in Ukrainian [landless agricultural laborers], and some *serednіaki* in Russian or *seredniaky* in Ukrainian [middle peasants], for example—who actively supported the Bolsheviks and participated in the organization and operation of Soviet institutions (village and district soviets, for example) as well as Communist Party and Komsomol cells in their communities. At the same time, however, the pre-Revolutionary wealth of the Mennonites, their support for the German Army during World War I and the White Army during the Russian Civil War, and their organization of *Selbstschutz* (self-defense corps) units to defend their communities against anarchists and the Red Army during the Civil War convinced many Soviet authorities that a large segment of the Mennonite population included kulaks or *kurkuli* in Ukrainian (that is, more industrious peasants, who were sometimes in Russian called *ekspertniki*

[16] See http://fresno.libguides.com/locations, http://fresno.libguides.com/mla and http://fresno.libguides.com/c.php?g=210496&p=6838908

[17] See https://tabor.edu/about/center-mennonite-brethren-studies/

[18] See https://www.bac-lac.gc.ca/eng/services/theses/Pages/theses-canada.aspx; http://www.bac-lac.gc.ca/eng/search/Pages/library-search.aspx

[experts] in Ukraine), or *byvshie* (former people, such as former members of the landowning classes, factory owners, industrialists, and White army participants and supporters), sectarians, religious fanatics, and enemies of the regime. At the village level, Soviet authorities exhibited their anti-German antipathy by implementing discriminatory measures—such as higher tax-in-kind assessments and labor-service requirements—and inciting physical attacks against Mennonite communities. As a result of this antipathy and the miserable living conditions, approximately 20,000 Soviet Mennonites emigrated to North America in the 1920s (Toews, et al.; Martin, 15–19; Neufeldt, "The Public," 3–6).

The Bolshevik leadership also had trouble slotting Mennonites into one of its categories of acceptable national minorities. The Soviet government initially categorized Mennonites as Dutch but eventually treated them as Germans and accorded them the benefits of having a German national identity. As such, Mennonites had the right to use and teach the German language in their settlements. The Bolsheviks also permitted Mennonites to establish their own German national raiony (districts) in Ukraine in the 1920s. One was the Molochansk German national raion established in 1924, which included 136 settlements (59 Mennonite villages from the former Molotschna colony) and encompassed 174,910 hectares (142,300 cultivated hectares). By 1933 its population was 47,300 inhabitants, of which 30,100 were Mennonites and Germans, and 10,400 were Ukrainians; the Molochansk raion also had more than thirty communities populated by German-speaking Lutherans, Catholics, Baptists, and Adventists. The second German national raion was Khortytsia, which was formally recognized in 1929, encompassed 38 villages (including 18 Mennonite settlements), and had 44,700 hectares of land and a population of 19,750 people (12,365 Mennonites and Germans, 6,569 Ukrainians, 530 Russians, and 286 Jews) (see Neufeldt, "Collectivizing," 237–38).

Notwithstanding the benefits that came with having their own national raiony, Mennonite communities both inside and outside the Khortytsia and Molochansk raiony were also the targets of anti-German hostility. During the early years of Soviet dekulakization and collectivization (1928–29), an increasing number of Mennonites experienced dispossession, incarceration, and exile. To escape this tyranny, more than 9,000 Mennonites (as well as 2,481 Lutherans, 743 Catholics, and 95 Baptists and Evangelicals) fled to Moscow in a last-ditch effort to leave the country in the second half of 1929. Approximately 3,880 Mennonites were eventually able to emigrate, but 5,200 were either exiled or transported back to their home villages, where many were subsequently dekulakized and exiled. The emigration actions of these Mennonites raised questions about their loyalty; many were branded as kulaks, class aliens, foreigners, counter-revolutionaries, and saboteurs (see Peters; Dyck, 158–59; Neufeldt, "The Flight").

As the terror resulting from the government's dekulakization and collectivization campaigns intensified in the early 1930s, an increasing number of Mennonites sought positions in local government institutions and the Communist Party. In these roles, they served as the government's foot soldiers in identifying, disenfranchising, dispossessing, and incarcerating Mennonite and non-Mennonite kulaks and other enemies of the state in their communities. To demonstrate their loyalty to their superiors, Soviet Mennonite officials often dekulakized their co-religionists first, and frequently in higher percentages than their non-Mennonite neighbours. Mennonites who worked for the state also facilitated the collectivization of their communities, and ensured that Mennonite landholdings, livestock, agricultural equipment, and possessions were transferred to newly established collective farms (*kolkhoz* in Russian, *kolhosp* in Ukrainian), whether they were populated by Mennonite or non-Mennonite populations (see Neufeldt, "Separating"; Neufeldt, "The '*Zborni*'"; Neufeldt, "Reforging").

By spring 1930, every Mennonite community in Ukraine was collectivized. In the Khortytsia raion, for instance, every village had at least one collective farm, and some communities had two or three; all told, there were at least thirty-four kolkhozy, three communes, nineteen artels, and twelve associations for the joint cultivation of land (SOZy). Of the 3,822 households in the raion, 2,482 (64.9 per cent) were in kolkhozy: 239 households were in the commune, 1,445 in artels, and 798 in SOZy. There were also at least thirty-four Machine-Horse Stations (MHS) supplying agricultural machinery and horses to kolkhozy. The collectivization of Molochansk bore similarities to what had occurred in Khortytsia. In late 1930, Molochansk officials proudly reported that the raion had 127 kolkhozy, of which ninety-six were artels and thirty-one were SOZy; there was also a commune, fourteen dairy *fermy* (farm units), seventeen swine *fermy*, and several cattle associations. Eventually the raion established a sovkhoz, two *plemkhozy* (animal breeding sovkhozy), and two Machine Tractor Stations (MTS) (see Neufeldt, "Collectivizing," 218).

At the onset of the 1932–33 famine, many Mennonite-populated kolkhozy experienced poor agricultural production results, declining livestock herds, and increasingly desperate living conditions. Mennonites shared many of the same challenges and tribulations as their Ukrainian, Russian, and Jewish neighbors during the Holodomor, but what aggravated the Mennonite experience at this time was the increasing anti-German and anti-sectarian hostility that pervaded their communities, as well as other ethnic German villages (see Neufeldt, "The Public," 7–8, 11–12, 61–63). The discussion below will highlight what North American archival resources document the Mennonite experience during the 1932–33 famine in Ukraine.

II. Sources of Mennonite perspectives on the 1932–33 famine

The following table is a summary of the resources on Mennonite perspectives of the 1932–33 famine that are available in North American archives and libraries, and which are discussed in greater detail below the table.

Table 1. Archive / Library or Database

Type of Resource	MHSC	MBHC	MHA	CMBS	MCC Can	MAO	MHSBC	MHSA	MHSS	MAC		MCC US	BCMLA	MHL	HLA	CMBS Hi	GAMEO	MAID	GRanDMA	LA
1. DAZO (see description below)			•				•								•					
2. Letters																				
a) Der Bote			•			•	•													
b) Mennonitische Rundschau				•		•	•													
c) Zionsbote			•	•		•	•													
d) Other letter collections			•	•									•							
3. Personal papers and diaries																				
a) Mennonite leaders				•									•	•						
b) Mennonites			•			•	•	•	•	•			•		•	•				
4. Oral Interviews						•	•													

5. Mennonite Relief Efforts			•	•								•	•							
6. Nazi Records				•																
7. Photographs	•		•															•		
8. NKVD and KGB files			•																	
9. Encyclopedia Articles	•																•			
10 Genealogical and other databases													•						•	
11. Dissertations																				•

DAZO — Derzhavnyi Arkhiv Zaporizhs'koi Oblasti (State Archive of Zapori-zhia oblast) in Zaporizhia, Ukraine
MHSC — Mennonite Historical Society of Canada Archives
MBHC — Mennonite Brethren Historical Commission
MHA — Mennonite Heritage Archives
CMBS — Centre for Mennonite Brethren Studies
MCC Can — Mennonite Central Committee Canada Archives
MAO — Mennonite Archives of Ontario / Milton Good Library
MHSBC — Archives of the Mennonite Historical Society of British Columbia
MHSA — Archives of the Mennonite Historical Society of Alberta
MHSS — Archives of the Mennonite Historical Society of Saskatchewan
MAC — Mennonite Archival Commons
MCC US — Mennonite Central Committee United States Archives
BCMLA — Bethel College Mennonite Library and Archives
MHL — Mennonite Historical Library / Goshen College Archives
HLA — Hiebert Library and Archives
CMBS Hi — Center for Mennonite Brethren Studies (Hillsboro)
GAMEO — Global Anabaptist Mennonite Encyclopedia Online — see description below

MAID — Mennonite Archival Image Database (MAID) — see description below
GRanDMA — Genealogical Registry and Database of Mennonite Ancestry — see description below
LA — Library and Archives Canada

A) *The DAZO collection*
There are many perspectives on the Mennonite Holodomor experience, and in North America one of the best collections of sources documenting this experience is the archival collection from the State Archive of Zaporizhzhia oblast in Zaporizhzhia, Ukraine.[19] This collection—hereafter the "DAZO collection"—is available in the MHA, MHSBC, and HLA and includes more than 125,000 microfilmed documents (on 125 reels) written in Russian, Ukrainian, and German. A significant percentage of the documents deals with the Soviet Mennonite experience in villages in the Khortytsia national German raion, and in a small number of villages in the Molochansk German national raion.[20]

What is invaluable about the DAZO collection is that it includes a selection of key government, Communist Party, and kolkhoz records that document the political, social, economic, agricultural, cultural, and religious life of Mennonites during the Holodomor. These records include the names and roles of some of the key Khortytsia and Molochansk Mennonites who participated in the management of their raiony and villages during the famine. Many of these Mennonites worked in the following organizations: raion soviets (RS) and village soviets (*rady* in Ukrainian); Communist Party organizations (raion-level party organizations [RC], as well as party cells in the villages, MTS, kolkhozy, and factories); village *potrebsouizy* (consumer associations); *kombedy* (Committees of the Village Poor or CVP); *Raboche-krest'ianskaia inspektsiia* (Workers' and Peasants' Inspection Committees or *Rabkrin*); Komsomol cells; MTS and MHS; the People's Court; the *Raizemotdel* (Raion Land Division Committee); the *Raikoopzerno* (Raion Grain Association); the *Raiposevtroika* (Raion Seeding *Troika*); the

[19] See https://portal.ehri-project.eu/countries/ua. During the Soviet period this archive was known as the Gosudarstvennyy Arkhiv Zaporozhskoy Oblasti, and consequently this archival collection is sometimes identified by this Russian name. Other names used to identify this archival collection include "State Archive of the Zaporozhe Region," "Zaporozhe Archives (A.S. Tedeev) Collection," and "Zaporoshje Regional Archives."
[20] Harvey L. Dyck (University of Toronto) and Alexandr S. Tadeev (State Archive Zaporizhzhia, Ukraine) compiled this archival collection in the 1990s. In 2001 the Centre for Russian and East European Studies (University of Toronto) produced a collection guide titled "Mennonites in Southern Ukraine, 1789–1941: A Guide to Holdings and Microfilmed Documents from the State Archive of the Zaporozhe Region."

Raisel'bank (Raion Rural Bank); the *Raitorgotdel* (Raion Market Commission); the *Raikolkhozzernosoiuz* (Raion Kolkhoz Grain Union); the *Raimetodburo (*Raion Curriculum Office), local Young Pioneer organizations, *Rote Ecke* (Red Corner cultural centre),. *Bauernheime* (peasant clubs), *Lesenhallen* (reading rooms) and *Kollektivistheime* (collective farm clubs).[21] The DAZO collection also includes information about how these Mennonite administrators responded to the developing famine conditions in their communities. Some of these administrators included Mennonite women, and the records in the DAZO collection illustrate the unique challenges they faced in balancing the demands of their political superiors vis-à-vis the interests of their communities and families.[22]

There were a host of reasons why Mennonites sought employment with the Soviet state at this time, and the records in the DAZO collection illuminate some of them. A small number did so because of their idealism or their desire to serve their communities, while other Mennonites sought a government position because it provided a steady income, regular food rations, job security, and the benefits that came with social mobility, including promotion within the government and Communist hierarchy, better housing, and/or educational opportunities. During the famine years, some Mennonites also sought state employment to avoid dekulakization—a punishment that applied not only to kulaks but to anyone accused of being a fascist, Hitlerist, foreigner, advocating emigration to the West, accepting aid from the West, stealing from a kolkhoz or the state, participating in sabotage, or falling out of favor with local officials.[23] But holding on to a government or Party post was not easy, and as the famine continued even those Mennonite officials who had exemplary government or party records lost their positions, often because of had to do with their ethnic German identity (Neufeldt, "Collectivizing," 222–29; Neufeldt, "Separating," 232–34).

The DAZO collection also documents the frenetic, unplanned, and oppressive government measures that local officials implemented to enforce nefarious economic, agricultural, and social policies and directives emanating from Moscow and Kharkiv. The DAZO collection provides forensic evidence of the rationale for and implementation of a host of campaigns and regulations that proved both disastrous and deleterious. These included the state's agricultural produce procurement campaigns,[24]

---

[21] DAZO: fond R-235, opis 4, sviazka 36 (hereafter DAZO: R-235/4/36); DAZO: R-235/4/53, 56, 62, 211; R-235/1/730, 757, 781, 808, 811, 813, 815, 823; R-235/2/61, 133, 138; R-3452/1/18, 20-1; R-286/1/107-9, 111, 114, 115-16, 118, 120, 123, 170, 190, 192, 207, 216, 232, 242, 254, 227, 228-29, 394, 397-98, 406, 416; PR-7/1/132.

[22] DAZO: R-286/1/114, 123, 170, 216, 232, 242, 398, 406; R-3452/1/18, 24.

[23] DAZO: R-3452/1/2-3; 235/3/23; 286/1/114, 166, 170, 216, 232, 242, 398, 406.

[24] DAZO: R-286/1/115, 122-23, 142, 166, 229, 256; R-3452/1/9, 18, 20-21.

mobilization-of-the-means campaigns,[25] the fight-for-seed campaigns,[26] onerous taxes and financial obligations,[27] anti-religious campaigns,[28] and restrictive laws and passport regulations that made life unnecessarily harsh for Mennonites during the famine (see Danilov et al., 3:453, 525, 541, 575, 562, 634; Berman, 29; Davies et al., 165; Kulchyts'kyi, *Holodomor,* 62; Shearer, 193, 243, 278–84; Kessler, 477; Beattie, 254–55). A key government official in implementing and enforcing these measures was I. K. Penner, a Mennonite Communist Party member who served as chairman of the Molochansk RS between January and October 1932. His actions and directives helped to facilitate famine conditions in a number of Molochansk communities and ensured that large numbers of Mennonites and non-Mennonites in his jurisdiction were expelled from their government positions and kolkhozy and subsequently dekulakized, arrested, or exiled.[29] Penner was eventually removed from his position and replaced by the non-Mennonite Wilkel, but by 1934 the chairmanship of the Molochansk RS was again in Mennonite hands when the Mennonite Communist Party member Wiebe held the post.[30]

Penner and Wiebe were not the only senior Mennonite officials whose management decisions exacerbated the famine in Mennonite communities. In the Molochansk RS and RC, some of the other key Mennonite leaders included Vasilii V. Martens (Molochansk MTS chairman), Hamm, Schmidt, Tiessen, Warkentin, Bergen, and Schmid.[31] The DAZO records outline many of

25 DAZO: R-3452/1/18, 21, 24; R-286/1/115, 120, 123, 166, 170.

26 DAZO: R-3452/1/24.

27 DAZO: R-3452/1/9, 18, 20-21, 24; R-286/1/115, 166, 229, 392.

28 DAZO: R-286/1/116, 192.

29 DAZO: 3452/1/18, 20-21; R-286/1/118, 229.

30 DAZO: R-3452/1/20-21; R-286/1/107, 114-16, 120, 130, 166, 170, 216, 229, 237, 394; R-235/1/808; R-235/3/48; R-3452/1/3, 13-14, 20.

31 Some of the Mennonte party organizers in kolkhozy belonging to the Molochansk MTS in 1933–34 included: Goerzen (party member since 1931; served as representative in Muntau area); Hiebner (party member since 1927; worked in the Executive Committee of Molochansk RS); J. P. Schmidt (party candidate member since 1932); Schulz (party candidate member since 1931; GPU party cell member); V. A. Schulz (party member since 1928; member of Militsia party cell; employee in People's Court [*Narsud*]); Plett (member of the Fabrikerweise party candidate group; chairman of Liebenau village soviet); T. T. Foth (party candidate member since 1932; member of Waldheim territorial party cell; chairman of Gnadenfeld village soviet); D. K. Unruh (party candidate member since 1932; member of Ohrloff kolkhoz candidate group; chairman of Ohrloff kolkhoz); A. P. Goerzen (party member since 1931; member of Muntau party candidate group); Lorenz (party candidate member since 1931; member of Heidelberg party candidate group; chairman of Heidelberg village soviet); E. A. Klassen (party member since 1930; member and secretary of Molochansk Soviet Party school party cell); F. F. Funk (party candidate member since 1932; a member of Molochansk Soviet Party school); Schmidt (party candidate member since 1932; member of Molochansk Soviet Party school); J.P. Pankratz (party candidate member since 1932; member of Molochansk Soviet Party school);

their administrative decisions, reports, directives, and activities, including their participation in raion Communist Party *troikas* (three-person extrajudicial tribunals) that conducted surprise inspections of local kolkhozy, reported the names of administrators and members who lagged behind in procurement deliveries, and punished those who permitted the unauthorized release of grain and produce to *kolkhozniki*.[32] Mennonites employed in the Control Commission of the Molochansk raion branch of *Rabkrin* also played pivotal roles in the administration of government policies in the Molochansk raion. This commission, which included the Mennonites Penner, Hamm, Martens, Schmidt, Tiessen, Warkentin, Bergen and Schmid, issued the lion's share of the government directives dealing with the grain, meat, and agricultural procurement process; seeding, weeding, threshing, and grain schedules; state taxes and obligations; and identification and punishment of those accused of stealing kolkhoz property or maliciously sabotaging the implementation of the grain procurement plans.[33]

Records specifying the roles and responsibilities of Mennonites working in and leading MTS and MHS operations in Molochansk and Khortytsia can also be found in the DAZO collection.[34] Controlled by the RC, each MTS operation dictated not only dictated the cultivation and harvest schedules of every kolkhoz in their respective jurisdictions but also the activities of subordinate party organizations in the kolkhozy, factories, party schools, and Komsomol organizations.[35] This infiltration network

---

P.A. Suderman (party candidate member since 1932; member of Molochansk Soviet Party school); Possen (Gossen?; party member since 1932; member of Molochansk MTS party cell; chairman of Lichtenau kolkhoz); Hildebrandt (party member since 1931; member of Waldheim MTS party cell); N. N. Fast (party candidate member since 1931; member of Waldheim MTS party cell); P. K. Koehn (party candidate member since 1930; member of Waldheim MTS party cell); J. J. Regier (party candidate member since 1932; member of Waldheim MTS party cell; chairman of Gnadental artel); A. K. Schmidt (party member since 1925; member of Sovetskaya party cell); N. N. Boldt (party member since 1918; member of Hierschau candidate group; chairman of Hierschau kolkhoz). DAZO: R-286/1/406.

[32] DAZO: R-3452/1/20-21, 24; R-286/1/115, 120, 166, 251.

[33] DAZO: R-3452/1/20; R-286/1/115.

[34] DAZO: R-286/1/115, 119, 130, 148, 167, 170, 248, 399, 406, 416; DAZO: R-226/1/8.

[35] Party cells under the supervision of the Molochansk MTS political department in 1933 included: Hochstadt party group; Efimovka party group; Gigant commune party group, Heidelberg party group, Blumental candidate group, Batrak candidate group, Prischib candidate group, Muntau candidate group, Ohrloff candidate group, Tiefenbrunn party Komsomol group, Friedrichsfeld party Komsomol group, Benovoe party Komsomol group, Trudolubimovka party Komsomol group, Leitershaugen party Komsomol group, Neu-Nassau party Komsomol group, Petershagen party Komsomol group, Reichenfeld party Komsomol group, Tiege party Komsomol group, Kronsfeld party Komsomol group, Nikolaifeld party Komsomol group, Pokaznoe party Komsomol group, Zelenai party Komsomol group, Grüntal party organization, Neubeorn party organization, Fischau party organization, Lichtenau party

ensured that the MTS leadership received regular reports on the success and failure of these organizations in meeting the government's increasingly outlandish expectations during the famine.[36]

The RS, RC, *Rabkrin,* and village soviets also recruited MTS and Komsomol members—including many Mennonites—to serve as activists in local kolkhozy. During the Holodomor, the activists performed a host of functions, including the following: spying on, intimidating, and publicly belittling underperforming kolkhoz administrators and *kolkhozniki*; implementing government policies on the kolkhozy; participating in grain raids with in the kolkhozy; identifying *kolkhoznik*s who hid grain and other agricultural produce or who committed acts of sabotage; ensuring that Hitlerists, kulaks, class aliens, foreigners, and saboteurs were expelled from the kolkhozy and subjected to criminal sanctions; organizing socialist competitions within the kolkhoz to improve production; implementing measures to broaden the political consciousness of *kolkhozniki*; and vetting applications for membership in the kolkhozy.[37]

Scholars will also find a wide array of documents in the DAZO collection concerning Mennonite life in the kolkhoz during the famine. These documents include the minutes of meetings and committees of the administration, membership, work teams, and women's organizations of Mennonite-populated kolkhozy.[38] These documents tell us something about how Mennonites carried out their duties as kolkhoz chairmen, secretaries, economists, and foremen,[39] and their responsibilities on the kolkhozy audit commission, committees, and working groups. What soon becomes evident from the records is that even the most dutiful and hard-working Mennonite administrators and *kolkhozniki* found it impossible to meet government and party expectations, and were ruthlessly and publicly denounced when they fell short. In many cases, the administrators were "unelected" from their

---

organization, Grozni Pacaar party organization. Petrovksy party organization and N-Lubimovka party organization. DAZO: R-286/1/416.

[36] Mennonite secretaries of Komsomol cells in the Molochansk MTS in 1934 included Bauman at Tiegenhagen; Dyck at Tiege; Unruh at Blumenort; Lorenz at Heidelberg; Winter at Friedrischsfeld; Fröse at Alt-Schöntal; and Franzen at Rosenort. DAZO: R-286/1/192. Mennonite secretaries of Komsomol cells in the Waldheim MTS in 1934 included: Lenzman at Gnadenheim; Dyck at Landskrone; Lohrenz at Grossweide; Plett at Liebenau; Hein at Sparrau; Janzen at Hamburg; and Bartel at Tractor Brigade No. 16. DAZO: R-286/1/192.

[37] DAZO: R-3452/1/9, 20, 24; R-286/1/115, 166, 256.

[38] In the DAZO collection, the most complete records on day-to-day kolkhoz life dealt with following village collective farms: Ohrloff, Tiege, Rosenort, Blumenort, and Kultura. Ohrloff, Tiege, Rosenort and Blumenort were largely populated by Mennonites, while Kultura was populated by Ukrainians. DAZO 286/1/192.

[39] DAZO: R-286/1/251, 416; R-3452/1/9, 18.

positions after a short period of service, and they and their families were summarily expelled.[40]

The day-to-day operations of Mennonite-populated kolkhozy during the famine are also documented in the DAZO collection. The archival records describe, often in minute detail, the seeding and harvest timetables that dominated the kolkhoz calendar and work plans, the repair schedule of agricultural machinery, the scheduled weeding, and the herculean efforts that each kolkhoz undertook to meet the demands of local authorities.[41] They also provide invaluable eyewitness information on a host of kolkhoz activities and events including: the precipitous decline of livestock herds and poultry flocks in 1932–33;[42] the organization and management of work teams;[43] the recruitment of children into seeding and weeding "brigades";[44] the organization of guards and spy networks to prevent theft and sabotage;[45] the relentless "socialist competitions" between kolkhozy to outperform each other;[46] the inequitable systems used to determine how *kolkhozniki* were compensated for their labor;[47] the roles of the kolkhoz *Rote Ecke,*[48] *Kollektivisheim,*[49] and *Red Kollegium*[50] in providing political and cultural literacy to the *kolkhozniki*; the celebration of national holidays (for example, "Day of Harvest and Collectivization" and "Day of the Proletarian Revolution"); and the continuous purported infiltration of kulaks, Hitlerists, and foreigners into kolkhozy and the processes used to expel them.

The relentless struggle for life and death that Mennonite *kolkhozniki* experienced during the famine is also recorded in the DAZO collection. The records provide insights into how Mennonite kolkhoz families did their best to cope with declining food rations, and the resulting illness and premature deaths that followed. There are also records on how Mennonite women participated in kolkhoz life, how they were mistreated by administrators and foremen, what they did to feed their families or secure better accommodations, and how some Mennonite women provided housekeeping and sexual services to Mennonite and non-Mennonite kolkhoz administrators in exchange for more food or special favors. One can also

---

40 DAZO: R-286/1/251.
41 DAZO: R-3452/1/18, 20; R-286/1/118, 166, 170, 416.
42 DAZO: R-3452/1/20.
43 DAZO: R-3452/1/21; R-286/1/251.
44 DAZO: R-286/1/123, 251; R-3452/1/18.
45 DAZO: R-3452/1/9, 18, 20, 24.
46 DAZO: R-3452/1/24.
47 DAZO: R-3452/1/9, 18.
48 DAZO: R-286/1/251, 142.
49 DAZO: R-286/1/251, 232, 142; R-3452/1/21.
50 DAZO: R-286/1/142, 170; R-226/1/29.

locate records detailing the experience of Mennonite kolkhoz children in kolkhoz nurseries, kindergartens, and schools. A small number of records document the experiences of elderly, handicapped, and ill Mennonites on the *kolkhoz*, but because they were marginal members, records detailing their lives during the famine are limited.[51]

Punishments meted out to Mennonite-populated kolkhozy and individual Mennonite *kolkhozniki* who did not meet government expectations are also documented in DAZO. By late 1932, *kolkhozniki* were required to surrender a portion of their meager annual food rations to help the kolkhoz meet its obligations,[52] and when these efforts proved insufficient, every kolkhoz was required to rej-thresh straw, scour harvested fields for any grain left behind, and conduct additional grain searches for the state.[53] Any kolkhoz accused of hiding grain or refusing to comply with the government's procurement policy was harshly penalized; in some cases, the penalty was fifteen times higher than the original quota. And when a kolkhoz failed to pay a penalty, the chairman ordered his *kolkhozniki* to make up the shortfall. If the *kolkhozniki* failed to meet expectations, then the kolkhoz chairman was personally liable for all deficiencies and could be prosecuted in the People's Court as a saboteur and enemy of the state. All under-performing kolkhozy were added to the *Schwarz Tafel* (Black Table), a published list of the worst-performing kolkhozy in the region. Special penalties for a blacklisted collective included the closure of its goods store, the prohibition of its *kolkhozniki* purchasing goods at other stores, and the withdrawal of the kolkhoz's access to state credit or loans.[54]

Underperforming Mennonite *kolkhozniki* were harshly punished, often for the most innocuous offenses. These punishments included an inordinate deduction in the number of earned workdays and food rations, additional work assignments, or expulsion.[55] Expulsion did not always mean a permanent ban from re-entry into a *kolkhoz*. Some expelled Mennonite *kolkhozniki* were permitted to reapply for admission so long as they disclosed why they had been previously expelled and the past offenses were not serious. The applicants also had to provide written references substantiating their good character, in addition to acknowledging their contrition for their past offenses and promising to behave in an exemplary

[51] DAZO: R-3452/1/18, 20, 24; R-286/1/122, 141.
[52] DAZO: R-3452/1/9, 18, 24.
[53] DAZO: R-3452/1/20-21.
[54] DAZO: R-3452/1/20-21, 24; R-286/1/251.
[55] DAZO: R-286/1/118, 130; R-3452/1/18, 24.

manner. Why did these Mennonite expellees reapply for admission? Life in the kolkhoz, albeit extremely difficult, was often better than life outside.[56]

Anti-German hostility existed in Ukraine in the 1920s and 1930s, but it increased significantly after Hitler came to power in Germany in early 1933. The DAZO collection documents this intensification of hostility in the Khortytsia and Molochansk communities and the manner in which local Soviet authorities made Mennonite and other ethnic-German populations the objects of their derision and attacks, accusing of them of being Hitlerites, fascists, Nazi agents, and enemies of the regime bent on destroying the USSR. In 1933–34, for example, Molochansk officials reported on the alarming growth in the number of fascists and Hitlerists in Mennonite-populated kolkhozy. They also warned that some of these Mennonite Hitlerists had secured important leadership positions in *kolkhozy* and local soviet organizations: more specifically, they claimed that Hitlerists and class-alien elements now constituted 40 percent or more of the population at Molochansk, at least twenty-three kulaks and Hitler agents reportedly worked as kolkhoz chairmen in the raion, and 547 of the 1,664 households located in the Waldheim MTS area were kulaks. The worst supposedly kulak-infested, Hitlerite villages included the Mennonite villages of Alexandertal, Schonau, Ohrloff, Reichenfeld, Lichtenau, Grossweide, Rückenau, Lichtfeld, Münsterberg, Gnadenfeld, and Blumstein. To address this crisis and root out what the regime claimed to be Nazi enemies, as well as kulaks and foreigners, the Molochansk RS, RC, village soviets, *Rabkrin*, Komsomol cells, schools, and women's organizations participated in regular anti-fascist campaigns. Soon Mennonite names appeared in large numbers on government lists of kulaks, Hitlerists, class aliens, foreigners, Left Deviationists and Trotskyites.[57] This frenzied anti-German hostility added an additional dimension of repression and hardship to the Mennonite experience of the 1932–33 famine—something which most Ukrainians and other non-Germans did not experience during the Holodomor.

There were a host of reasons why Khortytsia and Molochansk officials were certain that so many Mennonites were Hitler's agents, fascists or Trotskyites. A large number of Mennonites were classified as kulaks or *podkulaks* (kulak agents or hirelings, *pidkurkul* in Ukrainian) who supported the White Army during the civil war, organized *Selbstschutz* units to arm and defend themselves against the Red Army, and wanted to see the end of the USSR. A large number of Mennonite communities were also located in the German national raion, and were therefore accused of being natural allies of Hitler. Many Soviet Mennonites also had relatives who had

[56] DAZO: R-3452/1/9, 18, 24.

[57] DAZO: R-286/1/129, 144, 146, 148, 165-67, 169, 170, 214, 280; R-3452/1/9.

emigrated to the West in the 1920s and continued to maintain contact with them. During the early 1930s, these Soviet Mennonites received letters (with foreign currency) and food parcels from these relatives, as well as food parcels and financial support from German relief organizations (for example, *Brüder in Not*) and German government agencies. Molochansk government records in the DAZO collection indicate that a large number of foreign letters and parcels were addressed to Mennonite residents in Grossweide, Mariaheim, as well as in settlements supervised by the Waldheim village soviet—confirmation from the Soviet regime's perspective that these communities were deeply infected with Hitlerist and fascist groups working to agitate pro-Hitler support among their fellow *kolkhozniki*.[58] And with the foreign currency that these Soviet Mennonites received from the West, they purchased commodities at the state-operated Torgsin stores.[59] Based on these facts, local officials intensified their anti-German measures toward Mennonites, preventing them from participating in local soviet organizations and *kolkhozy*, and in some cases arranging for their arrest and exile.[60]

The Communist Party purge of its membership initiated in 1933 exacerbated the Mennonite experience of the famine. This purge was initiated to expel "class-aliens," "hostile elements," "degenerates" and "double dealers" who were perceived to have flooded the party and to ensure that the decisions of the party's Central Committee were being implemented at the local level. At the same time that the party purge was proceeding, the government created a Soviet Control Commission to undertake parallel investigations and purges of class aliens, hostile elements, kulaks, Hitlerists and other degenerates who had infiltrated non-party state and economic bodies. The DAZO collection sheds light on the rationale, processes, and outcomes of the purges in the Molochansk raion, and which reached a frenzied pace in June and July, 1934, just as the Holodomor was waning in intensity.[61] Included in DAZO are the minutes of purge commission hearings investigating Mennonite party members and candidates,[62] and confirming which Mennonites were verified (i.e., allowed to remain in the party) or summarily removed from the Molochansk party organizations, party cells in the local MTS (Molochansk/ Waldheim MTS), factories, Komsomol organizations, and party schools. What is clear from these records is that anti-German hostility was an important factor in

[58] DAZO: R-286/1/167, 170, 192, 194, 392.
[59] DAZO: R-286/1/167, 192, 251.
[60] DAZO: R-286/1/251.
[61] DAZO: R-3452/1/20.
[62] DAZO: R-286/1/170.

ensuring that large numbers of Mennonites were purged from party and government institutions.[63]

The DAZO collection provides documentation concerning the experiences of Mennonites living outside the kolkhozy during the famine—that is, Mennonites who never joined a kolkhoz because of religious or ideological reasons,[64] who were denied entry because they were considered to be kulaks, foreigners, Hitlerists, or class alien elements,[65] or had previously been expelled.[66] Non-kolkhoz Mennonites were often accused of a host of crimes against the state, including receiving Hitlerist aid or working as Hitlerist agents, acting as a corrupting influence on local *kolkhozniki*, organizing religious cults to distract *kolkhozniki*, agitating citizens to emigrate to the West, receiving foreign aid, or unlawfully purchasing commodities at the Torgsin store.[67] Unfortunately, the DAZO documents provide little information as to how these non-kolkhoz Mennonites survived the daily challenges of life during the famine.

Finally, the DAZO documents provide insights on the relationships between Mennonites and their non-Mennonite neighbors during the famine—whether those neighbors were Ukrainians, Russians, Jews, or Germans or were from Orthodox, Baptist, Lutheran, Adventist, or Catholic religious backgrounds. For example, there are detailed records of the meetings and agricultural affairs of the Kultura Collective Farm, a Ukrainian-populated kolkhoz that had regular dealings with Mennonite kolkhozy in the Ohrloff village soviet in the Molochansk raion.

B) Soviet Mennonite letters

Heart-wrenching, desperate, and despondent—some of the adjectives that describe the tone and content of the letters that Mennonites in Ukraine wrote to their relatives in the West during the 1932–33 famine. Often imbued with religious themes and occasionally with apocalyptic images, the letters were written by Mennonites who knew that their death or the death of loved ones was imminent; in many respects, these letters were their last testaments. Such letters also provide first-hand Mennonite perspectives on the brutality of kolkhoz life; the oppressive results of grain searches and declining food rations; the life-saving contents and benefits of food packages and letters (often with foreign currency) from the West; Mennonite attempts to purchase food commodities on the black market and

---

[63] DAZO: R-286/1/148, 169-70, 182, 188, 190-92, 207, 214, 216, 252, 256, 406, 416.
[64] DAZO: R-286/1/192.
[65] DAZO: R-286/1/24, 118, 120, 142, 189, 192, 214; R-3452/1/20, 24.
[66] DAZO: R-286/1/167, 189, 192, 214.
[67] DAZO: R-286/1/167, 189, 192, 197, 214.

in the state-operated Torgsin stores; the increasing reliance of Mennonites on vermin, weeds, and tree bark as food sources; the expulsion of Mennonites from the kolkhozy; and the devastating impact of illness and starvation deaths on Mennonite families.

The largest and perhaps most diverse collections of these letters were published in three North American Mennonite periodicals: *Der Bote*[68] (MHA, MAO, MHSBC), *Die Mennonitische Rundschau*[69] (CMBS, MAO, MHSBC), and *Zionsbote*[70] (CMBS, MHA, MAO, MHSBC). Collectively, these periodicals contain excerpts from more than a thousand letters written by Soviet Mennonites to their relatives in North America in the late 1920s and early 1930s. While the editors of these periodicals redacted many letters prior to their publication, the excerpts nonetheless provide very personal and intimate Mennonite reflections on their tribulations and losses during the famine.

The number of published letters decreased significantly after Hitler's rise to power in January 1933. One reason was the Soviet government's efforts to break contacts between Soviet populations and the West. How was this accomplished? According to documents in the DAZO collection, government officials employed Mennonites and non-Mennonites in local Communist cells to vet incoming and outgoing Mennonite correspondence and confiscate any correspondence to the West.[71] The Soviet regime also employed postal censors to screen and block Mennonite letters coming into and leaving the USSR.

Other important collections of Soviet Mennonite letters written during the Holodomor include *The Bargen Letter Collection* (MHA),[72] *B.H. Unruh Reports and Papers* (CMBS), and *B. H. Unruh Papers, 1920–59*[73] (BCMLA).

C) Diaries, personal papers and oral interviews

Mennonite diaries, personal documents, and oral interviews also provide important perspectives on the 1932–33 famine. Of these, the diaries and personal papers of Mennonite leaders in North America and Europe are especially interesting. These leaders organized relief and financial aid for Mennonites in Ukraine, lobbied government and non-governmental agencies in the West to provide help to those in Ukraine, and served as a lifeline between many Soviet Mennonites and their co-religionists in the

---

[68] *Der Bote* was a weekly periodical published by the Algemeine Konferenz, in Winnipeg, MB.

[69] *Die Mennonitische Rundschau* was a bi-weekly periodical first published by Mennonite Publishing Company in Elkhart, Indiana, and later by the Rundschau Publishing House (later "Christian Press") in Winnipeg, MB.

[70] *Zionsbote* was published by the Mennonite Brethren Publishing House, Hillsboro, Kansas.

[71] DAZO: R-286/1/391.

[72] See: https://www.mharchives.ca/holdings/papers/Bargen%20Letter%20collection.htm

[73] See http://mac.libraryhost.com/?p=collections/controlcard&id=100

West. Some of these leaders (for example, Benjamin H. Unruh) ingratiated themselves with Nazi leaders in order to assist their co-religionists in Ukraine (see Goossen, 123–24, 139–40, 143, 147). These Mennonite leaders also circulated Soviet Mennonite letters to their families and Mennonite publications in the West. For example, the *B. H. Unruh Reports and Papers* (CMBS) and the *B. H. Unruh Papers, 1920–59* (BCMLA) document B. H. Unruh's tireless efforts to aid Soviet Mennonites during the famine and include many excerpts from Mennonite letters sent from Ukraine. Other collections that include Soviet Mennonite letters are the *Cornelius F. Klassen Fonds*[74] (CMBS); *Benjamin B. Janz Fonds*[75] (CMBS); *Cornelius Krahn Papers*[76] (BCMLA); *Walter Quiring Papers, 1932–1950*[77] (BCMLA); and *Harold Stauffer Bender Papers, 1919–1962*[78] (MHL).

The diaries, personal papers, and oral interviews of Mennonites who lived in Ukraine during the famine, and North American and European Mennonites who corresponded with Soviet Mennonites during the Holodomor, are also invaluable. Given the nature of these personal documents, many of them provide limited perspectives on Mennonite life during the Holodomor—that is, they often focus on the experiences of Soviet Mennonites who lived in one or two villages or family communities. These collections include: *Peter J. Dyck (1879–1947) Collection*[79] (MHA); *Anganetha Wiebe (1873–1947) Fond*[80] (MHA); *Jacob J. Niebuhr (1874–1956) Collection*[81] (MHA); *Twentieth Century Russian Mennonite Memoirs of War and Immigration*[82] (MAO); *Russian Mennonite Immigrants Oral History Project*[83] (MAO); *Women Without Men Oral History Project*[84] (MAO); *Soviet Mennonite Memoirs and Family Histories*[85] (MAO); *Video recordings of Soviet*

---

[74] See http://cmbs.mennonitebrethren.ca/personal_papers/klassen-cornelius-f-1894-1954/

[75] See http://cmbs.mennonitebrethren.ca/personal_papers/janz-benjamin-b-1877-1964/

[76] See https://mla.bethelks.edu/holdings/fndng/ms/ms165.htm

[77] See http://mac.libraryhost.com/?p=collections/findingaid&id=294&q=&rootcontentid=7088#id7088

[78] See http://mac.libraryhost.com/?p=collections/controlcard&id=207

[79] See https://www.mharchives.ca/holdings/papers/Dyck,%20John%20P.%20fonds.htm

[80] See: http://www.mennonitechurch.ca/programs/archives/holdings/papers/Wiebe,%20Aganetha%20(1873-1947)%20fonds.htm

[81] See https://www.mharchives.ca/holdings/papers/Niebuhr,%20Jacob%20J..htm

[82] See https://subjectguides.uwaterloo.ca/c.php?g=695566&p=4931956 and https://uwaterloo.ca/mennonite-archives-ontario/personal-collections

[83] See https://uwaterloo.ca/mennonite-archives-ontario/sound-recordings-oral-history-projects/russian-mennonite-immigrants-oral-history-project

[84] See https://uwaterloo.ca/mennonite-archives-ontario/sound-recordings-oral-history-projects/women-without-men

[85] See https://primo.tug-libraries.on.ca/primo_library/libweb/action/search.do?vl(freeText0)=+Mennonites+-+Soviet+Union+-+Biography&vl(397444793UI0)=sub&vl(631150464UI1)=all_items&vl(1UIStartWith0)=exact

Mennonite Survivors (MHSBC); *Diaries and Letters of Soviet Mennonites* (MHSBC); *Kronswiede Village Collection, 1919–c1973*[86] (MHSA); *Alfred Klassen Fonds*[87] (MHSA); *Henry Peters Fonds*[88] (MHSA); *Katherine (Goerzen) Peters Collection* (MHSA); *Diaries and Letters of Soviet Mennonites* (MHSA); *Diaries and Letters of Soviet Mennonites* (MHSS); *Abram Penner Papers, 1904–1940*[89] (BCMLA, MHC); *Isaac B. Fast and Aganetha Unruh Fast Papers, 1911–1935*[90] (BCMLA); *Helen Penner Lingenfelder Papers, 1920–1940*[91] (BCMLA); *Gerhard J. Toews and Susanna Toews Papers, 1928–1941*[92] (BCMLA); *Helena Graewe Warkentin Papers, 1917–1940*[93] (BCMLA); *Papers of J. J. and Anna Dick, 1915–1980*[94] (HLA); *John B. Toews Library of Historical Materials* (MHSBC); and *D. M. Hofer and the Famine in Russia* (CMBS Hi).

D) Mennonite and international relief efforts

As was noted above, Mennonites in North America and Europe provided material aid (e.g., food packages) and financial assistance to their families and co-religionists suffering during the Ukrainian famine. Mennonite aid agencies, as well as international religious and relief organizations, also sent aid to Ukraine. According to some Soviet Mennonites, the food packages—which often included flour, sugar, salted pork, pasta, powdered milk, and occasionally coffee—made the difference between life and death for their families. With foreign currency received in letters from the West, Mennonites purchased food and other supplies, often at skyrocketing prices, on the black market or in the state-operated Torgsin stores that demanded payment for goods in foreign currency. Shortly after Hitler's rise to power in Germany, much of this Western aid unfortunately dwindled as local Communist Party cells in Ukraine often confiscated Western food and cash for the benefit of themselves or the Soviet state (see Neufeldt, "The Fate," 244).

The archival collections that provide documentation on North American and, to a lesser extent, European Mennonite relief efforts for

&fn=search&tab=default_tab&mode=Basic&vid=WATERLOO&scp.scps=scope%3a(CGC)&ct=lateralLinking

86 See https://mennonitehistory.org/kronswiede-collection-1919-c1973-2-cm/

87 See http://mennonitehistory.org/alfred-klassen-fonds-1929-1933-8-cm-franz-peter-klassen

88 See http://mennonitehistory.org/henry-peters-fonds-c-1910-1963-9-cm-photographs-and-correspondence/

89 See http://mac.libraryhost.com/index.php?p=collections/controlcard&id=53

90 See http://mac.libraryhost.com/index.php?p=collections/controlcard&id=204

91 See http://mac.libraryhost.com/?p=collections/controlcard&id=319

92 See http://mac.libraryhost.com/index.php?p=collections/controlcard&id=99

93 See *http://mac.libraryhost.com/index.php?p=collections/controlcard&id=80*

94 See http://encore.fresno.edu/iii/encore/record/C__Rb1116936__Sa%3A%28%22dick%2C%20j%22%29__Orightresult__U__X4__T?lang=eng&suite=cobalt

Mennonite communities in Ukraine include: *Russian Relief Collection*[95] (MCC US); *Correspondence of Levi Mumaw* (MCC US); *B. H. Unruh Reports and Papers (CMBS); B. H. Unruh Papers, 1920–59 (BCMLA); Canadian Mennonite Board of Colonization Documents*[96] (MHA). International relief efforts are also documented in *B. H. Unruh Reports and Papers (CMBS)* and *B. H. Unruh Papers, 1920–59* (BCMLA).

E) Nazi records and perspectives

Another perspective on the Mennonite experience during the Holodomor can be found in records located in the *Captured German War Documents Collection* (CMBS). Prepared by the *Reichsministerium für die besetzten Ostgebiete* (headed by Sonderkommando Dr. Karl Stumpp) in 1942–43, this collection includes field notes, family lists, village reports, and questionnaires on Mennonite and ethnic German communities (in the Khortytsia, Nikopol, Kronau [Kherson], Zagradovka [Kherson], and Kryvyi Rih areas) in Ukraine between 1917 and 1942. Although this collection does not include detailed documentation on Mennonite life in the early 1930s, the village reports provide some useful numerical and statistical information about the dekulakization and collectivization of Mennonite communities, the number of families exiled from each village in the 1930s, and village mortality rates during the Holodomor.

F) Photographic perspectives

North American archives currently contain few photographic images of the Mennonite Holodomor experience (MHSC, MHA); the majority of them can be found in the *Mennonite Archival Image Database* (MAID).[97] The good news is that this online collection is continuing to locate and post more digital images of the famine experience, and over time will provide academics with more photographic perspectives of the famine.

G) Other sources and perspectives

Other sources that academics should consider consulting include the *Global Anabaptist Mennonite Encyclopedia Online* (GAMEO),[98] a database with articles on "Soviet Mennonites" and "famine." Although many of these articles are dated and cursory, it is expected that GAMEO editors will increasingly incorporate more current research and sources on the Mennonite experience during the Holodomor.

---

[95] See File IX-01-3.

[96] See https://www.mharchives.ca/holdings/organizations/CMBoC_fonds.htm

[97] See https://archives.mhsc.ca/

[98] See https://gameo.org/index.php?title=Welcome_to_GAMEO

Two other databases with resources on the Holodomor include: a) the GRanDMA database (Genealogical Registry and Database of Mennonite Ancestry),[99] which contains disparate genealogical information on Soviet Mennonite families; and b) the *German Mennonite Sources Database* (BCMLA), a digital collection of documents published by or about Mennonites in Germany between 1800 and 1950 that includes some sources on Soviet Mennonites.[100]

Another potentially important source of information is the *NKVD and KGB Files*[101] (MHA), a collection that is currently being prepared by the Centre for Transnational Mennonite Studies (Winnipeg, MB) and which will include NKVD and KGB files on Soviet Mennonites arrested during the Great Terror. Some of the NKVD files contain information on Soviet Mennonites and their experiences during the Holodomor.

Finally, academics should also consider consulting dissertations (LA) on the Mennonite experience during Soviet collectivization and the Holodomor; they refer to a wide array of primary and secondary resources related to these important topics.

III. Some final observations

Collectively the archival collections and databases described above provide a variety of perspectives on Mennonite life during the famine, the relief efforts of Mennonite and international organizations, and the unique challenges and anti-German hostility that Mennonites faced during this period. The DAZO collection, for example, is especially useful in delineating the government's administration (and the roles of Mennonites therein) of a number of Mennonite communities in the Molochansk and Khortytsia raiony, and the day-to-day challenges of life on the collective farm during the famine. These records confirm that while Mennonites shared many of the same experiences and challenges as their Ukrainian, Russian, and Jewish neighbors during the famine, the anti-German hostility that Mennonites and other ethnic-German groups experienced at this time intensified their tribulations and made their Holodomor experiences unique.

But these North American archival collections also have their limitations. First, they are not a substitute for the records in state and former NKVD/KGB archives in Ukraine, and it is imperative that academics spend more time examining the records in these Ukrainian archives to better understand the Mennonite Holodomor experience both inside and

99 See https://www.grandmaonline.org/GW-ASP-5/GWHelp/GW-GMPopup.asp

100 See https://mla.bethelks.edu/gmsources/gmsources.php

101 See https://news-centre.uwinnipeg.ca/all-posts/kgb-files-offer-information-on-missing-mennonites/

outside the Khortytsia and Molochansk raiony. The DAZO collection, for instance, does not include all of the relevant documents from the Zaporizhzhia State Archive, and the documents in this collection only deal with a limited number of Mennonite settlements in the Khortytsia and Molochansk raiony; they do not include records on the many Mennonite communities beyond the borders of these two raiony.

Another limitation of the North American archival collections is that many are incomplete. The very restrictive Soviet borders in the 1930s made it difficult for correspondence and other records to make their way to the West, especially after Hitler came to power in early 1933. Moreover, North American and European Mennonite organizations were also not always diligent about preserving records and correspondence related to their leadership and relief organizations, as well as their collaborations with international relief bodies and government agencies in the 1930s and 1940s. Many of the letters in Mennonite periodicals and the B. H. Unruh Reports were heavily redacted by Unruh or the editors of the periodicals and are therefore fragmentary. The result is that these letters generally present a Mennonite victims' narrative that makes no mention of Mennonite participation in the government, party, and kolkhoz administration of the Holodomor.

Some of the records in the North American archives are also difficult to read; a significant number of DAZO records, for instance, were written in cursive script, often in Russian or Ukrainian, and with poor quality ink on poor quality paper. Apart from typed letters published in Mennonite periodicals or in the B.H. Unruh reports, most of the Soviet Mennonite letters were written in German, cursive, Gothic script. In some cases, the authors of these letters wrote to their loved ones in a coded language, imbued with secondary meanings not readily understood by Soviet censors, to make it less likely that Soviet authorities would confiscate the letters. Deciphering these documents can often prove challenging for modern-day academics not familiar with these languages or codes.

And what must be done to facilitate more research on Mennonite experiences of the famine? A more concerted effort must be undertaken to digitize primary source documents in Ukrainian state and former NKVD/KGB archives—especially with sources dealing with Mennonite communities not covered by the DAZO collection—and to make them broadly available for future researchers to access. A focused effort to collect and upload digital images of photographs of the Mennonite famine experience is also required.

There is also a need for academics to participate in more collaborative projects related to this topic—especially in terms of comparing and contrasting Mennonite Holodomor experiences with those of other ethnic groups (for example, Ukrainians, Russians, or Jews) or religious persuasions (for instance, Catholics, Orthodox, Lutherans, Baptists, and Adventists). These collaborations would also yield a deeper understanding of the following topics: how did the rise of Hitler, anti-German hostility, and anti-sectarian hostility in Ukraine affect the Mennonite experience in ways that were different from the experiences of other ethnic and religious groups; what were the international Mennonite relief efforts during the famine and how did Mennonite collaboration with government and non-government agencies affect the delivery of aid to their Soviet co-religionists; what was the extent of Mennonite interaction with Torgsin stores and how were they punished for patronizing these stores; to what extent did Soviet Mennonites rescue non-Mennonites from starvation and how commonplace was it for Mennonites to adopt orphaned non-Mennonite children into their families; what do the Mennonite letters confiscated by local Communist Party cells and Soviet censors reveal about the Mennonite famine experience; how was the 1933–34 purge experience of Mennonites different from that experienced by other ethnic groups in Ukraine; what were the mortality rates in Mennonite communities during the famine; and how did the Holodomor and ethnic hostility impact the subsequent Soviet Mennonite experience?

Finally, academics must also undertake more research in the Bundesarchiv and other archives in Germany to better appreciate how German politics, international relations, and relief efforts impacted the Mennonite Holodomor experience. This research will invariably reveal more about the roles of North American and European Mennonite leaders (especially Benjamin H. Unruh) and Mennonite relief organizations in their participation in international relief efforts, which included German government and relief agencies (such as *Brüder in Not*), Nazi-party relief agencies, as well as international Ukrainian, Baptist, Lutheran, and Quaker relief agencies. This research will expand the current understanding of some of the lasting consequences of the Holodomor on Mennonite populations, including the intergenerational transmission of trauma from Mennonite Holodomor survivors to their descendants, many of whom escaped to Germany during and after World War II or who eventually emigrated to Germany as *Aussiedler* (emigrants) or *Umsiedler* (resettlers) during the 1970s–90s and thereafter.

Archives

Derzhavnyi Arkhiv Zaporizhs'koi Oblasti (State Archive of the Zaporizhzhia oblast) in Zaporizhzhia, Ukraine.

Mennonite Historical Society of Canada Archives.

Mennonite Brethren Historical Commission.

Mennonite Heritage Archives.
Centre for Mennonite Brethren Studies.
Mennonite Central Committee Canada Archives.
Mennonite Archives of Ontario / Milton Good Library.
Archives of the Mennonite Historical Society of British Columbia.
Archives of the Mennonite Historical Society of Alberta.
Archives of the Mennonite Historical Society of Saskatchewan.
Mennonite Archival Commons.
Mennonite Central Committee United States Archives.
Bethel College Mennonite Library and Archives.
Mennonite Historical Library / Goshen College Archives.
Hiebert Library and Archives.
Center for Mennonite Brethren Studies (Hillsboro).
Global Anabaptist Mennonite Encyclopedia Online.
Mennonite Archival Image Database.
Genealogical Registry and Database of Mennonite Ancestry.
Library and Archives Canada.

Bibliography

Beattie, Robert. "A Great Turn that Never Happened: A Reconsideration of the Soviet Decree of Labor Discipline of November 1932." *Russian History* 13, nos. 2–3 (Summer-Fall 1986): 235–57.

Berman, Harold. *Soviet Criminal Law and Procedure*. Cambridge, MA: Harvard Univ., 1972.

Beznosov, Alexander. "Kulak, Christian, and German: Ukrainian Mennonite Identities in a Time of Famine, 1932–1935." In *Minority Report: Mennonite Identities in Imperial Russia and Soviet Ukraine Reconsidered, 1789–1945*, edited by Leonard G. Friesen, 260–86. Toronto: Univ. of Toronto Press, 2018.

Bezo, Brent, and Stefania Maggi. "Living in 'Survival Mode:' Intergenerational Transmission of Trauma from the Holodomor Genocide of 1932–1933 in Ukraine." *Social Science & Medicine* 134 (2015): 87–94.

Comerford, Vincent, Lindsay Janssen, and Christian Noack. *Holodomor and Gorta Mór: Histories, Memories and Representations of Famine in Ukraine and Ireland*. Cambridge: Cambridge Univ. Press, 2013.

Danilov, V.P., R.T. Manning, L. Viola et al., eds. *Tragediia sovetskoĭ derevni: kollektivizatsiia i raskulachivanie: dokumenty i materialy v 5 tomakh, 1927–1939*. Moskva: Rossiĭskaia polit. ėntsiklopediia, 1999–2006, vol. 3.

Davies, R.W., and Stephen Wheatcroft. *The Years of Hunger: Soviet Agriculture, 1931–1933*. New York: Palgrave, 2004.

Dietsch, Johan. "Textbooks and the Holocaust in Independent Ukraine: An Uneasy Past." *European Education* 44, no. 3 (2012): 67–94.

Dyck, Harvey L. "Collectivization, Depression and Immigration, 1929–1930." In *Empire and Nations: Essays in Honour of Frederic H. Soward*, edited by Harvey L. Dyck and H. Peter Krosby, 144–60. Toronto: Univ. of Toronto Press, 1969.

Goossen, Benjamin W. *Chosen Nation: Mennonites and Germany in a Global Era*. Princeton, NJ: Princeton Univ. Press, 2017.

Himka, John-Paul. "Making Sense of Suffering: Holocaust and Holodomor in Ukrainian Historical Culture, and: Holod 1932–1933 rr. v Ukraïni iak henotsyd/Golod 1932–1933 gg. v Ukraine kak genotsid [The 1932–33 Famine in Ukraine As a Genocide] (Review)." *Kritika: Explorations in Russian and Eurasian History* 8, no. 3 (2007): 683–94.

Kas'ianov, Georgii. "The Holodomor and the Building of a Nation." *Russian Social Science Review* 52, no. 3 (2011): 71–93.

Kessler, Gijs. "The Passport System and State Control over Population Flows in the Soviet Union, 1932–1940." *Cahiers du Monde russe* 42, nos. 2–4 (Apr–Dec 2001): 477–503.

Klid, B. "Why Is It Important to Study the History of the Holodomor—the Genocide of the Ukrainian People." *Storìnki Istoriï* (2017).

Krahn, Cornelius. "Ukraine." *Global Anabaptist Mennonite Encyclopedia Online*. 1959. https://gameo.org/index.php?title=Ukraine&oldid=143088. Accessed October 28, 2019.

Kulchytskyi, Stanislav. *Holodomor in Ukraine 1932–33: Interpretation of Fact*. Kyiv: National Academy of Sciences of Ukraine, 2008.

— "The Holodomor of 1932–33: How and Why?" *East/West: Journal of Ukrainian Studies* 2, no. 1 (2015): 93–116.

Kuryliw, Valentina. *Holodomor in Ukraine, the Genocidal Famine 1932–1933: Learning Materials for Teachers and Students*. Toronto, ON: CIUS, 2018.

Marochko, V. I., ed. *Sil's'kohospodars'kyĭ soiuz nashchadkiv hollands'kykh vykhodtsiv na Ukraïni (1921–1927): zbirnyk dokumentiv i materialiv*. Kyiv: Instytut istoriï Ukraïny, 2000.

Martin, Terry. "The Russian Mennonite Encounter with the Soviet State, 1917–1955." *Conrad Grebel Review* 20 (Winter 2002): 5–59.

Moore, Rebekah. "'A Crime against Humanity Arguably without Parallel in European History': Genocide and the 'Politics' of Victimhood in Western Narratives of the Ukrainian Holodomor." *Australian Journal of Politics & History* 58, no. 3 (2012): 367–79.

Neufeldt, Colin P. "Collectivizing the *Mutter Ansiedlungen*: The Role of Mennonites in Organizing Kolkhozy in the Khortytsia and Molochansk German National Districts in Ukraine in the late 1920s and early 1930s." In *Minority Report: Mennonite Identities in Imperial Russia and*

Soviet Ukraine Reconsidered, 1789–1945, edited by Leonard G. Friesen, 211–59. Toronto: Univ. of Toronto Press, 2018.

— "The Fate of Mennonites in Ukraine and the Crimea during Soviet Collectivization and the Famine (1930–1933)." PhD diss., University of Alberta, 1999.

— "The Flight to Moscow, 1929: An Act of Mennonite Civil Disobedience." *Preservings* 19 (December 2001), 35–47.

— "The Public and Private Lives of Mennonite Kolkhoz Chairmen in the Khortytsia and Molochansk German National Raĭony in Ukraine (1928–1934)." *The Carl Beck Papers in Russian and East European Studies* no. 2305 (January 2015): 1–87.

— "Reforging Mennonite *Spetspereselentsy*: The Experience of Mennonite Exiles at Siberian Special Settlements in the Omsk, Tomsk, Novosibirsk and Narym Regions (1930–33)." *Journal of Mennonite Studies* 30 (2012): 269–314.

— "Separating the Sheep from the Goats: The Role of Mennonites and Non-Mennonites in the Dekulakization of Khortitsa, Ukraine (1928–1930)." *The Mennonite Quarterly Review* 83, no. 2 (April 2009): 221–91.

— "The '*Zborni*' of Khortytsia, Ukraine: The Last Stop for Some Kulaks En Route to Stalin's Special Settlements." *Journal of Ukrainian Studies* 35–6 (2011–12): 207–23.

Shapoval, Yuri, ed. *The Famine-Genocide of 1932–1933.* Kingston: Kashtan, 2005.

Shearer, David. *Policing Stalin's Socialism: Repression and Social Order in the Soviet Union, 1924–1953.* New Haven, CT: Yale Univ., 2009.

Stark, Renate. "Holodomor, Famine in Ukraine, 1932–1933: A Crime against Humanity or Genocide?" *Irish Journal of Applied Social Studies* 10, no. 1 (2010): 20–30.

Toews, John B., and Paul Toews, eds. *Union of Citizens of Dutch Lineage in Ukraine (1922–1927): Mennonite and Soviet Documents.* Fresno, CA: Centre for Mennonite Brethren Studies, 2011.

New Research on Government Responses

Bearing Witness to the Holodomor: Eyewitness and Survivor Collections of the Early Cold War Period (1947–55)

Olga Andriewsky

How do people remember events that 'did not occur'? How do people remember what is meant to be forgotten?" These questions were famously posed by the anthropologist Rubie S. Watson in the 1990s, in the midst of what she called "a feast of remembrance" that followed the collapse of Communism.[1] Among the many "forgotten" histories that emerged in Ukraine at the time was the story of the Holodomor, the Terror-Famine that had killed millions of people in 1932–33. Of course, the Holodomor had never been quite forgotten—and particularly not by those who had experienced or witnessed the devastation. Both within and beyond the Soviet Union, as we can now see, the active construction and transmission of a social memory of the Terror-Famine continued—unevenly, sometimes surreptitiously, and often with great difficulty—over the course of many decades.[2]

This article will focus on survivor and eyewitness accounts of the Holodomor produced between 1947 and 1955, when the Terror-Famine was "first remembered."[3] Specifically, I highlight four collections that were created in North America—in most cases, incidentally—during the post-War decade. Indeed, none of these collections were originally conceived as

---

[1] Rubie S. Watson, *Memory, History, and Opposition under State Socialism*, School of American Research Advanced Seminar Series (Sante Fe, NM-Seattle: School of American Research Press; distributed by University of Washington Press, 1994): 6.

[2] The history of Holodomor memory in the Soviet Union before 1985 has yet to be fully studied. There are numerous examples—such as Vassily Grossman's novel, *Everything Flows,* begun in the 1950s—that indicate the existence of a "hidden" social memory. For a history of Holodomor memory in the diaspora in the 1980s, see Frank Sysyn, "The Ukrainian Famine of 1932–3: The Role of the Ukrainian Diaspora in Research and Public Discussion," in *Studies in Comparative Genocide*, ed. Levron Chorbajian and George Shirinian (New York-London: Palgrave Macmillan, 1999), 182–215.

[3] In the post-war era, the subject of the Holodomor was first raised publicly in 1946—before the start of the Cold War—by Ivan Bahrianyi, a writer from Soviet Ukraine and himself a refugee —in *Chomu ia ne khochu vertatys' do SSSR? (*Winnipeg, 1946) ("Why Do I Choose Not to Return to the U.S.S.R?"). His essay became, in effect, the "manifesto" of the Ukrainian refugees, as Marta Dyczok has put it.

"Holodomor projects." Rather, they owe their very existence to the convergence of two significant developments. First, there was the presence in the Displaced Person (DP) camps in Germany and Austria of a large number of refugees from the Soviet Union (est. 250,000), both Ukrainian and non-Ukrainian, who had lived through the era of de-kulakization, collectivization, and famine. Many of the Soviet Ukrainian refugees were former prisoners of war or *Ostarbeiter*, workers who had been forcibly deported to Germany as slave laborers during the War.[4] Second, and no less importantly, the collections came into being because *a public space* suddenly opened up after 1945 in which stories of the Famine-Terror could be told—and legitimized.[5] In contrast to 1933, when an active—and quite formidable—international campaign to bring attention to the plight of starving millions had been defused in official circles in the West, the Cold War created a variety of public settings in which survivors and eyewitnesses could openly bear witness to the suffering and political violence that had marked the lives of so many people.[6]

***

The most unusual of the four sets of eyewitness accounts is the so-called Oseredok collection. It was the first to be amassed—and the last to be re-discovered. (The content relating to the Holodomor within the collection only came to the attention of historians in the last decade.) Oseredok is the

---

[4] There is an unfortunate tendency to conflate Ukrainian refugees from interwar Poland and Rumania with those from the Soviet Union and to treat them as a monolith. Each population had distinct and complex origins and posed a different set of political challenges for the Allies at the end of the War. See Gerard Daniel Cohen, *In War's Wake: Europe's Displaced Persons in the Postwar Order* (New York: Oxford University Press, 2011); Marta Dyczok, *The Grand Alliance and Ukrainian Refugees* (Houndmills, Basingstoke, Hampshire: Macmillan Press, 2000); Mark Wyman, *DP: Europe's Displaced Persons, 1945–1951* (Philadelphia: Balch Institute Press, 1989); George Fischer, "The New Soviet Emigration," *The Russian Review* 8, no. 1 (1949): 6–19.

[5] On the problematic nature of testifying about political violence, see Claire Hackett and Bill Rolston, "The Burden of Memory: Victims, Storytelling and Resistance in Northern Ireland," *Memory Studies* 2, no. 3 (2009): 355–76. See also Boaz Cohen, "Holocaust Survivors and the Genesis of Holocaust Research," in *Beyond Camps and Forced Labour: Current International Research on Survivors of Nazi Persecution* (Osnabrück: Secolo-Verlag, 2008):) 290–300 and his "Holocaust Testimonies and Historical Writing Debates, Innovations, and Problems in the Early Postwar Period," *Yad Vashem Studies* 45, no. 2 (2017): 159–84.

[6] On the 1933 campaign, see, for example, Milena Rudnyts'ka, "Borot'ba za pravdu pro velykyi holod," *Svoboda*, nos. 134 and152, July 16 and August 9, 1958. The campaign reached the League of Nations but, according to Rudnytska, who led the effort, was stymied by the British and French, who were intent on signing trade agreements with the Soviet Union. See also Marco Carynnyk, "Blind Eye to Murder: Britain, the United States and the Ukrainian Famine of 1933," in *Famine in Ukraine 1932–1933*, ed. Roman Serbyn and Bohdan Krawchenko (Edmonton: Canadian Institute of Ukrainian Studies, 1986).

Ukrainian Cultural and Education Centre in Winnipeg (Canada). It was founded in 1944 as a museum and library by the Ukrainian National Federation of Canada. In early 1947, on the initiative of the émigré historian Dmytro Doroshenko, Oseredok announced a memoir writing competition. Doroshenko had spent the interwar period in Czechoslovakia and Poland and had himself just arrived in Winnipeg from a DP camp in Germany, where he had been elected President of the Ukrainian Free Academy of Sciences (November 1945). He was a capable memoirist in his own right and, in 1947, was in the midst of writing the second volume of his reminiscences (*Moï spomyny pro davnie-mynule, 1901–14 roky*; My Recollections of a Distant Past, 1901–1914).[7]

The memoir writing competition was aimed primarily at Ukrainian refugees living in the DP camps in Germany and Austria—regardless of their country of origin (i.e., interwar Poland, Rumania, Czechoslovakia, or the Soviet Union). (By this time, the policy of forcible repatriation of Soviet citizens by the Americans and British authorities had ended and they now came under the protection of the International Refugee Organization.) Oseredok placed a number of advertisements in the Ukrainian language press in Europe in 1947 and 1948 urging readers to record their recollections *of the War*:[8]

Write your memoirs!

We live in historic and terrible times. Someday, much will be written about our era. The writing of history will require accurate and truthful memoirs about contemporary events, accounts by various people—workers, farmers, teachers, professors, political leaders, artists and generally people from all walks of life.-

All of this is still fresh in your memory but will slowly fade…For this reason we ask: write down accurately what you yourself have lived through or what you have witnessed with your own eyes during the last War. The recollections can be long or short. It can be a reminiscence about one particular event.

---

[7] Doroshenko first published his memoirs of the Revolution in 1923. Dmytro Doroshenko, *Moï spomyny pro davnie-mynule, 1901–1914 roky* (Winnipeg: Tryzub, 1949). Thomas M. Prymak, "Dmytro Doroshenko: A Ukrainian Émigré Historian of the Interwar Period," *Harvard Ukrainian Studies* 25, no. 1/2 (2001): 31–56; Leonid Bilets'kyi, *Dmytro Doroshenko: Ukraïns'kyi vchenyi* (Winnipeg, 1949).

[8] "Pro konkursovi pratsi Oseredku Ukraïns'koï kul'tury i osvity," Oseredok. Fond I.: Konkurs spohadiv 1947–1948. Doroshenko, at the time, was writing a chapter on World War II for a new edition of Ivan Krypiakevych's *Velyka istoriia Ukraïny*, which would be published in Winnipeg in 1948.

The competition committee thus cast the net very widely, urging people from all regions and backgrounds to relate their experiences. "Don't worry if it is difficult for you to write. Write what you can. All of this will all be useful for [future] historians and writers." (Oseredok reassured prospective authors that their identities would be protected, if they so desired.[9]) Monetary prizes were to be awarded for the top entries—with the winner receiving $75 (equivalent to approximately $1,000 in current value).

ПИШІТЬ СВОЇ СПОГАДИ!

Ми живемо у великій і грізній добі. Про нашу добу колись будуть дуже багато писати. Для історії потрібно буде матеріялів, точно і вірно записаних спогадів про теперішні події, записок різних людей — робітників, селян, учителів, професорів, політиків, артистів, взагалі людей з кожного стану життя.

Все це ще свіже в пам'яті, але поволі буде затемнюватися. А шкода, щоб багато з того, що ще може бути точно записане з пам'яти, пропало. Тож просимо: запишіть точно те, що Ви самі пережили, або те, що діялося на Ваших очах від початку недавньої війни. Спомини можуть бути довгі або короткі. Може бути спомин і про одну якусь подію.

Записане надсилайте до Бібліотеки й Музею. Все присланне буде уважно розглянене, покляссоване і старанно збережене. Автор споминів повинен зазначити, що з присланим треба зробити. Коли деякі описані особи потребують охорони поки що, то хай автор згадує їх під прибраними іменами. Ключ до таких імен Музей буде держати, згідно з бажанням автора, в тайні, до зазначеного часу.

Не журіться тим, що Вам тяжко писати. Пишіть так, як можете й вмієте. Знайте, що все записане придасться для істориків і письменників.

Шліть все, що носить на собі печать українського духу до:

Осередок Української Культури й Освіти
Library and Museum,
Ukrainian Cultural and Educational Centre,
P. O. Box 3001,
Winnipeg, Mann., Canada

The idea of a memoir writing competition was remarkable in North America at the time. Until the late 1960s, with rare exceptions, the historical profession in the West was not interested in eyewitness accounts by "ordinary people." (The very first Oral History program, established by Allan Nevins at Columbia University in 1948, focused on elite subjects, that is, the famous and the powerful.[10]) In East Central Europe, however, efforts to record history "from below" had begun a generation earlier, after World War I and the revolutionary upheavals that followed. Doroshenko, as an active and long-time participant in the Ukrainian national movement before and during the Revolution, was acutely aware that history can easily "get lost" or distorted without documentation. He belonged to a generation of Ukrainian political activists who had made it their particular objective, beginning in the early 1920s, to chronicle for posterity the extraordinary events they had lived through.[11] The Oseredok memoir writing competition,

---

[9] Ultimately, eleven authors received prize money. "Vyslid konkursu na spomyny," Oseredok. Fond I.: Konkurs spohadiv 1947–1948. The advertisement quoted above appeared in *Nedilia,* March 22, 1947.

[10] Thomas L. Charlton, Lois E. Myers, and Rebecca Sharpless, eds. *Thinking About Oral History: Theories and Applications* (Lanham, MD: Altamira Press, 2006), 28–34.

[11] Virtually all of the members of the competition committee at Oseredok had been involved in the revolutionary events in Ukraine between 1917 and 1921 before subsequently emigrating to Canada. The committee included Dmytro Doroshenko, Paul Macenko, Leonid Biletsky, Mykyta Mandryka, Dmytro Kyslytsia, Mykhailo Pohoretsky, Wasyl Topolnytsky, and Yurii Diakunchak. Kyslytsia, the youngest member of the committee (b. 1912), was himself a

in this respect, was a continuation—and an expansion—of an ongoing history writing project.[12]

In all, the committee received sixty-five entries by the end of March 1948.[13] Most of the authors, reflecting the breakdown of the refugee population in the DP camps, were originally from eastern Galicia, i.e., Western Ukraine. Few actually wrote about World War II, or strictly about the War. In the course of the competition, as the first entries began to arrive, the committee, in fact, revised the terms of the contest to encourage submissions that went well beyond the 1939–45 period.[14] Some of the submissions focused on World War I and Revolution of 1917, others wrote about the 1930s. One author began his account in the 1890s. Some authors submitted novels or short stories; one entry was in the form of a poem. Some wrote in Russian; one memoir was written in Polish. Fedir Pihido [pseud. Pravoberezhnyi], the eventual winner of the competition, had in fact entered two manuscripts—a 200-page-long account of life in Kyiv province during the German occupation (which began with the Babyn Yar massacre) and a separate description of the Holodomor (*8,000,000 — 1933 rik na Ukraïni*).[15]

Indeed, what makes the Oseredok collection unique among Holodomor accounts is the unmediated nature of the texts. Authors had full control over their manuscripts. They chose what to write about and were able to express themselves in their own style and language and to construct their own meaning. There was no special effort to collect accounts of the Holodomor—and yet the Terror-Famine figured in virtually all of the manuscripts submitted by refugees from Soviet Ukraine. In almost every instance, however, the Holodomor was framed as part of a much larger story of persecution which included the Revolution, the "catastrophe of collectivization," and/or the Stalinist Terror. As Fedir

---

refugee from Soviet Ukraine, a Holodomor survivor, and one of the first DPs to arrive in Canada. "Vyslid konkursu na spomyny," Oseredok. Fond I.: Konkurs spohadiv 1947–1948.

12 Mykhailo Hrushevsky, the dean of Ukrainian historians, had himself encouraged this endeavor and, after his return to Kyiv in 1924—now the Ukrainian S.S.R.—helped launch a monumental project, *Za sto lit* [Over the Course of One Hundred Years], to publish primary sources and first-hand accounts relating to the social and cultural history of Ukraine in the 19th and early 20th c. under the auspices of the Academy of Sciences of Ukraine. See Mark von Hagen's introduction to Pavlo Khrystiuk, *The Ukrainian Revolution, 1917–1919: A Documentary Analysis* (forthcoming); *Za sto lit.* 6 vols., *Materiialy z hromads'koho i literaturnoho zhyttia Ukraïny XIX i pochatku XX stolittia* (Kyiv: Derzhavne vydavnytstvo Ukrainy, 1927–1930).

13 "Vyslid konkursu na spomyny," Oseredok. Fond I.: Konkurs spohadiv 1947–1948.

14 See the description in *Novyi shliakh*, March 3, 1948.

15 Pihido's account of World War II in Ukraine was used extensively by Karel Berkhoff in his book *Harvest of Despair: Life and Death in Ukraine under Nazi Rule* (Cambridge: Harvard University Press, 2004).

Pihido summarized in *The Stalin Famine*, nearly half of the people in his native village of Staiky (pop. 6,500) in Kyiv province had disappeared between 1918 and 1939. "This number is made up of those who were killed, who died of hunger, who were tortured to death in the polar slave labour camps, or who vanished without leaving any trace."[16]

Oseredok became, in this inadvertent way, the first repository for eyewitness accounts of the Holodomor. Even after the close of the competition, new submissions arrived for several years. Fedir Pihido [Pravoberezhnyi] (1888–1962) and Dmytro Solovei (1888–1966), two of the contest winners—and eyewitnesses in their own right—took the initiative to collect first-hand accounts of the Holodomor among Soviet refugees in the Western Zone of Germany and to send them along to Winnipeg for preservation.[17] Both men, in fact, had an unusually broad grasp of the cataclysm that had engulfed the Ukrainian countryside between 1928 and 1933. Both were in a position to view events "from above" as well as "from below" as they unfolded. Pihido had headed the planning division of the Kyiv regional Trust of the Building Materials Industry, "Budmaterial," and in this capacity, had travelled widely in the early 1930s. (He had an intimate understanding of the human costs as well—his own mother and sister had died during de-kulakization, while five other family members perished during the Holodomor.[18]) Solovei, for his part, had served as a department head with the Central Statistical Administration of the Ukrainian S.S.R. in Kharkiv (1925–33)—the agency charged with compiling statistical information and providing analysis about the economy and population of the Republic—and thus had had access to data that indicated the true extent of the devastation. (Each of the four directors under whom Solovei had served in the Statistical Administration was subsequently executed in 1937–38.[19]) For both men,

---

[16] F. Pigido-Pravoberezhny, *The Stalin Famine: Ukraine in the Year 1933* (London: Ukrainian Youth Association in Great Britain, n.d.), 18.

[17] Materials that arrived after the competition were archived separately. See Oseredok, f. 3. Fond Dmytra Solov'ia (1949–1952) and f. 4. Fond Pihido-Pravoberezhnoho.

[18] F. Pravoberezhny, "Churches in Vologda Become Shelters for the De-Kulakized," in *The Black Deeds of the Kremlin: A White Book; The Great Famine in Ukraine 1932–33*, ed. S. O. Pidhainy, vol. 2 (Detroit: DOBRUS [Democratic Organization of Ukrainians Formerly Persecuted by the Soviet Regime in U.S.A.], 1955), 189–90; Roman Serbyn and Iurii Shapoval, "Fedir Pihido ta ioho spohady," in *Velyka Vitchyzniana viina* (Kyiv: Smoloskyp, 2002), http://exlibris.org.ua/vvv/article-beg.html

[19] *Oseredok*. f. III: Fond Dmytra Solov'ia (1949–1952). Dmytro Solovei's published works on the Great Famine include [D. Sova], *Holod na Ukraïni* (Blomberg, Germany: n.p., 1948); *Stezhkamy na Holhotu. Vynyshchennia v Ukraïni mil'ioniv liudei terorom ta shtuchnym holodom v 1929–1933 rokakh*, (Scranton: Narodnia volia, 1952); *Holhota Ukraïny* (Winnipeg: Nakladom "Ukraïns'koho Holosu", 1953); *The Golgotha of Ukraine* (New York: Ukrainian Congress

documenting, explaining, and publicizing the Holodomor became a personal mission in the post-War era. The Oseredok memoir writing competition gave them and other Soviet refugees an opportunity to "remember what was meant to be forgotten."[20]

The Oseredok competition also gave Holodomor survivors and eyewitnesses a platform to reach a North American audience, many of whom had little comprehension of what the refugees had experienced or why they had fled. The opening of Oseredok and the memoir writing contest were, for example, reported in the Winnipeg press.[21] (The Western Canadian press, in general, covered the activities of Ukrainian organizations—Communist and non-Communist—on a regular basis at this time.) The winning entries were subsequently serialized and published in *Novyi shliakh* and other Ukrainian-language newspapers—and Pihido's winning submissions, including an English-language translation of his account of the Terror-Famine, soon appeared as separate publications.[22] Indeed, at a time when the refugees were a subject of growing interest across North America—and not only among Ukrainians—Oseredok helped put a human face on the new immigrants who were beginning to arrive in ever larger numbers.

***

As the Cold War gained momentum, Soviet refugees became the focus of ever greater attention. In Western political, military, and intelligence circles they came to be seen as an important source of information on the workings of the Soviet Union—"an inside source"—at a time when intelligence about life in the Soviet Union was extremely difficult, if not impossible, to obtain.[23] For Holodomor survivors, this meant new

---

Committee of America, 1953); D. F. Solovei, *Skazaty pravdu: try pratsi pro holodomor 1932–1933 rokiv* (Kyiv and Poltava: [s.n.], 2005). See also Iurii Shapoval, "Dmytro Solovei ta holovna tema ioho zhyttia," *Dzerkalo tyzhnia*, no. 31/559 (August 13–19, 2005). On the Statistical Administration under Stalin, see Alain Blum and Martine Mespoulet, *L'anarchie bureaucratique. Pouvoir et statistique sous Staline* (Paris: La Découverte, 2003).

[20] In his 1988 Report to Congress, James Mace singled out the great value of the work of Solovei and Pihido. See United States Commission on the Ukraine Famine, *Investigation of the Ukrainian Famine, 1932–1933: Report to Congress* (Washington: U.S. G.P.O., 1988): 9–16.

[21] "Ukrainians Build Library," *Winnipeg Tribune*, January 31, 1948.

[22] F. [Fedir Pihido] Pravoberezhnyi, *8,000,000. 1933-yi rik na Ukraïni* (Winnipeg: Ukrainian Cultural & Educational Centre, 1951); F. Pihido-Pravoberezhnyi, *Velyka vitchyzniana viina* (Winnipeg: Novyi Shliakh, 1954); F. Pigido-Pravoberezhny, *The Stalin Famine: Ukraine in the Year 1933.* (London: Ukrainian Youth Association in Great Britain, n.d.).

[23] At the time, Soviet refugees were interviewed by U.S., British, French, and Turkish intelligence agencies. George Fischer, "The New Soviet Emigration," *The Russian Review* 8, no. 1

opportunities to talk about the Terror-Famine—and to a much wider audience. In this way, the story of the Holodomor quickly became enmeshed in the Cold War discourse after 1948.

The largest, most ambitious, and most successful project to exploit the refugees for research purposes was, of course, the Harvard Project on the Soviet Social System, also known as the Refugee Interview Project (RIP).[24] It was launched in 1949 by a group of social scientists at Harvard University with funding from the United States Air Force. Between 1950 and 1953, the Harvard team interviewed several thousand Soviet refugees living in West Germany, Austria, and the United States. They administered 2,000 questionnaires and conducted 700 in-depth interviews. In an attempt to get a representative sample of the population, the Harvard team recruited various sub-groups of the population by class, nationality, gender, and age. (Approximately 24 percent of the participants were Ukrainian.)

Unlike the Oseredok collection, the Harvard Project was designed to produce a specific outcome. The interviews were tightly scripted. Questions focused on the structures and functions of Soviet institutions—on how collective farms worked, for example—rather than on the life experiences of the respondents.[25] For the purposes of the project, discussing the Holodomor was considered off-topic, a digression, not relevant to the ultimate goals of the RIP.

What the researchers quickly discovered, however, was that the refugees had their own stories to tell—and were determined to tell them. Though never asked about the famine of 1932–33, they talked about it, nonetheless. For many of the Soviet refugees, collectivization, de-kulakization, and the "Great Famine" were—clearly defining moments in their lives. As Merle Fainsod, a Harvard political scientist sent to Germany in 1949 to conduct preliminary research, observed in his field notes:

> Whenever I have spoken to simple people the first thing that they all want to talk about is just this: how Stalin purposely created a famine. This

---

(1949): 6–19; David C. Engerman, *Know Your Enemy: The Rise and Fall of America's Soviet Experts* (Oxford: Oxford University Press, 2009) esp. ch. 2.

[24] See Engerman, ch. 2. The original collection of materials related to the Harvard Project on the Soviet Social System is currently housed at the H.C. Fung Library in the Davis Center for Russian and Eurasian Studies Collection, Harvard University. Part of the collection is available in digitized form at https://library.harvard.edu/collections/hpsss/index.html

[25] For a list of questions and categories used in the interviews, see Harvard Project on the Soviet Social System, "Qualitative File Manual of A-Schedule Materials." Second-Run Edition (#2) http://nrs.harvard.edu/urn-3:FHCL:936791; "Qualitative File: A-Schedule Category Listings," http://nrs.harvard.edu/urn-3:FHCL:961058; Qualitative File Manual of B-Schedule Materials and Friedrich-Fainsod Materials. First-Run Edition (#5) http://nrs.harvard.edu/urn-3:FHCL:939141.

> idea has become so deeply imbedded in the minds of the peasants in particular, that I feel safe in saying that it has become part of the folk saga of the Ukraine, with more legendary importance than any of the positive achievements of the Communist regime in that region. It is a large and ineradicable part of the historical thinking of the peasants. The point is that the blame is squarely heaped on "Stalin and the Communists," with complete justification.[26]

The interviews illustrate how central "the Great Famine" was to the memory of those who had experienced it. The stories recorded from the survivors—when the interviewer made the effort to note their statements—were tales of separation, loss, of shattered families, destroyed communities, impossible choices. And they were also stories of violence and cruelty—of people being forcibly deprived of their homes, their livelihood, their food, their lives.[27] Doubt less this accounts for the vehemence with which the respondents often confronted their interviewers. The famine, as so many of the survivors were determined to explain to the researchers, did not *just happen*. It was an *artificial famine* triggered by state policies rather than natural causes — set in motion, as many believed, by policies aimed at their destruction.

Hunger and the search for food, in general, are themes that runs through virtually every interview. The words "hunger," "famine," and "starvation" [*golod* in Russian] appear in the transcripts 1,643 times. Some of the respondents spoke about the famine of 1921, others remembered starving during the German occupation, a few spoke of the post-war famine in 1946–47. Yet, in the personal narratives of many of the respondents, both Ukrainian and non-Ukrainian, rural and urban, the early 1930s—often referred to simply as "the years of famine"—emerge as a distinct period.

Indeed, what is unique about the Harvard project are the comments *by non-Ukrainians* on the famine of 1932–33 in Ukraine. *Nearly every refugee*—whether Ukrainian or non-Ukrainian—who had lived in the Ukrainian SSR mentioned the famine of 1932–33 in the course of their interview. One of the refugees interviewed by the Harvard Project was, in fact, an Odesa lawyer, a self-identifying Russian, who in 1933 had defended women charged with cannibalism.[28]

---

[26] Interestingly, Fainsod himself had spent 1932 in the Soviet Union on a Sheldon Traveling Fellowship. Harvard Project on the Soviet Social System digital collection: interviews and manuals, 1950–1953, fun0001. H.C. Fung Library, Harvard Library, Harvard University. https://id.lib.harvard.edu/ead/c/fun00001c00966/catalog

[27] How much was lost in transcription will also never be known. The interview records were in most cases based on notes taken by the interviewers, who were assisted by translators.

[28] HPSS, Schedule A, Vol. 12, Case149, 9.

Perhaps most significantly, the Harvard interviews show the degree to which the respondents thought about the famine of 1932–33 in *regional* and not just *class* terms. In the 1930s, rumors of "famine in Ukraine" (as distinct from "famine in the countryside") reached well beyond the borders of the Ukrainian SSR. In some cases, this information was reported by individuals who had been sent to Ukraine in 1932–33 in an official capacity. In other cases, it was Ukrainians fleeing to the RSFSR who helped spread the word. The famine, in the minds of those who had lived through those years, whether in Ukraine or Leningrad or Moscow, had a defined location, a distinct geography. It was "famine in Ukraine" or "famine in Ukraine and the Kuban and the Don."[29] And this makes the Harvard collection—however flawed—exceptional for the study of the Holodomor.

***

It was, above all, the opportunity to engage in the political process that galvanized the Ukrainian diaspora during the early years of the Cold War—and provided Holodomor survivors and eyewitnesses with new forums in which to testify officially, in public.[30] The first opening in this regard was the campaign to ratify the Genocide Convention. The Ukrainian Congress Committee of America (UCCA, est. 1940), an umbrella organization representing (non-Communist) Ukrainian-American groups and organizations from 26 different states and 100 communities, began promoting the Holodomor as a genocide in 1948.[31] (The United Nations General Assembly approved the Convention on the Prevention and Punishment of the Crime of Genocide on Dec. 9, 1948.) From 1949 on, the UCCA worked closely with Rafael Lemkin, the author of the Convention—who no doubt knew about the Terror-Famine from his time working in Berezhany (Interwar Poland, now Western Ukraine) in the 1930s, when it was widely reported in the press—to help push for ratification in both the U.S. and Canada. (Canada signed on to the Convention in January 1951, owing in part, as Lemkin himself recognized, to the efforts of the UCCA and

---

[29] Famine in Ukraine, by my calculations, is mentioned in over 115 interviews, sometimes in passing, other times at great length.

[30] As Hackett and Rolston observe (pp. 362–65), there is a crucial distinction between the official processes in which victims of political violence participate and the beliefs, expectations, and needs of the victims themselves.

[31] See *The Story of the Ukrainian Congress Committee of America (1940–1951)* (New York: Ukrainian Congress Committee of America, 1951), 47–55; Prof. T.S. [T. Sosnovyi], "Soviet Genocide of the Ukrainian People," *Ukrainian Quarterly* IV, no. 4 (1948): 325–38. The *Ukrainian Quarterly* is an official publication of the Ukrainian Congress Committee of America.

its Canadian counterpart, the Ukrainian Canadian Committee [now Ukrainian Canadian Congress].[32])

On February 9, 1950, when the Senate Foreign Relations Committee in the U.S. held hearings to discuss ratification of the Genocide Convention, two representatives from the Ukrainian-American community appeared before the Committee in person. Lev Dobriansky, a faculty member in the Department of Economics at Georgetown University and newly elected (American-born) President of the Ukrainian Congress Committee of America, gave a broad overview of "Soviet exterminations" dating from 1920 to the post-War period and linked Soviet (and Imperial Russian) territorial expansion and consolidation of power to the "systematic annihilation" of the non-Russians. Like Lemkin himself, Dobriansky conceived of the genocide of Ukrainians as a long-term process which had begun with attacks against the Ukrainian intelligentsia and continued to the present day, including the Bolsheviks' liquidation of the Ukrainian Catholic Church and clergy in the newly annexed territories of Western Ukraine.[33] The second representative, Antonii Batiuk (1894–1978), President of the Ukrainian Workingmen's Association, focused more narrowly on the famines of 1921–22 and 1932–33 in Soviet Ukraine. As part of his testimony, Batiuk submitted witness statements about the Holodomor from fifteen newly arrived Ukrainian immigrants.[34]

---

[32] On Lemkin and Ukrainians, see "Prof. Lemkin diakuie U.K.K. za pidtrymku aktsiï proty narodovbyvstva," *Svoboda*, May 21, 1952; Raphael Lemkin, *Totally Unofficial: The Autobiography of Raphael Lemkin*, ed. Donna-Lee Frieze (Yale University Press, 2013), 191–92; Roman Serbyn, "Lemkin on Genocide of Nations," *Journal of International Criminal Justice* 7, no. 1 (2009): 123–30; Douglas Irvin-Erickson, *Raphael Lemkin and the Concept of Genocide* (Philadelphia: University of Pennsylvania Press, 2017); John Cooper, *Raphael Lemkin and the Struggle for the Genocide Convention* (Basingstoke [England], New York: Palgrave Macmillan, 2008).

[33] Lev Dobriansky (1918–2008) became a key figure in Washington circles. In the early 1950s he aligned himself with the "rollback" camp—i.e., those political thinkers, like James Burnham, and Senators and Congressmen like Charles Kersten, who supported active measures to "liberate" Eastern Europe from Communism. For the proponents of "rollback," refugees were regarded as crucial to the success of the project. See, for example, Lev Dobriansky, *The Non-Russian Nations in the U.S.S.R.: Focal Point in America's Policy of National Liberation.* Extension of Remarks of Hon. Brien McMahon of Connecticut in the Senate of the United States, Thursday, May 15, 1952 (Washington, D.C.: United States Government Printing Office, 1952). Dobriansky's influence in foreign policy circles waned after 1954, when Kersten lost his seat and when, after Stalin's death, President Eisenhower shifted to a policy of "containment." He nonetheless remained active in ethnic politics and the UCCA for many years. In 1959, he authored the Captive Nations Week Resolution.

[34] *Genocide Convention: Hearings before the United States Senate Committee on Foreign Relations, Subcommittee on International Convention on the Prevention and Punishment of the Crime of Genocide*, 81st Congress, 2nd sess., on Jan. 23–25, Feb. 9, 1950 (Washington: U.S. G.P.O., 1950), 319–413, 454–68. See also William S. White, "Senators Wind Up Genocide Hearing," *The New York Times*, February 10, 1950.

The witness statements—unlike the Oseredok submissions and the Harvard interviews—were carefully curated to support the case for genocide. They were brief, summarizing in one or two paragraphs the mass deaths that survivors had seen with their own eyes. The witnesses did not appear before the committee, their testimony was translated into English, read into the hearings, and published in the Congressional record. Dobriansky and Batiuk also submitted supporting documents that had first been collected during the 1933 campaign—the July 1933 appeal of the Ukrainian Greek Catholic Bishops of Western Ukraine; the appeal of Cardinal Innitzer of Vienna; the 1933 appeal of Ukrainian Socialists in Western Ukraine and abroad; the 1934 Fish Resolution; the Report of Dr. Ammende, the General Secretary of the Congress of European Minorities; as well as excerpts from accounts of the famine by William Chamberlain and Gareth Jones. As Dobriansky remarked, "In truth we have waited twenty years to be given this sort of opportunity to present the case of systematic Soviet genocide of the Ukrainian nation."[35]

***

For Holodomor survivors and eyewitnesses determined to tell their story, however, the high point of the early Cold War was, no doubt, the Hearings of the House Select Committee on Communist Aggression, the so-called Kersten Committee. The hearings provided the émigré political refugees with the opportunity to testify directly, in a sympathetic and powerful setting. (Charles J. Kersten, Republican representative from Wisconsin and Chair of the Committee, was a fervent anti-Communist, an outspoken champion of the East European refugees, and a leading advocate for the policy of "rollback," i.e., the "liberation" of Eastern Europe from Communism.[36]) Initially created in 1953 to examine the Soviet annexation

---

[35] *Genocide Convention*: 319, 455–60. One of the members of the political board of UCCA in 1950 was Vasyl Mudry, a former editor of the Lviv newspaper *Dilo* and member of Parliament in Poland in the interwar period, who had played a leading role in 1933 in the international campaign to bring attention to the Holodomor.

[36] Kersten came to national prominence in 1951 with the so-called "Kersten Amendment" to the U.S. Mutual Security Act, which called for the annual appropriation of $100 million dollars to fund liberation movements in Eastern Europe. His interest in East European issues began in Milwaukee—his Congressional district included a sizable Polish population. As his obituary in *The Ukrainian Weekly* noted ("Congressman Kersten, Friend of Ukrainians, Dies," November 11, 1972), Kersten became interested in Ukrainian issues in 1949 through his contacts with Prof. Roman Smal-Stocki, who taught at Marquette University, and later, in Washington, with Lev Dobriansky. Margaret M. Manchester, "Charlie Kersten's War: A Catholic Crusader Goes to Congress," *Cold War History* 21, no. 2 (2021): 121–38. On the policy of rollback, see Stephen Long, "Strategic Disorder, the Office of Policy Coordination and the Inauguration of U.S. Political Warfare against the Soviet Bloc, 1948–50," *Intelligence and National Security* 27, no. 4

of the Baltic states, this committee was quickly authorized—with active support from the Ukrainian-American community—to investigate "the subversion and destruction of free institutions and human liberties in all other areas controlled, directly or indirectly, by world communism."[37]

Unlike the Senate hearings on the Genocide Convention, which had been short-lived, contentious, and ultimately did not lead to ratification, the Kersten Committee proved exceptionally effective. It met for a year and a half, held over forty hearings, conducted more than three hundred interviews, collected 1,500 submissions, produced 27 reports, and received widespread coverage in the media. Indeed, many of the hearings were broadcast on Radio Free Europe and Voice of America. The work of the committee focused mainly on the Communist takeovers in Eastern Europe—Poland, Czechoslovakia, Romania, Hungary, Bulgaria, etc. In the summer and fall of 1954, however, the committee travelled to Munich, New York, and Chicago to hold special hearings on "the treatment of non-Russians within the Soviet Union." (Separate hearings were held in New York in September 1954 for Jews from the Soviet Union.)[38]

Of the sixty-eight witnesses who testified about "the treatment of non-Russians within the Soviet Union," thirty-seven individuals spoke—many through interpreters—about Ukraine. They included prominent intellectuals, religious leaders, former government officials, professionals, journalists, workers, and farmers. Some, like Prof. Lev Dobriansky, appeared as expert witnesses; most spoke from personal experience. They described in systematic fashion the Bolshevik takeover of Ukraine, the arrests of intellectuals and ordinary people, the destruction of the churches and religious life, mass deportations, concentration camps, torture, and mass killings (the Vinnytsia massacre of 1937–38, the NKVD prison mass

---

(2012): 459–87; Gregory Mitrovich, *Undermining the Kremlin: America's Strategy to Subvert the Soviet Bloc, 1947–1956* (London; Ithaca, NY: Cornell University Press 2000); Peter Grose, *Operation Rollback: America's Secret War Behind the Iron Curtain* (Boston, MA: Houghton Mifflin 2000).

[37] Readers of *Svoboda* and *The Ukrainian Weekly* were urged, for example, to contact their Congressional representative in support of expanding the scope of the Com-mit-tee's investigations. See *Svoboda/The Ukrainian Weekly,* March 20, 1954, 3; House Select Committee on Communist Aggression, *Summary Report*, 83rd Congress, 2nd sess. (Washington: U.S. G.P.O., 1955), 1–3; Jonathan H. L'Homedieu, "Baltic Exiles and the U.S. Congress: Investigations and Legacies of the House Select Committee, 1953–1955," *Journal of American Ethnic History* 31, no. 2 (2012): 41–67.

[38] *Preliminary Inventory of the Records of the Select Committee on Communist Aggression, 83rd Congress,* compiled by George P. Perros. The National Archives. National Archives and Records Service. General Services Administration (Washington, D.C., 1959), 1–3, 11. The Committee and the hearings were covered in the national and local press, particularly in the Midwest, and received considerable attention in the "ethnic" press. See, for example, *Svoboda*, Feb. 12, March 13, May 7, August 18, 27, 1954.

executions in Western Ukraine in 1941)—as well as the continued resistance of the Ukrainian people. In some cases, the identities of the witnesses were kept secret for fear of reprisals against family and relatives who had remained in the Soviet Union.[39]

The "artificial famine" of 1932–33 figured prominently in the testimonies about Ukraine, framed as part of this larger narrative of state violence, persecution, and terror. Fedir Pihido—the winner of the Oseredok competition in 1948—was one of the first witnesses to testify during the Munich hearings and spoke at some length, offering an overview of the Soviet policies that had led to the Holodomor and the death of millions of people. Other survivors described in intimate terms the struggle to feed themselves and their families, the desperate measures people took to try to survive, the loss of family and neighbors. Several mentioned instances of cannibalism.

The testimony presented at the hearings was subsequently published as a special 370-page report, one of ten such interim reports produced by the Committee.[40] Interviews were further supplemented with written testimonies, documents, and publications which—though not published—were listed in the report as exhibits and formally entered into the committee's permanent record. Formal submissions included, for example, volume 1 of *The Black Deeds of the Kremlin,* a collection of 100 personal testimonies by victims of Stalinist repression, terror, and famine in Ukraine.[41]

Yet the official record represents only part of the evidence produced for the hearings. As generally noted in the *Preliminary Inventory of the Records,* "Because of the want of time, the Committee declined the offers of testimony of hundreds of other witnesses."[42] Forty-seven Ukrainian testimonials that did not make it into the official record have nonetheless been preserved in the National Archives in Washington, D.C. Additional eyewitness accounts relating to the Holodomor are preserved among the Charles J. Kersten Papers at Marquette University.[43]

---

[39] *Eighth Interim Report: Hearings before the United States House Select Committee to Investigate Communist Aggression. Investigation of Communist Takeover and Occupation of the Non-Russian Nations of the U.S.S.R.,* 83 Congress, 2nd sess. on June 30, July 1, Oct. 11–14, 18, 19, 1954 (Washington: U.S. G.P.O., 1954).

[40] Ibid.

[41] The thematic organization of the Kersten Committee testimony by Ukrainian witnesses replicated, in large measure, *The Black Deeds of the Kremlin: A White Book* (Toronto, 1953). This cannot be considered a coincidence. A number of individuals who were involved in the publication of *The Black Deeds,* including the editor, Semen Pidhainy, appeared as witnesses before the Kersten Committee. On the publication of this volume, see Bohdan Klid, "The Black Deeds of the Kremlin: Sixty Years Later," *Genocide Studies International* 8, no. 2 (2014): 224–35.

[42] *Preliminary Inventory:* 3.

[43] See Bohdan Klid, "Cold War Politics in the United States and Ukrainian Testimonies before the US House Select Committee on Communist Aggression in 1954." Paper presented at the

***

1955 marked the end of a remarkable decade of activity on the part of Holodomor survivors and eyewitnesses. As they made the transition from refugees to citizens, they demonstrated a powerful sense of agency, seizing every opportunity they could to bear witness to the political violence that had shattered the lives of many millions of people. Of course, not everyone spoke out. Some suffered in silence, fear, or guilt—often with a sense of sorrow that they had been unable to save members of their own family, relatives, or neighbors.[44] Others, however, were committed and determined to reveal to the world the terrible things they had seen and experienced.

The early Cold War empowered these refugees to tell their stories. It also provided them with a receptive audience willing to recognize and validate their suffering.[45] This convergence of circumstances found perhaps its fullest and most lasting expression with the publication of the second volume of *Black Deeds of the Kremlin* (1955), a 712-page collection of reports and personal testimonies devoted "solely to one theme, the preparation and realization of a terrible famine in the Ukraine in the years 1932–1933, the so-called organized famine."[46] Compiled, edited, and published by recently arrived Soviet Ukrainian refugees—and funded and translated into English with the help of the Ukrainian diaspora—the book was clearly aimed at an American audience. Charles J. Kersten, the Chair of the House Select Committee on Communist Aggression, for example, wrote the introduction.

The emergence of the story of the Holodomor during the early Cold War and its ultimate association with one particular political camp limited the impact of the revelations, however. In the eyes of many, the testimony—indeed, the very fact of a Ukrainian famine—appeared tainted by its links with the most hawkish wing of the Republican Party.[47] Once the U.S.

Congress of the Humanities and Social Sciences, Canadian Association of Slavists, University of British Columbia, May 27, 2019. The additional testimonies can be found at Records Relating to the Russian and Non-Russian Nations of the U.S.S.R., March — October 1954, Select Committee on Communist Aggression. 1954–12/1954, 83rd Congress, Records of the U.S. House of Representatives, Record Group 223, National Archives Building, Washington, DC.; Marquette University, Department of Special Collections and University Archives. Charles J. Kersten Papers. Series 6: House Select Committee on Communist Aggression, 1951–1955, Box 2 & 3.

[44] This was a common theme in survivor accounts. See, for example, "The Testimony of Witness H," *Eighth Interim Report,* 45–49. See also Hackett, 358–59.

[45] This audience included, crucially, refugees from other parts of Ukraine as well as the Ukrainian diaspora.

[46] *The Black Deeds of the Kremlin: A White Book. The Great Famine in Ukraine 1932–33*, 2: v.

[47] Ironically, the main popularizers of the Holodomor after the War—the circle of Eastern Ukrainians around Ivan Bahrianyi that included Fedir Pihido and Dmytro Solovei—were social democrats who saw themselves as heirs to the progressive socialist movement that had

abandoned the policy of "rollback" and its proponents lost their influence, the public space for discussing the Terror-Famine was greatly constricted. In an era when eyewitness accounts by ordinary people were not treated seriously by the historical profession in the West, the ample evidence provided by Holodomor survivors and eyewitnesses failed to receive scholarly attention.[48] It was only in the 1980s, in an altogether different intellectual and political environment, that historians began to acknowledge the gravity of the stories that the refugees had told more than three decades earlier.

Bibliography

Antons, Jan-Hinnerk. "Displaced Persons in Postwar Germany: Parallel Societies in a Hostile Environment." *Journal of Contemporary History* 49, no. 1 (2014): 92–114. http://www.jstor.org/stable/43697290.

— "The Nation in a Nutshell? Ukrainian Displaced Persons Camps in Postwar Germany." *Harvard Ukrainian Studies*, no. 1–2 (2020): 177–211.

Bahrianyi, Ivan. *Chomu ia ne khochu vertatys do SSSR?* Winnipeg: Komitet Ukraintsiv Kanady, 1946.

Berkhoff, Karel C. *Harvest of Despair: Life and Death in Ukraine Under Nazi Rule*. Cambridge, Mass.: Belknap Press of Harvard University Press, 2004.

Bilets'kyi, Leonid. *Dmytro Doroshenko: Ukraïns'kyi vchenyi.* Winnipeg, 1949.

The Black Deeds of the Kremlin: A White Book; The Great Famine in Ukraine 1932–33. Edited by S. O. Pidhainy. Vol. 2, Detroit: DOBRUS (Democratic Organization of Ukrainians Formerly Persecuted by the Soviet Regime in U.S.), 1955.

Blum, Alain, and Martine Mespoulet. *L'anarchie bureaucratique. Pouvoir et statistique sous Staline.* Paris: La Découverte, 2003.

Carynnyk, Marco. "Blind Eye to Murder: Britain, the United States and the Ukrainian Famine of 1933." In *Famine in Ukraine 1932–1933*, edited by Roman Serbyn and Bohdan Krawchenko, 109–38. Edmonton: Canadian Institute of Ukrainian Studies, 1986.

created the Ukrainian National Republic in 1917. They were anti-Soviet, to be sure, but not "nationalists" and repeatedly clashed with the radical nationalists from Western Ukraine in emigration.

[48] In the more than sixty articles and books that came out of the Harvard Project on the Soviet Social System, the famine in Ukraine did not receive any significant attention—evidence the researchers collected notwithstanding. This can be partly explained by the design of the study. The researchers were not interested in history per se; they were interested in "the system." But, as the Fainsod quote above suggests, it was also due to a basic mistrust of what "the simple people" had to say.

Charlton, Thomas L., Lois E. Myers, and Rebecca Sharpless, eds. *Thinking About Oral History: Theories and Applications*. Lanham, MD: Altamira Press, 2006.

Cohen, Boaz. "Holocaust Survivors and the Genesis of Holocaust Research." *Beyond Camps and Forced Labour: Current International Research on Survivors of Nazi Persecution* (2005): 290–300.

— "Holocaust Testimonies and Historical Writing Debates, Innovations, and Problems in the Early Postwar Period." *Yad Vashem Studies* 45, no. 2 (2017): 159–84.

Cohen, Gerard Daniel. *In War's Wake: Europe's Displaced Persons in the Postwar Order.* New York: Oxford University Press, 2011.

"Congressman Kersten, Friend of Ukrainians, Dies," *The Ukrainian Weekly*, November 11, 1972.

Cooper, John. *Raphael Lemkin and the Struggle for the Genocide Convention.* New York: Palgrave Macmillan, 2008.

Dobriansky, Lev E. *The Non-Russian Nations in the U.S.S.R.: Focal Point in America's Policy of National Liberation. Extension of Remarks of Hon. Brien Macmahon of Connecticut in the Senate of the United States.* Washington, D.C.: United States Government Printing Office, Thursday, May 15, 1952.

Doroshenko, Dmytro. *Moï spomyny pro davnie-mynule, 1901–1914 roky.* Winnipeg: Tryzub, 1949.

Dyczok, Marta. *The Grand Alliance and Ukrainian Refugees.* St. Antony's Series. Houndmills, Basingstoke, Hampshire: Macmillan Press, 2000.

Engerman, David C. *Know Your Enemy: The Rise and Fall of America's Soviet Experts.* Oxford: Oxford University Press, 2009.

Fischer, George. "The New Soviet Emigration." *The Russian Review* 8, no. 1 (1949): 6–19.

Fond Dmytra Solov'ia (1949–1952), Fond III. Oseredok Archives, Winnipeg, Manitoba, Canada.

Grose, Peter. *Operation Rollback: America's Secret War Behind the Iron Curtain.* Boston: Houghton Mifflin, 2000.

Grossman, Vasiliĭ, et al. *Everything Flows.* New York Review Books, 2009.

Hackett, Claire, and Bill Rolston. "The Burden of Memory: Victims, Storytelling and Resistance in Northern Ireland." *Memory Studies* 2, no. 3 (2009): 355–76.

Harvard University, The Harvard Project on the Soviet Social System Online [HPSSS]. https://library.harvard.edu/sites/default/files/static/collections/hpsss/index.html

Holian, Anna Marta. *Between National Socialism and Soviet Communism: Displaced Persons in Postwar Germany.* Ann Arbor: University of Michigan Press, 2011.

Irvin-Erickson, Douglas. *Raphael Lemkin and the Concept of Genocide.* Philadelphia: University of Pennsylvania Press, 2017.

Klid, Bohdan. "The Black Deeds of the Kremlin: Sixty Years Later." *Genocide Studies International* 8, no. 2 (2014): 224–35.

— "Cold War Politics in the United States and Ukrainian Testimonies before the US House Select Committee on Communist Aggression in 1954." Paper presented at the Congress of the Humanities and Social Sciences, Canadian Association of Slavists, University of British Columbia, May 27, 2019.

Konkurs spohadiv, 1947–1948, Fond I. Oseredok Archives, Winnipeg, Manitoba, Canada.

Lemkin, Raphael. "Soviet Genocide in the Ukraine." In *Holodomor: Reflections on the Great Famine of 1932–1933 in Soviet Ukraine,* Appendix A, pp. 235–42. Kingston: Kashtan Press, 2009.

— *Totally Unofficial: The Autobiography of Raphael Lemkin.* Ed. by Donna-Lee Frieze. Yale University Press, 2013.

L'Homedieu, Jonathan H. "Baltic Exiles and the U.S. Congress: Investigations and Legacies of the House Select Committee, 1953–1955." *Journal of American Ethnic History* 31, no. 2 (2012): 41–67.

Long, Stephen "Strategic Disorder, the Office of Policy Coordination and the Inauguration of US Political Warfare against the Soviet Bloc, 1948–50." *Intelligence and National Security* 27, no. 4 (2012): 459–87.

Manchester, Margaret M. "Charlie Kersten's War: A Catholic Crusader Goes to Congress." *Cold War History* 21, no. 2 (2021): 121–38.

Mitrovich, Gregory. *Undermining the Kremlin: America's Strategy to Subvert the Soviet Bloc, 1947–1956.* London; Ithaca, NY: Cornell University Press, 2000.

Pigido-Pravoberezhny, F. [Fedir Pihido]. *The Stalin Famine: Ukraine in the Year 1933.* London: Ukrainian Youth Association in Great Britain, n.d.

Pihido-Pravoberezhnyi, F. [Fedir Pihido]. *Velyka vitchyzniana viina.* Winnipeg: Novyi Shliakh, 1954.

Pravoberezhnyi, F. [Fedir Pihido]. *8,000,000. 1933-yi rik na Ukraïni.* Winnipeg: Ukrainian Cultural & Educational Centre, 1951.

Preliminary Inventory of the Records of the Select Committee on Communist Aggression, 83rd Congress. Compiled by George P. Perros. The National Archive. National Archive and Records Service. General Services Administration. Washington, D.C.: 1959.

"Prof. Lemkin diakuie U.K.K. za pidtrymku aktsiï proty narodovbystva," *Svoboda*, May 21, 1952.

Prof. T.S. [T. Sosnovyi]. "Soviet Genocide of the Ukrainian People." *Ukrainian Quarterly* IV, no. 4 (1948): 325–38.

Prymak, Thomas M. "Dmytro Doroshenko: A Ukrainian Émigré Historian of the Interwar Period." *Harvard Ukrainian Studies* 25, no. 1/2 (2001): 31–56.

Rudnyts'ka, Milena. "Borot'ba za pravdu pro Velykyi Holod." *Svoboda*, no. 134–152 (July 16–August 9, 1958).

S-vii, Dm. [Solovii, Dmytro]. "Skil'ky liudnosty zahynulo na Ukraïni pid chas shtuchno stvorenoho holodu 1932–33 rr.". *Ukraïns'ki visti*, no. 18 (1950).

Serbyn, Roman, and Iurii Shapoval. "Fedir Pihido ta ioho spohady." In *Velyka Vitchyzniana viina* Kyiv: Smoloskyp, 2002. http://exlibris.org.ua/vvv/article-beg.html.

Serbyn, Roman. "Lemkin on Genocide of Nations," *Journal of International Criminal Justice* 7, no. 1 (2009): 123–130.

Shapoval, Iurii. "Dmytro Solovei ta holovna tema ioho zhyttia." *Dzerkalo tyzhnia*, no. 31/559 (August 13–19, 2005).

Solovei, D. F. *The Golgotha of Ukraine.* New York: Ukrainian Congress Committee of America, 1953.

— *Holhota Ukraïny.* Winnipeg: Nakladom "Ukrains'koho Holosu", 1953.

— *Skazaty pravdu: Try pratsi pro Holodomor 1932–1933 rokiv.* Kyiv and Poltava: [s.n.], 2005.

— *Stezhkamy na holhotu. Vynyshchennia v Ukraïni mil'ioniv liudei terorom ta shtuchnym holodom v 1929–1933 rokakh.* Scranton, PA: 1952.

Sova, D. [Dmytro Solovei]. *Holod na Ukraïni.* Blomberg, Germany, 1948.

The Story of the Ukrainian Congress Committee of America (1940–1951). New York: Ukrainian Congress Committee of America, 1951.

Sysyn, Frank. "The Ukrainian Famine of 1932–3: The Role of the Ukrainian Diaspora in Research and Public Discussion." In *Studies in Comparative Genocide*, edited by Levron Chorbajian and George Shirinian, 182–215. New York–London: Palgrave Macmillan, 1999.

"Ukrainians Build Library," *Winnipeg Tribune*, January 31, 1948.

United States. Commission on the Ukraine Famine. *Investigation of the Ukrainian Famine, 1932–1933: Report to Congress.* Washington, U.S. G.P.O., 1988.

United, States. *Genocide Convention: Hearings before the United States Senate Committee on Foreign Relations, Subcommittee on International Convention on the Prevention and Punishment of the Crime of Genocide, Eighty-First Congress, Second Session, on Jan. 23–25, Feb. 9, 1950.* Washington: U.S. G.P.O., 1950.

United States. Congress. House Select Committee on Communist Aggression. *Eighth Interim Report: Hearings before the United States House Select Committee to Investigate Communist Aggression. Investigation of*

Communist Takeover and Occupation of the Non-Russian Nations of the U.S.S.R., Eighty-Third Congress, Second Session, on June 30, July 1, Oct. 11–14, 18, 19, 1954. Washington, D.C., 1954.

— *Summary Report of the Select Committee on Communist Aggression: House of Representatives, Eighty-Third Congress, Second Session, under Authority of H. Res. 346 and H. Res. 438.* Washington, D.C.: U.S. G.P.O., 1955.

United States. Congress. House Select Committee on Communist Aggression.

Watson, Rubie S. *Memory, History, and Opposition under State Socialism.* Santa Fe, NM: School of American Research Press, 1994.

White, William S. "Senators Wind Up Genocide Hearing." *The New York Times*, February 10, 1950.

Wyman, Mark. *DP: Europe's Displaced Persons, 1945–1951.* Philadelphia: Balch Institute Press, 1989.

Za sto lit. 6 vols. Kyiv: Derzhavne vydavnytstvo Ukrainy, 1927–1930.

The Holodomor and Canada's Response: Archival Findings

Serge Cipko

In July 1934, the *Winnipeg Free Press* published an editorial about the visit to Canada of Ewald Ammende. Ammende was the honorary secretary of the Vienna-based Interconfessional and International Relief Committee for the Starving Districts of the Soviet Union, and the stated purpose of his visit to North America was to bring groups together for joint action in the event of a recurrence of famine. Among other things, the *Winnipeg Free Press* editorial cautioned that the story of "millions of human beings dying of starvation" was one that could not "lightly be put aside." And in Western Canada, it stressed, "we must be doubly aware of it ... because of the thousands of our fellow-citizens to whom these provinces are not places on a map but connected by ties of association and of blood."[1]

There indeed were a good many people in Canada who had such "ties of association and of blood," as the *Winnipeg Free Press* put it. Ammende himself made this observation in his book *Human Life in Russia*, when he referred to the many Ukrainians, Russians, Germans, and Jews in Winnipeg alone who had ancestral connections with Soviet territories.[2] Official statistics confirm such observations. The 1931 Canadian census counted 225,113 Ukrainians and 88,148 Russians in Canada as a whole. There were also 473,544 Germans, including Mennonites, and 156,726 Jews in Canada, and some among these two groups had origins in Soviet territories. The population of Canada at that time was 10,376,379.[3] Considering this significant population factor, one might expect to find famine-related materials in archives across Canada. This paper discusses the sorts of materials discovered in various archives when carrying out the research for my book *Starving Ukraine: The Holodomor and Canada's Response* and new findings since then.

Perhaps one of the first places that one would expect a historian to turn to during a study of Canada and the Holodomor is Library and Archives Canada in Ottawa. Indeed, this is where a good portion of the archival material that was applied to the book originated. A key collection perused there was the R. B. Bennett Papers. Richard Bedford Bennett was the prime

[1] "Famine over Russia," *Winnipeg Free Press*, July 26, 1934, 13.
[2] Ewald Ammende, *Human Life in Russia* (London: G. Allen & Unwin, [1936]).
[3] *Canada Year Book 1933* (Ottawa: King's Printer, 1933).

minister of Canada between 1930 and 1935. During those years, relations between the Soviet Union and Canada were strained. In 1931, the Bennett-led Conservative government imposed a partial embargo on trade with the Soviet Union. In response, the Soviet Union imposed a complete embargo on imports from Canada. Two particularly interesting items in the vast collection are a letter that Katharine Marjory Stewart-Murray, Duchess of Atholl, wrote to the Canadian prime minister in 1934 and his reply to her. The Duchess of Atholl was a British Member of Parliament for the constituency of Kinross and West Perthshire in Scotland. Her letter to Prime Minister Bennett concerned the matter of the admission of the Soviet Union to the League of Nations, which was to be debated in Geneva on 17 September 1934. She expressed the opinion that it would be an act of hypocrisy if the league allowed the USSR to enter it without anything said about the conditions there. In his reply, Bennett intimated that he was aware of the famine from first-hand information received in western Canada. As it turned out, even though Canada voted in favor of admitting the USSR to the League of Nations, Bennett instructed Oscar Skelton, the undersecretary of state for external affairs, to bring up the famine during the debate in Geneva, which Skelton did. The Oscar Douglas Skelton Fonds was another collection in Library and Archives Canada that was mined for the book.[4]

It is important to note that the Duchess of Atholl had earlier raised the matter of the famine in the British House of Commons on July 5, 1933, citing the reports of British journalists Gareth Jones and Malcolm Muggeridge. It is also noteworthy, though, that politicians in Canada learned about the famine from local sources before Jones's story broke on March 29, 1933. Nearly two weeks earlier, on March 16, 1933, the Legislative Assembly of Saskatchewan adjourned its regular affairs to discuss the issue of the famine. The Mennonite board in Rosthern, Saskatchewan, was said to be receiving, on average, 700–800 letters a week from the Soviet Union. The discussion in Regina about the famine was extensively covered in the Canadian mainstream press.[5] It prompted a letter to the editor by Wolodymyr S. Plawiuk, which was published in the *Edmonton Journal* on March 20, 1933. Plawiuk drew attention to the many letters he said had been received from Ukraine by local Ukrainian community members, asking for grain and flour.[6]

[4] Serge Cipko, *Starving Ukraine: The Holodomor and Canada's Response* (Regina: University of Regina Press, 2017).

[5] "House Urges Canada Send Surplus Grain to Starving Russians," *Leader-Post* (Regina), March 16, 1933, 1, 14.

[6] "Soviets Refused Wheat," *Edmonton Journal*, March 20, 1933, 4.

When one hears of this number of letters, one wonders whether any of this correspondence has been kept anywhere. While Mennonite archives in Canada were not examined for my book,[7] I studied some letters published in the Mennonite newspaper *Der Bote* of Rosthern, Saskatchewan. In several instances, Canadian mainstream newspapers published excerpts of letters translated into English that were said to have come from the Soviet Union. The Ukrainian-language press in Canada also published some letters. In terms of original letters, reference in the book is made to German-language letters that have been preserved in the Provincial Archives of Alberta (Edmonton) and to one that has been retained in St. Vladimir's Ukrainian Orthodox Congregation Library and Archives in Calgary.

A related question is why so many letters were allowed to come to Canada, considering the practice of strict censorship in the Soviet Union. The answer may be found not in the archives but in a perceptive article in the *Calgary Herald*. Published in April 1933, it pointed out that not all news from the Soviet Union came by cable. It then shared a letter received by "a Calgary Russian from relatives in the Soviet Republic." The letter writer spoke of a "syndicate [in the city] where there are all kinds of merchandise and food to be bought cheap, but only for dollars. You send the money to the syndicate and they will send us as much goods as they feel like." The *Herald* commented that when one understood where the dollars would go and "guesse[d] how little the 'syndicate' will give for them to the sufferers," then it was not so difficult to comprehend why such letters were permitted to pass the censors.[8]

Plawiuk's letter to the editor in the *Edmonton Journal* also mentioned that an offer of collective aid was made by Ukrainian Canadian farmers to famine sufferers in Ukraine but was rejected by the Alliance of the Red Cross and Red Crescent Societies of the Soviet Union in September or October 1932. That refusal was highlighted in several of the anti-famine protest meetings that took place across Canada in 1933–34. In total there were around eighty such protest actions, organized mainly but not exclusively by Ukrainian groups. Typically, resolutions would be passed at such meetings and forwarded to provincial governments and to Ottawa, London (UK), Washington, DC, and Geneva. Copies of some of these resolutions can be found in Library and Archives Canada, but none were seen during visits to the provincial archives of Alberta, Saskatchewan, and Manitoba. In terms of community archives, there are draft copies of resolutions by the Ukrainian Sporting Sitch Association in the Demetrius

[7] Library and Archives Canada has a "Mennonite Collection" (C-15749), which was consulted.
[8] "Letter from Russia Paints Sad Picture," *Calgary Herald*, April 28, 1933, 24.

Elcheshen Fonds at the Ukrainian Cultural and Educational Centre (Oseredok) in Winnipeg.

The "syndicate" to which the *Calgary Herald* was referring was undoubtedly the Soviet state-run hard currency store known as the "Torgsin" (from the Russian words *torgovlia s inostrantsami*, which means "trade with foreigners"). Individuals in the Soviet Union could receive aid from abroad through the Torgsin system. In Canada, funds were collected and sent to committees such as the Committee to Aid Victims of the Famine in Ukraine headed by Elizabeth Skoropadsky in Berlin. Among other things, that committee sent postcards with a famine-related image to Canada for sale in order to raise money for assistance to families or individuals in Ukraine via the Torgsin method. A copy of that postcard (reproduced in the book) can be found in the Demetrius Elcheshen Fonds at Oseredok.

Besides the Demetrius Elcheshen Fonds at Oseredok, not many materials related to the Holodomor were located in community archival collections elsewhere in Canada. A response to an enquiry made about the holdings of the Archives of the Ukrainian Orthodox Church of Canada in Winnipeg seemed to indicate that there is no documentation there related to the Holodomor for the years 1932–34, and there is little in the Ukrainian Catholic Archeparchy of Winnipeg Archives. There are, though, some valuable items in the Michael Luchkovich Papers at the Ukrainian Canadian Archives and Museum of Alberta, Edmonton. These include letters that the Member of Parliament (MP) for Vegreville received from Lord Godfrey Walter Phillimore, Ewald Ammende, and others in 1934. Of particular interest is the letter that Ammende wrote to Luchkovich on July 24, 1934, in which he urged the MP to insist on Prime Minister Bennett to include him officially in the Canadian delegation to the League of Nations and to "come personally to Geneva in September."[9]

However valuable such archival sources may be, they do not always provide answers. For example, in June 1933 an editorial in the Edmonton Ukrainian-language newspaper *Ukraïns'ki visty* expressed dismay at the lack of any treatment of the famine in the parliaments of countries inhabited by Ukrainians, namely, Poland, Romania, Czechoslovakia, and Canada. Then, in November 1933 an editorial in the same newspaper again conveyed frustration, though this time it was at the perceived passivity toward the

[9] Cipko, *Starving Ukraine*, 193. After 2020, the Ukrainian Canadian Archives and Museum of Alberta ceased to exist. (See "UCAMA President Blames Governments for Project's Collapse," *New Pathway/Ukrainian News*, December 19, 2020, at https://newpathway.ca/ucama-president-blames-governments-for-projects-collapse/.) The Michael Luchkovich Collection was transferred to the Bohdan Medwidsky Ukrainian Folklore Archives in the Kule Folklore Centre at the University of Alberta.

matter by Canadian elected representatives of Ukrainian descent specifically.[10] In 1933, five individuals of Ukrainian descent held political office in Canada: one in the federal Parliament, two in the Legislative Assembly of Manitoba, and two in the Legislative Assembly of Alberta.[11]

When the famine was brought up in the Legislative Assembly of Saskatchewan in March 1933, action was urged. James G. Gardiner, the leader of the Liberal opposition, remarked that there was "no better way for the Anglo-Saxon countries to act than to provide 20,000,000 bushels of wheat." The federal government seems to have never directly commented on this proposal, but its position may be inferred from its standard responses to resolutions submitted by Ukrainian groups. They were told that the Canadian government could not organize relief "under the sovereignty of another government in the absence of any indication that such action would be acceptable to that government." From a letter dated March 27, 1933 that is among the Premier James Garfield Gardiner Papers at the Provincial Archives of Saskatchewan in Regina, it is clear that while Gardiner believed that the federal government should act in some way, he also was aware of the particular circumstances of the Soviet case. He described the Soviet Union as a state that was "so far apart from all the other great nations of the world ... as to render the bringing of assistance to their people so difficult as it is at present."[12] Cornelius W. Wiebe, a Mennonite who represented the constituency of Morden and Rhineland as a member of the Liberal Party, spoke about the famine in the Legislative Assembly of Manitoba on May 3, 1933. He proposed no specific action and made no motion in connection with the famine but did want to draw the legislature's attention to constituents who had learned of the plight of relatives in the USSR.[13]

Luchkovich raised the matter of the famine in the Canadian House of Commons, but later, on February 5, 1934. The question is why not earlier and why did the MLAs of Ukrainian origin not seem to have done so at all in their respective legislatures? It has not been possible to find the answer to this question in any of the archival materials inspected in Canada. However,

---

[10] "Do spravy nashoï uchasty v politychnim zhyttiu Kanady," *Ukraïns'ki visty*, November 22, 1933, 4.

[11] Michael Luchkovich, United Farmers of Alberta/Co-operative Commonwealth Federation, Vegreville, Alberta. Manitoba: Nicolas Volodymir Bachynsky, Liberal-Progressive, Fisher; and Nicholas Apoluner Hryhorczuk, Liberal-Progressive, Ethelbert. Alberta: Peter Miskew, United Farmers/Liberal, Victoria electoral district; and Isidore Gorecky, United Farmers, Whitford. Both Luchkovich and Miskew attended and spoke at a protest against the famine in Willingdon, Alberta, on November 5, 1933.

[12] Cipko, *Starving Ukraine*, 42.

[13] "Great Privations in Russia Told to Legislature," *Winnipeg Free Press*, May 4, 1933, 3.

there is possibly a clue in an archival collection beyond North America. The one in question is the Ukrainian Bureau in London collection in the Polish Institute and Sikorski Museum (London, UK).[14] The Ukrainian Bureau in London operated between 1931 and 1940 was directed by Vladimir Kysilewsky, who was born in western Ukraine and emigrated was to Canada in 1925. I was aware of the Vladimir Julian Kaye (Kysilewsky) Fonds in Library and Archives Canada, and that collection was consulted for my book, but I was unaware of the Ukrainian Bureau in London collection until recently. That collection in London includes correspondence between Kysilewsky and Luchkovich. In a letter to Luchkovich dated May 30, 1932, Kysilewsky drew attention to the Imperial Economic Conference that would convene in Ottawa in July and suggested that a deputation of Ukrainian representations be assembled that could put the case of Ukrainians in Europe before the British delegation. In a second letter, dated May 31, 1932, Kysilewsky enclosed copies of letters that he had sent to Canadian MLAs of Ukrainian descent. He noted that the British press was becoming more interested in Soviet Ukraine, where the population was experiencing hunger while the Soviet regime prepared to continue its practice of "dumping" grain in the world market. He thought that Canada likewise would become more interested in Ukraine. In his reply to Kysilewsky, Luchkovich intimated that he had spoken to Albertan MLAs Isidore Goresky and Peter Miskew and both were of the opinion, which he seemed to share, that since it was an economic conference and not a political one, and centred only on matters of trade, it might in fact do the Ukrainian cause harm rather than good by raising it at the wrong moment and place. Perhaps the reticence of the MPs and MLAs during 1933 could be explained to some degree by the cautious attitude expressed in Luchkovich's reply. In any event, Kysilewsky did not accept the view that the Ukrainian question would be out of place in the conference in Ottawa. In a subsequent letter to Luchkovich, he clarified that he had in mind Soviet as well as Polish Ukraine. He argued that Soviet Ukraine was relevant to the conference because Soviet wheat was being dumped in Europe in competition with Canadian grain, and this was only possible because "Ukrainian peasants have had their own supplies taken from them and are in a terrible starving condition."[15]

There were journalists from Canada in the Soviet Union during the time of the famine and some materials pertaining to two of them, Carleton J. Ketchum and Pierre van Paassen, have been kept in Library and Archives

---

[14] See the article on this subject by Roman Wysocki elsewhere in this volume.

[15] Polish Institute Archives and Sikorski Museum, Kolekcja 433, no. 136. Letters from Vladimir Kysilewsky to Michael Luchkowich, May 30 and 31, 1932, and reply from Michael Luchkovich to Vladimir Kysilewsky, July 5, 1932.

Canada. In a book about Ukraine and its diaspora during 1932–33, Mykhailo Marunchak wrote about the Western correspondents who helped the cause of Soviet propaganda through their writings about the famine. Two names mentioned were Walter Duranty of the *New York Times* and Pierre van Paassen of the *Toronto Star*.[16] Thus, it is worthwhile briefly discussing van Paassen in the light of archival findings and an analysis of his journalistic and other writings.

In August 1933, the Netherlands-born van Paassen, a *Toronto Star* journalist, was assigned to investigate reports of the famine, specifically in Ukraine. By that time, van Paassen had already established an international reputation as a correspondent. In 1933 the *Toronto Star* was banned in Nazi Germany for a series of articles he authored that were critical of the regime and its treatment of Jews and other groups. The *Star* apparently became the first "American" newspaper to be banned by Hitler.[17] Apart from the *Star*, van Paassen's reports about Ukraine were also published in other Canadian newspapers.

An unfinished biography of van Paassen forms part of the Hugh Whitney Morrison Fonds at Library and Archives Canada. In that unpublished biography, Morrison, who worked as a reporter for the *Toronto Star*, wrote that van Paassen had "reported in generally favourable terms on the energy and spirit of the Russian people" but that "his observations on the famine in the Ukraine got him in temporary trouble." The famine had apparently "disturbed him but did not wholly dissuade him of the laudable aims of the Bolshevik revolution." Van Paassen acknowledged the famine's existence, but had been able to see "a quite different face of Communist behavior."[18]

One of van Paassen's articles was titled "Ukraine Practically Won over to Soviet Farm Plan," datelined "Krumenchuk,"[19] Ukraine, and published on September 13, 1933. The opening sentences read as follows:

> What happened in this district [Kremenchuk] last winter and this spring would form a sorrowful and indeed a harrowing recital. I need only say that there was nothing to eat when everyone will understand that the adjective "harrowing" is no exaggeration. Witnesses from all walks of life, some of whom had also lived through the horrors of the 1921 famine on

---

[16] Mykhailo H. Marunchak, *Natsiia v borot'bi za svoie isnuvannia: 1932 i 1933 v Ukraïni i diiaspori* (Winnipeg: UVAN, 1985), 30.

[17] Michael Hanlon, "A Dangerous Job—Since the Boer War a Century Ago, The Star Has Sent Correspondents to Cover Foreign Skirmishes, Big and Small," *Toronto Star*, November 11, 2002, C01.

[18] Cipko, *Starving Ukraine*, 87–88.

[19] Likely the town of Kremenchuk (Rus.: Kremenchug), a rural district centre in Poltava oblast.

> the Volga, tell me that the privations in the Ukraine did not quite reach the privations of that earlier catastrophe when ten millions died of hunger and typhus. But all admit, with more or less frankness, that the situation from January up to a few weeks ago was calamitous. Strange to say there is little evidence of it left today. I am therefore unable, happily, to give an eye-witness account of a famine.[20]

The Ukrainian Bureau in London may have read that article before it invited van Paassen to visit and tell more about his Ukraine experiences. Louise Gibson of the bureau wrote to him at an address in Paris on November 2, 1933, and asked that he let them know when he would visit Great Britain. The bureau, she said, would welcome the opportunity to discuss the situation in the Soviet Union with him.

In his reply, which, together with Gibson's letter, is among the papers of the Ukrainian Bureau's collection in London, van Paassen wrote about his reporting on the famine. He began his letter, dated November 8, 1933, by stating to Gibson that her name was not unfamiliar to him, as he thought he had seen it in "the course of that long drawn-out controversy in the Manchester Guardian." Van Paassen claimed that he was anxious to launch a "sort of pro-Ukrainian campaign" in the newspapers he served in Canada and the United States, but he could not do anything if his hands were "not upheld." These newspapers included the *Montreal Eagle*, *St. Catherines Journal*, *Toronto Star*, and *Winnipeg Free Press* in Canada and the *Atlanta Constitution*, *Boston Globe*, *Milwaukee Journal*, *Philadelphia Record*, and *St. Louis Post-Dispatch* in the United States—which had a total readership, he estimated, of some four million. The editors, Van Paassen said, were "eagerly scanning" the letters received, and the playing up of a particular subject depended on "whether they receive commendatory letters or even controversial letters from readers." He then turned specifically to the *Toronto Star*, to which Gibson had made reference in her letter. That "very influential" newspaper, he said ("in strict confidence"), was "out and out pro-Soviet," which was "its right" and "Yet it printed ten articles on the situation in the Ukraine by me." Van Paassen described that situation thus in his letter:

> I said without beating about the bush that the situation was gruesome, that in one village Kr[e]menchuk nearly all the inhabitants had died last winter and this spring from hunger and that I personally saw six corpses—in the company of a man named Gregory Lazorson, my guide, an old Bolshevik, a member of the party, but one whose enthusiasm of the years

[20] "Ukraine Practically Won over to Soviet Farm Plan," *Toronto Daily Star*, September 13, 1933, 1 and 4.

before has dwindled into nothing and which has even changed into a blind rage against the Stalinian regime. He was my guide for three consecutive years on trips through the Ukraine. Please do not use his name in any connection, for that would mean disaster to him and his family. I saw pitiful examples of what happens when Soviet citizens talk too much to foreigners. Only think of the staff of the Hotel Novo-Moskowskaya, all in the GPU jail this year. Many of them were friends of mine and lovely people. I remarked upon their absence this year and was given no explanation, until I met the wife of one of the officials, whom I had accompanied the year before to the Ballet, now begging in the streets with a dying baby on her arms. She told me the story which I later verified.

Van Paassen then drew attention to his last article in which he predicted a bad winter in Ukraine, and proceeded to remark on a lack of public commentary by the Ukrainian community:

> Now when such articles are followed by complete silence on the part of Ukrainians living in Toronto, for instance, there is no response whatever, for the Communists also keep mum. The less said, the less will be known, is their motto. When I was recently in Jugo-Slavia and criticized events there, the Croats in Toronto rallied to my support and the remainder of the series of articles on that country leaped into prominence. I am not concerned about my own standing or fame or anything of the kind. But for the sake of their own cause, why do not the Ukrainians come forward and write letters stating their own view of the matter, complementing my findings with reports they have in their possession from relatives etc? The Toronto Star very reluctantly printed those articles on hunger and destitution in Ukrainia. The paper was in the midst of a campaign urging the establishment of normal trade relations between Canada and the USSR, so naturally, my stories were not encouraging, to say the least. One gentleman in Toronto, I noticed, came to my assistance, a Greek-Orthodox priest, and I was grateful to him. But that was all. The Star had other writers print columns upon columns of material from the Moscow Daily News showing the immense progress being made in the social, scientific and industrial field in the USSR. This was like a counterblast to my stuff. And since there was no support for my allegations, the others won out. I was discredited. Yet I was on the spot and saw while they were merely repeating, parrot-like, what they had seen in official soviet [*sic*] publications.

Van Paassen then called on the Ukrainian community to say something in response to the articles he wrote that would appear in future issues of the *Toronto Star*:

> The last articles have not as yet appeared in Toronto and if you have any acquaintances there among the Ukrainian people, or anywhere in Ontario, for the Star circulates largely through the whole province, please urge

them to say something in letters to the editor. Not for my sake, but for the sake of their own kinsmen at home. There lies the whole secret of getting your point of view into print in America. Editors fight shy of independent reporters, men who go out free-lancing, but they do print letters from their readers, no matter what they say. One paper I forgot to mention which also ran the Ukrainian series is the Syracuse Herald, of Syracuse NY.

The foreign correspondent and columnist went on to say that he was about to travel, and he also distanced himself from Édouard Herriot, the former prime minister of France, who had recently returned from a visit to Ukraine and dismissed any talk of a famine:

> I am writing you in haste. I am on the point of travelling to Constantinople, but will be back here in Paris in a few weeks' time[.] I have lived here for the last ten years, first as correspondent of the N.Y. World, and then as travelling correspondent for the papers above named, which are served through a syndicate. My views on Russian affairs have had some repercussions in the USA and Canada (I say this without boasting), because formerly I was completely in sympathy with the Soviets, but not since I went deeper, that is to say since I finally found the key to unlock the minds of the people, and they began to talk more freely. I was in Ukrainia simultaneously with M. Herriot. No wonder he is enthusiastic. The man was surrounded by a wall of hangers-on.

Van Paassen closed his letter by informing that he had been invited to deliver talks in the United States on the very subject of Ukraine:

> After my return from Turkey I leave for America (in January), where I have been invited to lecture — 172 engagements from New York to San Francisco — on this very subject of Ukrainia. I hope to say a good word for the martyred peasants of that country in the course of my lectures, but anticipate much opposition form the other side, which will most likely call me a traitor and a turn-coat and all that. C'est la vie!
>
> Some day I would so much like to talk with you. Can we not arrange a meeting?[21]

The November 8, 1933 letter is revealing for many reasons. Among other things, van Paassen referred to a debate in the *Manchester Guardian*, in which the Ukrainian Bureau took part. The exchange was likely the one that occurred during September 1933, which followed announcements

[21] Polish Institute Archives and Sikorski Museum, Kolekcja 433, no. 327. Letter from Louise Gibson to Pierre van Paassen, on November 2, 1933, and reply from Pierre van Paassen to Louise Gibson, November 8, 1933.

about a new bountiful harvest in the Soviet Union.[22] Although he had been assigned to investigate the reports about famine in Ukraine, van Paassen did not take part in the debate. However, he did write about it in his column, the "World's Window," in the *Syracuse Herald*. Letters had come from people in the Soviet Union describing famine in the USSR but the American educator, writer, and YMCA leader Sherwood Eddy found no such conditions, said van Paassen. He then went on to intimate that,

> I noticed Dr. Eddy in Moscow two months ago with a large party of tourists. They were staying at the Hotel Novo-Moskovskaya and the party even had a private dining room at its disposal, where important Soviet people also came to lecture and harangue them on various phases of life in this country.

Van Paassen noted Eddy's comment in the *Manchester Guardian* that under his leadership his tourist group had split into four sections and embarked on an unsuccessful search for the famine. But where, van Paassen asked, did they go? He then provided the following commentary about the famine—a narration that contained much that was reminiscent of his letter to the Ukrainian Bureau:

> Everybody in Russia admits that conditions in the Ukraine and the North Caucasus were bad last winter. Many will go further and say that they were terrible. Right in the same Novo-Moskovskaya Hotel a man came to me, an old revolutionary, a trusted servant of the Soviet government, who told me, when my room had been bolted and locked (he insisted on this, not I) that millions had died of starvation last winter and this spring. I could give his name here, but that would be the end of him, so I won't. That was the first intimation I had that something was seriously amiss in the Ukraine. Not an enemy, not a foreign spy or an ex-Bourgeois, a real Bolshevik, came to tell me. "But," said I to him, "if it is that bad and you people are yourselves aware of it, why don't you protest against the policy of collectivization which has produced this disaster." And he replied: "Eighty per cent of the members of the Communist party are disgusted with Stalin's policy, but they dare not open their mouths. The first who protests is thrown out, his food-card is taken away and he is left to starve. For a

[22] The exchanges in the *Manchester Guardian* comprised: Louise Gibson, "Famine in Soviet Ukraine," September 2, 1933, 15; Joan Beauchamp "The Harvest in Russia — Managed Tours", September 7, 1933 18; Sherwood Eddy, "The Harvest in Russia — This Year and Last," September 8, 1933, 18; Louise Gibson, "The Harvest in Russia — Cases of Starvation" and Z.H. Coates, "The Soviet Press," September 13, 1933, 18; Joan Beauchamp, "M. Herriot's Statement," G.H. Barber, "Improved Conditions," Wilfred Wellock, "An Impression of Kiev," and John Jagger, "A Visit to the Ukraine," September 18, 1933, 16; and J. Baker White, "The Harvest in Russia — Some Famine Areas," September 25, 1933, 16.

> group to protest leads to the fate of the Trotskyists, exile and prison. What are we to do? The situation is terrible. I am keeping my relatives alive in the North Caucasus with packages of food. I have seen corpses lying in the streets of the village of Kr[e]menchuk. All the inhabitants of that place have either died of hunger or they have fled.

Van Paassen closed by saying that what he wrote would be dismissed as anti-Soviet propaganda. But he was "merely giving what I was told by a man who still occupies an important position in Moscow."[23]

The November 8, 1933 letter is important, too, because it raises the question of language facility. As van Paassen was about to set off on his investigative trip to Ukraine, the *Edmonton Bulletin*, one of the newspapers that published his articles on the USSR, announced that because the journalist spoke "both German and Yiddish, he will be able to converse freely with the natives."[24] Many years later, Frank Rounds, in reviewing van Paassen's book *Visions Rise and Change* (about religion in the USSR) in the *New York Tribune*, wrote that the latter was vague about the dates of his visits to the Soviet Union and was "silent on the subject of his knowledge of the Russian language." Because the book was replete with interviews and short conversations with local people, "this question of the language barrier," Round wrote, "inevitably arises in a reviewer's mind."[25] The letter to the Ukrainian Bureau in London does not offer any clues about van Paassen's knowledge of Russian or Ukrainian, but it does indicate that he was accompanied in his trips to Ukraine by a guide. In his *Syracuse Herald* column van Paassen includes an interview with "a real Bolshevik." In this instance, it was the latter who saw the "corpses lying in the streets of the village of Kr[e]menchuk." In the letter to Louise Gibson, van Paassen wrote that he "personally saw six corpses" in that place ("in the company of…an old Bolshevik").[26]

To what degree did the *Toronto Star* constrain van Paassen? While the newspaper may have been opposed to the R.B. Bennett-led Conservative government's policies on trade with the Soviet Union and ran upbeat stories about progress in that vast state, it did publish, as front page news, Gareth Jones's declaration (via H.R. Knickerbocker) that the Soviet Union was in the grip of a catastrophic famine. By coincidence, a story by van Paassen, on Nazism and the Ku Klux Klan, was also featured on the same page. The Knickerbocker piece in late March 1933 emphasized that Jones considered that the famine was proving to be as disastrous as the one of 1921, that the Welsh journalist spoke

[23] Pierre van Paassen, "World's Window," *Syracuse Herald*, September 23, 1933, 4.

[24] "Pierre Van Paassen to Send Hot Cables," *Edmonton Bulletin*, August 14, 1933, 1.

[25] "Religion's Role in Old and New Russia," *New York Tribune*, October 9, 1955, E6.

[26] Polish Institute Archives and Sikorski Museum, Kolekcja 433, no. 327. Letter from Pierre van Paassen to Louise Gibson, November 8, 1933.

Russian fluently, and that the death of millions from starvation, "murderous terror and the beginning of serious unemployment" was imminent.[27]

Of interest, too, is van Paassen's statement that only one Ukrainian, an Orthodox priest, supported him, presumably in the letters to the editor pages of the *Toronto Star*. He undoubtedly had in mind the letter by Rev. Dmytro Leschisin published under the heading of "Ukrainian Independence" in the *Toronto Star* on September 28, 1933. This letter was written in reaction to another published in the *Toronto Star* by Ivan N. Petelka, which, in Rev. Leschisin's words, glorified the Soviet regime in Ukraine. Among many other things, Leschisin wrote that "to what extent the Ukrainian workers and peasants are satisfied with the Soviets I have only to refer the readers to the recent reports from the Ukraine by such able correspondents as Mr. P. van Paassen, an article by Dr. E. Am[m]ende, general secretary of the [C]ongress of European National[ities] and a host of others." Yet while Rev. Leschisin mentioned van Paassen in this manner, a representative of another Ukrainian church, Rev. L.A. Standret of the Ukrainian Presbyterian Church, was not impressed by the journalist's writings. He was one of the speakers at a rally held at St. George's Hall (Albert Street) in Oshawa, Ontario, on October 13, 1933, that protested "the fiendish plan of the Soviet government to exterminate the greater part of the Ukrainian population by means of famine and massed deportation to Siberia." According to the *Oshawa Daily Times*, "Rev. Mr. Standret called out some correspondents, like Pierre Van [Paassen], who had writte[n] fallacious accounts of the events in the Soviet Union." "One cannot expect," the newspaper quoted him as saying, "to hear facts from a correspondent who is feasted by the Moscow foreign commissar and who was sen[t] over to justify the stand his paper had taken in regard to the Soviet regime."[28]

Later, in November 1936, van Paassen returned to the subject of the famine in an article published in the *Atlanta Constitution* titled "Fascists in Russia." The article concerned the recent arrests in the Soviet Union of persons, "probably most of them...German...concerned with Ukrainian nationalism," charged with producing fascist propaganda. On the famine, van Paassen wrote: "In 1932, when there was a big famine, we were kept cooling our heels in Moscow and told that everything was lovely." He said that the *Manchester Guardian*, in "referring to that famine recently, remarked that it was the 'greatest mystification of history.'" According to van Paassen, the *Manchester Guardian* asserted that no one outside the

---

[27] H.R. Knickerbocker, "Russia is in Grip of Great Famine Millions Dying," *Toronto Star*, March 29, 1933, 1.

[28] "Ukrainian Mass Meeting Makes Strong Protest," *Oshawa Daily Times*, October 16, 1933, reprinted in *Svoboda* (Jersey City, NJ), November 6, 1933, 4.

USSR had heard about it. "This is not quite true," van Paassen told his readers, "Many of us knew definitely that there was a famine in Ukraine but we had no definite data to go by."[29]

The article in the *Manchester Guardian* that van Paassen likely had in mind was the editorial titled "Repression in Russia" (prompted by the Sergei Kirov murder and aftermath events) that was published on December 27, 1934. That editorial opened as follows: "The evolution of contemporary Russia proceeds in a darkness far deeper than the darkness of the Third Realm. For a long time the Russian Dictatorship was able to conceal from the eyes of the world what was incomparably the biggest economic calamity that had afflicted Europe for more than a decade—the Russian famine of 1932. No such feat of concealment has ever been accomplished by any other European country in modern times."[30] By the time van Paassen's piece appeared in the *Atlanta Constitution* in 1936, the *Manchester Guardian* also had reviewed William Henry Chamberlin's book *Russia's Iron Age*. The reviewer, F.A.V., said in part: "Although this famine [that afflicted southern regions of the USSR in 1932–33] was the greatest economic disaster in Europe since the Russian famine of 1921...the very fact that the famine occurred at all was, and still is, denied by the Russian authorities and by so-called friends of Russia." The reviewer added that Chamberlin showed "that hunger was an instrument of policy in the hands of the Russian Government, and that the famine could have been relieved if that Government had wished to relieve it, instead of using hunger to force the peasantry into the 'collective farms.'"[31]

Earlier in 1936, the pro-Communist U.S. newspaper, the *Daily Worker*, ran a Federated Press report by van Paassen about famine, not in the Soviet Union but in neighbouring Poland. That country, he wrote, had "3,000,000 registered unemployed plus three million Jews who are systematically being starved to death, plus a famine of unprecedented severity." In Polissia, where, he claimed, famines were an annual occurrence, starvation was currently being accompanied by an "epidemic of typhus and infantile paralysis."[32]

Standret's views about van Paassen were probably shared by a November 1936 letter-writer in the *Winnipeg Tribune* who signed off as "Ukrainian Subscriber." The latter was reacting to an article about Ukraine by Harrison Brown ("People are Happy in Glorious Ukraine"). The letter-writer said that Brown reminded him of van Paassen, "whose despatches were

[29] Pierre van Paassen, "The World's Window: Fascists in Russia," *Atlanta Constitution*, November 30, 1936, 4.

[30] "Repression in Russia," *Manchester Guardian*, December 27, 1934, 8.

[31] F.A.V., "A Balanced Book on Russia," *Manchester Guardian*, February 19, 1935, 5.

[32] "Polish Millions Starve While Nations Arms," *Daily Worker*, April 30, 1936, 31.

filling the columns of Canadian and American newspapers not so long ago." Where now was that journalist, "Ukrainian Subscriber" asked? "Passed into oblivion," the latter remarked, and "of the newspapers of this country probably only the columns of the Toronto Star are still open to him. It appears that Mr. V[a]n Paassen's misrepresentations of facts have caused most self-respecting newspapers to close their pages to his misinformations."[33]

As it happened, the *Toronto Star* also parted ways with van Paassen. In an article titled "Best of Us Sometimes Get Fooled," Jim Foster of the *Toronto Star* included as an example van Paassen and his writings about the Spanish Civil War. "Compelling, authentic dispatches from Spain's civil war," he wrote, were filed by van Paassen but "then came an acute embarrassment." The *Catholic Register*, in September 1936, according to Foster, "charged that van Paassen was no longer in Spain but in Paris, inventing news or rewriting others' reports." Following an investigation, van Paassen was dismissed.[34]

There does not seem to be any evidence that a lecture tour that focused on Ukraine ever occurred, and van Paassen does not say very much about the famine in the several books that he wrote in subsequent years. But the letter that he penned to the Ukrainian Bureau in London is an example of what one may discover in little-known archival collections.

Archives

Instytut Polski i Muzeum im. gen. Sikorskiego 1933, Biuro Ukraińskie w Londynie 1931–1939, London, U.K.

Bibliography

Ammende, Ewald. *Human Life in Russia*. London: G. Allen & Unwin, [1936].

Canada Year Book 1933. Ottawa: King's Printer, 1933.

Cipko, Serge. *Starving Ukraine: The Holodomor and Canada's Response*. Regina: University of Regina Press, 2017.

"Do spravy nashoï uchasty v politychnim zhtyttiu Kanady." *Ukraïns'ki visty*, November 22, 1933, 4.

"Famine over Russia." *Winnipeg Free Press*, July 26, 1934, 13.

Foster, Jim. "Best of Us Sometimes Get Fooled." *Toronto Star*, April 1, 1992, A1.

"Great Privations in Russia Told to Legislature." *Winnipeg Free Press*, May 4, 1933, 3.

[33] "People Not Happy in 'Glorious Ukraine,'" *Winnipeg Tribune*, November 30, 1936, 9.

[34] Jim Foster, "Best of Us Sometimes Get Fooled," *Toronto Star*, April 1, 1992, A1.

Hanlon, Michael. "A Dangerous Job—Since the Boer War a Century Ago, The Star Has Sent Correspondents to Cover Foreign Skirmishes, Big and Small." *Toronto Star*, November 11, 2002, C01.

"House Urges Canada Send Surplus Grain to Starving Russians." *Leader-Post* (Regina), March 16, 1933, 1, 14.

Knickerbocker, H. R. "Russia is in Grip of Great Famine Millions Dying," and Pierre van Paassen, "Naziism [sic] Embodies Ideals Followed by Ku Klux Klan." *Toronto Star*, March 29, 1933, 1.

"Letter from Russia Paints Sad Picture." *Calgary Herald*, April 28, 1933, 24.

Marunchak, Mykhailo H. *Natsiia v borot'bi za svoie isnuvannia: 1932 i 1933 v Ukraïni i diiaspori*. Winnipeg: UVAN, 1985.

"People Not Happy in 'Glorious Ukraine.'" *Winnipeg Tribune*, November 30, 1936, 9.

"Pierre Van Paassen to Send Hot Cables." *Edmonton Bulletin*, August 14, 1933, 1.

"Repression in Russia." *Manchester Guardian*, December 27, 1934, 8.

Rounds, Frank. "Religion's Role in Old and New Russia." *New York Tribune*, October 9, 1955, E6.

"Soviets Refused Wheat." *Edmonton Journal*, March 20, 1933, 4.

"Ukrainian Independence." *Toronto Star*, September 28, 1933, 6.

"Ukrainian Mass Meeting Makes Strong Protest." *Oshawa Daily Times*, October 16, 1933, reprinted in *Svoboda* (Jersey City, NJ), November 6, 1933, 4.

van Paassen, Pierre. "The World's Window: Fascists in Russia," *Atlanta Constitution*, November 30, 1936, 4.

— "Polish Millions Starve While Nations Arms," *Daily Worker*, April 30, 1936, 3.

— "World's Window," *Syracuse Herald*, September 23, 1933, 4.

— "Ukraine Practically Won over to Soviet Farm Plan," *Toronto Daily Star*, September 13, 1933, 1 and 4.

"Willingdon Citizens Protest gainst Bolshevik Regime in Ukraine," *Vegreville Observer*, November 15, 1933, 5.

'A Trial of Strength against the Restive Peasantry': What the Germans Knew about the Great Famine in the USSR and How They Perceived It

Paolo Fonzi

Publications of non-Soviet documents on the Great Famine are a genre in its own right with a fairly long tradition. The first round of published collections of documents, including British, Italian, and German diplomatic reports, appeared before 1990.[1] Foreign diplomatic reports were particularly precious for historians at that time, as most Soviet sources were still inaccessible to scholars. In the 1990s, after the collapse of the USSR and the archival revolution that followed, further publications of this kind made Polish, Romanian, and Vatican records known to the wider public.[2] The vitality of the genre, even after the opening of the Soviet archives and the possibility of accessing "direct evidence," attests to the persisting relevance of these kinds of documents. There are several reasons for this. As I will show in the following pages, foreign documents often contain important insights, not despite but because of their particular, non-Soviet perspective. Being neither perpetrators nor victims of the violence they saw unfolding before their eyes, foreign observers provided in many instances a more neutral view of those events. Moreover, because they were often based on first-hand information gained via alternative sources to official channels, they provide a view from below that is often absent in other kinds of sources.

The importance of foreign sources is not limited to providing information about the famine itself. In fact, they allow a different topic to be

---

[1] M. Carynnyk et al., eds., *The Foreign Office and the Famine: British Documents on Ukraine and the Great Famine of 1932–1933* (Vestal, N.Y.: Limestone Press, 1988); D. Zlepko, *Der ukrainische Hunger-Holocaust* (Sonnenbühl: Verlag Helmut Wild, 1988); A. Graziosi, *Lettere da Kharkov: La carestia in Ucraina e nel Caucaso del Nord nei rapporti dei diplomatici italiani, 1932–33* (Turin: Einaudi, 1991), 30. Some of the documents that figure in this collection first appeared in French translation. See A. Graziosi, "Lettres de Kharkov : La famine en Ukraine et dans le Caucase du Nord à travers les rapports des diplomates italiens, 1932–1934," *Cahiers du Monde Russe* 30, nos. 1–2 (1989): 5–106.

[2] J. J. Bruski, *Hołodomor 1932–1933: Wielki Głód na Ukrainie w dokumentach polskiej dyplomacji i wywiadu* (Warsaw, 2008); A. D. McVay and L. Luciuk, *The Holy See and the Holodomor: Documents from the Vatican Secret Archives on the Great Famine of 1932–1933 in Soviet Ukraine* (Toronto: The Kashtan Press, 2011); A. Basciani, "From Collectivization to the Great Famine: Eyewitness Statements on the Holodomor by Refugees from the Ukrainian SSR, 1930–1933," *Holodomor Studies*, no. 3 (2011): 1–27.

addressed, namely, how the Great Famine was perceived in other countries. Despite the increasing limitations placed on the freedom of movement of people, goods, and information in the 1930s, which amounted to a pronounced "de-globalization,"[3] the Great Soviet Famines of the 1930s were a transnational phenomenon, inasmuch as foreign states and the public opinion of other countries played a role in co-determining their course. Although foreign governments were in no position to influence Soviet internal affairs directly, even if they had wanted to—by 1932–33 most countries had improved their relations with the USSR and were unwilling to put them at risk by denouncing the famine—campaigns aimed at publicizing the starving of millions in the USSR were activated around the world.[4] Moreover, relief operations on behalf of specific national or religious groups in the famine areas were initiated by political or religious organizations.[5] Therefore, even if the Great Famine of the 1930s is a patent instance of "humanitarian non-intervention," it did unleash a series of actions and transformations in other countries that still await a study focused on comparison and entanglements (*histoire croisée*).[6] All these operations were, for obvious reasons, part and parcel of the tense and conflicted environment of the 1930s and were inspired by political, religious, or nationalistic agendas. They had an impact on the unfolding of the famine and the social conflict stemming from it within the Soviet Union, as foreign aid allowed many to survive the dire conditions of the famine while exposing the recipients to persecution by the Soviet authorities.

---

[3] J. Osterhammel and N. P. Petersson, *Globalization: A Short History* (Princeton: Princeton University Press, 2005), 99–106.

[4] On Ewald Ammende's activism, see S. Bamberger-Stemmann, *Der Europäische Nationa-litätenkongreß 1925 bis 1938: Nationale Minderheiten zwischen Lobbyistentum und Großmachtinteressen* (Marburg and Lahn: Verl. Herder-Inst., 2000); M. Housden, *On Their Own Behalf: Ewald Ammende, Europe's National Minorities and the Campaign for Cultural Autonomy, 1920–1936* (Amsterdam and New York: Rodopi, 2014); idem, "Ewald Ammende and the Organization of National Minorities in Inter-war Europe," *German History* 18, no. 4 (2000): 439–60. On Poland, see R. Wysocki and P. Redko, "Reactions to the Famine in Poland," *Harvard Ukrainian Studies* 30, nos. 1/4 (2008): 49–67.

[5] To date, only the history of the Mennonites has been the object of a wide number of scholarly studies. See C. Neufeldt, "Through the Fires of Hell: The Dekulakization and Collectivization of the Soviet Mennonite Community (1928–1933)," *The Journal of Mennonite Studies* 16 (1998): 9–32; idem, "Separating the Sheep from the Goats: The Role of Mennonites and Non-Mennonites in the Dekulakization of Khortitsa, Ukraine (1928–1930)," *The Mennonite Quarterly Review* 83, no. 2 (April 2009): 221–91; T. Martin, *The Russian Mennonite Encounter with the Soviet State, 1917–1955* (Waterloo, Ont.: Conrad Grebel University College, 2001), 31–39. For detailed discussion of the reports sent by the German agricultural attaché Otto Auhagen, see E. Warkentin, "The Mennonites before Moscow: The Notes of Dr. Otto Auhagen," *The Journal of Mennonite Studies* 26 (2008): 199–218.

[6] M. Werner and B. Zimmermann, *Beyond Comparison: Histoire Croisée and the Challenge of Reflexivity, History and Theory* 45, no. 1 (February 2006): 30–50.

Unraveling this dense web of people and organizations spanning many countries can greatly improve our understanding of the history of the interwar period. Moreover, it can enhance our understanding of how the perception of the famine and, more generally, of Stalin's modernization affected the cultural and political history of other countries.[7] In short, pursuing these avenues will foster the trans-nationalization of Holodomor studies by adding new lines of inquiry to the issues traditionally at the center of their interest.

The aim of this paper is to provide some insights into German sources related to the Great Famine. While a number of publications on this subject already exist,[8] in my opinion German records have not received the attention they deserve from scholars. Inasmuch as the amount and quality of information reaching Germany during the famine was hardly matched by any other major power of the time, there is still a need for a more detailed study. Apart from a few exceptions,[9] students of Germany have shown little interest in the Great Famine, leading a German scholar to speak of a "denied intertwining."[10] Even though Eastern European history is an established academic field in Germany, its contribution to the understanding of the relations between Germany and the Soviet Union has largely focused on

---

[7] In this regard studies have been written on how the question of how Stalin's modernization was perceived by social scientists in the USA is investigated in David C. Engerman, Modernization from the Other Shore. American Intellectuals and the Romance of Russian Development (Cambridge Mass., 2004), 144–243.

[8] A selection of German diplomatic reports on the famine was published in Zlepko, *Der ukrainische Hunger-Holocaust* (the same documents were published in Ukrainian translation by A. I. Kudriachenko, *Holodomor v Ukraïni 1932–1933 rokiv za dokumentamy politychnoho arkhivu Ministerstva zakordonnykh sprav Federatyvnoï Respubliky Nimechchyna* (Kyiv: Natsionalnyi instytut stratehichnykh doslidzhen, 2008). For an article based on German diplomatic reports, see O. Wenzel, "Holodomor: Stalins Genozid in der Ukraine 1932–1933," in *Berichten der Deutschen Botschaft Moskau und des Generalkonsulats Charkow, Zeitschrift des Forschungsverbundes SED-Staat*, no. 27 (2010): 5–24.

[9] B. Falk's dissertation on Soviet cities during the famine is one such exception (Barbara Falk, Sowjetische Städte in der Hungersnot 1932/33. Staatliche Ernährungspolitik und städtisches Alltagslebene [Köln, 2005]). Stephan Merl, who has written several studies on the history of the peasantry in the USSR, has published a few articles on the famine. See S. Merl, "Entfachte Stalin die Hungersnot von 1932–1933 zur Auslöschung des ukrainischen Nationalismus? Anmerkungen zu neueren westlichen Veröffentlichungen über die 'ukrainische' Hungersnot," *Jahrbücher für Geschichte Osteuropas* 37, no. 4 (1989): 569–90; idem, "War die Hungersnot von 1932–1933 eine Folge der Zwangskollektivierung der Landwirtschaft oder wurde sie bewußt im Rahmen der Nationalitätenpolitik herbeigeführt?" in G. Hausmann and A. Kappeler, eds., *Ukraine: Gegenwart und Geschichte eines neuen Staates* (Baden-Baden, 1993), 145–66.

[10] G. Hausmann, *Verweigerte Verflechtung: Die ukrainische Hungersnot 1932–1933 in der deutschsprachigen Historiographie*, in Alfred Eisfeld, Guido Hausmann, and Dietmar Neutatz, eds., *Hungersnöte in Russland und in der Sowjetunion 1891–1947: Regionale, ethnische und konfessionelle Aspekte* (Essen, 2017).

World War II, the occupation, and the violent policies aimed at the extermination of Jews and other groups. Until the publication of the first comprehensive study on the Great Famine in 1986, namely, Robert Conquest's *The Harvest of Sorrow*, this lack of interest was not a peculiarity of Germany but rather common among non-Ukrainian historians. Following this seminal study and, even more importantly, the fall of the Soviet Union, the historiography on the Great Famine has grown markedly, becoming an established field in international scholarship. The persistent gap in German scholarship is therefore surprising in light of this relatively recent trend. The reasons for this are manifold, one of them being the fact that German historiography after 1990 has been strongly involved in the elaboration of a new national identity. As Stefan Berger has pointed out,[11] in post-1990 Germany there has been a clear trend toward the re-nationalization of the historical perspective, stemming from the need to redefine national identity in the light of reunification. Since the Nazi regime had exploited, in its anti-Bolshevik campaigns, the famine theme both before and during the occupation of the USSR, this subject did not seem to fit into German post-reunification identity searching and thus remained relatively understudied.[12]

In the following pages I will focus mainly on German diplomatic records. But I will also touch upon sources of a different nature that, as already mentioned, played a key role in transmitting information to Germans and in shaping their perception of the famine. This contribution will address three issues:

First, the amount and quality of information that Germans had about the famine. In this context, I will look at what I call "the politics of information" about the famine conducted by the German Foreign Office (*Auswärtiges Amt*) between 1932 and 1933.

Second, the contents of diplomatic dispatches, how the German diplomatic corps made sense of the famine, and the patterns of perception that shaped their explanations.

And third, the impact that knowledge of the famine had on Germans and its possible long-lasting consequences.

---

[11] S. Berger, *The Search for Normality: National Identity and Historical Consciousness in Germany since 1800* (Oxford, 2002); idem, "A Return to the National Paradigm? National History Writing in Germany, Italy, France, and Britain from 1945 to the Present," *The Journal of Modern History* 77, no. 3 (September 2005): 629–78.

[12] G. Hausmann and T. Penter, "Instrumentalisiert, verdrängt, ignoriert: Der Holodomor im Bewusstsein der Deutschen," *Osteuropa* 70," nos. 3–4 (2020): 193–214.

I

The extent to which information from the Soviet Union reached the outside world in 1932–33 was very limited, as the Bolshevik authorities had a firm grip on the border-crossing movement of information and people, and on the circulation of foreigners within the country. In this context of general scarcity, Germany was comparatively one of the countries with the largest information network in the Soviet Union, and its public opinion had, on average, a better knowledge of Soviet internal affairs than most other countries. It is hardly surprising, therefore, that German news reports were often used as sources by the foreign press.[13]

The main reason for this lies in diplomacy. Germany was the first major power to establish relations with the Bolshevik state, with the 1922 Treaty of Rapallo. Throughout the 1920s and the early 1930s the two outsiders of the Versailles international system leveraged this special relationship, which was kept alive even in the immediate aftermath of the Nazi seizure of power, in order to raise their status in the international system. This explains why at the time of the famine Germany had seven diplomatic missions in the Soviet Union, three of which were located in Ukraine (Odesa, Kharkiv, Kyiv, Moscow, Leningrad, Novosibirsk, and Tbilisi), whereas most European states had few if any representatives outside the Soviet capital.[14] German sources, however, were also varied, comprising a wide array of informants apart from diplomats—namely, ordinary citizens who maintained contacts both with institutions in Berlin and with German diplomatic proxies. In the Soviet Union there were sizeable groups of Germans, both German citizens (*Reichsdeutsche*) and so-called persons of German descent (*Deutschstämmige*)—German colonists who for the most part had settled in the Russian Empire in the eighteenth century. There are hardly any reliable statistics on the number of ethnic Germans living in the Soviet Union. Whereas the 1926 Soviet census registered 1.24 million ethnic Germans, the German Embassy in Moscow calculated that in 1934 this number had shrunk by one-quarter.[15] As for German citizens, in 1930 there were 11,327 in the whole USSR, 5,554 of whom were in Ukraine,[16] where many

13 W. Müller, "Russlandberichterstattung und Rapallopolitik: Deutsch-sowjetische Bezie-hungen, 1924–1933, im Spiegel der deutschen Presse" (PhD dissertation, Saarbrücken, 1983); C. Mick, *Sowjetische Propaganda, Fünfjahresplan und deutsche Russlandpolitik 1928–1932* (Stuttgart: Steiner Verlag, 1995).

14 P. Fonzi, "Non-Soviet Perspectives on the Great Famine: A Comparative Analysis of British, Italian, Polish, and German Sources," *Nationalities Papers* 48 (May 2020): 444–59.

15 "The German Peasants in the Soviet Union," September 23, 1934, Politiches Archiv Auswärtiges Amt (hereafter PA AA R83854).

16 German Embassy in Moscow, "Die Reichsdeutschen in der Union der SSR," December 18, 1930, PA AA R60202.

Germans had settled in the countryside as farmers. Although many re-emigrated under the pressure of dekulakization and collectivization, in 1935 the number of German citizens in the USSR still stood at 6,000, 2,500 of whom were in Ukraine.[17]

German colonists were a valuable source of regular reporting to the consulate about what was occurring in the countryside. This allowed the German diplomatic corps, unlike those of other countries, to gather precise information on developments outside cities. For instance, at the peak of the Ukrainian famine in 1933 the German Consul in Kyiv reported that approximately 50 German peasants visited the consulate every day to ask for assistance, and on these visits crucial knowledge was obtained about the terrible conditions the peasants were facing. Moreover, the numerous Germans who sought refuge in Germany after 1929, either as German citizens or because they had managed somehow to leave the Soviet Union, were systematically interrogated by the Gestapo upon their arrival. The material thus collected was kept in the files of several institutions; it was used for intelligence purposes but also in anti-Bolshevik publications.[18] At the height of the famine ethnic Germans sent a considerable number of letters (so-called *Hungerbriefe*) to Germany, a large number of which were addressed to religious institutions. In addition, ethnic Germans who emigrated to Germany upon their arrival forwarded letters received from their relatives in Ukraine to the Foreign Office. Also, many addressees living in Germany wrote to the German Foreign Office on behalf of their relatives, forwarding the letters they had received.

Apart from information *strictu sensu*, it must be noted that unlike other countries which regarded Soviet internal affairs as something distant and

[17] German Embassy in Moscow, "Die Reichsdeutschen in der Union der SSR," Stand von November 1935, PA AA R83854. See also W. Mensing, "Sowjetbürger werden oder packen—Stalin und der Exodus der Russlanddeutschen im Spiegel der Akten des Auswärtigen Amts,".*Jahrbuch für historische Kommunismusforschung* (2015) 217–35. According to a report by the Geheime Staatspolizeiamt in 1939, 5,000 were still living in the Soviet Union. See W. Mensing, "Die Vernehmungsprotokolle der '"Rußlandrückkehrer'eine unausgeschöpfte Fundgrube im Politischen Archiv des Auswärtigen Amts,." *Jahrbuch für Forschungen zur geschichte der Arbeiterbewegung* (III) (2003): 154–70.

[18] K. Krupinski, *Rückkehrer berichten über die Sowjetunion* (Berlin: Stollberg, 1942). Krupinski's book is based on 3,400 Gestapo interrogations. Information on the gathering of these data is in BA R6/147. A second report, which was based on the same source but not published, described the conditions of the ethnic Germans in the Soviet Union. See PA AA R127509. Since many interrogations contained information on the famine of 1932–33, they were excerpted by the Ministry of the Interior and collected separately, in order to be used in anti-Communist propaganda. See BAB R58/3493. According to Wilhelm Mensing, who has systematically analyzed a large number of the original interrogations, the famine of 1932–33 does not figure prominently in the accounts of the German returnees (Mensing, "Sowjetbürger werden oder packen," 217–35.

pertaining exclusively to the field of foreign affairs, the presence of significant numbers of ethnic Germans in the USSR compelled Germany to perceive the famine as a problem directly affecting national politics. The feeling of a shared bond with Soviet ethnic Germans, who were part of the "imperial legacy" in German national history, had been strongly revived during World War I and was heightened by several crises, such as the one in 1929 when 15,000 Mennonites targeted by the first wave of dekulakization gathered on the outskirts of Moscow pleading to be allowed to leave for Germany. Their request was granted after lengthy negotiations.[19]

Interestingly, Germany was one of the few countries where an organized relief operation with the participation of government representatives was in place. Started already during the Mennonite crisis, the operation was systematized in 1933, when several religious, charitable, and pro-ethnic German organizations, led by a strong initiative from the Mennonite community, set up an umbrella relief committee known as "Brüder in Not" (Brethren in Need).[20] It took charge of collecting funds from state agencies and private donors, and organized the delivery of food packages and money transfers to starving Germans via the Soviet foreign-currency Torgsin shops. In order to identify the Germans in need of relief, a central card file of all "hunger letters," complete with senders' addresses, was kept at the German Foreign Office. The operation ran, with increasing difficulties owing to Soviet bans on the delivery of packages, from 1933 to the German attack on the USSR in 1941. In 1933 a British diplomat, struck by the efficiency of Reich institutions in caring for their ethnic kin, wrote that "the ethnic network that most functions to convey information, aid requests, and aid is the German one."[21]

Another source of information was the large community of émigrés from the former Russian Empire living in Germany. These asylum seekers arrived in Germany in several waves between 1919 and 1923. Estimates

---

[19] The literature on these events is fairly extensive. See, e.g., Mick, *Sowjetische Propaganda*, 356–70; J. Oltmer, "Volksdeutsche fremder Staatsangehörigkeit: Grenzen privilegierter Migration in der Weimarer Republik," in *Handbuch Staat und Migration in Deutschland seit dem 17. Jahrhundert*, ed. J. Oltmer (Oldenburg: De Gruyter, 2015), 483–502.

[20] The committee set up a "working committee" comprised of representatives of all participating organizations., including the Nationalsozialistische Volkswohlfahrt (National Socialist People's Welfare), the Evangelical Charity Organizations, the German Caritasverband, Mennonites, and several organizations for the preservation of relations with ethnic Germans, e.g., the Volksbund für das Deutschtum im Ausland and the Deutscher Schutzbund für das Grenz- und Auslandsdeutschtum (founded in 1919), one representative of the Foreign Office, and one from the German Red Cross. See Deutsches Rotes Kreuz, Betr. Hilfswerk "Brüder in Not" für notleidende deutsche Volksgenosse im Auslande, June 21, 1933, PA AA R127510.

[21] Sir Esmond Ovey, British Ambassador in Moscow, to Simon, March 13, 1933, in Carynnyk et al., *Foreign Office and the Famine*, doc. no. 24.

differ widely, but their numbers in 1925 might have been as high as 500,000, thus constituting a large multi-ethnic community. Though it greatly decreased in the following years, the number of refugees from Russia still amounted to 100,000 in 1933, with a strong concentration in Berlin, which became home to a large number of cultural organizations, newspapers, magazines, and publishing houses—testifying to the intellectual vitality of this community.[22]

Finally, Germany had a long tradition of cultural contacts with the Russian Empire and the Soviet Union, which found expression in a significant number of scholarly institutions dealing with the history and politics of Eastern Europe and the Russian Empire. Whereas the field of *Osteuropäische Geschichte* (Eastern European History) began to establish itself increasingly in the German academic landscape in the early twentieth century, after World War I and notably after 1933, so-called *Ostforschung* (East-related research) came to be the dominant approach in the study of Eastern Europe. Unlike the former, *Ostforschung* was marked by a politicization aimed at revising the Versailles order.[23]

Among the actors that had access to information from the Soviet Union, the most relevant was the diplomatic corps. The *Auswärtiges Amt* controlled the most relevant source of information, namely, diplomatic proxies. Many of the reports on the famine that appeared in the press at the time reproduced parts of diplomatic dispatches sent by German consuls. This points to the fact that, far from establishing a monopoly on the information flow from the Soviet Union, the German Foreign Office worked as a sort of floodgate or, in other words, a key node of an information network stretching from the Soviet Union to Germany. Therefore, the question arises as to the ways by which and the reasons why information collected in the Soviet Union that reached the Foreign Office in Berlin was handed over by the diplomatic corps to other state and non-state actors.

The behavior of the Foreign Office in relation to the dissemination of news about the famine was conditioned by the state of Soviet-German relations at the time. In 1933 diplomats of the Foreign Office still regarded the Rapallo policy—namely, the maintenance of good relations with the Soviet Union—as a key element of German foreign policy.[24] Rapallo had

---

22 K. Schlögel, ed., *Berlin: "'Stepmother' among Russian Cities,"* in *Russian-German Special Relations in the Twentieth Century: A Closed Chapter?* (Oxford and New York: Berg, 2006), 43–76.

23 E. Mühle, "Ostforschung: Beobachtungen zu Aufstieg und Niedergang eines geschichtswissenschaftlichen Paradigmas," *Zeitschrift für Ostmitteleuropa-Forschung* 46, no. 3 (1997): 317–50; Markus Krzoska, "Ostforschung," in Ingo Haar and Michael Fahlbusch, eds., *Handbuch der völkischen Wissenschaften* (Munich, 2008), 452–63.

24 S. Slutsch and C. Tischler, eds., *Deutschland und die Sowjetunion 1933–1941* (Munich: OldenbourgVerlag, 2013).

helped Germany out of the isolation in the years immediately following World War I, and had allowed it to regain international prestige. In addition, friendship with the Soviet Union was seen as a means to deflect the possibility of a military invasion from Poland through an alliance with its major enemy, a policy that in internal documents was called *Rückendeckung* (rear cover policy). As Hitler's rise to power threatened to strain German-Polish relations, German diplomats were convinced that it was even more important to keep in place the Soviet "rear cover" against Poland while preparing for war.

Hitler's rise to power between 1932 and 1933 was feared as a major threat to the Rapallo policy, because the National Socialist Party had a clear anti-Bolshevik agenda and had openly demonstrated its program of eastward expansion. Yet, in the first years of his rule Hitler sought to posture as a moderate politician in foreign affairs. Thus, he gave the Foreign Office staff ample room for maneuvering, and stressed continuity instead of rupture in foreign relations. His decision in May 1933 to ratify the German-Soviet Neutrality and Nonaggression Pact, which had been renewed in 1931, seemed to point in this direction. Nevertheless, moderation soon gave way to a more aggressive course. From 1934 Hitler imposed a stronger grip on German foreign policy, thereby irreparably souring relations with the Soviet Union. However, this course of events was not foreseeable in 1933, and therefore German diplomats, especially those belonging to the so-called "Russia Desk" of the Foreign Office, initially believed in the possibility of keeping the Rapallo policy alive.[25]

This attitude on the part of German diplomats affected their "politics of information" about the famine in two ways. First, they tried as much as possible to curb the spread of news about the famine in German society. Instead, anti-Bolshevik propaganda conducted by several non-state institutions was used as evidence of the famine in order to campaign against Communism. For example, in the summer of 1933 a "protest meeting against the starving of the Germans in Russia" was called by several organizations, among them the NSDAP. These campaigns placed Germany's relations with the Soviet Union under great strain, inasmuch as the Bolsheviks never admitted to the existence of a famine in their country. The Foreign Office thus had to silence this kind of mobilization and avoid giving the impression that it was in any way involved in it.

This "prudence" in disseminating information had its limitations. Like all other Reich institutions, the Foreign Office conducted or supported a

---

[25] For detailed discussion of the Russia Desk during the Weimar years, see I. Sütterlin, *Die "Russische Abteilung" des Auswärtigen Amtes in der Weimarer Republik* (Berlin: Duncker & Humblot, 1994).

policy directed against the Communist Party or the remnants of the communist movement after it was suppressed by the Nazi government. To this end, it was important to release news about the real conditions in what the German communists idealized as the "Soviet paradise," such as news about the famine. Moreover, the German Foreign Office had no monopoly on information. Therefore, it had to take into account the fact that German public opinion was informed through other channels of the catastrophe unfolding in the Soviet Union. For instance, in 1933 the Brethren in Need committee launched a "public collection" (*Reichssammlung*) to raise money to be sent to ethnic Germans. Booklets featuring pictures of the famine were circulated among German citizens to motivate them to contribute to the collection. It was impossible, therefore, to completely deny the existence of a famine in the Soviet Union.

As a result of these two contrasting aims, namely, keeping Rapallo alive and releasing news of the famine, the Foreign Office adopted a cautious strategy of disseminating information, sometimes even distributing copies of consular dispatches to a select number of institutions and non-state actors (for example, churches), in order to prevent any uncontrolled leaking of news. For example, copies of consular dispatches were sent to the Evangelical Church, which were then used to raise money for the relief operation for ethnic Germans. However, these documents circulated as "reports from a reliable informant," their true provenance—local consular proxies—being thus concealed.

This information policy was successful to some extent. The German government was not particularly outspoken in denouncing the famine publicly. Several episodes connected to the leaking of news about the famine strained German-Soviet relations, but they never led to a diplomatic crisis.

The second aspect of the information policy relates rather to the content of the dispatches themselves. There is evidence that German consuls were advised by the Foreign Office to moderate their reporting on the famine, in order to avoid the impression that the Soviet Union was about to collapse under the weight of unrest in the countryside.[26] The Russia experts at the Foreign Office did this because they sought to convince the new National Socialist rulers in Berlin that the Bolsheviks would remain in power in the years to come and that it was therefore advisable to come to terms with them.

The same attitude also informed the way that diplomatic dispatches dealt with nationality issues. In his early writings Alfred Rosenberg,

---

[26] See, e.g., the exchange of letters between Andor Hencke and Fritz von Twardowski, the latter reprimanding the consul because of his too-pessimistic reporting about the famine, in PA AA R27438.

director of the *Außenpolitisches Amt* (Foreign Policy Office) of the NSDAP, had argued that the party should support the cause of the nationalities oppressed by Great Russian chauvinism. In the wake of the Nazi seizure of power, rumors that Rosenberg was working on plans to detach Ukraine from the Soviet Union began to circulate in Germany and abroad. Indeed, in the first months of Nazi rule Russian émigré circles approached the new rulers (contacts with the NSDAP had been established as early as the 1920s) with a view to forging an alliance with the National Socialists.[27] Therefore, the Russia experts at the Foreign Office tried in their reporting to show that the nationalities factor did not play a significant role in the outbreak and geographical distribution of the famine.

In sum, the Foreign Office's attitude was to try to influence the perception of the famine by the National Socialist rulers and German public opinion in order to ensure continuity in foreign policy. This was done by dampening to some extent the impact of the news about the famine on German society.

II

As Andrea Graziosi points out in an article that provides new insights into the interpretation of the Soviet famines,[28] in order to understand the multilayered nature of these events one must distinguish between two different but closely interrelated aspects. On one level, in the 1930s there was the general phenomenon of food insecurity and famines deriving from the particular way in which collectivization and industrialization were conducted. On a second level, there were specific processes, such as the dramatic acceleration of the famine in 1931–33, which affected specific areas to an unprecedented degree and the methods that the state used to tackle this crisis. The way that diplomats reported the famine attests to their clear understanding of this multilayeredness.

As for the first level, within the Foreign Office the possible outcome of Soviet industrialization had been broadly discussed since its inception. This is due to the fact that this institution was particularly concerned with the consequences of forced industrialization for the stability of the Soviet economic and political systems and thus with the impact of these internal developments on diplomatic and economic relations with the Reich. It is no

---

[27] H.-A. Jacobsen, *Nationalsozialistische Außenpolitik 1933–1938* (Frankfurt am Main: Alfred Metzner Verlag, 1968), 85 and ff; S. Kuusisto, *Alfred Rosenberg in der nationalsozialistischen Aussenpolitik, 1933–1939* (Helsinki: Suomen Historiallinen Seura, 1984), 108–19.

[28] A. Graziosi, "The Soviet 1931–1933 Famines and the Ukrainian Holodomor: Is a New Interpretation Possible, and What Would Its Consequences Be?" *Harvard Ukrainian Studies* 27, nos. 1/4 (2004–2005): 97–115.

surprise, then, that German reports show an acute awareness early on that Soviet industrialization was heading toward a major crisis. A telling instance of this is a meeting of state officials and representatives of the German conglomerate IG Farben in February 1930, during which the latter presented data and observations collected during travels in the Soviet Union. Already at this early stage they believed that collectivization would result in a strong decrease in crop yields the following spring. In their opinion, Ukraine and the south of Russia would suffer relatively less than other regions because of their particularly fertile soil. This expectation, as we know, would prove wrong. In other respects, however, the forecast by IG Farben's representatives was quite interesting and accurate. They believed that collectivization would "disrupt agriculture" and lead to a major political crisis. This crisis could be manifested in two forms: either a military coup or a famine that might lead to a popular uprising. However, in discussing this second outcome, most of those present came to the conclusion that the "central power *had* the possibility of handling the situation to the effect that only local famines and local starving *would* take place," thereby lowering the chances of a general uprising and preventing a collapse of the Bolshevik system.[29]

A common trait of the memoranda written after the inception of collectivization is the clear understanding that a major component of this process was the human factor, namely, the peasants' attitude to collectivization. German diplomats understood early on that behind the economic problems there was a struggle between the state and the peasants, the latter resisting collectivization, which they perceived as a new form of serfdom. (The expression *Leibeigenschaft* is used in many German reports.) In their dispatches German diplomats provided different views on this struggle. Some pointed to intentional resistance by the peasants in response to the war waged by the Bolshevik system against them. In some cases, diplomats showed sympathy to the peasant world, especially when talking about German peasants.

In most reports, however, they demonstrated understanding of the necessities that had forced the Soviet authorities to start modernization from above, although they criticized the specific way that the Bolshevik leadership had steered the process of industrialization. Many reports emphasized that peasant resistance was the product of their backward mentality, their natural indolence, or their deeply entrenched, individualistic mindset—attitudes that prevented them from adapting fully

[29] Meeting at the Reich Ministry of Economics on the state of the Soviet economy. Employees of the German firm IG Farben report impressions gained during their stay in the USSR, February 21, 1930, PA AA R29276.

to the modernization of Soviet agriculture. The German consul in Kharkiv, for example, wrote in December 1933 that the cause of the famine was that the regime "had decided to carry out collectivization too early, too fast and with insufficient means, thus throwing agriculture into great disarray and, because of other factors, overlooking the fact that according to Stalin himself 'cadres decide everything' and disregarding the issue of whether twenty-two million Ukrainian peasants would follow him or show understanding of and collaborate with the new collective economic form [which went against] their deep-rooted individualistic ideology."[30]

Although they despised Bolshevism as a political system, German diplomats shared the Bolsheviks' view of the peasant world as a place of backwardness and somehow even admired the Soviet Communists' ability to modernize the country in such a short span of time. In this they were not alone. During the Great Depression the Soviet Union was admired throughout the world, as it was the only country that was spared an economic slump and, moreover, was even able to make a huge leap toward industrialization.[31] Even in Fascist Italy, Soviet industrialization was regarded with keen interest by groups of intellectuals, especially those who had traveled to the Soviet Union.[32] Yet, German diplomats did not consider peasants as a mere relic of the past, an attitude that mirrored widespread pro-agrarian currents in Germany at the time.[33] On the whole, German reports do not display a complete aversion toward the countryside but rather a sort of idealization of the good peasant, embodied by the German colonist with his percipient attitude to modernization, as opposed to the huge mass of backward "Slavic" peasants. A passage from a report from Kharkiv clearly expresses this position: "Both from a theoretical and a practical point of view, socialized agriculture is surely justified as a necessary substitute for the small and unproductive economic units [...] But the small crop yields and big losses show that the people of the countryside in their majority have not yet taken the predestined way [*vorgezeichneten Weg*], but that, instead, they remain outside and have not yet undergone the change of mindset necessary to achieve better results."[34]

A thread running through all the dispatches is the attempt by the diplomats to establish which causal factor was responsible for the famine. In

---

30 German Consulate in Kharkiv, "Jahresbericht. Die allgemeine Lage in der Ukraine," December 11, 1933, PA AA Moskau 348.

31 For a short overview, see M. Mazower, *Dark Continent: Europe's Twentieth Century* (London: Allen Lane–Penguin Books, 1998), 117–28.

32 See, e.g., P. L. Bassignana, *Fascisti nel paese dei Soviet* (Turin: Bollati Boringhieri, 2000).

33 K. Bergmann, *Agrarromantik und Grossstadtfeindschaft* (Meisenheim am Glan: Hain, 1970.

34 German Consulate in Kharkiv, "Die allgemeine Lage in der Ukraine," September 30, 1932, PA AA Moskau 348.

this respect, it is interesting to note that most diplomatic dispatches do not see any trade-off between an intentionalist and a structuralist explanation of the famine.[35] On the one hand, the famine was explained by German consuls as a complex series of socioeconomic processes stemming from the decision to conduct industrialization at breakneck speed. On the other, the idea was also widespread that the Soviet regime had exploited the famine as a means of crushing the peasants' resistance to collectivization. In a passage from his 1979 memoirs Andor Hencke, the German consul in Kyiv between 1933 and 1935, expressed the prevailing view among German diplomats about the famine with this incisive passage: "The Muscovite dictator certainly did not want a famine, if only for the fact that his way of thinking was too realistic to understate the danger for his state arising from it. The world knows that Stalin did not dread any risks in internal policy when, in his eyes, a substantial goal was at stake. However, he has never increased on purpose the difficulties already given in the way therein."[36]

A key figure in the history of the German perception of the Great Famine is Otto Schiller, Attaché for Agricultural Issues at the German Embassy in Moscow. A long-serving expert in Soviet affairs, Schiller had close contacts with the network of cultural associations known as *Ostforschung*, which eventually led to his posting in occupied Ukraine during the war as an agrarian expert of the *Wirtschaftsstab Ost*, in charge of devising the new agrarian system to be introduced after the re-privatization of collective property.[37] During the 1932–33 famine Schiller reported constantly to Berlin, providing information about the development of Soviet agriculture collected during long trips he made in his own car. A typical route of one of his road trips stretched for 4,200 km, covering the following localities: Homel (Gomyel), Chernihiv, Kyiv, Bila Tserkva, Kamianka, Zinovievsk (now Kropyvnytsky), Bobrynets, Kryvyi Rih, Vysokopillia, Nikopol, Dnipropetrovsk (now Dnipro), Zaporizhzhia, Melitopol, Molochansk, Berdiansk, Mariupol, the Donbas, Kharkiv, Kursk, Orel, Tula, Roslavl, and Moscow.[38] Travelling entirely on his own, Schiller was able to

---

[35] For a similar attitude in Polish reporting, see J. J. Bruski, "In Search of New Sources: Polish Diplomatic and Intelligence Reports on the Holodomor," in *Holodomor and Gorta Mór. Histories, Memories and Representations of Famine in Ukraine and Ireland*, ed. Christian Noack, Lindsay Janssen, and Vincent Comerford (London: Anthem Press, 2012), 215–30.

[36] A. Hencke, *Erinnerungen als Deutscher Konsul in Kiew in den Jahren 1933–1936* (Munich: Ukrainische Freie Universität, 1979), 29.

[37] C. Gerlach, "Die deutsche Agrarreform und die Bevölkerungspolitik in den besetzten sowjetischen Gebieten," in C. Gerlach and C. Dieckmann, *Besatzung und Bündnis: Deutsche Herrschaftsstrategien in Ost/ und Südosteuropa* (Berlin and Göttingen: Verlag der Buchläden, 1995), 9–60.

[38] O. Schiller, "Die Ernteaussichten in einigen Gebieten Zentralrußlands," July 17, 1933, PA AA R94408.

circumvent the control of the Soviet authorities and to interview peasants unimpeded, gaining first-hand information not available in the press. This led to several conflicts with the Soviet authorities, even though Schiller tried his utmost to avoid them. After he was threatened with expulsion several times, he had to leave the USSR in 1936.

In his memoranda Schiller portrayed in great detail the dire conditions of the peasants and the depopulation of entire regions. Far from providing mere descriptions, his memoranda contain systematic inquiries into key issues, such as the intensity of the famine in different regions, from which he tried to make sense of mortality variations. In his opinion, a major reason for the discrepancies in mortality rates was the different cultural and economic development achieved by the population of different areas and between different ethnic groups within the same area. In Ukraine, for example, Schiller noted that German colonists were affected less severely by the famine than Ukrainian and Russian peasants.[39] He explained this by pointing out the exceptional performance of independent German peasants in previous years, which had resulted in a larger accumulation of capital stock. When the famine broke out, German colonists were able to sell these assets, acquiring the means to survive the food crisis for a longer period of time than others.

One major factor that Schiller recognized behind such variations was a political one. For example, he pointed to the differences in mortality rates between Ukraine and the North Caucasus. The latter, according to his estimates, was affected more severely than Ukraine. In his view, one of the causes of this variation in the geographical distribution of the starving was what he termed the "political use of the famine," that is, an intentional strategy of food denial to break down resistance. The regions that had suffered more were those where an uncompromising anti-Soviet attitude was present, as, for example, in the Cossack regions of the North Caucasus. There, the decrease in agricultural output and large-scale deportations of the population had resulted in a reduced workforce and completely disrupted agriculture.

Schiller also spoke of the "political use of the famine" in explaining how the Soviet authorities overcame the crisis of 1932–33. In the summer of 1933, in an effort to assess the crop prospects for the following harvest, which he expected to be higher than in the previous year, he concluded: "The crop in the S[oviet] U[nion], however, like everywhere, is dependent not only on weather but also on the work of people. It cannot be denied that this year people employed in agriculture are working much more than last

39 The idea that the German colonists had achieved an outstanding level of economic and social development was quite common in German writings about the USSR.

year. This fact is particularly surprising considering that the food supply of the people this year is considerably worse and that the hunger catastrophe has negatively impacted not only the attitude of the people for work but also their physical ability."[40]

The reason for this change was the introduction of the general "labor service duty," a form of forced labor. However, even more important was the use of grain distribution by the state to a selected number of regions as political leverage. Schiller observed that in the winter of 1932–33, when the famine had reached its peak, the state had begun distributing both food and seedstocks. The distribution of aid followed a clear political strategy, aimed at forcing people to work in the fields.

The correlation between nationality issues and famine is a recurring topic in many of the diplomatic reports sent to Berlin from the USSR. Most diplomats clearly saw the *turnaround in the Kremlin's nationalities policy* that had taken place in those years, a policy that had also increasingly targeted Germans and was regarded with great concern in diplomatic circles. German dispatches also show a clear awareness that a "national interpretation," to use Terry Martin's apposite expression, had taken hold within the Bolshevik leadership, namely, the idea that separatist tendencies in Ukraine stood behind the procurement crisis.[41] Yet, they believed that targeting nationalism for the failure of crop collection was a means of crushing opposition to Moscow rather than a goal in and of itself. Just as any expression of discontent was labeled as Trotskyism, so too in Ukraine any demand for support of the Ukrainian language or culture was considered a deviation from the party line and a weakening of the center's control over the peripheries.[42]

Another passage from Hencke's memoirs helps synthesize the predominant view among German diplomats at that time: "Hatred of the Muscovite lords pervaded the people. Here my impression was that outrage against the Bolshevik order, with its far-reaching impact on the life of each individual, was much stronger than the feeling of national oppression. Moscow was fully aware of the several causes of this tension. By emphasizing the Ukrainian issue under the aspect of high treason, the Kremlin endeavored to distract from the burning problems of economic hardship."[43] In a memorandum of 1933 Schiller treated this issue

[40] O. Schiller, "Die Ernteaussichten in einigen Gebieten Zentralrußlands," July 17, 1933, PA AA R94408.

[41] T. Martin, *The Affirmative Action Empire: Nations and Nationalism in the Soviet Union, 1923–1939* (Ithaca, N.Y.: Cornell University Press, 2001), 273–308.

[42] See, e. g., General Consulate Kharkov, "Politischer Jahresbericht," December 6, 1935, PA AA Moskau 348.

[43] Hencke, *Erinnerungen als Deutscher Konsul*, 31.

particularly systematically. He noted that there was a widespread idea among the peasants that the state's handling of the famine was swayed by Great-Russian chauvinism. However, he dismissed this hypothesis, pointing to the fact that in Ukraine no preference was accorded to Russian peasants. Instead, for economic reasons the mortality rate showed a clear cleavage in favor of German colonists, as we have seen, and disadvantaged both Ukrainian and Russian peasants. Schiller concluded: "The suffering of the German peasants has been caused by the Soviet agricultural policy. This, however, is directed against the peasantry of the S[oviet] U[nion] as a whole, with no regard for national differences as far as these are not linked with social and economic differences.[44]

As for nationalism within Ukraine, most German diplomats stressed that nationalist feelings in the republic were rather a product of the famine and discontent with the Soviet regime. In their view, opposition to Bolshevism was more important than purely nationalist goals, such as the struggle for independence or for unification with Western Ukraine, then under Polish rule. Several reasons account for this view. First, as I stated earlier, the Foreign Office sought to counter Rosenberg's policy toward the non-Russian nationalities in the Soviet Union. Moreover, there was a widespread idea that Moscow's grip on the other republics through the party structure did not allow the development of any nationalist movement. Another reason lies in the prevalence of a "master nation" bias, which saw in the Ukrainian national peasant identity a second-class nationalism, as opposed to what they perceived as a higher degree of national consciousness among Germans and, in particular, German colonists.

III

As already mentioned, the famine became the subject of Nazi propaganda only after 1935, when the regime unleashed a fierce anti-Bolshevik campaign.[45] During the wartime occupation of Ukraine collaborationist newspapers, such as *Nova Ukraina*, dealt extensively for the first time with the famine of 1932–33 in Ukraine, providing the very first estimates of deaths. In 1942 the first scientific investigation of the famine was conducted by Stepan Sosnovyj, an agrarian expert from Kharkiv, and partly

---

[44] O. Schiller, "Die Auswirkung der bolschewistischen Wirtschaftspolitik auf den Umfang und die Verteilung der Hungersnot," July 15, 1933, PA AA R94408.

[45] See, e. g., Fritz Dittloff, "Die Hungerkatastrophe in der Sowjetunion im Frühjahr 1933 und ihre Gründe," in Alfred Laubenheimer, ed., *Und du siehst die Sowjets richtig: Berichte von deutschen und ausländischen "Spezialisten" aus der Sowjet-Union* (Berlin, 1935), 315–22.

published published in the occupation press.[46] Yet, looking at several publications of the time, one is tempted to say that the famine was never perceived as a discrete phenomenon, as a humanitarian catastrophe standing apart from all other concomitant phenomena, such as collectivization, dekulakization, and the ensuing purges; the perception of the latter probably overshadowing that of all other previous occurrences. The famine was regarded instead as part and parcel of a particular perception of Bolshevism as a dehumanizing and Asiatic process of barbarization. It is noteworthy in this respect that the authors of a propaganda booklet issued by the Eastern Division (*Ostabteilung*) of the *Aussenpolitisches Amt* merely allude to the famine in trying to account for the demographic changes that had occurred in Ukraine since the last available census.[47]

Knowledge of the famine, however, affected Germany in several ways. First, it dashed any remaining hopes that the Bolshevik power would evolve toward "normalization," an idea that had informed the choices of many members of the Foreign Office since the inception of industrialization.[48] The ruthlessness with which the Soviet power had dealt with the peasants' opposition to collectivization had prevented the collapse of the Bolshevik regime. Yet, many reports stressed that the use of force could not work forever and that in order to integrate the peasants fully into the Soviet system the state had to raise their living standard. As Schiller put it in one of his reports, even a moderate improvement in the food supply system in the catastrophic situation of 1933 could gain the peasants' goodwill. "Never has it been as easy as now," he concluded, "for whatever government to win over the Soviet population by few means."[49]

As mentioned at the beginning of this essay, the perception of the famine as a disruptive crisis of the Soviet state strengthened those currents within the German leadership, which viewed the souring of Soviet-German relations as an inevitable outcome of the National Socialists' rise to power. The perception of the famine cemented the idea among many Germans that the Soviet system was characterized by an unstable internal structure and that it was based on coercion to such an extent that any external strike

---

[46] Hausmann and Penter, "Instrumentalisiert, verdrängt, ignoriert," 208–10; T. Penter and D. Tytarenko, "Der Holodomor, die NS-Propaganda in der Ukraine und ihr schwieriges Erbe," Vierteljahrshefte für Zeitgeschichte 69, no. 4 (2021): 633–67.

[47] G. von Mende, *Die Völker des Ostraumes* (Berlin: Stollberg, ca. 1942), 24. A second publication on Ukraine does not mention the famine at all. See Die Bücherei des Ostraumes. Ukraine (Berlin: Stollberg 1942).

[48] Mick, *Sowjetische Propaganda*, 311.

[49] O. Schiller, "Die Ernteaussichten in einigen Gebieten Zentralrußlands," July 17, 1933, PA AA R94408.

might cause it to crumble in on itself—the very notion that in 1941 had nurtured the idea that the Soviet Union would immediately collapse upon the German invasion.[50] Although German diplomats tried their utmost to check this idea by stressing the solid foundation of the Soviet system, their very endeavors to counter this opinion support the fact that it was slowly taking root in the German leadership.

The famine also contributed to the shaping of particular perceptions, not only those related to the Soviet Union but more generally to a particular view of modernization that was to have lasting effects in the years to come. As Susanne Heim and Ulrike Schatz have argued, the ideas and experiences gathered in the Soviet Union during collectivization, dekulakization, and famine were seminal for many German experts, crystallizing the idea that "agrarian overpopulation" as a major obstacle to modernization had to be addressed by all possible means, including violent population transfers. Population experts, economists, and students of Eastern Europe who came to play a key role in the occupation of the Soviet Union after 1941 embraced the idea that Soviet modernization, though marred by the "uncivilized" "Russian" toughness with which it was conducted, was to be regarded as a model experience.[51] Writing on Soviet agricultural development in 1941, Otto Bräutigam, director of the Russia Desk of the Foreign Ministry Economic Department prior to 1936, remarked that this subject had aroused his interest because the Soviet Union had tackled an issue common to Eastern and Western Europe, namely, the modernization and reduction of overpopulation in the countryside. He noted, however, that the Bolsheviks had solved these problems with their own methods (which the Germans themselves were to adopt), that is, the extermination of millions of peasants, arguing that the experiment was worth analyzing because of its unprecedentedness.[52] Bräutigam's argument is a typical instance of foreign perception of the Soviet Union during the early 1930s, when it was regarded as a "developing country" where the authorities could experiment with ideas of social engineering.

Last but not least, the famine contributed enormously to the strengthening of the bond between the German Reich and Russian-Germans, which became a decisive factor in the Germans' wartime occupation policy in Eastern Europe.[53] This is especially true for the

---

[50] See the essays in *Das Rußlandbild im Dritten Reich*, ed. Hans-Erich Volkmann (Cologne: Böhlau, 1994).

[51] S. Heim and U. Schatz, *Berechnung und Beschwörung: Überbevölkerung—Kritik einer Debatte* (Berlin: Verlag der Buchläden Schwarze Risse, Rote Strasse, ca. 1999), 85–89.

[52] O. Bräutigam, *Die Agrarpolitik der Sowjetunion* (Berlin: Deutsche Informationsstelle, 1942).

[53] The pro-German or pro-National Socialist attitude of the Russian Germans is a very contested issue that has given rise to a strongly politicized discussion. A study by Meir

organization Brethren in Need, which operated until the German invasion of the Soviet Union, but with increasing difficulty. The USSR was not the only place where a strong connection with ethnic Germans was established prior to World War II. Throughout Eastern and South-Eastern Europe, the Reich set up centralized institutions to assist all Germans abroad. Yet, the famine created a particular bond, one that was based on extensive material assistance that reached approximately 36,000 families up to 1941.[54] It may be said that in the same years that Germany was turning eastwards—the expression used by Michael Burleigh[55] to denote the collective leaning of the German culture toward an imperial expansion in the East—ethnic Germans in the USSR were turning westwards, with Germany assuming the features of a "caring" power. The German Consul in Kyiv stressed as early as December 1933 the political gains earned by Germany for assisting the starving Germans. In a letter intercepted by the GPU he wrote:

> No other nation in the world gave proof of its ties with its compatriots living in Russia in such a planned manner and on such a wide scale, moreover, without directy involving itself (as Germans). In fact thousands of Germans were saved from the worst of the famines, and with thousands more a boundless trust for their old fatherland was born. A more effective demonstration against the anti-German campaign of lies and slander

---

Buchsweiler focuses on the question whether Ukrainian Germans were convinced National Socialists and acted as a fifth column in the Soviet Union. No reliable sources allow us to establish this aspect with certainty. However, the question seems to be ill-defined. For Germans living in the Soviet Union at the time, the existence of a staunch anti-Bolshevik regime in Germany became conflated with their strong orientation toward that country for other reasons. Germanness, National Socialism, and anti-communism can be separated only from today's point of view. During the war they strongly overlapped. What is more interesting is the fact that for many Russian-Germans the material assistance provided by Germany was a strong motivation for their fidelity to National Socialism. This is revealed by the results of a survey conducted by the Canadian Mennonite journal *Der Bote* in the interwar years, which show how the Mennonites felt committed to Germany for the relief efforts that had been provided in 1929. See M. Buchsweiler, *Ethnic Germans in the Ukraine towards World War II: A Case of Double Loyalty?* (Tel-Aviv: Diaspora Research Institute: Society for Jewish Historical Research, 1980), 92.

[54] "Bericht des Verbandes für Evangelische Auswandererfürsorge über das Evangelische Hilfswerk 'Brüder in Not' an den notleidenenden Reichs- und Volksdeutschen in der Sowjetunion 1929–1941, erstattet in der Mitgliederversammlung des Evangelischen Vereins für deutsche Ansiedler und Auswanderer von Else Schmidt," 3.12.1941, PA AA R127511. The "imperial" dimension of German politics in Europe during the interwar period is a much-discussed topic. For a fruitful approach stressing the importance and peculiarity of the self-consciousness of the Germans as a "'trans-cultural actor' or, to be more precise, at least a member of a trans-imperial nation," see E. R. Dickinson, "The German Empire: An Empire?" *History Workshop Journal* 66 (2008): 129–62.

[55] M. Burleigh, *Germany Turns Eastwards: A Study of Ostforschung in the Third Reich* (New York: Cambridge University Press, 1988).

unleashed by the Bolsheviks was not possible. In fact, a most widespread cultural propaganda campaign has been carried out which has also borne fruit with the Russian, Ukrainians, Poles and other nat[tional] minorities. The Soviet citizens of Slav origin living in our consular region look with envy at their brothers in misery, the Germans, whose poverty is not only the subject of resolutions and not only the subject of discussion in all possible forums, but who receive active aid from the donations flowing in from the fatherland. It is known to me that in numerous requests [for aid] received by the local Polish Consulate, the population of Polish descent continually points to the German example, with no results, however. In creating attitudes favorable for the Germans, it is obviously a very beneficial circumstance that regardless of the related accusations in the area of foreign policy, the available aid is offered exclusively under the German flag. Not only for humanitarian reasons and national ties, but also from the propaganda perspective, it would be highly desirable for the organization "Brethren in Need" to be able to continue its work also in the future for as long as it proves possible.[56]

Else Schmidt, who was in charge of running the relief operation until 1941, notes in her final report (1941) on the results achieved by Brethren in Need:

> In the last years, when the Soviet Union more and more sealed itself off hermetically from the outside world, when almost all letter exchanges with the Soviet Union came to a standstill, our deliveries were almost the only possibility of keeping the link with a part of the ethnic Germans and bringing them, besides material help, also the valuable spiritual message: "You have not been forgotten in your old homeland." Without doubt we have contributed to consolidating ideally the basic attitude of the ethnic German peasant in the Soviet Union against communism. Some German colonies that now have been freed by the German Wehrmacht have been included in our operation for years.[57]

It can also be said that the peculiarity of the famine was due to the fact that German public opinion recognized to an unprecedented extent the suffering of those whom they considered their "brothers of blood." In addition to the propaganda about the famine, the *Reichssammlung* of 1933, in support of the starving Germans, gave the population a concrete sense of

---

[56] D. Boyko, *Holodomor: The Great Famine in Ukraine, 1932–1933* (Warsaw: Institute of National Remembrance, Commission of the Prosecution of Crimes against the Polish Nation, 2009), d. 185, 499.

[57] "Bericht des Verbandes," 3.12.1941, PA AA R127511, AA R127511.

what was happening. This also established a bond that was to have important consequences in the following years.

Archives

Politiches Archiv Auswärtiges Amt (hereafter PA AA R83854).
PA AA R127511.
PA AA R60202.
PA AA R83854.
PA AA R127510
PA AA R94408.
PA AA Moskau 348.
PA AA R27438
Carynnyk et al., *Foreign Office and the Famine*, doc. no. 24.

Bibliography

Bamberger-Stemmann, S. *Der Europäische Nationalitätenkongreß 1925 bis 1938: Nationale Minderheiten zwischen Lobbyistentum und Großmachtinteressen*. Marburg and Lahn: Verl. Herder-Inst., 2000.

Basciani, A. "From Collectivization to the Great Famine: Eyewitness Statements on the Holodomor by Refugees from the Ukrainian SSR, 1930–1933." *Holodomor Studies*, no. 3 (2011): 1–27.

Bassignana, P. L. *Fascisti nel paese dei Soviet*. Turin: Bollati Boringhieri, 2000.

Berger, S. "A Return to the National Paradigm? National History Writing in Germany, Italy, France, and Britain from 1945 to the Present." *The Journal of Modern History* 77, no. 3 (September 2005): 629–78.

— *The Search for Normality: National Identity and Historical Consciousness in Germany since 1800*. Oxford: Berghahn Books, 2002.

Bergmann, K. *Agrarromantik und Grossstadtfeindschaft*. Meisenheim am Glan: Hain, 1970.

Boyko, D. *Holodomor: The Great Famine in Ukraine, 1932–1933*. Warsaw: Institute of National Remembrance, Commission of the Prosecution of Crimes against the Polish Nation, 2009.

Bräutigam, O. *Die Agrarpolitik der Sowjetunion*. Berlin: Deutsche Informationsstelle, 1942.

Bruski, J. J. "In Search of New Sources: Polish Diplomatic and Intelligence Reports on the Holodomor." In *Holodomor and Gorta Mór. Histories, Memories and Representations of Famine in Ukraine and Ireland*, edited by Christian Noack, Lindsay Janssen, and Vincent Comerford, 215–30. London: Anthem Press, 2012.

Bruski, J. J., ed. *Hołodomor 1932–1933: Wielki Głód na Ukrainie w dokumentach polskiej dyplomacji i wywiadu*. Warsaw: PISM, 2008.

Buchsweiler, M. *Ethnic Germans in the Ukraine towards World War II: A Case of Double Loyalty?* Tel-Aviv: Diaspora Research Institute: Society for Jewish Historical Research, 1980.

Burleigh, M. *Germany Turns Eastwards: A Study of Ostforschung in the Third Reich.* New York: Cambridge University Press, 1988.

Dickinson, E. R. "The German Empire: An Empire?" *History Workshop Journal* 66 (2008).

Dittloff, Fritz. "Die Hungerkatastrophe in der Sowjetunion im Frühjahr 1933 und ihre Gründe." In *Und du siehst die Sowjets richtig: Berichte von deutschen und ausländischen "Spezialisten" aus der Sowjet-Union,* edited by Alfred Laubenheimer, 315–22. Berlin: v. A. Laubenheimer, 1935.

Fonzi, P. "Non-Soviet Perspectives on the Great Famine: A Comparative Analysis of British, Italian, Polish, and German Sources." *Nationalities Papers* 48 (May 2020): 444–59.

Gerlach, C. "Die deutsche Agrarreform und die Bevölkerungspolitik in den besetzten sowjetischen Gebieten." In *Besatzung und Bündnis: Deutsche Herrschaftsstrategien in Ost/ und Südosteuropa,* edited by C. Gerlach and C. Dieckmann, 9–60. Berlin and Göttingen: Verlag der Buchläden, 1995.

Graziosi, A. "Lettres de Kharkov: La famine en Ukraine et dans le Caucase du Nord à travers les rapports des diplomates italiens, 1932–1934." *Cahiers du Monde Russe* 30, nos. 1–2 (1989): 5–106.

— *Lettere da Kharkov: La carestia in Ucraina e nel Caucaso del Nord nei rapporti dei diplomatici italiani, 1932–33.* Turin: Einaudi, 1991.

— "The Soviet 1931–1933 Famines and the Ukrainian Holodomor: Is a New Interpretation Possible, and What Would Its Consequences Be?" *Harvard Ukrainian Studies* 27, nos. 1/4 (2004–2005): 97–115.

Hausmann, G. "Verweigerte Verflechtung: Die ukrainische Hungersnot 1932–1933 in der deutschsprachigen Historiographie." In *Hungersnöte in Russland und in der Sowjetunion 1891–1947: Regionale, ethnische und konfessionelle Aspekte,* edited by Alfred Eisfeld, Guido Hausmann, and Dietmar Neutatz. Essen: Klartext, 2017.

Hausmann, G., and T. Penter. "Instrumentalisiert, verdrängt, ignoriert: Der Holodomor im Bewusstsein der Deutschen." *Osteuropa* 70, nos. 3–4 (2020): 193–214.

Heim, S., and U. Schat. *Berechnung und Beschwörung: Überbevölkerung—Kritik einer Debatte.* Berlin: Verlag der Buchläden Schwarze Risse, Rote Strasse, ca. 1999.

Hencke, A. *Erinnerungen als Deutscher Konsul in Kiew in den Jahren 1933–1936.* Munich: Ukrainische Freie Universität, 1979.

Housden, M. "Ewald Ammende and the Organization of National Minorities in Inter-war Europe." *German History* 18, no. 4 (2000): 439–60.

— *On Their Own Behalf: Ewald Ammende, Europe's National Minorities and the Campaign for Cultural Autonomy, 1920–1936*. Amsterdam and New York: Rodopi, 2014.

Jacobsen, H.-A. *Nationalsozialistische Außenpolitik 1933–1938*. Frankfurt am Main: Alfred Metzner Verlag, 1968.

Krupinski, K. *Rückkehrer berichten über die Sowjetunion*. Berlin: Stollberg, 1942.

Krzoska, Markus. "Ostforschung." In Ingo Haar and Michael Fahlbusch, eds. *Handbuch der völkischen Wissenschaften*, 452–63. Munich, 2008.

Kuusisto, S. *Alfred Rosenberg in der nationalsozialistischen Aussenpolitik, 1933–1939*. Helsinki: Suomen Historiallinen Seura, 1984.

Carynnyk, Marco, Lubomyr Y. Luciuk, and Bohdan S. Kordan. *The Foreign Office and the Famine: British Documents on Ukraine and the Great Famine of 1932–1933*. Vestal, N.Y.: Limestone Press, 1988.

Martin, T. *The Affirmative Action Empire: Nations and Nationalism in the Soviet Union, 1923–1939*. Ithaca, N.Y.: Cornell University Press, 2001.

— *The Russian Mennonite Encounter with the Soviet State, 1917–1955*. Waterloo, Ont.: Conrad Grebel University College, 2001.

Mazower, M. *Dark Continent: Europe's Twentieth Century*. London: Allen Lane–Penguin Books, 1998.

McVay, A. D., and L. Luciuk. *The Holy See and the Holodomor: Documents from the Vatican Secret Archives on the Great Famine of 1932–1933 in Soviet Ukraine*. Toronto: Kashtan Press, 2011.

Mensing, W. "Die Vernehmungsprotokolle der "Rußlandrückkehrer'eine unausgeschöpfte Fundgrube im Politischen Archiv des Auswärtigen Amts." *Jahrbuch für Forschungen zur geschichte der Arbeiterbewegung* (III) (2003): 154–70.

— "Sowjetbürger werden oder packen—Stalin und der Exodus der Russlanddeutschen im Spiegel der Akten des Auswärtigen Amts." *Jahrbuch für historische Kommunismusforschung* (2015): 217–35.

Merl, S. "War die Hungersnot von 1932–1933 eine Folge der Zwangskollektivierung der Landwirtschaft oder wurde sie bewußt im Rahmen der Nationalitätenpolitik herbeigeführt?" In *Ukraine: Gegenwart und Geschichte eines neuen Staates*, edited by Hausmann G. and Kappeler A., 145–66. Baden-Baden: Nomos, 1993.

— "Entfachte Stalin die Hungersnot von 1932–1933 zur Auslöschung des ukrainischen Nationalismus? Anmerkungen zu neueren westlichen Veröffentlichungen über die 'ukrainische' Hungersnot." *Jahrbücher für Geschichte Osteuropas* 37, no. 4 (1989): 569–90.

Mick, C. *Sowjetische Propaganda, Fünfjahresplan und deutsche Russlandpolitik 1928–1932*. Stuttgart: Steiner Verlag, 1995.

Mühle, E. "Ostforschung: Beobachtungen zu Aufstieg und Niedergang eines geschichts-wissenschaftlichen Paradigmas." *Zeitschrift für Ostmitteleuropa-Forschung* 46, no. 3 (1997): 317–50.

Müller, W. "Russlandberichterstattung und Rapallopolitik: Seutsch-sowjetische Beziehungen, 1924–1933, im Spiegel der deutschen Presse." PhD dissertation, Saarbrücken, 1983.

Neufeldt, C. "Separating the Sheep from the Goats: The Role of Mennonites and Non-Mennonites in the Dekulakization of Khortitsa, Ukraine (1928–1930)." *Mennonite Quarterly Review* 83, no. 2 (April 2009): 221–91;

— "Through the Fires of Hell: The Dekulakization and Collectivization of the Soviet Mennonite Community (1928–1933)." *Journal of Mennonite Studies* 16 (1998): 9–32.

Oltmer, J. "Volksdeutsche fremder Staatsangehörigkeit: Grenzen privilegierter Migration in der Weimarer Republik." In *Handbuch Staat und Migration in Deutschland seit dem 17. Jahrhundert*, edited by J. Oltmer, 483–502. Oldenburg: De Gruyter, 2015.

Osterhammel, J., and N.P. Petersson *Globalization: A Short History*. Princeton: Princeton University Press, 2005.

Schlögel, K., ed., Berlin: 'Stepmother' among Russian Cities." In *Russian-German Special Relations in the Twentieth Century: A Closed Chapter?*, 43–76. Oxford and New York: Berg, 2006.

Slutsch, S. and Tischler, C., eds. *Deutschland und die Sowjetunion 1933–1941*. Munich: OldenbourgVerlag, 2013.

Sütterlin, I. *Die "Russische Abteilung" des Auswärtigen Amtes in der Weimarer Republik*. Berlin: Duncker & Humblot, 1994.

Volkmann, Hans-Erich, ed., *Das Rußlandbild im Dritten Reich*. Cologne: Böhlau, 1994.

von Mende, G. *Die Völker des Ostraumes*. Berlin: Stollberg, ca. 1942.

Warkentin, E. "The Mennonites before Moscow: The Notes of Dr. Otto Auhagen." *Journal of Mennonite Studies* 26 (2008): 199–218.

Wenze, O. l., "Holodomor: Stalins Genozid in der Ukraine 1932–1933." In *Berichten der Deutschen Botschaft Moskau und des Generalkonsulats Charkow, Zeitschrift des Forschungsverbundes SED-Staat*, no. 27 (2010): 5–24.

Werner, M. and B. Zimmermann. *Beyond Comparison: Histoire Croisée and the Challenge of Reflexivity. History and Theory* 45, no. 1 (February 2006): 30–50.

Wysocki, R. and Redko, P. "Reactions to the Famine in Poland." *Harvard Ukrainian Studies* 30, nos. 1/4 (2008): 49–67.

Zlepko, D. *Der ukrainische Hunger-Holocaust*. Sonnenbühl: Verlag Helmut Wild, 1988.

— *Der ukrainische Hunger-Holocaust.* Translated by A. I. Kudriachenko. In *Holodomor v Ukraïni 1932–1933 rokiv za dokumentamy politychnoho arkhivu Ministerstva zakordonnykh sprav Federatyvnoï Respubliky Nimechchyna*. Kyiv: Natsionalnyi instytut stratehichnykh doslidzhen, 2008.

International Reception

The *Voyage Enchanté* of Édouard Herriot in Ukraine

Iryna Dmytryczyn

> No one, I am sure, could have made such a trip with an -honest desire to learn the truth and escaped the conclusion that the Ukrainian countryside had experienced a gigantic tragedy.
>
> W. H. Chamberlain, *The Ukraine; A Submerged Nation* (New York: Macmillan, 1944)

Edouard Herriot, mayor of Lyon, twice Prime Minister of France and three times President of Parliament, went to the Soviet Union in August–September 1933. He stayed in Soviet Ukraine for five days, from August 26 to 30, and was a total of fifteen days in the country. He arrived at Odesa, went to Kyiv on the 27th, Kharkiv on the 28th, and visited the Dniprohes dam on the 29th before travelling to Moscow, where he spent most of his trip. In Ukraine, he moved at a fast pace, one city per day, with train travel at night in two cars placed at his disposal.[1]

Despite the historical importance of this journey, the numerous works—mostly laudatory—dedicated to Herriot do not expand on the journey. They either ignore it or barely mention it.[2]

Preparations and trip organization

At a time when workers' delegations were going to the USSR continuously and were being followed by distinguished guests, the trip of a prominent Western politician stood out as a unique occurence.[3] The decision to invite Herriot was taken by the Soviet Embassy in Paris in June 1933, because of

[1] "Le voyage de M. Herriot," *Le Temps*, August 31, 1933.

[2] For example, Herriot's trip is mentioned in 17 lines of 629 pages in Michel Soulié, *La vie politique d'Édouard Herriot* (Armand Colin, 1962); and 2 lines of 327 pages in Serge Berstein, *Édouard Herriot ou la République en personne* (Presse de la Fondation Nationale des Sciences Politiques, 1985), 196.

[3] Thanks to VOKS (Soviet Society of Contacts with foreigners, founded in 1925), almost 100,000 visitors came during the 1920s and 1930s. Michael David-Fox, *Showcasing the Great Experiment: Cultural Diplomacy and Western Visitors to the Soviet Union, 1921–1941* (Oxford: Oxford University Press), 1.

"his great Franco-Soviet and even international political importance."[4] Indeed, Herriot had always been favourably disposed to the USSR and never failed to underline this.[5] Released from his government obligations after his cabinet fell in December 1932, Herriot made the trip privately, even if it was obvious that he planned a return to major politics. The break also allowed him to circumvent protests that an official trip would have invariably raised, had it even taken place.

The main goal of Édouard Herriot's trip seems to have been to deny the existence of famine in Ukraine.[6] The Soviet embassy prepared meticulously for the visit, gathering precise reports on Herriot's personality, his career, and even his reading. In Moscow, the preparations were supervised by Stalin himself, as evidenced by his correspondence with his plenipotentiary in Ukraine, Lazar Kaganovich. Thanks to archival documents, we know that nothing was left to chance, including the choice of routes, interpreters, hotels and places to visit, protocol nuances, and the right tone to adopt.

During his trip, Herriot was closely watched and a real *cordon sanitaire* was organized around him from the very moment he was on the boat.[7] Once he was in Ukraine, foreign diplomats were kept out of the way, making it impossible for them to contact the guest.[8] Receptions were carefully

---

[4] Sophie Coeuré, *La grande lueur à l'Est, Les Français et l'Union Soviétique, 1917–1939* (Paris: Seuil, 1999), 171.

[5] After his month-long trip to Russia in September 1922, he was one of the engines of France's recognition of the USSR in 1922 (which took effect in 1924, when he came to power). A supporter of the Franco-Soviet alliance against Germany, he signed the Franco-Soviet Treaty of Non-Aggression and Non-Interference on November 29, 1932, with the Soviet ambassador.

[6] Marcel Rosenberg in a letter to Nikolay Krestinskiy on August 15, 1933 wrote: "The false information about the famine was mainly about Ukraine, and that is why it would be desirable to show him a *sovkhoz* or a collective farm in Ukraine. If we don't do it when he crosses Ukraine, if we show him these things elsewhere, it can lead to incorrect statements (...) It is very important to show him something exemplary with regard to the countryside. In Crimea, there is no harm in showing him Livadia, but the main thing remains the good choice of a collective farm and the skillful organization of a conversation with peasants" (Coeuré, *La grande lueur à l'Est*, 173).

[7] Stalin suggested that Balytskyi, head of the GPU of the Ukrainian SSR, follow Herriot during his stay in Ukraine. See Oleg Khlevniuk et al., eds., *Stalin i Kaganovich, Perepiska, 1931–1936* (ROSSPEN, 2001), 311, 317). On the organisation in Odesa see Liudmyla Aulova et al., eds., *Holodomor 1932–1933 rokiv v Ukraïni za dokumentamy GDA SBU* (Tsentr doslidzhen' vyzvol'noho rukhu, 2010), 298).

[8] This information is provided by the complaints from the Polish and German consulates in Kharkiv and Kyiv. See Jan Jacek Bruski, *Holodomor 1932–1933. Wielki Glod na Ukrainie w dokumentach polskiej dyplomacji i wywiadu* (Warszawa: Polski Instytut Spraw Miedzynarodowych, 2008), 394; Vasyl Marochko, ed., *Natsional'na knyha pamiati zhertv holodomoru 1932–1933. Misto Kyiv* (Kyiv: Fenix, 2008), 88.

organized, as were the crowds who applauded him as he passed. The famine-ravaged cities of Kyiv[9] and Kharkiv had been cleaned up.[10]

It is possible to follow the journey step by step through reports in the French and Soviet (Russian and Ukrainian) press.[11] Reports by the security services are also available. These allow us to look backstage. The testimonies of those who attended as spectators complete the picture.

What did he do and see?

While on August 21, five days before his arrival, the Soviets were still wondering about the possibility of visiting a kolkhoz (collective farm) "given the state of the economy in this sector" (Coeuré 173),[12] Herriot was finally able to visit two collective farms in Ukraine.[13] These were the "*Chervonyi promin*" ("Red Ray"; *Krasnyi luch* in Russian) in Biliaivka village, 45 km from Odesa, and the "International" kolkhozes in the village of Khortytsia in south-eastern Ukraine.[14]

---

[9] See the testimony of the German consul in Kyiv, A. Hencke, on August 31, 1933. Marochko, *Natsional'na knyha,* 88. See also the testimony of Harry Lang, an American journalist of the *Jewish Daily Forward*, who made a journey to study the situation of Jews in different countries. For translations into English of Lang's articles, see Bohdan Klid and Alexander J. Motyl, eds., *The Holodomor Reader: A Sourcebook on the Famine of 1932–1933 in Ukraine* (Edmonton and Toronto: Canadian Institute of Ukrainian Studies Press, 2012), 117–37).

[10] See the dispatch of Sergio Gradenigo, Royal Consulate of Italy, Kharkiv, 31.05.1933, in Andrea Graziosi, ed., *Lysty z Kharkova. Holod v Ukraïni ta na Pivnichnomu Kavkazi v povidomlenniakh italiis'kykh dyplomativ 1932–1933* (Kharkiv: Folio, 2007), 158. See also testimonies of Polish diplomats: Robert Kusnierz, "The Question of the Holodomor in Ukraine of 1932–1933 in the Polish Diplomatic and Intelligence Reports," *Holodomor Studies* 1, no. 1.

[11] See Iryna Dmytrychyn, *Le voyage de Monsieur Herriot. Un épisode de la Grande Famine 1932–1933* (Paris: Harmattan, 2018).

[12] Coeuré, *La grande lueur à l'Est*, 173.

[13] Another visit, to the "October Revolution" collective farm in the Kyiv region near Brovary, was reportedly canceled at the last moment. It provides valuable information because of testimony concerning the preparations, which perfectly illustrate the staging that was probably similar elsewhere. See Semen Pidhainy, ed., *The Black Deeds of the Kremlin, A White Book*, Vol. 2, *The Great Famine in Ukraine in 1932–1933* (Toronto: 1955), 93; and Robert Conquest, *The Harvest of Sorrow; Soviet Collectivization and the Terror-Famine* (London: Arrow Books, 1988), 339. No other information about this planned visit was found.

[14] He attended the operation of an electric threshing machine and took the opportunity to give advice, an episode which was widely reported by the Soviet press and which he later gave great pleasure in describing to reporters, one of whom wrote: "Édouard Herriot is a good economist, continues the Soviet correspondent: he noticed at the first glance what the collective farmworkers who trampled daily the wheat spilled on the ground had not noticed" ("M. Herriot professeur d'agriculture," *Le Nouvelliste de Lyon*, September 8, 1933).

He was also shown "*Verbliud*" ("Camel"), a model *sovkhoz* (Soviet state farm) located about 40 kilometers from Kharkiv in the Rostov region, where they tried to dazzle him, offering him a ride on a combine harvester, while "above the French hosts flew an airplane attached to the agricultural service which was doing its inspection." This set of technical

In Biliaivka, according to the GPU chief of Odesa, "everything he saw in the collective farm made a good impression." Herriot "had a female collective farm worker sit by his side," kissed everyone, lent himself to photographers and operators, joked and savored a "good" lunch in a peasant house.[15] He left after a few hours, with two embroidered *rushnyky*, while eighteen embroidered shirts "brought from the NKVD" were offered to him as he was boarding the train leaving Odesa for Kyiv.[16] Herriot asked questions, felt filled sacks to make sure they contained wheat, showed satisfaction at the answers and wrote them down in his little notebook.[17]

Overall, Herriot was a very accommodating guest.[18] The fears of Soviet officials who had gone to so much trouble proved unnecessary: what they did not manage to hide from Herriot, he managed to hide from France.[19] If we cannot blame him for the reception and staging by the Soviets, for the close surveillance of which he was the subject, he still cannot be completely forgiven, above all for his claims of objectivity and protestations that he enjoyed total freedom during his trip. He always put forward these claims in his declarations.[20]

---

advancements produced on the French hosts "a very strong impression." *Bulletin périodique de la presse russe*, August 9 to September 14, 1933 (MEAE, Europe 1930–1940, vol. 923, fol. 440); "M. Herriot à Rostov," *L'Humanité*, September 1, 1933.

[15] *Les renseignements spéciaux de GPU de la RSS d'Ukraine sur le séjour d'Édouard Herriot, ancien premier-ministre de la France à Odessa*, 28 August 1933, par le chef de la section régionale d'Odessa de la GPU Kaminsky et le chef du groupe opérationnel Boretsky (HDA SBU, Odessa, spr. 71, vol. 8, ark. 111–16) in Iouriy Chapoval, ed., *Holodomor des années 1932–1933 en Ukraine: une tragédie inconnue* (Kyïv, Éditions parlementaires d'Ukraine, 2008), 158. See also Report of Com. Leplevsky *About the Édouard Herriot's visit in Odessa*, August 29, 1933: H-DA SBU, f. 65, spr. 71, vol. 8, ark. 117–29 (187–99).

[16] Chapoval, *Holodomor des années 1932–1933 en Ukraine*, 158.

[17] Report of Com. Leplevsky.

[18] The German consul in Odesa asserted that Herriot was "noticeably ready to be duped." Aulova et al., *Holodomor 1932–1933 rokiv*, 301.

[19] For example, the Soviet report regretted that the delegation had observed a demonstration by the "Hammer and Sickle" collective farm of electric threshing machines, which were "worn, chipped and obviously, badly repaired." Herriot, however, emphasized that all the tools in the collective farms were moving electrically. Velychko's report, August 31, 1933, Tsentralnyi Derzhavynyi Arkhiv Hromads'kykh Obiednan' Ukrainy (hereafter cited as TsDAHOU), f. TsK KPU n°1, op. 20, spr. 6204, ark. 51; "M. Herriot, de retour à Lyon parle de l'U.R.S.S.," *L'Humanité*, September 14, 1933; "M. Édouard Herriot, revenant de Russie, a traversé hier Paris. Il exprime, en arrivant à Lyon, son admiration pour l'œuvre accomplie par l'Union soviétique," *L'Oeuvre*, September 14, 1933.

[20] He stated: "The first words that were addressed to us on Russian soil were: 'Tell us what you want to see and nothing will be hidden from you.' "M. Herriot est rentré de Russie. Le maire de Lyon est arrivé hier soir en gare de Brotteaux. La foule lui a ménagé une enthousiaste réception," *Lyon Républicain*, September 14, 1933.

In fact, from the outset Herriot was manipulator as much as manipulated.[21] When, for example, he declared, "Before my departure I was given the name of a village afflicted by the plague," this was a double lie: no one had told him about such a village, and the famine, which was not confined to "a village," was obscured by the misnomer "plague" that softened or even hid the reality.[22]

The return: What he said

Upon his return Herriot gave numerous interviews and lectures in which he commented favourably on the USSR.[23] Regarding famine, his remarks underwent a significant evolution, from silence to denial. When asked in Moscow about the Soviet agricultural system, Herriot had declared that he could not speak, having seen "only one *sovkhoz* and two kolkhozes of unequal value." However, his first reaction to a question on the subject when he was outside Soviet borders, in Riga, was "The Russian famine, I do not believe it."[24]

When he got off the train in Paris on September 6, he waxed eloquent on the subject of Ukraine: "I crossed Ukraine. Well! I tell you that I saw it as a garden in full bloom, a beautiful garden with black and rich soil that was covered, over considerable expanses, by magnificent harvests. It is said, you say, that this country is at this time saddened. I cannot talk about what I did not see. However, I was driven to the places that were said to be suffering. But I only found prosperity. Everywhere they beat with ardor at the electric thresher."[25]

At a banquet of the Radical Party on September 17, he was more aggressive on the topic, warning against slanders against a "formidable" people who "are industrializing," and he targeted Germany without naming

---

[21] He even conjured incredible stories about wagons specially fitted for mothers, "with showers, small wash houses, electric drying cabinets, milk coolers." Édouard Herriot, *L'Orient* (Paris, Hachette, 1934), 319.

[22] "M. Herriot est rentré de Russie. Le maire de Lyon est arrivé hier soir en gare de Brotteaux. La foule lui a ménagé une enthousiaste réception," *Lyon Républicain*, September 14, 1933.

[23] For example: "There, as in France, we see well cultivated land, cleanly dressed men, free and proud young people, magnificent children ... that some cities are even models of urbanism. It is obvious that this does not exclude ungrateful regions, secret miseries. But what about the rest of Europe? What about France itself?" Caspar-Jordan, "La vraie Russie," *Lyon Républicain*, September 15, 1933. The comparison itself is already manipulative.

[24] Compare this to his statement: "Mais oui, le peuple russe souffre de la famine!" *Le Nouvelliste de Lyon*, September 15, 1933. The conflation of "Russian" and (presumably) Soviet is also manipulative, as it obscures and denies the specificity of the Ukrainian situation.

[25] "M. Édouard Herriot à Lyon," *Le Temps*, September 15, 1933; "Le retour à Lyon de M. Herriot," *Le Progrès* (Lyon), September 14, 1933.

it.[26] On September 19, during his Vichy address, Herriot was even more explicit about who he felt was behind the information about the famine: "The Russian famine, which is agitated like a scarecrow, is only the suspect product of Hitler's propaganda."[27]

Thus, Herriot swept aside the famine issue, arguing in favor of the industrial achievements of the Soviet Union but also laying charges against those who sought to "colonize" Ukraine. His finger was pointed toward Berlin, which accused him of being fooled by the Soviet authorities. Herriot turned the argument in his favor by arguing that if Hitler's Germany was unhappy, it meant that he was on the right track.[28] In 1933–34 this argument worked perfectly.

On the famine issue, Herriot completely accepted the Soviet argument, a fact that interested Soviet parties immediately noticed, as is testified by Velychko's report: "As far as I could judge, as much through conversations as through exchanges with Herriot, on the famine issue, he has acquired the firm conviction that we have no famine and, (...) he is convinced that we are providing him with correct information on the past and how we overcame difficulties; moreover, he sees in the fact that we have overcome these difficulties a major sign of collectivization's true success."[29] One can legitimately ask to what extent these internal Soviet documents are to be taken literally, knowing that the author of the statements was responsible for successfully chaperoning Herriot and therefore had to provide the correct line. However, in view of the result obtained, namely Herriot's

---

[26] "This is not the time to describe the effort of these people. I only warn you against legends that have the same origin as the slanders I have often spoken of. When they maintain that the Ukraine that I have traveled through is devastated by famine and at the same time when they offer to colonize it, well, I can answer you that I saw a people who made a great effort, a people who industrialized, who took science for law, who made education mandatory. I saw a people who, on one of their great rivers, built an extremely powerful hydroelectric plant, the second [most powerful] in the world. "M. Herriot parle de l'U.R.S.S.: "J'ai vu un peuple qui fait un formidable effort... dit-il à une manifestation radicale dans l'Indre," *L'Humanité,* September 18, 1933. The *Petit Parisien* version slightly differs: "When I read that Ukraine is devastated by famine, it means one is thinking of colonizing it." G.-Th. Girard, "M. Édouard Herriot fêté dans l'Indre parle de son voyage dans les Balkans et en Russie," *Le Petit Parisien,* September 18, 1933; "Retour de Russie. M. Herriot fait éloge du régime soviétique," *Le Nouvelliste de Lyon,* September 18, 1933. *Le Matin*'s report from this meeting contains a sentence that became famous: "When one maintains that Ukraine is devastated by famine, I only shrug." "M. Édouard Herriot relate au Blanc son voyage en Russie au cours d'un banquet radical-socialiste," *Le Matin,* September 18, 1933.

[27] "Le témoignage d'Herriot sur l'U.R.S.S.," *L'Humanité,* September 22, 1933. L'*Humanité* highlighted the quotation. See also "M. Herriot a fait à Vichy une conférence sur les Soviets," *Le Nouvelliste de Lyon,* September 20, 1933.

[28] "Les déclarations de M. Édouard Herriot," *Le Temps,* September 16, 1933.

[29] TsDAHOU, f. TsK KPU n°1, op. 20, spr. 6204, fol. 52 (Velychko's Report, August 31, 1933).

statements on the famine, we must admit that the mission of persuasion was completely successful.[30]

The true triumph, however, came with a letter by Herriot sent from Lyon on September 21, 1933 to Gelfand, the GPU's eye and his personal companion on the trip:

> Once again, I want to thank you for all the good care that you provided for us. We have become friends, and, as for me, I am delighted. Since my return, I have been working on putting my notes in order for the book I will publish. I have already given two lectures: one in Indre, the other in Vichy, in front of a vast social public. Both here and there, the reception was very favorable, despite the threats that I had received. I will continue the fight. To be specific, *Le Matin* has published the enclosed photograph. Unless I'm mistaken, it's a photo from 1921, exhibited at the Revolution Museum, which has been disguised. Send me quickly, please, a reproduction of that photo. I want to show how they mislead public opinion. If you have any other documents on the alleged famine in Ukraine, send them to me: I will make good use of them.[31]

This is undoubtedly the picture of a child published on the front page of *Le Matin* on September 17, 1933, taken from the cover of a pamphlet published in Germany calling for help for the Soviet Germans.[32] There is no further information about this request. Its existence alone, however, shows Herriot's willful involvement in the famine negation enterprise in Ukraine.

From then on, the name of Édouard Herriot and his declarations served as references in the debate around the famine, provoking protests among some and awe or jubilation, among others.[33]

---

[30] We can give credit to the reporter's observations: "When we arrived in the 'Internationale' commune where there were gathered, in addition to the workers, many members of the commune and more generally peasants of B(olchaïa) Khortitsa, Herriot noticed their good health, well fed and happy air, and he said: 'Look at these hungry people' and looking at the crowd in the cities and the stations he repeatedly said: 'Here it is, the famous Ukrainian famine!'" Ibid.

[31] Coeuré, *La grande lueur à l'Est,* 182.

[32] "On quête outre-Rhin pour nourrir les petits Allemands fixés en Russie," *Le Matin*, September 17, 1933. The article ends with the question: "How to reconcile the collections made in Germany to feed the little Germans of Ukraine with the statement that there is nothing lacking in this eastern 'Beauce'?"

[33] Charles de Peyret-Chappuis denounced "the conspiracy of silence": "Despite compromises and slogans, an hour comes, however, when the truth is revealed. Already, in recent months, weakened echoes have reached French ears of events in Ukraine and the North Caucasus. The foreign press, through the English, German, Swiss, Belgian newspapers every day exposed with growing spread of the scourge... Soon, the big French organs will in turn awaken public attention to the new famine devastating large territories twice the size of ours. [...] *It is unlikely to remain silent any longer about a terrible situation, reaching a population of 30 million souls*

Reception and reactions

Édouard Herriot's trip provoked many reactions in Ukrainian and Russian émigré circles in France, which numbered at the time tens of thousands, including many intellectuals and politicians who intended to continue the fight against the Moscow of Lenin and Stalin. The two emigrations each pursued its objective: a Great Russia on one side, and an independent Ukraine on the other. They did not join efforts and their reactions to the trip were not identical.

The Russian emigration engaged in a controversial exchange with Herriot through its press organ, the daily *Vozrozhdenie* (Renaissance). Herriot responded with barely veiled arguments and accusations.[34] The Ukrainian emigration in France was alerted to the famine by its publication *Tryzub* (Trident).[35] Alexander Choulguine (Oleksandr Shulhyn) gave an important interview to *Figaro*, in which he made references to Herriot explicitly but cautiously.[36] The different Ukrainian communities in Europe and on the international scene, particularly in Geneva, had criticized the silence of the International Red Cross and bodies within the League of Nations like the Office of National Minorities and the Committee of International Women's Organizations. The dealings of émigrés with these organizations were complicated, especially after

---

and constituting a real shame inflicted on a world that claims to be civilized" Charles de Peyret-Chappuis, "Ce que M. Édouard Herriot se gardera bien de dire au retour de son 'triomphal voyage';" "La famine en Ukraine," *L'Ordre*, September 10, 1933.

[34] "This campaign has another origin, another meaning, another reach. The most discerning reader will observe that by the very admission of the editors of these articles, this information—whether or not transmitted by the Russian newspaper in Paris, *La Renaissance*—comes from Berlin and the Hitler network. Also from Berlin comes the whole campaign on the so-called famine in Ukraine, well made to move generous souls, at once macabre and obnoxious, and in order to produce an effect of horror using certain photographic documents of the long-ago famine that we had ourselves noted, but in 1922! And the reason for this campaign? It's easy to find out, if one bothers to read the review *Volk und Reich*, published at the expense of the German government and specifically devoted to Eastern European issues. In one of its last issues, this review publishes a long article in which it advocates the constitution of a Ukrainian State which would be supported by Germany and England." Édouard Herriot, "Etudes russes," *L'Information financière, économique et politique*, November 1, 1933.

[35] The weekly *Tryzub* (1925–40), the political organ of the Ukrainian government-in-exile, dedicated many pages to the famine of 1932–34. See, for example, "Do p. Edvarda Erio, Odvertyi lyst prof. Ukraïnskoï Hospodars'koï Akademiï v Podiebradakh O. I. Bochkovs'koho," *Tryzub*, no. 33, September 17, 1933, 10 (French version: "Après le 'triomphal' voyage en U.R.S.S.: La voix de l'Ukraine suppliciée: celle que M. Édouard Herriot n'a pas entendue ou n'a pas voulu entendre," *L'Ordre*, September 23, 1933); Viacheslav Prokopovych, "Danse macabre," *Tryzub*, no. 41, November 12, 1933, 10.

[36] D. le Lasseur, "La famine en Ukraine," *Le Figaro*, October 16, 1933.

Herriot's declarations, and did not produce any desired results.[37] Even so, *Le Matin* was able to conclude:

> Geneva has therefore encountered inevitable procedural difficulties. Nevertheless, the tragic fact of the Ukrainian famine has been confirmed and practically recognized by the 76th session of the Council of the League of Nations.[38]

The *Trident* was pragmatic regarding the outcome of its struggle on the international scene: "We must note that indeed no international legal standard exists (as long an international convention on human rights does not exist) on which the League of Nations could have relied to stop this appalling crime, or at least protest against it."[39]

None of the people who travelled with Herriot contradicted him—neither the senator of Isere Joseph Serlin, the deputy of the Marne Alfred Margaine, the deputy of the Rhone Jules Julien nor the diplomat and former deputy chief of Herriot's cabinet Marcel Ray. Ambassador Alphand, Herriot's chief of staff at the Ministry of Foreign Affairs and appointed by him to Moscow, was effusively for the cause of rapprochement. In his dispatches, Alphand steered the ministry away from discussing the famine, suggesting that there would have been at most only a few difficulties, an "imbalance" that the peasants themselves had been responsible for—all hatched by Hitler's Germany.

Of the two journalists in the delegation, only Georges Luciani went to Ukraine: he seems to have been totally caught up in the mystification, judging by his articles in *Le Petit Parisien* and *Le Temps*.[40] Géneviève Tabouis joined

[37] See on this subject the Archives of the League of Nations in Geneva. Also the memoirs of Milena Rudnytska, who had an interview with the president of the Council of the League of Nations, Johan Ludwig Mowinckel, who indicated that none of the fourteen representatives of the member countries denied the fact of the famine, but that pushed by the interests of economic and political cooperation with the Soviet Union, they preferred to hide behind formal pretexts. Bohdan Klid and A.J. Motyl, eds., *The Holodomor Reader: A Sourcebook on the Famine of 1932–1933 in Ukraine* (Toronto: Canadian Institute of Ukrainian Studies Press, 2012), 166.

[38] Henri de Korab, "L'effroyable problème de la famine en Ukraine a été posé hier par M. Mowinckel devant le conseil de la Société des nations" (*Le Matin*, September 30, 1933); "La misère et la famine en Russie," *Le Nouvelliste de Lyon*, October 1, 1933.

[39] *Tryzub* (Paris), no. 37, October 15, 1933, 7.

[40] Here is an example: "The trip will have been useful in the reconciliation between France and the USSR; it was good that a brilliant representative of our culture, a universally known politician, capable in his simplicity and the cordiality of his ways of winning people's sympathies, came to Moscow and heard French words there." Georges Luciani, "M. Herriot a achevé son voyage d'études en U.R.S.S.," *Le Petit Parisien*, September 10, 1933. On his return to France, Luciani learned Ukrainian and worked on Ukrainian subjects as an academic specialist on Eastern Europe.

Herriot only in Russia. Nevertheless, she devoted several articles to Ukraine and the harvest, taking part in Herriot's famine denial enterprise.[41]

Main publication of the trip

Only a few months after his return, Édouard Herriot published a book, in March 1934, at Hachette. *L'Orient* tells the story of his journey between Turkey, the Soviet Union, and Latvia. Ukraine occupies Chapter VII, a total of 29 pages of 418.

Before tackling the collective farm visit, Herriot explains the Soviet agricultural organization and the difference between collective farms (kolkhozes), state farms (*sovkhoz*es), and individual enterprises. He seems to be following memos provided by the authorities. The story of the visit is lyrical and moving, with a profusion of details, and above all, the affirmation of an abundant harvest.[42] "They do not know where to house the wheat."[43]

---

[41] "It is difficult to imagine the intensity of the state propaganda for agricultural development when one hasn't seen it. On the central square of each city, huge blackboards stand, illuminated at night by spotlights, with the harvest results for each district, each city, each farm written hour by hour. The crowd throngs before these boards as before war press releases. The 'good farms' are written down in a red column, the 'bad' in a black column. Likewise, on each farm—and, moreover, in each factory or plant—the good workers are registered every day with their output and their wage bonuses, while alongside these 'decorated' are noted the infamous lazy and the incapable. In the city as in the countryside, it's only about the harvest. Speakers are heating up the population in open air rallies: the children themselves are led in columns to the farms and paraded in front of the tractors waving red flags." "In this Soviet Canaan land, the harvest is always good, even when the previous year, it was bad in the rest of the territory. And the State, to which the vast majority of the land belongs, wishing to redistribute the wheat equally throughout the Union, completely empties Ukrainian elevators—this is why the Ukrainian [citizens] can be hungry near the earth's wealth, which seem paradoxical to us !" "L'Oeuvre en U.R.S.S. Ce que j'ai vu en Ukraine, grenier de l'Union soviétique," *L'Oeuvre*, September 21, 1933.

[42] "In order to show us a kolkhoz in Ukraine, we are led to the Dnister, about forty kilometers from Odesa. After crossing the German village of Freudenthal...we travel through the open fields,—in what heat and in what dust!—in the midst of peasants busy threshing the harvest. We count about a hundred of them, men, women and children. The sound of voices mingles with the noise of three engines. Wearing canvas clothing, combed, with a white kerchief, eyes protected by glasses, bare feet, nimble and lively, the women feed the threshing machines. Back and forth endlessly. A canteen prepares the harvesters' meal; a Red Cross station has been set up to treat possible injuries. Plenty of life and even cheerfulness. Large white clouds are slowly navigating across the sky." Édouard Herriot, *L'Orient* (Paris: Hachette, 1934), 164. "We visit the Bil[i]aivka Kolkhoz: 2 500 hectares, 286 houses, 1 200 workers. Which crops? Wheat, corn, vegetables, grapevines. Four brigades have been formed: for cereals, one for the vegetable gardens, one for vineyards, one for milk and its by-products. The collective organization receives the tractors, the threshing machines, the combines, the trucks [...]. After the harvest, the cooperators first discharge their obligations to the State; then they share, according to the work done by each, after having reserved what's necessary for the seed grain." Herriot, *L'Orient*, 164.

There are also descriptions of peasant houses, which are described as containing a radio and portraits of Stalin and Lenin, of the "shock brigades" and their work of educating the peasants.

In these descriptions of collective farming there is everything to reassure a French spirit: good organization, freedom of movement, punishment of abuses. The system is described as logical and clear: paid work and protected peasants. The reader is relieved not to find scenes of food requisitioning and cannibalism, deportations, slave labor, or images of death and starvation. Today's reader can only wonder what drove Herriot to make France believe in the omnipresence of machinery in the Ukrainian countryside, or the existence of Red Cross posts in village fields during the harvest? Did he not have the slightest doubt of a staging? No suspicions about the people's love for their leaders, whose portraits he could see everywhere?

This book, whose preface was written in March 1934, can be considered the official record and the main source of information about his journey, presented in the way he wished. His "message" can more readily be found in this book than in his declarations immediately upon returning.

Reasons

Édouard Herriot needed this trip and the recognition, both national and international, that its political success was likely to procure him.[44] At the same time, the Soviet Union sought to assert a radiant image of a country that was worthy of joining the concert of nations, and to silence reports about the famine. Both parties were interested in making the trip successful and neither was looking for controversy.

Herriot's journey was wholly a success. The Soviets were wrong to worry: what they could not hide, Herriot's favorable optics erased.[45] The goal sought by Stalin's regime would not have been fully achieved without

---

[43] Herriot, *L'Orient*, 166.

[44] Brodovsky's report proves that the Soviets were perfectly aware of this: "The general impression based on personal observations and things heard by those around Herriot is as follows: the main purpose of Herriot's journey is to justify his policy towards the USSR. Therefore the appreciation he had previously given for our development and, secondly, the current strengthening and broadening of Franco-Soviet relations." TsDAHOU, f. CC PCU n°1, 20, vol. 6204, fol. 49 (Brodovsky-Krestinsky, received September 1, 1933).

[45] When Herriot was Minister of Foreign Affairs and during the year 1933, before his departure, French diplomats had received information on collectivization from the embassy in Moscow, on its progress and its failures. Warnings about the famine had been issued since the spring of 1932: the peasant uprisings in Ukraine, the convictions of senior officials of the Commissariat for Agriculture, etc. The accuracy and lucidity of the dispatches sent by the French ambassadors Jean Herbette (1924–1931) and François Dejean (1931–1933) allow one to understand that Herriot and the French decision-makers were fully informed about the situation in Ukraine. See MEAE, Europe 1930–1940, vol. 942, 1045, 1046, 1054, 1062.

the participation, voluntary or involuntary, of the French visitor. His personality was used, his testimony instrumentalized.[46] He lent himself to the deception with his "guilty indulgence."[47] Herriot agreed to play a role in the show organized for him and in which he was one of the extras; without him and the part he performed on his return, the success of the sinister staging would not have been such an unqualified achievement.

Thirty years after the regime's fall, Soviet archives are still not accessible on this issue. However, the available evidence on the efforts to mislead Herriot, and the political imperatives to which he believed he should submit, cannot absolve him of responsibility for the final result.

If he did not see much, it was because that suited him. The problem was not in his lack of awareness but in his claim that the famine was a product of hostile propaganda. Even if this was a "suggested lie," Herriot fully adopted it and did not question it.[48] His name was invoked henceforth and thrown in the face of all those who tried to speak of the famine: he never attempted to distance himself from such exploitation of his words.[49]

Herriot undertook the journey with two ideas: peace and rapprochement with the USSR—or rather, the idea of peace through rapprochement with the USSR. He unquestionably saw enough to have

---

[46] "M. Herriot's wonder has removed the last hesitations of the average Frenchman." Claire Charles-Geniaux, "La jeunesse russe," *Lyon Républicain*, September 25, 1933. "M. Herriot, who has readings, knows what the old regime represents. He had already been to Soviet Russia and could, on his last trip, make comparisons, so useful in order to learn. As head of government, he had had to study particularly Russian affairs and their complications... Moreover, it turns out that left-winger though he is, he showed a certain severity for Marxism. If we represent him as having gone there with eyes shut, which traveler would we trust to have an idea about a foreign country." Jean-Jacques Caspar-Jordan, "La vraie Russie," *Lyon Républicain*, September 15, 1933. "If a former president of the Council, informed by his embassy, can be so delusional by himself about Russia's prosperity..." Louis Rougier, *Peut-on savoir la Vérité sur l'Expérience Soviétique?* (Besançon: Librairie Chaffanjon, 1937), 34. "Whom will we trust, we radicals, to judge the USSR, if it weren't President Herriot's competence and authority?" Rodolphe Arthaud, *L'U.R.S.S. vue et jugée par un radical* (Paris: Éditions des AUS, 1939).

[47] The expression comes from Alfred Fabre-Luce and was used against Georges Duhamel and his *Voyage de Moscou* published in 1927: "I criticize the author of the Voyage de Moscou for not having more strongly underlined the deep, irreducible, moral opposition which separates communism from the free intelligence. I regret that he thus encouraged in the Western elite the progress of a guilty indulgence." Alfred Fabre-Luce, *Russie 1927* (Paris: Bernard Grasset, 1927).

[48] An expression from Pierre Pascal in the foreword to Yvon's book, *Ce qu'est devenue la Révolution russe* (Paris: La Révolution prolétarienne, 1936).

[49] See, for example, the following: "The main source of the slanders concerning the famine in the USSR are the 'letters from the Soviet Union' released in the press of the White Guards. Herriot himself established that these letters are forgeries by political opponents." "L'église et la 'famine en Russie,'" *Des faits sur l'Union Soviétique*, no. 13, January 1934.

doubts.[50] But the "mental sorter" of which Koestler spoke had done its work: the observed images could not have diverted him from what he believed to be in the interest of France.

To undersatnd Herriot's views on the Soviet issue one has to take into account the European situation, where the advent of Hitler created threats and materialized fears of a new war. The Franco-Soviet rapprochement took "an anti-German turn" in the middle of 1933.[51] From 1934, the French political scene was dominated by the principle of unity in antifascist action and carefully avoided any criticism of Stalinism. For many, defending the USSR was synonymous with fighting Nazism, and conversely, undermining the USSR was seen as supporting Hitler's regime.

To the political motives and personal ambitions of Herriot must be added the Franco-Soviet agreement, whose fate was decided at the precise moment of his travels, although it had been discussed for many years.[52] A Protocol to the Provisional Trade Agreement was signed at the Quai d'Orsay on August 26, 1933, the same day that Herriot landed in Odesa.[53] He pleaded for the reestablishment of a Marseille-Odesa link; the boats would have brought phosphates from Algeria and returned to France loaded with "Ukrainian durum wheat."[54] To admit the existence of famine would not have facilitated these projects.

An ideological sensibility is also to be taken under consideration. Herriot might have been receptive to Soviet rhetoric that constantly referred to the French Revolution and the ideal of social progress, and which referred pointedly to oppressive kulaks.[55] Many minds of the time accepted that the

---

[50] We have testimonies which assert that Herriot had been exposed to images of the misery, even of the famine, in particular when he visited Saint Sophia Cathedral in Kyiv. Along the way, he found himself in front of ruins: "Amidst the ruins, an old woman in rags was cooking something on a small fire in a small cauldron, and beside her sat a famished little boy of about five years old." TsDAHOU, f. TsK KPU n°1, op. 20, spr. 6204, ark. 51 (Velychko's Report, August 31, 1933). See also the German consul's testimony on Herriot's meeting with the homeless in the streets of Kyiv. A. Hencke, Kyiv, August 31, 1933, *Natsional'na knyha pamiati,* 88. Herriot never mentioned these episodes.

[51] Sabine Dullin, *Des hommes d'influences. Les ambassadeurs de Staline en Europe 1930–1939* (Paris: Payot, 2001), 118.

[52] See: MEAE, vol. 1057, fol. 84, fol. 92, fol. 95, fol. 106. There were two parts to the agreement, political and economic, which were to be signed simultaneously.

[53] MEAE vol. 1058, fol. 3 and fol. 110. This volume contains many other documents reflecting the negotiations' progress. It is to be noted that the USSR emphasized its wheat exports: fol. 39.

[54] TsDAHOU, f. CC PCU n°1, 20, vol. 6204, fol. 56 (Velychko's report, August 31, 1933).

[55] During the emblematic exchange of greetings in the Museum of the Revolution in Moscow, when its director mentioned the inspiration of the French Revolution, Herriot answered: "My companions and I have not forgotten the series of great revolutions that established the history of France. This is why we observe with deep and sincere sympathy the efforts that you

birth of the "new world" could not be accomplished without suffering or error.[56] The French Radical Party, which was founded by Herriot, was leading the rapprochement with Moscow, and each time the horizon cleared for the USSR in France, it occurred under the auspices of this leftist party.[57] Between the blind and the naive, the convinced partisans and the strategists of supporting the "lesser evil", the declarations of Édouard Herriot contributed to marrying different strands of pro-Sovietism.[58]

We will probably never know to what extent Herriot believed what was told him about the pernicious nature of the kulaks and the joys of collective farm life. However, it is clear that Herriot knew a great deal more than he admitted. His silence was not proof of his ignorance but of the contrary.

Consequences

The case of Édouard Herriot raises the question of a politician's responsibility for decisions where error borders on criminal complicity. Fortified by his eyewitness status, Herriot dismissed as Nazi supporters all those who tried to tell the truth or help starving people. He endorsed the tactics of the Soviet Union and provided support for the regime. The Stalinist propaganda machine would no doubt have succeeded even if Herriot had told the truth, but Herriot and the enchanted pilgrims among whom he occupied a place of choice played their useful role. We have at least two proofs that his trip prevented the arrival of relief and had consequences likely to amplify the human disaster. In a report to the Sûreté on the Congress of National Minorities in Berne, we learn that the Soviet Union was inclined to recognize the famine "by explaining it as caused by transport disorder and the activity of 'saboteurs.'"[59] But that was, stresses the report in parentheses, before Herriot's visit. Similarly, in debates at the International Red Cross, his denials were an argument of sufficient weight to counterbalance many alarmed voices.[60]

---

have made in the fight against absolutism and that you demonstrate in the construction of the new society." "M. Herriot à Moscou," *L'Ere nouvelle*, September 4, 1933.

[56] Quoting Romain Rolland: "Despite the disgust, despite the horror, despite the ferocious mistakes and crimes, I go to the child, I take the newborn: he is the miserable hope of humans' future." Serge Berstein, *La France des années 30* (Paris: Armand Colin, 2011), 118.

[57] Sabine Dullin speaks about a "radical Soviet milieu" and, at the end of her work on the Franco-Soviet game of influence, delivers a severe verdict on certain members including Édouard Herriot. Dullin, *Des hommes d'influences*.

[58] David Caute, *Le communisme et les intellectuels français, 1914–1966* (Paris: NRF-Gallimard, 1967).

[59] Archives Nationales de France (Centre d'Accueil et de Recherche des Archives Nationales — CARAN: Série F7.

[60] During the Red Cross meeting of October 5, 1933, where the question about famine was discussed: "M. de Haller signals Herriot's testimony talking about Ukraine's magnificent crops in the articles he publishes. The CR will lose all authority if it embarks on this adventure."

Undoubtedly, the situation of famine in August-September 1933, attenuated by the harvest, was no longer at its peak. Herriot, however, managed to prevent the arrival of relief, which even near the end of 1933 could have saved lives. Essentially, at the time no one could know when the famine was going to end. Moreover, the efforts to help continued and in 1935 one of those who was still urging international organizations to act argued that "the words of Mr. Herriot constitute to this day a serious impediment for all people who, moved by humanitarian considerations, fight to spread the truth and help those suffering from famine in the Soviet Union."[61]

Robert Conquest spoke about Édouard Herriot's "irresponsibility."[62] The French philosopher Raymond Aron saw the occidental admiration for the Soviet regime as being governed by three factors: political irresponsibility, scientific misconception, and moral fault.[63] Herriot perfectly embodies all three.

Archives

Archives Nationales de France (Centre d'Accueil et de Recherche des Archives Nationales — CARAN): Série F7.

Archives du Ministère de l'Europe et des Affaires Etrangères (MEAE), Europe 1930–1940, vol. 923, 942, 1045, 1046, 1054, 1062.

Haluzevyi Derzhavnyi Arkhiv Sluzhby Bezpeky Ukrainy, fond 65, opys 71, sprava 8.

Tsentraln'yi Derzhavnyi Arkhiv Hromads'kykh Obiednan' Ukrainy, fond TsK KPU n°1, opys 20, sprava 6204.

Bibliography

Ammende, Ewald. *Human Life in Russia*. Cleveland: John T. Zubal, Inc., 1984.

Aron, Raymond. *L'Opium des intellectuels*. Paris: Pluriel, 2010.

Arthaud, Rodolphe. *L'U.R.S.S. vue et jugée par un radical*. Paris: Éditions des AUS, 1939.

Roman Serbyn, "The Great Famine of 1933 and the Ukrainian Lobby at the League of Nations and the International Red-Cross," *Holodomor Studies* 1, issue 1 (winter-spring 2009): 125. The judgement of Ewald Ammende was the following: "His action had a disastrous influence on the emerging desire to bring help to Russia [*sic*] which was beginning to be felt in many countries." Ewald Ammende, *Human Life in Russia* (Cleveland: John T. Zubal, Inc. Publishers, 1984), 221.

[61] Ammende, *Human Life*, 257.

[62] "The irresponsibility shown must have greatly encouraged Stalin in his view of the gullibility of the West, on which he was to play so effectively in later years." Robert Conquest, *The Harvest of Sorrow* (London Arrow books, 1988), 314.

[63] Raymond Aron, *L'Opium des intellectuels* (Paris: Pluriel, 2010), xiv.

Aulova, Ludmyla, Vasyl' Danylenko, and Valentyna Lavreniuk, eds. *Holodomor 1932–1933 rokiv v Ukraïni za dokumentamy GDA SBU*. Lviv: Tsentr doslidzhen' vyzvol'noho rukhu, 2010.

Berstein, Serge. *Édouard Herriot ou la République en personne*. Paris: Presse de la Fondation Nationale des Sciences Politiques, 1985.

Berstein, Serge. *La France des années 30*. Paris: Armand Colin, 2011.

Bruski, Jan-Jacek. *Holodomor 1932–1933. Wielki Glod na Ukrainie w dokumentach polskiej dyplomacji i wywiadu*. Warsaw: Polski Instytut Spraw Miedzynarodowych, 2008.

Caute, David. *Le communisme et les intellectuels français, 1914–1966*. Paris: NRF — Gallimard, 1967.

Chapoval, Iouriy [Iurii/Yuri Shapoval], ed. *Holodomor des années 1932–1933 en Ukraine: une tragédie inconnue*. Kyiv: Éditions parlementaires d'Ukraine, 2008.

Coeuré, Sophie. *La grande lueur à l'Est, Les Français et l'Union Soviétique, 1917–1939*. Paris: Seuil, 1999.

Conquest, Robert. *The Harvest of Sorrow: Soviet Collectivization and the Terror-Famine*. London: Arrow Books, 1988.

Dmytrychyn, Iryna. *Le voyage de Monsieur Herriot. Un épisode de la Grande Famine 1932–1933*. Paris: Harmattan, 2018.

Dullin, Sabine. *Des hommes d'influences. Les ambassadeurs de Staline en Europe 1930–1939*. Paris: Payot, 2001.

Fabre-Luce, Alfred. *Russie 1927*. Paris: Bernard Grasset, 1927.

Graziosi, Andrea, ed. *Lysty z Kharkova. Holod v Ukraïni ta na Pivnichnomu Kavkazi v povidomlenniakh italiis'kykh dyplomativ 1932–1933*. Kharkiv: Folio, 2007.

Herriot, Édouard. *L'Orient*. Paris: Hachette, 1934.

Khlevniuk, Oleg, Robert Devis [Davies], L. Kosheleva, E. Rees, and L. Rogovaia. *Stalin i Kaganovich, Perepiska, 1931–1936*. Moscow: ROSSPEN, 2001.

Klid, Bohdan, and A. J. Motyl, eds. *The Holodomor Reader; A Sourcebook on the Famine of 1932–1933 in Ukraine*. Toronto: Canadian Institute of Ukrainian Studies Press, 2012.

Lang, Harry. *Vpechatleniia amerikanskogo zhurnalista o sovetskoi Rossii*. Paris, 1933.

Kusnierz, Robert. "The Question of the Holodomor in Ukraine of 1932–1933 in the Polish Diplomatic and Intelligence Reports." *Holodomor Studies* 1, no. 1.

L'Humanité Russie d'Aujourd'hui

L'information financière, économique et politique

L'Oeuvre

l'Ordre

Le Figaro

Le Progrès

Lyon Républicain
Le Matin
Le Nouvelliste de Lyon
Le Petit Marseillais
Le Petit Parisien
Le Temps
Marochko, Vasyl, ed. *Natsional'na knyha pam'iati zhertv holodomoru 1932–1933. Misto Kyiv.* Kyiv: Fenix, 2008.
Pidhainy, Semen, ed. *The Black Deeds of the Kremlin, A White Book*, vol. 2, *The Great Famine in Ukraine in 1932–1933.* Toronto: Dobrus, Grove Press, 1955.
Rougier, Louis. *Peut-on savoir la Vérité sur l'Expérience Soviétique?* Besançon: Librairie Chaffanjon, 1937.
Soulié, Michel. *La vie politique d'Édouard Herriot.* Paris: Armand Colin, 1962.
Serbyn, Roman. "The Great Famine of 1933 and the Ukrainian Lobby at the League of Nations and the International Red-Cross." *Holodomor Studi-es* 1, no. 1 (winter-spring 2009).
Tryzub
Vozrozhdenie
Yvon. *Ce qu'est devenue la Révolution russe.* Paris: La Révolution prolétarienne, 1936.

The American Yiddish Daily *Forverts* on Privation in Soviet Ukraine: Experiences and Reflections

Gennady Estraikh

Two people played tangible roles in shaping the American Jewish narrative about the famine in Ukraine in the early 1930s: Mendel Osherowitch and Harry (Herts) Lang. Both were born in 1888 as subjects of the Russian imperial state, and both in their youth emigrated to the United States, became successful journalists and writers, working on the staff of the highest-circulation New York Yiddish daily *Forverts* (Forward). Established in 1897 as a voice of the socialist labor movement, the newspaper printed 275,000 copies in the late 1920s. America's entry into the economic crisis and the imposed restrictions on immigration contributed to the decline of its circulation to 170,000 in the late 1930s. Nonetheless, *Forverts* continued to run its operations as the most influential Jewish newspaper, though it had to cut editorial-staff wages and use the reserve fund accumulated in the "fat years."[1]

After initially welcoming the revolutionary events of 1917, the journalistic newspaper through the 1920s was transformed into a bitter critic of the Soviet regime and generally of Communism, especially when it became utterly clear that the Kremlin ideologues did not have plans to introduce democratic forms of governance. At the same time, the Soviet Union remained in the focus of its detailed coverage, thus catering to the interests of the newspaper's readers, the majority of whom were immigrants born in what used to be the Russian Empire. Among the contributors, it was rather common to be fluent in Russian. Abraham Cahan, editor-in-chief of *Forverts*, himself a product of a Russian-language school, spoke Russian at home with his wife, Anna Bronstein, an alumna of a Kyiv *gymnasium*. In any case, journalists of *Forverts* usually did not need interpreters when they visited the Soviet Union.

"Talking to people," paying attention to quotidian aspects of life was the method advocated by Cahan, who himself practiced it during his trips, including his and Bronstein's three-month long sojourn in the Soviet Union

[1] Baruch Vladeck, "Der Forverts durkh di krizis-yorn," *Forverts*, April 25, 1937, p. 2; Joseph Chaikin, *Yidishe bleter in Amerike: a tsushtayer tsu der 75 yoriker geshikhte fun der yidisher prese in di Fareynikte Shtatn un Kanade*. Sh. Shklarski, 1946, 295.

in 1927.[2] Indeed, encounters with people usually provided material for a readable, informative, and even historically valuable narrative. On the negative side, this method carried the danger of picking up rumors, including extravagant ones, which circulated in the country.

Neither Osherowitch nor Lang pioneered the discussion in the pages of *Forverts* concerning problems faced by Soviet peasants, especially after being herded into collective farms (*kolkhozes*). Even before serializing their Soviet travelogues, *Forverts* published pertinent materials, either written by the newspaper's own contributors or lifted from other outlets. The Jewish Telegraphic Agency was an important provider of information. In addition, the newspaper regularly featured comprehensive overviews of the Soviet press. Significantly, the *Jewish agricultural colonization* in Ukraine and in the Crimea (then part of the Russian republic) remained one of the central topics of Jewish public interest worldwide and enjoyed heavy sponsorship from American organizations, most notably the American Jewish Joint Distribution Committee, or JDC. The newspaper had one more motive for writing about Soviet villagers' travails: in its ideologically motivated coverage of events in the Soviet Union, the dramatic transformation of the agricultural sector and its failures vividly illustrated fundamental flaws of Communism.

The situation in Soviet Ukrainian villages was not in the main focus of Osherowitch and Lang. They both—and their readers—were more interested, first, in the life of Soviet Jews and second, in the country's general mood. However, their travelogues, and, the circumstances of their publication and reception, provide material for analyzing various aspects of the famine in Ukraine and its reporting.

Mendel Osherowitch, 1932

In the spring of 1932, Osherowitch—by that time known as a novelist, historian, playwright, and translator from Russian and Hebrew—spent five weeks in the Soviet Union. This was Osherowitch's first trip to his home country since he left it more than two decades earlier. Born in Trostianets, now in Vinnytsia (Russian: Vinnitsa) province of Ukraine, Osherowitch wrote prolifically on Russia and Russian culture, and—as a good Ukrainian speaker—was reputed to be a competent expert in Ukrainian history and current affairs. His proficiency in Russian and Russian literature developed just before his emigration, as distance learning student (*ekstern*) in Odesa preparing to take examinations for a certificate of Russian secondary school education.[3]

---

[2] Daniel Soyer, "Abraham Cahan's Travels in Jewish Homelands: Palestine in 1925 and the Soviet Union in 1927," in Gennady Estraikh and Mikhail Krutikov, editors, *Yiddish and the Left* (Legenda, 2001), 56-79.

[3] Mendel Osherowitch, "Geshikhtes fun mayn lebn", *Forverts*, 1945, 393.

In early 1932, besides visiting Moscow and several other Soviet cities and towns, mainly in Ukraine, Osherowitch went to villages and travelled as a third-class train passenger, in order to get a first-hand impression of the situation and to have direct conversations with peasants on a variety of themes. It was the trip of a self-guided tourist rather than an officially accredited journalist. He might have made the necessary arrangements through one of the agencies linked with the Soviet state-run Intourist agency. Most probably it was through the travel bureau of the New York-based Amalgamated Bank, founded in 1923 as a "socialist bank" by the Amalgamated Clothing Workers of America, a heavily Jewish trade union. The bureau published advertisements in *Forverts*, hailing the trips as inexpensive, "affordable to everyone" opportunities to see Soviet Russia.

On his way back from the Soviet Union, Osherowitch shared his reflections with a correspondent of the Yiddish daily *Unzer ekspres* (Our Express), which was based in Warsaw but had local editions in several cities of Poland. It is highly likely that the interviewer was Israel Joshua Singer (the elder brother of the later Nobel Prize winner Isaac Bashevis Singer), a Warsaw correspondent of *Forverts* who also wrote for *Unzer ekspres*. Singer's own 1926 travelogue, *Nay-Rusland: bilder fun a rayze* (New Russia: Impressions of a Journey), was serialized in the *Forverts* and came out in Vilna (Vilnius) in book form in 1928. According to *Unzer ekspres*, the long years of Osherowitch's life in America had not weakened his love of Russia, "even now when the country is being led by the Bolsheviks." Hence his decision to go and see how people lived there. In addition, he longed to see his mother, four sisters, and two brothers.[4]

Osherowitch's articles, full of trenchant observations, were serialized in *Forverts* from April to August 1932 and then shaped the book *Vi mentshn lebn in sovet Rusland* (How People Live in Soviet Russia), published in January 1933. In the introduction, Osherowitch repeated his claim of having a positive attitude toward "Russian culture and Russian idealism." As a socialist, he "wanted to see how socialism was being built in the country where I was born and which I never stopped loving."[5] Only a small part of the book is devoted to the situation in the rural areas of Ukraine. In fact, he stressed that the same sad picture of village life could be seen in central Russia and the Don region.[6]

Osherowitch had come to the conclusion that young Soviet citizens (presumably, he meant the Jews, particularly those who lived in Moscow and other cities) were generally content with their lives. In his opinion, no

---

[4] [Şinger, Israel Joshua.] "A lebediker grus fun soviet-rusland," *Unzer ekspres*, April 8, 1932, 6.
[5] Mendel Osherowitch, "Vi mentshn lebn in sovet rusland", *Forverts*, 1933, 6–7.
[6] Ibid., 133.

more than five percent of them would have emigrated to the United States if they were allowed to do this. The elderly people, on the other hand, would have probably preferred to leave the country. The desire of the youth to stay in the country did not stem from what could be characterized as satisfaction with their life conditions. Rather, Osherowitch described them as people overwhelmed with a kind of religious "Hasidic exaltation." This state of mind made it possible to be ill-fed, badly clothed and miserably lodged, but at the same time happy with having access to education and career opportunities, and full of enthusiasm for constructing a new society.

It was shocking to Osherowitch to see the dire straits in which Soviet citizens found themselves in Ukraine. Known for its fertile land and favorable growing climate, Ukraine was, nevertheless, among the areas most hard hit by famine. In many villages, peasants were swollen from hunger and dying from lack of food. In search of subsistence, they filled railway stations and roamed from one place to another. The situation in urban areas of the country, including Ukraine, was different and generally not as catastrophic as in the villages. That made the town-village divide even bigger than before and further polarized urban dwellers, including Jewish ones, and non-Jewish peasants.

Osherowitch included in his travel notes a description of an observed conversation between an elderly Ukrainian peasant and a young Jewish urbanite. Clearly, the American journalist's sympathies were on the side of the former. While the peasant complained that his family had not eaten bread for two weeks and that his village did not have horses or seeds to enable him and other villagers to plant future crops, the Jewish young man blamed [Ukrainians] for hiding grain needed for fulfilling the country's industrialization plans. The peasant predicted that the situation would only worsen in 1933, because by that time all the horses and many people would die. He shrugged off the young man's argument that tractors would replace farm labor: "Talking is the only thing you can do. Nothing else."[7]

Still, to Osherowitch's surprise, many of the peasants he spoke to were full of hope for better times. He turned to a stereotype to explain this phenomenon, ascribing it to their proverbial patience and obedience. Like many other emigrants, he apparently perceived himself as an expert on Soviet life, though in fact, after the world war and civil war, followed by the radical social and economic transition from absolute monarchy to totalitarian Stalinism, it was a fundamentally different country. Besides, before his emigration Osherowitch's first-hand experience of life in the Russian empire had been limited mainly to deeply provincial locations, with

[7] Ibid., 142–45.

brief stints in Balta and Kishinev, and a longer one in Odesa. Five years earlier, on the eve of the Cahan Soviet trip, *Forverts* similarly extolled the editor-in-chief's expertise in the subject, arguing that by virtue of his "thorough knowledge of the Russian language and literature" and "a profound sympathy for the Russian masses," no American journalist was "better qualified to understand and interpret Soviet Russia than Abraham Cahan."[8] In fact, however, this was Cahan's first, and last, visit after thirty-five years of observations from afar through the prism of literature, common sense, and his understanding of Marxism.

Soviet life appeared to Osherowitch full of paradoxes. Some of them he encountered in Moscow, where, notwithstanding hunger in wide areas of the country, theatres staged an excellent selection of plays, while a few expensive restaurants provided food, service, and entertainment, including American jazz music.[9] In his *shtetl*, on the other hand, Osherowitch encountered a completely different paradox of Soviet life: from an elderly Jew, a former wealthy merchant, he heard that his son had implored the man to become poor in order to shed the second-class status of a *lishenets*, or disenfranchised. This status affected many aspects of life among those "non-proletarian elements," including Jews, whom the Bolshevik authorities deemed socially deficient. By becoming "poor," the family could be listed in a social category that opened doors for the young man to attend a Moscow university.[10]

In Berlin, Osherowitch's next stop on his way back to New York, he spoke—as reported by the Berlin correspondent of the Warsaw Yiddish daily *Haynt* (Day)—about the fissures in the relations between Jews and Ukrainians.[11] This topic was not new for *Forverts*. In 1918, Moyshe (Moissaye) Olgin, then a top journalist of the newspaper (after 1921 he became a prominent American communist), wrote that the relations between the Jews and the Ukrainians had developed "organically." The Jews looked down on the Ukrainians' traditions and religious practice, whereas the Ukrainians remained convinced of the Jews' culpability in crucifying Jesus. "However, this was a pale abstraction that existed in parallel with the full-blooded reality of life, which had formulated the rule that despite being different in many ways, the two different peoples had to live on the same

---

[8] Unsigned article 1. "Cahan on Russia." *Forverts*, October 23, 1927, English section, 1.

[9] Mendel Osherowitch, "Vi mentshn lebn in sovet rusland," *Forverts*, 1933, 46–47.

[10] [Singer, Israel Joshua.] "A lebediker grus fun soviet-rusland," *Unzer ekspres*, April 8, 1932, 6.

[11] Klinov, Yishayahu. "Yidn shikern—yidn arbetn—yidn veynen: nokh a bazukh in soviet-Rusland." *Haynt*, April 15, 1932, 3.

land"[12]. In his 1921 book *My Shtetl in Ukraine*, he wrote: "In my shtetl, the Gentile did not hate the Jew and the Jew did not hate the Gentile."[13]

A dozen years after the anti-Jewish atrocities of the civil war, which peaked in 1919, Osherowitch observed that on the surface, both ethnic groups lived and worked together rather amiably.[14] Meanwhile, religious practice and Yiddish usage had declined among young people, and generally the cultural divide was narrowing. Intermarriage was becoming increasingly common.[15] For all that, as a Jewish resident of Berdychiv (Berdichev in Russian) told Osherowitch, the relationship between the Jews and the Ukrainians was like a string stretched too tight on a fiddle. For instance, Jewish agricultural colonization was not popular among the Ukrainian population. The concerns of Jewish activists were raised too. *Forverts* mentioned one of their arguments: it was neither fair nor safe to move to the land that belonged historically to non-Jewish peasants.[16] Indeed, in the 1920s and early 1930s competition for land led to tension and even conflicts between Jewish and Ukrainian farmers (Kagedan). Some people speculated that should the Soviet regime fall, the Ukrainian peasants would massacre the Jewish colonists.[17]

Not long before Osherowitch's trip, in 1931, the establishment of Torgsin—the network of state-run hard currency stores—exacerbated the tensions between Jews and Ukrainians. Such stores were open to people who had hard currency, gold, or jewelry. Although the abbreviation Torgsin stood for "*torgovlia s inostrantsami*" (trade with foreigners), it also became widely known as "trade with Jews," because many Jews received remittances from their families abroad in hard currency. Probably even more consequential for forming an "ethnic image" of Torgsin was the preponderance of Jews, who often had experience in dealing with jewelry, among the staff of such stores.[18]

---

[12] Moyshe Olgin, "Yidishe un nit-yidishe kultur in dem zelbn land," *Forverts*, December 23, 1918, 5.

[13] Moyshe Olgin, *Mayn shtetl in Ukrayne*. M. Gurevich, 1921,75.

[14] In 1905, Osherowitch had survived a pogrom in Balta, near Odesa (Osherowitch, *Geshikhtes* 351–58).

[15] Among Ukrainian Jews, intermarriages were as high as 15 per cent in the mid-1930s (Konstantinov 52).

[16] Zalman Wendroff, "Vi es halt mit der yidisher kolonizatsye in Rusland," *Forverts*, August 30, 1926, section 2, 5.

[17] Zalman Wendroff, "Vayterdike argumentn far un kegn yidisher kolonizatsye in sovet-Rusland," *Forverts*, September 1, 1926, 7.

[18] Elena Sorokina, *Zoloto dlia industrializatsii: Torgsin.* (ROSSPEN, 2009), 163, 277–78, 444; Dar'ia Antsibor, "Fenomen 'torgsina': obraz evreia v narrativakh o Golodomore," in *Kontakty i konflikty v slavianskoi i evreiskoi kul'turnoi traditsii*, ed. Olga V. Belova, 282–97 (Moscow: Sefer, 2017).

A delicate issue was the help provided by foreign Jewish organizations. In 1928, which was a year of serious crop failures, the Moscow correspondent of the Jewish Telegraphic Agency wrote that the JDC would like to supply the colonists with flour with which to weather the crisis. But here it is confronted with a problem. "Why only the Jewish colonists? Why not the neighboring peasants whose position is just as grave? Why are the Jewish peasants any better than the Russian [sic; in fact, he was describing the situation in Ukraine] peasants?"[19]

Nonetheless, in the spring of 1932 the JDC, which after 1930 stopped its operations in Soviet Ukraine and focused on aiding the Crimean Jewish colonies, purchased 1,930 quintals (centners) of rye flour for distribution in all Jewish colonies of Ukraine, except from those in the Skadovsk area, Kherson province, which were not directly affected with food shortages.[20] Earlier, in 1929 Nathaniel Zalowitz, editor of the Sunday English section of *Forverts*, wrote: "Were it not for the continuous stream of money from the United States, heaven alone knows what would have happened to the two-and-a-half million Russian Jews!" This was his (overstated) impression derived from reading the 1929 Soviet travelogue, *Sovyet Rusland, vi ikh hob ir gezen* (Soviet Russia, How I Saw Her), also previously serialized in *Forverts*, by Nathan Chanin, chair of the Jewish Socialist Farband (Union) of the Socialist Party in America.[21]

Although access to Torgsin stores, which operated in 1931–36, helped many Jews to get through the period of food deprivation, contacts with foreign relatives not only caused envy among non-Jews but also made the "lucky Jews" targets of secret police attention and action. (My great-grandfather, a rabbi in one of the Jewish colonies in Ukraine, was kept incarcerated until the old man surrendered the ten dollars that he had most probably received from abroad.) In 1932, the Jewish press, including *Forverts*, wrote about the Soviet police's "dollar inquisition," namely requisition of privately held hard currency, targeting primarily those Jews who had relatives in the USA or elsewhere.[22] The newspaper published letters from Soviet Jews describing the travails associated with getting help through Torgsin outlets (Letters).

Osherowitch also went in Moscow to a Torgsin store, where following a friend's advice, he bought flour and some other commodities for his mother

---

[19] Boris Smolar, "Visitng the Jewish Colonies in Russia," *The Sentinel*, July 27, 1928, 13.

[20] "Otchet o deiatel'nosti Agrodzhointa za 1932 god." JDC Archive, Joseph A. Rosen Papers, file 70.1.

[21] Nathaniel Zalowitz, "How Do the Russian Jews Live?" *Forverts*, August 4, 1929, 12.

[22] Jacob Lestschinsky, "Naye dolar-inkvizitsye in sovet-Rusland," *Forverts*, November 13, 1932, 1.

and other relatives. In his notes we read that he felt downhearted carrying such things to Ukraine.[23]

The Ukrainian villages which he had a chance to visit looked neglected compared with how he remembered them from the time before emigration. One of the striking things to him was the disappearance of nicely painted houses, once part of the Ukrainian rural landscape. Villagers, now the most disadvantaged Soviet citizens, did not have any interest in decorating their homes, because they were not sure how long they were destined to live there. In addition, they feared drawing attention to themselves, lest they would be categorized and persecuted as kulaks.[24]

From Ukrainian peasants, coerced into membership in collective farms, Osherowitch heard that *panshchina*, or the previous labour obligations to the landlord, now seemed to them better than their working for the collective farm. They argued that their hatred of kolkhozes was stronger than the hatred they once felt towards their landlords.[25] Chanin wrote in 1929: "No one in Russia doubts that in a year's time, the experiment with kolkhozes will be deemed unsuccessful."[26] Indeed, on March 2, 1930 Stalin published an article, "Dizzy with Success," in which the dictator tried to mollify the peasants by admitting the harm done due to the "excesses" of collectivization and signaling a halt of the process. The *Forverts* digest of this article came out on March 3, under the title "Stalin Is Afraid of the Peasants and Orders Communists to Slow Down."[27]

However, the tactical retreat was not to last. Things changed—and quickly, because the real objective was "total collectivization." In July 1930, *Forverts* predicted that in the fall, the harvest would reveal a downside of the collectivization.[28] In fact, the harvest of 1930 happened to be the biggest in seventeen years. Severe problems, including the famine in Ukraine and other areas of country, developed later. In 1932, Osherowitz observed that while the *kolkhozniks* expected to get a share of the harvest sufficient to keep their families going for a year, many of them received from their kolkhoz only a meager amount of grain, which could feed them for merely a matter of weeks. The rest had to be delivered to the state.

It was painful for Osherowitch to see hungry children, who were "pale, debilitated, emaciated, and without any sign of the cheerfulness that is

---

[23] Mendel Osherowitch, "Vi mentshn lebn in sovet rusland", *Forverts*, 1933, 61, 64.

[24] Ibid., 133.

[25] Ibid., 134, 138–39.

[26] Nathan Chanin, *Sovyet Rusland, vi ikh hob ir gezen* (Veker, 1929), 149.

[27] Unsigned article 2. "Stalin hot moyre far di poyerim; heyst komunistn geyn pamelekh," *Forverts*, March 3, 1930, 1.

[28] Raphael Abramovitch, "Der sakh-hakl fun di tsen yor bolshevistishe[r] revolutsye," *Forverts*, November 8, 1927, 3.

characteristic of children in other countries."[29] He heard about riots, especially by women, which—contrary to his characterization of peasants as inherently stoical people—had erupted in various places but remained unreported in the Soviet press. Sometimes peasants would set fire to buildings that belonged to their kolkhoz, doing this as an act of protest.[30] The author recounted the stories he heard about starving peasants in Bratslav (35 miles from Trostianets) who broke down the doors of the granary and carried out all the grain. In Haisyn (25 miles from Trostianets), starving peasants went to starving Jews and urged them to do the same thing. The villagers cautioned the Jews: "If you are not with us, this means that you don't want this, and we will get even with you when the time comes."[31]

The situation in Osherowitch's home *shtetl* was depressing too. The local population lived in the shadow of the monument to hundreds of victims of the May 1919 pogrom, one of the bloodiest of the time. In the memory of local Jews, life was still divided into three periods: before, during, and after the pogrom, or, as they called it in Yiddish, *umglik*, or disaster.[32] In Osherowitch's description, life in Trostianets was not much better than in the surrounding villages:

> Poverty and desolation in the houses... Jews wear the same dirty and torn clothes as the villagers do, and the same worn fur hats. Jewish women wear the same ragged clothes as the village women. ... Nobody speaks loudly, nobody cries, nobody feels confident... Jews started drinking heavily. They drink on mornings, days and evenings, with meals and without; they drink not only on holidays and Saturdays but also on weekdays, drink and look for opportunity to drink more... Drinking is explained by the fact that bread costs 12 rubles 50 kopecks, whereas a liter of vodka costs 2 rubles. "We drink and forget that we are hungry..."
>
> One cannot feel Saturdays on the street. Only on rare occasions do Jews dress on Saturdays differently than on weekdays. Poverty, which prevents welcoming guests on Saturdays, creates acute discomfort in people... Jews gather in the only remaining synagogue on Rosh Hashanah and Yom Kippur. ... People tell that a year ago, one woman cried in the synagogue because her son, a Communist, Soviet clerk, worked on Yom Kippur. She asked the Almighty to forgive her son... It happens that religious parents

[29] Mendel Osherowitch, "Vi mentshn lebn in sovet rusland," *Forverts*, 1933, 140.

[30] Ibid., 137–38. For women's riots, see Viola 181–204.

[31] Wolf Moskovich, "Jewish American Writer Mendel Osherowitz's Impressions of His Trip to Ukraine in the Winter of 1932," https://ukrainianjewishencounter.org/en/jewish-american-writer-mendel-osherowitzs-impressions-of-his-trip-to-ukraine-in-the-winter-of-1932/

[32] Mendel Osherowitch, "Oyf a brider-keyver, vu es lign bagrobn finf hundert yidn," *Forverts*, May 15, 1932, 3.

no longer go to synagogue because of fear that they could spoil their children's careers in the Party or some profession.[33]

Osherowitch concluded his book by quoting a woman who had once participated in a revolutionary movement. Now she told him: "We are rotting here under the banner of a beautiful ideal."[34]

Harry Lang, 1933

Raphael Abramovitch, a prominent Menshevik and an opinion-shaping political journalist of *Forverts*, paid much attention to the relations between the Soviet regime and the peasantry. Time and again he repeated that instead of a proletarian revolution the Bolsheviks had followed their utopian vision and organized an uprising of peasants drafted in the tsarist army during World War I.[35] On the occasion of the tenth anniversary of the Bolshevik revolution, he stressed the importance of applying democratic methods to finding a compromise with the peasant class.[36] In 1930, the *New York Times* publicized Abramovitch's criticism of the Soviet farm collectivization drive as a "historic tragedy affecting tens of millions of people." He stressed that "dull and stubborn Stalin will stop at nothing. No cruelty will prevent him from continuing." As a result, the country was "being converted into a real hell not merely for the ex-bourgeois but likewise for the peasant."[37] Abramovitch's article in the *New York Times* is a rare example of transcending linguistic borders. Almost the entire corpus of the political journalism and travel observations written by *Forverts* contributors remains "hidden" in Yiddish. In this sense, Harry Lang's articles on his 1933 Soviet journey are exceptions.

Born in Lithuania, Lang became an active trade unionist in the United States. In 1917 he joined the staff of journalists on *Forverts*. Although his articles focused predominantly on problems of the American labor movement, he also wrote on other themes, combining journalism with fiction. Some of his "entertainment novels," including *The Unhappy Bride from Suffolk Street* (1931) and *The Struggle for a Mother* (1932), came out

---

[33] Victoria Khiterer, Jewish places in the Ukraine, A historical guide, https://www.jewishgen.org/Ukraine/PTM_Article.asp?id=21. Accessed February 29, 2020.

[34] Mendel Osherowitch, "Vi mentshn lebn in sovet rusland," *Forverts*, 1933, 392.

[35] Raphael Abramovitch, "Mensheviks un Bolsheviks," *Forverts*, April 30, 1922, 8–9; Raphael Abramovitch, *The Soviet Revolution, 1917–1939*, (Allen and Unwin, 1962), 89.

[36] For Abramovitch's role in *Forverts*, see Estraikh, "Die jiddischsprachige."

[37] Raphael Abramovitch, "'Drive to the Left' in Russia Seen as Menace to Country: Stalin, It Is Declared, Has for His Objective the Extermination of the Peasant," *The New York Times*, February 9, 1930, 5.

under the feminine pseudonym Iva Lazarus.[38] Yet the more visible trace he left in history is associated with his journey, which lasted nine months and covered about twenty countries, including, most notably, a two-week stay in the Soviet Union in the fall of 1933. Lang and his wife Lucy Robins Lang, a labor activist, travelled to the Soviet Union on a visa issued by the Soviet embassy in Berlin thanks to the intervention of Republican Senator William E. Borah of Idaho, who campaigned for the USA's recognition of the Soviet Union and therefore was highly valued by Moscow's policy makers.[39]

By the time of Lang's trip, the food situation in the Soviet Union had become much grimmer than in the spring of 1932, although even then it had looked rather devastating to Osherowitch. In October 1932, *Forverts* summarized on its front page the article in the *New York Herald Tribune*, "Peasants Feel Winter of Want in South Russia" (October 7, 1932) by Ralph W. Barnes, the newspaper's correspondent in the Soviet Union. This material appeared on the same day on the front page of *Forverts* under the title "Ukraine on the Cusp of Bitter Hunger this Winter." In December 1932, *Forverts* wrote about the ban on private trading of food and that this restriction would cause ruin to thousands of Jews involved in such operations.[40] Internal passports, introduced at the end of 1932, normally were not issued to village dwellers, making it illegal for them to leave the countryside. On January 22, 1933, the government issued the "directive on preventing mass departure of starving peasants," claiming that "this departure of peasants, as well as departure from Ukraine last year, was organized by enemies of Soviet power."[41]

In December 1932 my elder brother was born in a Jewish colony in Ukraine, and I grew up listening to stories about the hunger from which the community suffered at that time—in particular, about a life-saving bag of dried bread which my mother's sister somehow managed to send from the city of Stalino (renamed Donetsk in 1961). From fall 1932 to summer 1933, famine raged in Jewish colonies of Ukraine.[42] *Forverts* wrote about "purges"

---

[38] Ellen D. Kellman, "The Newspaper Novel in the Jewish Daily Forward (1900–1940): Fiction as Entertainment and Serious Literature" (Ph. D diss., Columbia University, 2000), 238–40.

[39] Lucy Lang (Fox) Robins. *Tomorrow is Beautiful.* (Macmillan, 1948), 260–75; David Shub, *Fun di amolike yorn: bletlekh zikhroynes* (CYCO, 1970), 803–4; Dana G. Dalrymple, "The Soviet Famine of 1932–1934," *Soviet Studies* 15, no. 3 (1964): 255, 262; Bohdan Klid, and Alexander J. Motyl, eds. *The Holodomor Reader: A Sourcebook on the Famine of 1932–1933 in Ukraine* (Canadian Institute of Ukrainian Studies Press, 2012), 117–34.

[40] Unsigned article 4. "Toyznter yidishe familyes in Rusland veln laydn fun farbot tsu farkoyfn produktn," *Forverts*, December 10, 1932, 1.

[41] David R. Shearer, and Vladimir Khaustov, *Stalin and the Lubianka: A Documentary History of the Political Police and Security Organs in the Soviet Union, 1922–1953* (Yale UP, 2015), 133.

[42] Elena Suchkova, "Sodeistvie Agro-Dzhointa zemledel'cheskoi kolonizatsii evreev v Ukraine," *Trudy po evreiskoi istorii i kul'ture*, 50, 2014, 57.

in the colonies among local functionaries accused of unauthorized distribution of wheat grain to local families and, as a result, of failure to fulfill the entire plan of grain supply to the state.[43]

Lang's travel notes began to appear in *Forverts* on November 25, 1933, eight days after the USA's diplomatic recognition of the Soviet Union. Cahan purposefully postponed publication until after the official announcement, on November 16, of the American decision. The editor was wary of critical portrayals of Soviet reality being interpreted as the newspaper's disagreement with President Franklin D. Roosevelt, who was very popular among Jewish socialists. As Osherowitch wrote later, Cahan believed that Roosevelt's "New Deal was a harbinger of a more liberal epoch in the history of the United States."[44] In introducing Lang's critical report, Cahan expressed the hope that the description of life in the Communist state would provide a convincing answer to the rosy accounts of those travelers who, in Cahan's words, saw Russia through the eyes of guides provided by the Soviet secret police. He wrote, "The Soviet government travel bureaus are a powerful, highly developed device for obscuring the Russian truth from thousands of foreigners whom they bring over—for [their purpose is] to obscure the facts and to spread propaganda through them."[45]

Published in twenty-five instalments, Lang's report about his Soviet trip in general and about the devastating famine in particular, especially in Ukraine, was well-written and contained many interesting observations, but it was hardly as compelling as the arguably more comprehensive and competent travel notes by Osherowitch. Significantly, in contrast with Osherowitch, Lang often had an official companion travelling with him, which made conversations with people less frank.

The issue of the believability of Lang's description, especially in its revised form, was raised not only in the Communist press.[46] Lang's article "Seen and Heard in the Villages of the Ukraine," published on December 27, 1933, suggested the following explanation of the mass starving to death: "The peasants refused to do anything, so no bread was delivered to them. In other words, it was a revolt; revolt by starvation, revolt by swollen bellies and revolt by mass death..."[47] In reality, people were dying, as a rule, not because they had revolted and were being punished for doing so but

---

[43] Unsigned article 3. "Farfolgungen oykh in yidishe sovet-farms in Ukrayne," *Forverts*, December 15, 1932, 1, 8.

[44] Mendel Osherowitch, "Abraham Cahan," *American Jewish Year Book*, 53, 1952, 529.

[45] Daniel Soyer, "Back to the Future: American Jews Visit the Soviet Union in the 1920s and 1930s," *Jewish Social Studies*, vol. 6, no. 3 (2000): 146.

[46] Nayer Tomid, "Food for Thinker," *Bnai Brith Messenger*, May 3, 1935, 6.

[47] Bohdan Klid and Alexander J. Motyl, eds. *The Holodomor Reader: A Sourcebook on the Famine of 1932–1933 in Ukraine* (Canadian Institute of Ukrainian Studies Press, 2012), 120–21.

because most of the meager harvest went to the state and the villagers were simply left without food. Lang's short visit to a Jewish kolkhoz, Red Star, not far from Kharkiv, made a sad impression on him. The *kolkhozniks* appeared to him as inmates rather than happy farmers. He compared them with poor Arab peasants in Palestine, fully dependent on their landlords. According to him, the *kolkhozniks* definitely had problems with a lack of food, especially meat, but there were no signs of real hunger.[48]

In the winter of 1932–33, when Lang's travel notes about the two weeks spent in the Soviet Union were serialized in *Forverts*, they did not become a sensation and probably therefore did not come out in book form. They did, however, cause a stir in April 1935, after being reprinted in revised form and translated into English in the *New York Evening Journal*, whose publisher, William Randolph Hearst, sought to use these revelations to attack Roosevelt's pro-Soviet policy. This was one of the *New York Evening Journal*'s several publications on this topic. Lang's article stood out by mentioning an estimate of six million dead.[49]

Hamilton Basso, a novelist and journalist, wrote: "It is certain that there was a general shortage of food throughout the country in 1932–33, and that it reached famine proportions in localized parts of the Ukraine, the Lower Volga and the North Caucasus." However, he attacked Hearst for saying "little about the food shortage when it actually occurred" and using it two years later as part of a political campaign (Basso). Indeed, the nature of the publication and the timing rather than the content of Lang's description were widely viewed as being downright scandalous. The Los Angeles-based *B'nai B'rith Messenger* ridiculed Lang for lending himself "to prostitution of his pen for a demagogue like Hearst," who was discredited, in particular, for his sympathies towards Hitler's fascism, "to which the Hearsts of America are trying to drive the American people."[50]

Particularly outraged were readers of *Forverts*. Numerous individuals and organizations, including Yiddish writers and journalists in Havana, Cuba, sent protesting letters. A group of Jewish socialists formed a Committee against the Hearst-Lang-Cahan Alliance. In all, it seems that the protests and outrage remained confined predominantly to Jewish circles. Characteristically, William Green, President of the American Federation of Labor, wrote to Baruch Charney Vladeck, Manager of *Forverts* and a towering figure in the American labor movement, on May 18, 1935: "It

---

[48] Harry Lang, "A bazukh in di yidishe 'kolkhozn' fun Ukrayne un Vaysrusland." *Forverts*, December 30, 1933, 3.

[49] Report to Congress. *Investigation of the Ukrainian Famine, 1932–1933*. U.S. Government Publishing Office, 1988, 178–79.

[50] Nayer Tomid, "Food for Thinker," *B'nai B'rith Messenger*, May 3, 1935, 6.

occurs to me that the question of importance was whether the articles were true and whether they stated facts rather than the question as to how they were given publicity."[51] By that time, *Forverts* had distanced itself from the publication in the *New York Evening Journal* (Unsigned articles 5 and 6), though hardly anyone believed that Lang would have done this without getting Cahan's approval.

Lucy Robins Lang recalled:

> Hell broke loose. ... Harry was held responsible for all the ideas that William Randolph Hearst had ever expressed. Reliable informants reported that Harry was likely to be assassinated, and friends in the garment workers' union escorted him to and from the office. ... Harry was expelled from the Socialist Party, and he was nearly fired from the *Forward*. Indeed, if Abraham Cahan had not stated that he would resign if Harry were dismissed, the end of the story might have been different.[52]

Meanwhile, in May 1935, Cahan faced an angry audience that filled Madison Square Garden for the 35th annual convention of the influential mutual aid association Workmen's Circle, which was closely linked with *Forverts*. The delegates booed the editor for allowing Lang to recycle his articles.[53] The publication in Hearst's newspaper led to Vladeck's resignation, which was later withdrawn.[54] Rumors circulated that readers were deserting *Forverts*. One headline read: "Lost 30,000 circulation because of the Harry Lang-Ab. Cahan escapade in the Hearst publications."[55]

So, why did Cahan allow the publication of Lang's articles, though he certainly knew that Jewish socialists hated Hearst vehemently, particularly for his "romance" with Hitler? It can be assumed that Cahan, who belonged to the rigidly anti-communist "Old Guard" in the ranks of the Socialist Party, did it in an attempt to discourage more radical "militants" from cooperation with communists in the climate of the Popular Front policy. In any case, the scandal around the publication had little to do with the suffering of Ukrainian peasants.

---

[51] Vladeck Archive. Baruch Charney Vladeck Papers and Photographs TAM.037. Box 4. Lang, Harry-Hearst Articles. The Tamiment Library & Robert F. Wagner Labor Archives. New York University.

[52] Lucy Lang (Fox) Robins, *Tomorrow is Beautiful* (Macmillan, 1948), 274–75.

[53] Unsigned article 7. "Workmen's Circle Convention Boos Cahan." *Jewish Advocate*, May 10, 1935, 5.

[54] Unsigned article 9. "Vladeck's Resignation," *B'nai B'rith Messenger*, July 12, 1935, 4.

[55] Phineas J. Biron, "Strictly Confidential." *B'nai B'rith Messenger*, May 17, 1935, 4.

Conclusions

It is generally difficult to detect much sympathy toward Ukrainian peasants in *Forverts* publications. Undoubtedly, Ukraine and Ukrainians did not prompt positive feelings among the majority of *Forverts* readers. Too fresh were the memories of the civil war pogroms. A case in point is the attitude of the *Forverts* milieu to Sholom Schwartzbard, whose assassination in May 1926 of Symon Petliura became very salient in the Jewish and non-Jewish public discourse.[56] The Mensheviks, including Abramovitch, decided to distance themselves from this act of revenge, seeing it as a deleterious manifestation of Jewish nationalism. Cahan, on the other hand, explained that deep in his heart he agreed with Abramovitch but could not publish his anti-Schwartzbard article because it would outrage his readership, who viewed Petliura's assassin as a national hero.[57] Characteristically, Osherowitch and many other Ukraine-born writers of the *Forverts* persisted in writing about their enduring love of *Russia* rather than Ukraine.

Harry Lang turned to the topic of the tragedy which later became known as the Holodomor rather accidentally. However, thanks to the availability of the 1935 English version of his travel notes, they attracted the attention of scholars and publicists. Roman Serbyn, a Canadian historian of Ukraine, "always favored the estimate of 6 million victims that Harry Lang of the Jewish daily *Forward* brought back to the United States; this was based on a discussion he [i.e., Lang] had in September 1933 with a high Soviet official in Kharkiv."[58] Osherowitch continued to write extensively on Ukraine during the entire span of his career and was known as a prominent figure in American organizations of Ukrainian Jewry (Estraikh, "Uderzhitsia evreiskaia Palestina"). His two-volume edition of *Shtet un shtetlekh in Ukrayne* (Cities and Towns in Ukraine) was widely advertised and reviewed in the Jewish press. Its publication would even lead to the convening of a conference of American Jews of Ukrainian origin.[59] In fact, Osherowitch wrote a narrative of the centuries-long martyrdom of Ukrainian Jewry, beginning from Bohdan Khmelnytsky's time. For him and the majority, if not all, of *Forverts* writers and readers, this aligned with their image of Ukraine—a place of suffering from the 1648 massacres to the pogroms of the late imperial period and the civil war, and finally to the "final solution" under the Nazi German occupation. It is no coincidence that 1942 saw a

---

[56] David Engel, ed. *The Assassination of Symon Petliura and the Trial of Scholem Schwarzbard, 1916–1927: A Selection of Documents* (Vandenhoeck & Ruprecht), 2016, 285.

[57] YIVO Archive. The Papers of Abraham Cahan, RG 1139, box 2, folder 36.

[58] Roman Serbyn, "Letter to the Editor," *Nationalities Papers* 40, no. 2 (2012): 291–92.

[59] Unsigned article 10. "Folks-konferents fun Ukrayner yidn in Amerike vert tsugegreyt," *Forverts*, December 8, 1961, 8.

new edition of Sholem Asch's novel *Kidesh hashem*, an epic of 1648 that was first serialized in *Forverts* in 1919. In 1943, following the Soviet government's decision to rename Pereiaslav as Pereiaslav-Khmelnytsky, Osherowitch described it as a step similar to renaming a town after Hitler.[60] It is hardly a wonder, therefore, that his Soviet travelogue can be read as a sad interlude between a catastrophe and an apocalypse.

Archives

Yidisher Visnshaftlekher Institut. Archive. The Papers of Abraham Cahan, RG 1139, box 2, folder 36.

Bibliography

Abramovitch, Raphael. "Der sakh-hakl fun di tsen yor bolshevistishe[r] revolutsye." *Forverts*, November 8, 1927, 3.

— "'Drive to the Left' in Russia Seen as Menace to Country: Stalin, It is Declared, Has for His Objective the Extermination of the Peasant." *New York Times*, February 9, 1930, 5.

— "Der kongres fun der komunistisher partey hot gutgeheysn Stalins politik, vayl Stalin hot azoy geheysn." *Forverts*, July 24, 1930, 5.

— "Mensheviks un Bolsheviks." *Forverts*, April 30, 1922, 8–9.

— *The Soviet Revolution, 1917–1939*. Allen and Unwin, 1962.

Antsibor, Dar'ia. "Fenomen 'torgsina': obraz evreia v narrativakh o Golodomore." In *Kontakty i konflikty v slavianskoi i evreiskoi kul'turnoi traditsii*, edited by Olga V. Belova, 282–97. Moscow: Sefer, 2017.

[Barners, Ralph W.] "Ukrayne oyfn shvel fun bitern hunger hayntikn vinter." *Forverts*, October 7, 1932, 1.

Basso, Hamilton. "Mr. Hearst's Apostolic Creed." *The New Republic*, May 8, 1935, 361.

Biron, Phineas J. "Strictly Confidential." *B'nai B'rith Messenger*, May 17, 1935, 4.

Chaikin, Joseph. *Yidishe bleter in Amerike*: *a tsushtayer tsu der 75 yoriker geshikhte fun der yidisher prese in di Fareynikte Shtatn un Kanade*. Sh. Shklarski, 1946.

Chanin, Nathan. *Sovyet Rusland, vi ikh hob ir gezen*. Veker, 1929.

[60] Mendel Osherowitch, "A shtot in Ukrayne oyfn nomen fun pogromshtik Bogdan Khmelnitski," *Forverts*, October 23, 1943, section 2, p. 5; October 25, 1943, section 2, 6; Gennady Estraikh, "Jews and Soviet Remythologization of the Ukrainian Hetman: The Case of the Order of Bohdan Khmelnytsky," in *Stories of Khmelnytsky: Competing Literary Legacies of the 1648 Ukrainian Cossack Uprising*, ed. Amelia M. Glaser, Stanford, CA: Stanford Univ. Press, 2015), 169-81, 176–77.

Dalrymple, Dana G. "The Soviet Famine of 1932–1934." *Soviet Studies* 15, no. 3 (1964): 250–84.
Unsigned article 1. "Cahan on Russia." *Forverts*, October 23, 1927, English section, 1.
Unsigned article 2. "Stalin hot moyre far di poyerim; heyst komunistn geyn pamelekh." *Forverts*, March 3, 1930, 1.
Unsigned article 3. "Farfolgungen oykh in yidishe sovet-farms in Ukrayne." *Forverts*, December 15, 1932, 1, 8.
Unsigned article 4. "Toyznter yidishe familyes in Rusland veln laydn fun farbot tsu farkoyfn produktn." *Forverts*, December 10, 1932, 1.
Unsigned article 5. "Mir hobn bakumen briv vegn Langs artiklen, velkhe geyen itst in di Horst tsaytung." *Forverts*, April 11, 1935, 1.
Unsigned article 6. "A vikhtike derklerung fun der Forverts asosieyshon." *Forverts*, April 23, 1935, 1.
Unsigned article 7. "Workmen's Circle Convention Boos Cahan." *Jewish Advocate*, May 10, 1935, 5.
Unsigned article 8. "An Idol is Destroyed." *B'nai B'rith Messenger*, June 7, 1935, 4.
Unsigned article 9. "Vladeck's Resignation." *B'nai B'rith Messenger*, July 12, 1935, 4.
Unsigned article 10. "Folks-konferents fun Ukrayner yidn in Amerike vert tsugegreyt." *Forverts*, December 8, 1961, 8.
Engel, David, ed. *The Assasination of Symon Petliura and the Trial of Scholem Schwarzbard, 1916–1927: A Selection of Documents*. Vandenhoeck & Ruprecht, 2016.
Estraikh, Gennady. "'Uderzhitsia evreiskaia Palestina—vozroditsia i Ukraina!': Pis'ma Nikifora Grigor'eva k Moiseiu Osherovichu." *Jews and Slavs* 19 (2008): 284–92.
— "Jews and Soviet Remythologization of the Ukrainian Hetman: The Case of the Order of Bohdan Khmelnytsky." In *Stories of Khmelnytsky: Competing Literary Legacies of the 1648 Ukrainian Cossack Uprising*, edited by Amelia M. Glaser, 169–81. Stanford, CA: Stanford Univ. Press, 2015.
— "Die jiddischsprachige New Yorker Tageszeitung *Forverts* und ihr Berliner Korrespondent Raphael Abramovitch." In *Judentum und Arbeiterbewegung: Das Ringen um Emanzipation in der ersten Hälfte des 20. Jahrhunderts*, edited by Markus Börner, Anja Jungfer, and Jakob Stürmann, 115–41. De Gruyter, 2018.
Kagedan, Allan L. "Soviet Jewish Territorial Units and Ukrainian-Jewish Relations." *Harvard Ukrainian Studies* 9, no. 1–2 (1985): 118–32.
Kellman, Ellen D. "The Newspaper Novel in the Jewish Daily Forward (1900–1940): Fiction as Entertainment and Serious Literature." Ph. D diss., Columbia University, 2000.

Khiterer, Victoria. Jewish places in the Ukraine, A historical guide, https://www.jewishgen.org/Ukraine/PTM_Article.asp?id=21. Accessed February 29, 2020.

Klid, Bohdan, and Alexander J. Motyl, eds. *The Holodomor Reader: A Sourcebook on the Famine of 1932–1933 in Ukraine*. Canadian Institute of Ukrainian Studies Press, 2012.

Klinov, Yishayahu. "Yidn shikern—yidn arbetn—yidn veynen: nokh a bazukh in soviet-Rusland." *Haynt*, April 15, 1932, 3.

Lang, Harry. "A bazukh in di yidishe 'kolkhozn' fun Ukrayne un Vaysrusland." *Forverts*, December 30, 1933, 3.

Lang, Lucy (Fox) Robins. *Tomorrow is Beautiful*. Macmillan, 1948.

Konstantinov, Viacheslav. *Evreiskoe naselenie byvshego SSSR v XX veke: sotsial'no-demograficheskii analiz*. n.p., 2007.

Lestschinsky, Jacob. "Naye dolar-inkvizitsye in sovet-Rusland," *Forverts*, November 13, 1932, p. 1.

Letters. "Di hor shteln zikh kapoyr lezndik dize fir briv fun sovet-Rusland tsu hige kroyvim," *Forverts*, December 24, 1932, p. 6.

Moskovich, Wolf. "Jewish American Writer Mendel Osherowitz's Impressions of His Trip to Ukraine in the Winter of 1932." https://ukrainianjewishencounter.org/en/jewish-american-writer-mendel-osherowitzs-impressions-of-his-trip-to-ukraine-in-the-winter-of-1932/. Accessed February 29, 2020.

Nayer Tomid. "Food for Thinker." *B'nai B'rith Messenger*, May 3, 1935, 6.

Olgin, Moyshe. "Yidishe un nit-yidishe kultur in dem zelbn land." *Forverts*, December 23, 1918, 5.

— *Mayn shtetl in Ukrayne*. M. Gurevich, 1921.

Osherowitch, Mendel. "Oyf a brider-keyver, vu es lign bagrobn finf hundert yidn." *Forverts*, May 15, 1932, 3.

— *Vi mentshn lebn in sovet rusland*. Forverts, 1933.

— "A shtot in Ukrayne oyfn nomen fun pogromshtik Bogdan Khmelnitski." *Forverts*, October 23, 1943, section 2, p. 5; October 25, 1943, section 2, 6.

— *Geshikhtes fun mayn lebn*. Forverts, 1945.

— *Shtet un shtetlekh in Ukrayne un andere teyln fun Rusland*. M. Osherowitch Jubilee Committee, 1948.

— "Abraham Cahan." *American Jewish Year Book*, 53, 1952, 527–29.

"Otchet o deiatel'nosti Agrodzhointa za 1932 god." JDC Archive, Joseph A. Rosen Papers, file 70.1.

Report to Congress. *Investigation of the Ukrainian Famine, 1932–1933*. U.S. Government Publishing Office, 1988.

Serbyn, Roman. "Letter to the Editor." *Nationalities Papers* 40, no. 2 (2012): 291–92.

Shearer, David R., and Vladimir Khaustov. *Stalin and the Lubianka: A Documentary History of the Political Police and Security Organs in the Soviet Union, 1922–1953*. Yale Univ. Press, 2015.

Shub, David. *Fun di amolike yorn: bletlekh zikhroynes*. CYCO, 1970.

[Singer, Israel Joshua.] "A lebediker grus fun soviet-rusland," *Unzer ekspres*, April 8, 1932, 6.

Smolar, Boris. "Visitng the Jewish Colonies in Russia," *The Sentinel*, July 27, 1928, 13.

Sorokina, Elena. *Zoloto dlia industrializatsii: Torgsin*. ROSSPEN, 2009.

Soyer, Daniel. "Back to the Future: American Jews Visit the Soviet Union in the 1920s and 1930s." *Jewish Social Studies* 6, no. 3 (2000): 124–59.

— "Abraham Cahan's Travels in Jewish Homelands: Palestine in 1925 and the Soviet Union in 1927." In *Yiddish and the Left, edited by Gennady Estraikh and Mikhail Krutikov, 56-79.* Legenda, 2001.

Suchkova, Elena. "Sodeistvie Agro-Dzhointa zemledel'cheskoi kolonizatsii evreev v Ukraine." *Trudy po evreiskoi istorii i kul'ture*, 50, 2014, 52–60.

Viola, Lynne. *Peasant Rebels under Stalin: Collectivization and the Culture of Peasant Resistance*. Oxford Univ. Press, 1996.

Vladeck, Baruch. "Der Forverts durkh di krizis-yorn." *Forverts*, April 25, 1937, 2.

Vladeck Archive. Baruch Charney Vladeck Papers and Photographs TAM.037. Box 4. Lang, Harry-Hearst Articles. The Tamiment Library & Robert F. Wagner Labor Archives. New York University.

Wendroff, Zalman. "Vi es halt mit der yidisher kolonizatsye in Rusland." *Forverts*, August 30, 1926, section 2, 5.

— "Vayterdike argumentn far un kegn yidisher kolonizatsye in sovet-Rusland." *Forverts*, September 1, 1926, 7.

Zalowitz, Nathaniel. "How Do the Russian Jews Live?" *Forverts*, August 4, 1929, 12.

The Holodomor and the Informational Work of the Ukrainian Bureau in London during 1932–34

Roman Wysocki

It is hard to believe that only three decades have passed since it became possible to open the archives where documents about the Holodomor in 1932–33 had been secreted up until the fall of one of the largest Communist empires and the establishment of the Ukrainian state on its ruins. Given earlier lack of access, for six decades it had been impossible to even look at the tragic history of many millions of human lives. As a consequence of totalitarian rule in the USSR, Ukrainian society's current knowledge of the Holodomor could not become an element of collectively cultivated memory. In the vast majority of cases today, it is a *post-memory,* shaped under the strong influence of historical studies.

It was only with the onset of the 1990s, alongside attempts to make public life in Ukraine more democratic, that historians were able to make use of the formerly Soviet archives to conduct their research with relative ease. Over the course of the last three decades, they have also acquired an ever-greater understanding of the extent to which information about the Holodomor was able to leak across the USSR's closely guarded borders during the 1930s. Not much was known about it then, but nevertheless enough to correctly identify the scale, cause, and perpetrators of the famine-catastrophe. As a result of received "leaks" there were also those (perhaps unjustly somewhat forgotten today) who raised the alarm and engaged in informing Western societies about the tragedy taking place in Ukraine. This paper looks at one such instance—the informational and publicity campaign of the Ukrainian Bureau in London, which sounded the alarm societies and governments in the West regarding events in Ukraine.

Among Ukrainian civil institutions, the Ukrainian Bureau in London was small, yet it was among the most significant contributors to disseminating the news of an ongoing famine disaster in Ukraine between 1932 and 1933. It was thanks to the information distributed by it and the actions taken by its small circle of employees that many British politicians first learned of the scale of the famine-catastrophe along the Dnipro. It behooves us today to assess the effectiveness of the Bureau's information activities, the information it had at its disposal, and its impact on consolidating knowledge of the Holodomor in Western society and the Ukrainian emigration.

The Ukrainian Bureau in London was a project that required significant financial resources for its realization. According to the official version, it was initiated and created by Jacob Makohin (1880–1956), who provided all of the funds necessary for its establishment and ongoing operation in London. *Notably,* he also financed a similar institution in Geneva, as well as representation for both bureaus in Prague. These centers also collaborated with people in Canada and Romania. Makohin's plans included establishing independent information centers in Vienna, Harbin, Shanghai, and Tokyo, but he was unable to realize these aims.

In the version propagated by Jacob Makohin, the creation of the Ukrainian Bureau in London was linked to his trip to Galicia, then part of the Second Polish Republic, in the autumn of 1930. This trip took place immediately after the "pacification" of several hundred Ukrainian villages undertaken by Polish military and police divisions. According to Makohin, seeing the consequences of the violence inflicted in Galicia on local Ukrainian peasants prompted him to establish an information bureau. With this institution's help, he wanted to publicize in the West information about the brutal methods employed by the Polish government toward an innocent Ukrainian population.

The Ukrainian Bureau in London began its operation on March 25th, 1931. It developed an active and effective practice unexpectedly quickly, which surprised many.[1] The initiative was not conceived as a long-term one. In correspondence with colleagues, Jacob Makohin asserted that he only intended to finance the bureau's work for the first two years, and that the burden of maintaining the office afterward should be taken over and shouldered by Ukrainian society. The notion of "taking over" fell on deaf ears, and indeed Makohin did not look for new, "strategic" sponsors for the bureau. In the end, he financed established information centers for longer, at least the next several years[2] and, in London's case, almost until the end of its existence. When he stopped financing the London Bureau's work in 1939, its administrator up until then, Vladimir J. Kaye (Kysilewsky), tried directing its activities for an additional period of time. The institution's end came right after the outbreak of World War II, when Kysilewsky left London and moved to Canada in 1940.

The London Bureau's bylaws dictated that its activities benefit Ukraine's independence cause. Makohin's surviving correspondence contains declarations prohibiting contact between the institution he founded, along with its employees, and any Russian, Polish, or Romanian

[1] Instytut Polski i Muzeum im. gen. Sikorskiego [henceforth: IPMS], Biuro Ukraińskie w Londynie 1931–1939: Kolekcja 433 [henceforth: BU], sygn. 1, s. 5. *J. Makohin to Doctor [V. Kysilewsky]*, 14.01.1936; sygn. 2, s. 22, В. Кисілевський, *Перегляд праці Українського Бюро в Лондоні в роки 1931–1932–1933.*

[2] "Українське Бюро в Женеві перестало існувати", *Час*, December 2, 1936, 3.

authorities.[3] They were also not allowed to work with communist groups regardless of their members' nationalities. Despite his "patriotic" declarations, however, the Bureau's founder was frequently accused of working as an agent. These accusations arose from doubts and ambiguities surrounding the source of his fortune the one which made possible, so to speak, the work of the information bureau. In Ukrainian political circles, he was suspected of acting on behalf of, variously, Soviet, German, British, Italian, or American intelligence.[4] Simultaneously, his activities also placed him within the sphere of interest of Polish, French, and British intelligence services.[5] Suspicion toward the Ukrainian Bureau's founder also stemmed from his unexpected appearance on the Ukrainian political scene, as a person unknown to the public and without a political past.

Information about Jacob Makohin (1880–1956) [6] was (and remains) relatively scant, and his biography is full of ambiguity.[7] It is known that he emigrated to North America in 1903 from then Austro-Hungarian territories and that he enlisted in the United States Marine Corps (USMC),[8] which he left in 1921 with the rank of Second Lieutenant. In 1920, Jacob Makohin married the eleven-years-younger Susan Fallon (1891–1976). During the 1930s, she very actively supported her husband, engaging personally with specific initiatives and handling correspondence and behind-the-scenes talks on his behalf.[9] Their marriage was often presented

---

[3] IPMS, BU, sygn. 2, s. 3, *Circular 1.a, s. 4, Statement of aims and principles of the Ukrainian Bureau.*

[4] *Hołodomor 1932–1933. Wielki Głód na Ukrainie w dokumentach polskiej dyplomacji i wywiadu*, ed. by J. J. Bruski (Warsaw, 2008), 438; "Пресове Бюро в Лондоні і комуністична робота", *Українське Слово*, no. 16, April 21, 1935, 1; М. Цеглинський, "Справа з Макогоном", *Робітнича Громада* 4 (1937): 12–16; *Tajne mafie ukraińskie*, Słowo Narodowe, December 17, 1937, 3; *II Rzeczpospolita wobec ruchu prometejskiego* 4, edited by P. Liber (Warsaw 2013), 389.

[5] Personnel files on Jacob Makohin were compiled by M.I.5. See The National Archives (hereafter NA), Security Service (hereafter KV) 2/1239, 2/1240.

[6] "Помер Яків Макогін, відомий діяч і меценат," *Свобода* 9, January 17, 1956, 1; Р. Кравець, "Яків Макогін," *Українська Думка* no. 24, December 3, 2011, 8.

[7] NA, KV 2/1240, Memorandum. Jacob Makohin alias Jacob Makolin alias Jacob Makohon alias Jack McOwen alias Count Jacob Razumofsky alias Prince Mazeppa; A. A. Zięba, *Lobbing dla Ukrainy w Europie międzywojennej. Ukraińskie Biuro Prasowe w Londynie raz jego konkurenci polityczni (do roku 1932)* (Kraków 2010), 181–207.

[8] NA, KV 2/1239, "Summary of information regarding Mr. and Mrs. Jacob Makohin; "Grandfather" of Marine Aviation Dies in Mass.," *Windward Marine* 41, January 27, 1956, 5; *United States Census, 1910*, https://familysearch.org/pal:/MM9.3.1/TH-1942-25141-44442-61?cc=1727033.

[9] R. Breitman, B. McDonald Stewart, and S. Hochberg, eds., *Advocate for the Doomed: The diaries and papers of James G. McDonald, 1932–1935* (Bloomington 2009), 470. After the arrival in Lviv of Susan Makohin on June 29, 1933 (in the company of English journalist Hubert Tilman), the Ministry of Foreign Affairs ordered the Embassy of the Polish Republic in London never again

as a political and social intrigue, however. Of particular significance in this respect was the moment when Jacob Makohin began to pose as Prince Razumowski and his wife was taken for a person from a wealthy family.[10]

The office of London's Ukrainian Bureau (not to be confused with the Ukrainian Press Bureau that existed in 1919–20) was located in Grosvenor Place (London SW1), initially in building no. 40 and later at no. 27, where it was moved in 1934. The latter building was bombed and destroyed during World War II, which is one reason why the fate of the Ukrainian Bureau's files is not fully known. It is known, however, that part of the documents remained at Jacob Makohin's disposal in his private collection. With the Bureau's closure, the files located in his room were divided into at least two parts, with Vladimir Kaye (Kysilewsky) taking one part to Canada. Beside the bureau's correspondence and Makohin's letters, these files contained press articles prepared by the bureau's employees. Of significance to this collection is Kysilewsky's surviving diary covering his time in London. The mentioned documents are presently kept in Canada's national archives in the Vladimir Julian Kaye (Kysilewsky) Fonds.

The major part of the Ukrainian Bureau's documents remained in London after its dissolution. Currently, it is held in the archives of the Polish Institute and Sikorski Museum (PISM). The institute was established under a slightly different name in May of 1945 in order to gather and store the collections of "all [Polish] government and military archival units" loyal to the Polish government-in-exile. The manner in which it came into possession of the Ukrainian documents is shrouded in mystery. One version maintains that they were given to the Polish side voluntarily by the Bureau's former director, namely Vladimir Kysilewsky. This story does raise some questions, however. Indeed, there is little doubt that the path these documents took in arriving at PISM was more complicated.

The materials stored at London's PISM form the *Ukrainian Bureau in London (no. 433)* collection. It presently contains 454 items that consist almost exclusively of typescripts, as well as of daily records that occupy several metres. After the collection was sorted, part of the documents was put in chronological order while files with correspondence between the main office and its subordinate units retained their old system of organization. The quantity of preserved documents both impresses and disappoints. On the one hand, what has survived are materials illustrating the internal functioning of London's Ukrainian Bureau and correspondence

---

to give her a visa. See Archiwum Akt Nowych (hereafter AAN), Ambasada RP w Londynie, sygn. 1254, s. 60.

[10] "Відбудеться виставка мистецької спадщини Якова та Сузанни Макогін-Розу-мов-ський," *Свобода* 274, December 16, 1978, 1.

between people who worked there and various Ukrainian and international groups. On the other hand, there is generally little chronological continuity in the preserved documentation and only selected periods are better represented. Gaps in the archived correspondence prevent learning about the Bureau's activities in detail, or even fully knowing how the Ukrainian question was presented on the international arena. It is not possible to fully recreate the ongoing work of the Ukrainian Bureau on the basis of the surviving materials.

A look at the inventory of the London collection reveals that of the specified individual archival units (files) only one, no. 199, is dedicated to the "famine in Soviet Ukraine." To some extent, documents included in files 108 (correspondence with Olgerd Bochkowsky), 297 (correspondence with Cardinal Innitzer), and 406 (English press cuttings) also relate to the problem of the Holodomor. The real scope of Holodomor-related materials in the collection is greater, however. Many of the archival units contain information about activities of the Ukrainian Bureau, and of its funders and employees, that were tied to an information campaign about the famine in Ukraine. The records do not contain documents that reveal new facts about the actions of the Soviet authorities and the events as they happened. They do contain, however, much information about the campaign to publicize the Holodomor in the West. In the main part, this is true of correspondence devoted to organizing protest action and to contacts with various Western and Ukrainian politicians, and more rarely of memorials and reports. Among the archived documents we find, for instance, an almost unknown typescript of Olgerd Bochkovsky's work about the famine in Ukraine prepared on request of the Ukrainian Bureau, which was to have been published in the English language.[11]

The activities of the Ukrainian Bureau in London are of interest to historians mainly in the context of its participation in the protest action related to the so-called "pacification" of Eastern Galicia in 1930[12] and the work of Vladimir J. Kaye (Kysilewsky). Analysis of records inherited from the bureau deepens our understanding of Ukrainian civic diplomacy and the means of conducting international publicity campaigns by the Ukrainian émigré communities at that time. The institution was extremely impactful

---

[11] This text was first published in 2020. See О. І. Бочковський, *Вибрані праці та документи*, Т. III (Київ: Україна Модерна, Дух і Літера, 2020), 77–142.

[12] A. A. Zięba, *Lobbing...*; idem, "Jacob Makohin i jego Ukraińskie Biuro Prasowe (1931–1939)", *Biuletyn Informacyjny Południowo-Wschodniego Instytutu Naukowego* 1 (1995): 65–67; idem, *Ukraińcy w Kanadzie wobec Polaków i Polski, 1914–1939* (Kraków, 1998), 316–24; O. T. Martynowych, "A Ukrainian Canadian in London: Vladimir J. (Kaye) Kysilewsky and the Ukrainian Bureau, 1931–40," *Canadian Ethnic Studies* 4/5 (2015): 263–288; Р. Скакун, *Пацифікація: польські репресії 1930 року в Галичині* (Львів, 2012), 118.

in this regard. It is not sufficiently known, however, as perfectly exemplified by the paucity of knowledge about its part in informing the Western world of the famine in Ukraine during 1932–33. The Ukrainian Bureau held a key position in that initiative, which was made possible, as the documents show, due to the personal engagement of its director, Vladimir Kysilewsky.[13] He was a talented individual, very organizationally nimble and of an independent mindset.[14] Without his participation, Makohin's and the Bureau's publicity activity would not have had significant results, with the latter's role diminished in value to become, perhaps, only a minor episode in the history of Ukrainian emigration.[15]

The informational and publicity campaigns of the Ukrainian Bureau in London, beside Kysilewsky and Jacob and Susan Makohin, also involved Cecil John L'Estrange Malone with his wife and Louise Gibson, a hired secretary.[16] In the past, the mentioned Col. Malone served in the Royal Navy and was a pioneer of British naval aviation, commnding seaplane carriers during World War I. After the war he visited Soviet Russia and became fascinated by Bolshevism. In 1920 he became the first representative of the Communist circles in the House of Commons, later joining the Labor Party and becoming a Member of Parliament under its auspices in 1928. For the Ukrainian Bureau, as the surviving correspondence confirms, his value was tied to his numerous personal contacts with the British establishment, which enabled Kysilewsky to distribute information among British politicians. It is also worth mentioning Kysilewsky's relationship with Prof. Robert William Seton-Watson. It was under the supervision of this renowned expert in Eastern European International Relations that the Ukrainian Bureau's director wrote his doctoral dissertation at London's School of Slavonic and East European Studies. Moreover, Malone and Seton-Watson recommended Kysilewsky for membership in the Royal Institute of International Affairs.[17]

Right before the Ukrainian Bureau in London became aware of the famine disaster along the Dnipro, it tried to initiate an anti-Soviet campaign. Kysilewsky's correspondence reveals that obstacles to its development included, besides limited staff, a shortage of first-hand information. This

---

[13] O. T. Martynowych, "A Ukrainian Canadian...", 263–88; П. І. Арсенич, "Уродженці Прикарпаття — дійсні та звичайні члени НТШ (1873–1989)", *Прикарпатський вісник НТШ*, 2009, no. 3, 233–34.

[14] NA, KV2/1239, *"Why Makogon's? Antonchuk's"*

[15] See NA, KV2/1239, *Russian Unnumberd*, Prague, October 12, 1933.

[16] R. Kuśnierz, "Propaganda radziecka w okresie Wielkiego Głodu na Ukrainie (1932–1933)", *Dzieje Najnowsze* 2004, no. 4, p. 42; "The Great Famine", *The Ukrainian Weekly*, no. 36, September 4, 1983, 7.

[17] O. T. Martynowych, "A Ukrainian Canadian...", 269.

issue also became noticeable during the information campaign undertaken in relation to the Great Famine, which exposed the mechanism and scope of the Bureau's activities. The Ukrainian Bureau did not aim to disseminate second-hand information, but instead tried to base its reports on eyewitness accounts. Despite this being set as the standard of work at the bureau, it was difficult to meet in practice.

The Ukrainian Bureau's impulse to begin working toward publicising the news of famine in Ukraine came with news of Soviet refugees arriving in Poland and Romania. It was the Ukrainian Assistance Committee in Romania that first tried to publicize information on this subject. On March 21, 1932, it issued a memo to the League of Nations, with a copy arriving also at the Ukrainian Bureau.[18] According to the data it presented, 1,055 refugees (including 506 children) arrived in Romania between the beginning of January and March 13, 1932. Romanian border guards had also witnessed 10 people being killed and 29 people being injured on the Soviet side, and it was suspected that an indeterminate number of people must have been killed *before* entering the border zone. The refugees who made it to the Romanian side repeatedly spoke of famine spreading across Ukraine in their accounts. Hnat Porokhivsky, an activist in a group of former Ukrainian National Army (UNR) soldiers in Bucharest, confirmed as much in his correspondence with Kysilewsky. "They all," he wrote in one of his reports, "are ethnically Ukrainian and Romanian. Only a thousand refugees managed to escape to the Romanian side, but many failed to do so and died from the bullets of Soviet border guards, or in the Dnipro, or on Ukraine's territory."[19]

In April 1932, new information started to arrive in London via Geneva and Prague, confirming the arrival of successive refugees from Soviet territories in Romania.[20] One of the people responsible for collecting data on these arrivals was Col. Demyd (Dmytro) Antonchuk, the London Bureau's representative in Prague and a former member of the Ukrainian Military Mission in Romania. Based on the information he provided, the Ukrainian Bureau in London supported a discussion in the House of Commons, announced on April 13 of 1932, on the subject of need for the League of Nations' intervention in aiding the mentioned refugees. During this discussion, a representative of the British government advised the parliamentarians that

[18] IPMS, BU, sygn. 198, 122–23, *Mémoire concernant les refugies Ukrainiens en Roumanie présente par LED délègues des organisations ukrainiennes, membres du Comite Consultatif des organisations prives pour les refugies*, Genève, March 21, 1932.

[19] IPMS, BU, sygn. 198, 153–57, Г. Порохівський, *Втікачі з України*, Бухарест. See also: *Мілена Рудницька. Статті, листи, документи*, упоряд. М. Дядюк (Львів, 1998), 394–95; "Pogrom włościan ukraińskich na pograniczu rumuńsko-sowieckim", *Wiadomości Ukraińskie*, nr 100/690, March 3, 1932, 2.

[20] IPMS, BU, sygn. 14, s. 77, *В. Кисілевський до Д. Антончука*, Лондон, 23.04.1932

the Ukrainian Assistance Committee in Romania has already intervened in the issue and the problem seemed to have been addressed.[21]

In reality, the situation was nowhere as good. The information received by the Ukrainian Bureau from its Prague representative indicated much greater numbers of refugees than those given in Porokhivsky's report. According to the former, the Ukrainian Assistance Committee had to care for approximately five thousand people UNR's and there were instances of the Romanian authorities deciding to return refugees into the hands of the Soviet government. The veracity of this information was confirmed by Mykola Trotsky, the former secretary of the Ukrainian People's Republic diplomatic mission in Vienna and now the director of the information bureau established by Makohin in Geneva. In one of the letters preserved in the London collection he wrote, "After the intervention of the Ukrainian Social Assistance Committee [in Bucharest], the government promised to stop turning back refugees on the condition that the Committee assume legal (obtaining documentation) and material responsibility for them." Since chances of securing support by means of seeking voluntary donations were slim, according to Trotsky, the mentioned Committee turned to the Nansen International Office for Refugees for help. An estimated one million lei were needed to support those who had already crossed the border. The Nansen Office agreed to allocate ten thousand Swiss francs (approx. 340 thousand lei) in aid, but on the condition that this amount will be returned within the next five years. Given the urgency of the issue, the Committee in Bucharest decided to accept the loan. At the same time, with the Ukrainian Bureau as an intermediary, it wanted to influence the British representative in the Nansen Office in order to improve the institution's stance toward Ukrainian requests.[22]

In June of 1932, the Ukrainian Bureau in London noted, "The English press has written much about the situation in the Ukraine [in recent weeks], and we have provided [it with] helpful materials."[23] The bureau did not have a decisive say in the content that British newspapers published in the end, but it did try to consistently supply them with their materials. In

---

[21] O. T. Martynowych, "A Ukrainian Canadian...", 273.

[22] IPMS, BU, sygn. 16, 56, *М. Троцький до Д. Антончука*, Женева, June 3, 1932.

[23] IPMS, BU, sygn. 14a, s. 116, *В. Кисілевський до Д. Антончика*, Лондон, June 7, 1932. In 1931, 194 texts on Ukraine and Ukrainians, among which 14 were about Soviet Ukraine, appeared in the British press. In the following years, the corresponding figures were 1932: 360 (231); 1933 (from January 1 to September 15 — 627 (472); 1934, altogether 750; 1935 — more than 1,000. See: IPMS, BU, sygn. 2, s. 36, В. Кисілевський, *Перегляд праці Українського Бюро в Лондоні за роки 1931–1932–1933*; "Propaganda ukraińska w Anglji", *Biuletyn Polsko-Ukraiński*, 1936, no. 35; В. Ю. Киселівський, "Українська справа у Анґлії", *Діло*, no. 18, January 24, 1935, 2–3.

organizing an informational and publicity campaign, it printed and distributed press reports in the Ukrainian language, which were sent to thirty recipients. It also published a monthly, five-page bulletin (in runs of 900 copies) and periodically prepared English-language press reports and reviews (in runs of 35 and 50 copies, respectively). The Bureau also aimed to supply selected British politicians with information, which is why on June 24, two days after the members of the House of Commons raised the issue of Soviet politics, it sent materials about the USSR, with thanks for supporting Ukrainians, to all participants in that discussion. [24]

British interest in the events in the USSR and the Soviet Ukraine opened new possibilities for the Ukrainian Bureau. In a letter dated October 12, 1932, Kysilewsky wrote to Susan Makohin that "Something is happening in Soviet Russia and all the London newspapers are full of reports about the arrests of leading Communist activists in Moscow. All of us need to observe these events and wait for the right moment for Ukrainians."[25] The letter's author was not yet aware of the real scope of the famine-catastrophe. The lack of reliable knowledge on the issue stemmed largely (but not exclusively) from the inability to establish steady contacts with people in Soviet Ukraine and from the effects of Soviet counterpropaganda.[26]

It was November 1932 by the time Makohin and Kysilewsky began to hold talks with British humanitarian organizations, without seeing any positive results, however, for the next several months. From the correspondence stored at PISM it transpires that the British elites were for a long time mostly indifferent toward news of the famine in Ukraine. It was only after the journalists Malcolm Muggeridge and Gareth Jones published in March of 1933 a report based on a visit to the hunger-stricken regions[27] in the British press (*The Manchester Guardian* and *The London Evening Standard*) that the work of the Ukrainian Bureau fell on fertile soil.[28]

Midway through 1933, Ukrainian communities, including the London Bureau, began to mobilize once again. The undertaken actions led to the establishment of both protest and relief committees. On July 19, 1933, Volodymyr Tselevych, a politician with the Ukrainian National Democratic Alliance (UNDO), wrote a letter to Jacob Makohin, who was then in Geneva,

---

[24] IPMS, BU, sygn. 2, k. 14–15, *Строго огірочний звіт діяльности Українського Бюро в Лондоні за місяць червень 1932 року*, June 30, 1932.

[25] IPMS, BU, sygn. 4, k. 262, *В. Кисілевський до Я. Макогона*, October 12, 1932.

[26] For a wider discussion see R. Kuśnierz, *Propaganda radziecka...*, 29–46.

[27] Ibidem, 42; O. T. Martynowych, "A Ukrainian Canadian...", 273.

[28] IPMS, BU, sygn. 5, s. 231, *В. Кисілевський до Я. Макогона*, Лондон, July 13, 1933. See also: [Укрбюро Лондон], "Анґлійська преса про голод на Кубані", *Діло*, no. 227, August 31, 1933, 4; [Укрбюро Лондон], "Анґлійська преса про голод на Україні", *Діло*, no. 244, September 17, 1933, 3.

about the anxiety among Ukrainian-Galician political and religious circles regarding the situation in Soviet Ukraine. The Ukrainian parties in the Second Polish Republic, with the support of the Metropolitan Andrei Sheptytsky and other Greek Catholic bishops, proposed organizing a protest action. It was to include the publication of an appeal to international opinion, two days of mourning, anti-Soviet manifestations, as well as fundraising for the refugees. It was thought that similar actions could take place also among the Ukrainian emigration and come hand in hand with the creation of local relief committees. In encouraging Makohin toward cooperation, Tselevych tried to convince him that the work of the press bureaus in Geneva and London was seen as very important in Lviv.[29]

In answering Tselevych's proposal, Makohin agreed with asserting the need for conducting a proper campaign. He also assured him of his readiness to support the proposed action, revealing in the process his deep conviction in the uniqueness of the institutions he was financing. He argued that, on the international arena, the action will make sense only after prior demonstrations of Galician residents. According to him, it was there that the centre for coordinating the protest and relief actions should be organized and a long-term plan of action worked out. Makohin contended in his response—as activists in Lviv were, in fact, aware—that in Galicia, where the peasant population dominated, anti-Soviet sentiment could be stirred only after the harvest, on the cusp of August and September, and that protests should therefore be organized at that time. He emphasized that émigré protest committees established before the onset of activities should not be issuing petitions to the League of Nations.[30]

Kysilewsky also presented his own reply to Tselevych's letter for Makohin to approve. He thought that the bureaus could join in the common action, but that all activities should be conducted in line with an earlier established plan. In the Galician lands, in his opinion, the protests should aim both at the terror in Soviet Ukraine and the activities of local, pro-Communist and pro-Soviet circles. The role of the bureaus, he argued, would be to monitor publications, prepare suitable press materials, publish an informational bulletin, and translate and distribute informational materials among non-Ukrainians. Due to the summer holidays in Britain, as he wrote, the initiation of the action should wait until after August. He also noted that the appeals being prepared by the Ukrainian Parliamentary

---

[29] IPMS, BU, sygn. 5, s. 237, *Копія В. Целевич до Добродія [Я. Макогін]*, Лондон, July 19, 1933.
[30] IPMS, BU, sygn. 5, s. 258–259, *[Я. Макогін] до В. Целевича*, Женева, July 26, 1933.

Representation in Poland must be based on factual evidence and should come with the public endorsement of church hierarchs.[31]

As the correspondence preserved at PISM shows, Makohin was displeased by the independent stance of Galician politicians. Convinced of the uniqueness of his work and the moral leadership that was supposedly his due in organizing the protests on the international arena, he was indignant in his comments about their actions—namely, concerning the decision to establish a protest committee made in Lviv without awaiting his reply.[32] The one-sided assessment of the situation, typical of Makohin's statements, and his tendency to position himself as a mentor revealed aspects of his character. He remained scrupulously silent in his correspondence about his becoming interested in the famine in Ukraine only after several months of the issue being discussed in Lviv. Moreover, the decision to create the Ukrainian Social Committee for Rescuing Ukraine (UKHRU) in Lviv, which was formed mainly by means of the UNDO, was already considerably late in relation to the chronology of events in Soviet Ukraine.[33]

Despite Jacob Makohin's negative stance, the Ukrainian Bureau in London dispatched a letter to the UKHRU on August 21, 1933, in which it "declared solidarity with the campaign" that had started in Lviv. The missive underlines that the bureaus financed by Makohin in London and Geneva "believe that the Ukrainian Parliamentary Representation and key institutions on Ukrainian territories, which directly and in actual fact represent millions of Ukrainian people, are solely called upon to take leadership of the rescue efforts." Kysilewsky, acting on behalf of the Ukrainian Bureau in London, declared his willingness to closely cooperate with the Lviv Committee and to contribute to efforts at informing the international audience "of the situation in Great Ukraine, where the Soviet Muscovite rulers brought the populace to death by starvation." He also promised to keep informing the British public about the work of the UHKRU. In closing, he announced that "in order to strengthen its statement of moral solidarity and support also materially, the Ukrainian bureaus place the sum of one hundred US dollars at the disposal of the UHKRU in Lviv."[34]

---

31 IPMS, BU, sygn. 5, s. 262–263, *Проект відповіді для Целевича*, Лондон, July 27, 1933. See also: IPMS, BU, sygn. 5, s. 265, *Я. Макогін до В. Кисілевського*, Женева, July 29, 1933.

32 IPMS, BU, sygn. 5, s. 266, *Я. Макогін до Доктора [В. Кисілевського]*, Женева, 1933.

33 "Український Громадський Комітет Допомоги Страждальній Україні", *Діло*, no. 195, July 28, 1933, 1. For further information see R. Kuśnierz, *Ukraina w latach kolektywizacji i Wielkiego Głodu (1929–1933)* (Toruń, 2005), 217–22.

34 IPMS, BU, sygn. 199, s. 38, *[В. Кисілевський] до Д. Левицького*, Лондон, August 21, 1933. See that same document: Biblioteka Narodowa [henceforth BN], Towarzystwo Naukowe im. T. Szewczenki [henceforth NTSz], mkf. 68694, 1453, *В. Кисілевський до Д. Левицького*, Лондон, August 21, 1933.

The above declaration was similarly received. A memo from the UHKRU administration, signed by Milena Rudnytska and Zenovii Pelensky, promised to inform the London bureau of embarked-upon actions.[35] Arriving at an understanding was important to both sides, but it meant decidedly more to the London bureau, since it ensured a better flow of the information that was indispensable to its functioning. In mid-August of 1933, Makohin wrote that it was necessary to begin efforts to send aid to the starving.[36] He saw an appeal published by the Lviv newspaper *Dilo* (Deed) under the title "Let's strike the great bell in alarm!"[37] which called for similar actions, as a declaration that was effective and consistent with his own position. Consequently—as he wrote to Kysilewsky—he was prepared to join, along with the bureaus under his command, the publicity campaign being coordinated from Lviv.[38] In reality, Makohin's position on the matter was not unequivocal. He complained notoriously in correspondence with colleagues that maintenance of the informational action he initiated two years previously has not been assumed by the Galician circles and that emerging financial limitations do not allow him to continue.[39]

Subsequent months brought the breakdown of protests actions on Galician lands. Before this happened, the Ukrainian Bureau in London received worrying news from Romania. Despite the appearance of new refugees and reports of the wave of hunger and terror in Soviet Ukraine,[40] the Romanian authorities had forbidden the organization of a protest rally in Bucharest. They also used preventative measures in announcing the confiscation of an issue of the Ukrainian newspaper *Chas* (Time) for including information about the famine.[41] The Ukrainian Bureau in London was also informed about the worsening of conditions for organizing protests in Czechoslovakia by, among others, Dmytro Antonchuk. As the director of the Ukrainian Bureau's branch in Prague wrote in a letter to Kysilewsky:

---

[35] IPMS, BU, sygn. 199, 38, *Український Громадський Комітет Рятунку України до Українського Бюра в Лондоні*, Львів, August 25, 1933.

[36] IPMS, BU, sygn. 5, s. 274, *Я. Макогін до Доктора [В. Кисілевського]*, Женева, August 15, 1933.

[37] "Биймо у великий дзвін на трівогу!," *Діло*, no. 212, August 14, 1933, 1.

[38] IPMS, BU, sygn. 5, 276, *Я. Макогін до Доктора [В. Кисілевського]*, Женева, August 16, 1933.

[39] IPMS, BU, sygn. 5, 279, *Я. Макогін до Доктора [В. Кисілевського]*, Женева, August 25, 1933.

[40] IPMS, BU, sygn. 199, 40–42, *Бюлетень Українського Телеграфного Агентства (Украінтаг)*, Букарешт, August 25, 1933.

[41] IPMS, BU, sygn. 14a, k. 332v, *Д. Антончик до В. Кисілевського*, Прага, August 8, 1933; sygn. 16, 213, *Д. Антончик до М. Троцького*, Прага, September 13, 1933; BN, NTSz, mkf. 68694, 1773, *Українськиц Громадський Комітет Рятунку України у Чернівцях до Українського Громадського Комітету Рятунку України*, Чернівці, September 2, 1933; R. Kuśnierz, *Ukraina...*, 222.

The conditions for working on behalf of the famine are perhaps more adverse here than anywhere else. Evidence: the previous week, the Czech press published over ten articles and information about the situation in Ukraine. This week, there is not one word about the famine. It seems likely that the media have received some directions. Officially and unofficially, the Bolsheviks have carried out a frantic counter-attack [...] Bolshevik agents have convened rallies and organized the unemployed to go to the Relief Committee and humanitarian institutions [in order to ask] for help by saying "Help us if you are so sensitive. There is no famine in Ukraine. The famine is among us."[42]

On August 26, 1933, during a meeting of Galician politicians belonging to the UKHRU, the idea of including the Ukrainian Bureau in London in the publicity campaign on an international arena was discussed.[43] Makohin was satisfied with the idea, despite objections raised about the way the campaign was organized. At the start of September, in correspondence with Kysilewsky, he once again mentioned the necessity of commencing preparations for an anti-Soviet campaign. In describing his vision for this campaign, he was simultaneously providing instructions for the ongoing work at the bureau. He also took the opportunity to inform Kysilewsky, and not for the first time, that he was ready to sever cooperation with the Galician politicians if they proved incapable of being non-partisan or of organizing the campaign. According to Makohin, a single individual should be entrusted with its direction, and he warned against giving that role to Milena Rudnytska (a member of the Sejm). He suggested that the campaign funding be sourced from relief funds for the starving. He also informed Kysilewsky that he had called for a meeting to take place on occasion of the organization of the Congress of Minority Nations.[44]

In September of 1933 in Geneva, during the above-mentioned congress, a meeting of all the attending Ukrainian politicians took place in the hotel apartment rented by Makohin.[45] During the meeting, Makohin was more favorable in his treatment of the Romanian parliamentarians, whom he

---

[42] IPMS, BU, sygn. 14a, 333, *Д. Антончик до В. Кисілевського*, Прага, August 18, 1933.

[43] IPMS, BU, sygn. 5, 282, *[В. Кисілевський] до Я. Макогона*, Лондон, August 31, 1933.

[44] IPMS, BU, sygn. 5, 284–85, *Я. Макогін до Доктора [В. Кисілевського]*, Женева, September 4, 1933.

[45] IPMS, BU, sygn. 5, 311, *[В. Кисілевський] до Д. Антончук, Лондон*, September 23, 1933; BN, NTSz, mkf. 68694, s. 145, *Українська Парламентарна Репрезентація до Українського Громадського Комітету Рятунку України*, Львів, 14 XII, 1933; "Sprawy kulturalno-oświatowe i społeczne. Ridna Szkoła. — Proświta. — Akcja antysowiecka. — Wszechukraiński kongres", Sprawy Narodowościowe, 1933, nr 5, 553; S. J. Paprocki, "Zjazdy Mniejszościowe. IX. Kongres Mniejszości Narodowych w Bernie," *Sprawy Narodowościowe*, 1933, no. 5, 590, 595, 596–97.

personally invited to London, than of the Ukrainians politicians from the Second Republic who played a key role in the protest campaign. The meeting did not lead to the coordination of activities, intensifying instead Makohin's personal conflict with the Sejm members Rudnytska and Pelensky.[46] In correspondence about the mentioned meeting with employees of the bureaus, Makohin explained that he would be interested in further supporting a shared protest campaign when he was convinced "that the campaign helps the starving and not the prestige of one part of the country, a political party, or in the worst case even individuals."[47]

Following his director's lead, Kysilewsky expressed his disappointment with the stance of the Galician activists.[48] Despite translating the just-published declaration of the Lviv UKHRU into English on his own initiative, he described it as pompous and pointless in a letter to Antonchuk.[49] He also wrote that "the Lviv committee for helping the starving drove me crazy and I was nearly ill because of it. They are incapable of conducting any campaign. They do not pursue any possibilities or try to do anything on their own."[50] It is unclear how sincere these remarks were, since the surviving correspondence reveals that he avoided this tone of criticism in contacts with people outside of the bureau, speaking almost positively about the work of the Galician politicians.[51]

Also in the first half of September of 1933, Kysilewsky started to intervene at the British Red Cross. In informing Makohin about it, he wrote that working in close cooperation with Col. Malone, he thus wanted to convince the International Red Cross to send a representative to the famine-stricken regions.[52] This task was treated very seriously, especially since Makohin assured he had credible information that, with the Red Cross' permission, a special British commission would go to the affected areas in order to assess the situation. He felt this would forge a path toward

[46] IPMS, BU, sygn. 6, s. 234, *Я. Макогін до В. Кисілевського*, Женева, October 22, 1934.
[47] IPMS, BU, sygn. 5, k. 304, *Я. Макогін до Д. Антончука*, Прага, September 22, 1933.
[48] The antagonism of Jacob Makohin to Milena Rudnytska most probably had a personal root. The delegate to the Sejm did not hesitate to point out that he did not merit trust and that he sought to play a self-assigned role in political life that he did not deserve. See NA, KV2/1239, *Extract from: -SF/75/Ukraine/1. 20*, December 14, 1933.
[49] Por.: IPMS, BU, sygn. 14a, 353, *Витяг з протоколу Празького Комітету Рятунку України з дня 16.X.1933*, Прага, 30.10.1933; sygn. 16, 215, *Д. Антончик до М. Троцького*, Прага, October 12, 1933.
[50] IPMS, BU, sygn. 14a, 340, *В. Кисілевський до Д. Антончука*, Лондон, September 25, 1933.
[51] IPMS, BU, sygn. 140, 18–19, *[В. Кисілевський] до О. Мельника*, Лондон, September 22, 1933.
[52] IPMS, BU, sygn. 5, 295, *[В. Кисілевський] до Я. Макогона*, Лондон, September 13, 1933.

a humanitarian action of the kind organized by Herbert Hoover during World War I.[53]

In response to the invitation, the Ukrainian politicians from Romania, namely senator Volodymyr Zalozetsky and deputy Yurii Serbyniuk, arrived in London in September of 1933.[54] According to Kysilewsky's account, both parliamentarians encouraged Makohin to finance the Ukrainian Bureau's operations independently and advised against handing its control over to the Galician politicians.[55] Makohin and Kysilewsky took advantage of their presence in London to inform the British about the situation in Ukraine and to create a British committee for famine relief.[56]

In the meantime, to encourage closer association with British circles, the Ukrainian Bureau established direct contact with the charitable organizations Save the Children Fund, the Federation of Jewish Relief Organizations, and the Society of Friends.[57] Surviving documentation reveals that discussions with them concerned, as was the case with the Red Cross, the dispatch of a representative to Ukraine for the purpose of a first-hand assessment of the situation. The Ukrainian Bureau's proposal met with support on the part of Jewish circles, which, indeed, were already sending aid to Jewish people in Ukraine.[58] Col. Malone took charge of these discussions, first meeting their representatives at his personal residence on September 29.[59] Kysilewsky as well as Senator Zalozetsky and Deputy Serbeniuk were also present at these talks.[60]

The second meeting of this informal committee took place on October 6th and again concerned matters of famine relief and the dispatch of a representative.[61] Its participants noted that Soviet authorities could not only deny entry to a delegation but also prevent the delivery of food aid. In the meantime, it had transpired that the International Red Cross could not bring aid to the starving; it could not work in the famine-struck regions without the official permission of the government and the cooperation of its

---

53 IPMS, BU, sygn. 5, 296–98, *Я. Макогін до Доктора [В. Кисілевського]*, Женева, September 15, 1933.

54 NA, KV2/1239, *CX/8825*, 02.10.1933; *PF.40371*, October 10, 1933.

55 IPMS, BU, sygn. 14a, 342, *В. Кисілевський до Д. Антончука*, Лондон, September 28, 1933.

56 [Укрбюро Льондон], *"Акція допомоги в Анґлії,"* *Діло*, ч. 264, 08.10.1933, 2.

57 IPMS, BU, sygn. 199, 54, *L. B. Golden to C. Malone*, London, 07.09.1933.

58 IPMS, BU, sygn. 199, 68, *Українське Бюро в Лондоні до Українського Громадського Комітету Рятунку України*, Лондон, 19.09.1933.

59 NA, KV2/1239, *CX/8825*, 02.10.1933; *PF.40371*, 10.10.1933.

60 IPMS, BU, sygn. 199, 60, *C. Malone to A. M. Kaizer*, London, 27.09.1933; 202, *Українське Бюро в Лондоні до Секретаря Українського Громадського Комітету Рятунку України*, Лондон, 09.03.1934.

61 IPMS, BU, sygn. 199, 62, *C. Malone to A. M. Kaizer*, London, October 1933.

local structures. In reporting on this, Kysilewsky wrote to the Lviv famine relief committee:

During the discussion, two possible methods of helping the Ukrainian people were considered:

> 1) By means of suitable publicity, [meaning] by publishing true facts about the famine in Ukraine, [as well as] by pressuring international public opinion, [to try and] force the Soviet government to engage in saving the starving. This method, however, will not accomplish its aim according to the British representatives, since a) the Soviet government does not take much heed of international public opinion, and b) it is not invested in protecting the Ukrainian peasant population;
>
> 2) The second means of aid would involve: a) a food drive, b) obtaining permission from Soviet authorities to deliver the collected resources (if possible without paying duties) to regions most in need of help, and c) distributing the collected and delivered food supplies.

Surviving documents reveal that representatives of English charities were in favor of the second method of providing aid. They all agreed that the fundamental problem in negotiations with the USSR was that they unequivocally denied the fact of the famine in Ukraine. During the discussions, it transpired that one of the British organizations was able to obtain a preliminary permission from Moscow to send aid. This compromise did not mean that the Soviet authorities acknowledged that a famine had taken place. Their permission was granted because, as Kysilewsky wrote, citing the words of an administrator at the Soviet embassy in London, "the current economic crisis did not bypass Ukraine and there are many people there in need of help." According to the Soviet diplomat, aid could only be delivered by official means, through the chain of foreign currency stores "Torgsin." In the British view, the collection and delivery of grain to the starving was a very expensive proposition since, among other reasons, there existed a risk of import duties being imposed on the sent aid at the border. It was agreed that more detailed information from Galicia, Volhynia, and Bukovyna was needed. Of interest was the type and amount of food that could be collected as part of the relief effort, how much time was necessary for its collection, and whether the Lviv UHKRU had already undertaken talks with Soviet officials.[62]

In reply, the UKHRU informed the Ukrainian Bureau in London that Ukrainian politicians from the Second Republic could not lead negotiations with the Soviet authorities. If anyone was to do it, it should be non-

---

[62] IPMS, BU, sygn. 199, 97–98, *Українське Бюро в Лондоні до Голови Українського Громадського Комітету Рятунку України*, Лондон, October 11, 1933.

Ukrainians, if the Soviet powers were to take them seriously. They also wrote that a food drive had not yet been announced for lack of permission to export the goods and out of concern that they would spoil. It was estimated, however, that they could collect five to seven carloads of grain along with some other food items. [63]

The Ukrainian Bureau's efforts for the joint, still informal British relief committee to influence the authorities in London bore fruit only after several weeks of overtures. On the 27th of October 1933, a delegation consisting of Col. Cecil Malone, Ethel Christie, and Alice Nike met with Laurence Collier, the director of the North Department in the Foreign Office. They asked him for the support of British authorities in efforts to dispatch a humanitarian mission to Ukraine. A little later, Captain Walter P. Legge, who was the Secretary of the Catholic Relief Committee for Russia, an organization linked to the Interfaith and International Committee to Help the Territories of the Soviet Union Suffering from Hunger established under the patronage of the Vienna Archbishop, Cardinal Innitzer, signed a letter to the League of Nations requesting that an investigation committee be sent to the USSR.[64]

On November 1, 1933, during another meeting of representatives of London's charitable organizations, including Col. Malone and Kysilewsky, the discussion concerned the results of talks conducted in Geneva with the leadership of the International Red Cross. A proposal to establish contact with Cardinal Innitzer's committee in Vienna was also considered. The British were wary of a person who was working with him, namely Ewald Ammende, whom they considered to be a Nazi sympathizer. Another issue at stake during the meeting was a proposal to utilise the contacts of Jewish organizations in Kyiv to assess the effectiveness of aid provided via the "Torgsin" stores. Also discussed was the unofficial information that a representative of one of the British organizations commenced efforts in Moscow to get permission to supply aid for the starving. During the talks, the matter of formalizing the committee was also raised and it was agreed this would happen at the next meeting on November 10.[65]

A meeting did take place on the set date, but a joint famine relief committee was not formed. Instead, a decision was made to gather within the span of three days a group of representatives of specific circles, and for them to

[63] IPMS, BU, sygn. 199, 101–102, *Український Громадський Комітет Рятунку України до Українського Бюро в Лондоні*, Львів, October 23, 1933.

[64] IPMS, BU, sygn. 6, 1. *[V. Kysilewsky] to J. Makohin*, January 2, 1934. See also: "The Catholic Relief Committee for Russia: An Appeal," *The Tablet*, no. 4926, October 6, 1934, 12; "The Famine in the Soviet Union," *The Tablet*, no. 4945, February 16, 1935, 21.

[65] IPMS, BU, sygn. 199, 113–14, *Minutes of meeting*, 01.11.1933.

commence work on the future organization's charter. The results of the talks in Vienna were also related at the meeting, meaning that despite previously raised objections, contact with Cardinal Innitzer's committee was established in the meantime. The discussion extended to the issue of commencing a monetary fundraiser. It was furthermore established that the future committee would have only English charitable organizations as its basis, without an official representative of the Ukrainian Bureau, which was meant to guard the committee from accusations of engaging in a political campaign.[66]

On December 6, 1933, representatives of the Save the Children Fund, the Federation of Jewish Relief Organizations, and the Society of Friends created the Advisory Committee for Relief in the Soviet Union.[67] As foretold, the Ukrainian Bureau was not allowed to officially participate in it, though allowance was made for Kysilewsky to become its member as a private individual.[68] The Advisory Committee was seen as a temporary structure by all of its founding bodies. They agreed to form a "broader" committee once financial resources began to come it, which would include known figures of the British political scene. The concept was in fact realized, with the newly established formation named the Russian Assistance Fund.[69]

In the second half of 1934, there were in fact two active British relief committees for the Ukrainian starving in London. The "narrow" committee was directed by Lord Willoughby Dickinson, while the "broad" one included representatives of various religious communities as well as the leadership of the former.[70] The Ukrainian Bureau did not approve of the name assumed by the committee, but this was not its greatest worry at the time. A competing anti-Soviet campaign started in London by Volodymyr Korostovets, Hetman Pavlo Skoropadsky's representative in Great Britain, became a source of the Bureau's serious concern.[71] Without virtually any resources, he had nevertheless managed to organize a campaign that gained publicity and had

---

[66] IPMS, BU, sygn. 199, s. 126–128, *Українське Бюро в Лондоні до Голови Українського Громадського Комітету Рятунку України*, Лондон, 13.11.1933.

[67] R. Kuśnierz, *Ukraina...*, 225; IPMS, BU, sygn. 199, 144, *[Українське Бюро] до Секретаря Українського Громадського Комітету Рятунку України*. For that same document in the original, see BN. Mf 68694, 1513, *В. Кисілевський до Секретаря Українського Громадського Комітету Рятунку України*, Лондон, 18.02.1934. The original intention was for the committee to be called the Advisory Committee for Relief in Russia. See IPMS, BU, sygn. 297, *Draft Constitution*.

[68] IPMS, BU, sygn. 199, 129, *L. B. Golden to C. Malone, London*, 22.11.1933.

[69] IPMS, BU, sygn. 199, 144, *[Українське Бюро в Лондоні] до Секретаря Українського Громадського Комітету Рятунку України*.

[70] IPMS, BU, sygn. 199, 359–60, *Українське Бюро до Секретаря Ділового Комітет Рятунку України*, Лондон, 14.07.1934.

[71] IPMS, BU, sygn. 199, 99, *А. Жук до В. Кисілевського*, Львів, 16.10.1933.

a strong impact on the British press. For a period of time, it even surpassed the efforts of the Ukrainian Bureau, which troubled Makohin.[72]

The Ukrainian Bureau could not participate directly in the work of the Russian Assistance Find, but its interests were represented there by Col. Malone, who had been chosen as the organization's honorary secretary, with the function of the treasurer assigned to Ethel Christie.[73] In the later stages, their roles were reversed, with Christie becoming the honorary secretary and Col. Malone becoming its chairman.[74] Not everyone saw the Advisory Committee for Relief in the Soviet Union, and later of the Russian Assistance Fund, as being independent from the Ukrainian Bureau. Some of the committee meetings were, in fact, held at the Bureau's premises.[75] Even Col. Malone thought that "the committee also belongs to the Bureau." Addressing this issue, Kysilewsky wrote that the Advisory Committee (or else the Assistance Fund) should not only function independently, but also that its members (alluding to Col. Malone) should not count on the Bureau to perform any work in their stead.[76]

As already mentioned, naming the organization the *Russian* rather than *Ukrainian* Assistance Fund prompted Kysilewsky to intervene. At the start of March 1934, in reporting on the effects of his efforts, he wrote to Makohin:

> Meetings of the Famine Committee in London are now more frequent. I demanded categorically that the name be changed. In response to my proposal the name was altered, but [only] in part. Now the committee really has two names and two types of letterhead have been printed. One reads *Russian Assistance Fund*, the other *Ukrainian Assistance Fund.* We will use the Ukrainian version of the letterhead. This entire *Fund* and its work are very inconvenient as they take up time I should be devoting to other aims.[77]

In December 1933, according to Kysilewsky's information, the Russian Assistance Fund was getting ready to start fundraising. It was also in talks with the Soviet "Torgsin," which had assured it that a 50 percent discount on food purchases would be given with the deposit of at least five thousand

---

[72] IPMS, BU, sygn. 6, 45, *Я. Макогін до В. Кисілевського*, Женева, 28.02.1934; sygn. 199, 394–95, *Українське Бюро в Лондоні до Секретаря Українського Громадського Комітету Рятунку України*, Лондон, 08.08.1934.

[73] IPMS, BU, sygn. 199, 202–03, *Українське Бюро в Лондоні до Секретаря Українського Громадського Комітету Рятунку України*, Лондон, 09.03.1934.

[74] IPMS, BU, sygn. 199, 389, *Russian Assistance Fund (Including Ukraine and North Caucasus)*.

[75] IPMS, BU, sygn. 6, 5, *В. Кисілевський до Я. Макогона*, Лондон, 09.01.1934.

[76] IPMS, BU, sygn. 6, 74, *В. Кисілевський до Я. Макогона*, Лондон, 26.03.1934.

[77] IPMS, BU, sygn. 6, 48, *В. Кисілевський до Я. Макогона*, Лондон, 03.03.1934.

British pounds.[78] The Fund was also in talks with representatives of the Soviet government regarding the delivery of aid in the form of grain. It sent the first food relief parcels to Ukraine only in the first half of 1934 and made the next shipment contingent upon receiving a delivery confirmation from the addressees.[79]

Without becoming directly involved in collecting the financial and material donations, the director of the Ukrainian Bureau in London concentrated his attention on preparing informational materials about the famine in Ukraine. He translated the documents, reports, feedback and petitions that he received from Lviv into English, as well as annotated them and sent to the press.[80] Some of the texts were distributed by Col. Malone, whose task was to deliver them to British politicians.[81]

The publication of information about the famine in Ukraine met with a Soviet counter-campaign in Great Britain. In writing to UHKRU, Kysilewsky noted: "The English press is exceptionally well-inclined toward the Ukrainian campaign. A lively discussion about the famine has taken place in the press. The Soviet authorities try to deny all news about the famine through its agents."[82] In a letter sent a few days later, he added: "The lack of authentic materials is extremely aggrieving [...]"[83] He reproached the politicians in Lviv for not providing him consistently with victims' reports.[84]

In response to Kysilewsky's complaints, the UHKRU in Lviv informed that it was unable to send new reports. Staffing issues in Lviv meant that there were no permanent employees who could tackle this job. The UKHRU admitted that refugees should be a valuable source of reports, but they were difficult to access.[85] As much as possible, Lviv provided news updates about refugees and copies of private correspondence with Soviet citizens. The Ukrainian Bureau exercized great caution when copying and distributing these materials. Suspicion regarding the authenticity of

---

[78] IPMS, BU, sygn. 140, 29, *[В. Кисілевський] до О. Мельника*, Лондон, 12.12.1933.

[79] IPMS, BU, sygn. 199, 10, *Український Громадський Комітет Рятунку України до В. Кисілевського*, Львів, 04.05.1934; R. Kuśnierz, *Ukraina...*, 225–26; *The Foreign Office and the famine...*, XXXVIII-XXXIX.

[80] See IPMS, BU, sygn. 199, 36, *Appeal by the Ukrainian Catholic bishops on behalf of the starving population of Soviet Ukraine.*

[81] IPMS, BU, sygn. 5, 385, *[В. Кисілевський] до Я. Макогона*, Лондон, 12.12.1933.

[82] IPMS, BU, sygn. 199, 55, *Українське Бюро в Лондоні до Голови Українського Громадського Комітету Рятунку України*, Лондон, 7.09.1933. See also: [Укрбюро], "Протиакція більшовиків в англійській пресі", *Діло*, no. 275, October 19, 1933, 2.

[83] IPMS, BU, sygn. 199, 13, *Українське Бюро в Лондоні до Голови Українського Громадського Комітету Рятунку України*, Лондон, 13.09.1933.

[84] IPMS, BU, sygn. 199, 91, *Українське Бюро в Лондоні до Секретаря Українського Громадського Комітету Рятунку України*, Лондон, 05.10.1933.

[85] IPMS, BU, sygn. 199, 95–96, *А. Жук до В. Кисілевського*, Львів, 07.10.1933.

received materials was apparent in the instance of the photographs sent by Alexander Wienerberger from Austria—which today are perhaps the best-known photographs of famine victims from Kharkiv. Col. Malone oversaw the process of passing them to the British press on the Bureau's behalf.[86] Kysilewsky did not have similar doubts about the veracity of information received from his mother, the senator Olena Kysilewsky. In one of his letters to Makohin, he wrote: "I have some news from Galicia. My mother has been to the Soviet border and spoke with the refugees. The Polish police sends many back to Bolshevia [*sic*], meaning toward certain death."[87]

The apogee of Kysilewsky's involvement in preparing information and propaganda materials about the famine in Ukraine came at the turn of December 1933 and January 1934. In a letter dated January 7, 1934, he wrote to Makohin:

> The Ukrainian Christmas is today but we do not have even a moment for rest. We have just finalized the matter of the petition. It has been sent to the press and all parliamentarians. I am sending a copy to Dr. Dm[ytro] L[evytsky] in Lviv. Tomorrow, I will prepare a press release about the petition. Such a task takes [a lot of] time [...].[88]

At the same time, Kysilewsky was preparing press summaries and editing the bulletin. It is worth mentioning that he was also helping to edit texts by people from outside the Bureau at this time. It was thanks to his personal involvement that *Peasant Europe*, a book by the British journalist Hubert Hessell Tiltman, was published. In the first half of 1934, in cooperation with the Lviv committee, Kysilewsky prepared an English version of Olgerd Bochkovsky's work about the famine in Ukraine.[89] A little

---

[86] IPMS, BU, sygn. 199, 230, *C. Malone to A. Wienerberger*, London, 03.05.1934, 232, *A. Wienerberger to C. Malone*, Slazburg-Maxglan, 08.05.1934; http://www.garethjones.org/soviet_articles/thomas_walker/muss_russland_hungern.htm [accessed: 07.04.2016]. The topic of photographic documentation of the Great Famine has been the subject of historical research. See, for example, R. Serbyn, "Photographic Evidence of the Ukrainian Famines of 1921–1923 and 1932–1933," *Holodomor Studies* 2 (2010), 63–94; J. Vogl, "*Alexander Wienerberger— Fotograf des Holodomor,*" "Dokumentationsarchiv des österreichischen Widerstandes," 2015, R. 2015, 259–72; and the HREC Holodomor Photo Directory: holodomor.ca/resources/hrec-photo-directory/

[87] IPMS, BU, sygn. 6, 39, *В. Кисілевський до Я. Макогона*, Лондон, 21.02.1934.

[88] IPMS, BU, sygn. 6, 4, *В. Кисілевський до Макогона*, Лондон, 07.01.1934.

[89] As a result of his reservations about the English variant of the text, its author decided not to publish it and sent typescript copies to select individuals. See IPMS, BU, sygn. 199, 17, *Український Громадський Комітет Рятунку України до Українського Бюро в Лондоні*, Лондон, 13.05.1934.

while earlier he independently published a small brochure endorsed by the Ukrainian Bureau in London titled *Facts about Ukraine*.[90]

In the spring of 1934, the Ukrainian Bureau's engagement in publicizing the famine in Ukraine weakened noticeably.[91] Afterward, it once again paid a lot of attention to the Ukrainian question in the Second Republic, raising the subject of autonomy and anti-Ukrainian discrimination and promoting the idea of the All-Ukrainian Congress. Starting in June 1934, in line with Makohin's assumptions, the main burden of coordinating the so-called famine campaign fell on the shoulders of the Bureau's representation in Prague.[92] In 1935, the issue of the famine was placed on the backburner of the London Bureau's activity, with its focus now on the organization of an English-Ukrainian Committee.[93]

The preserved documents from the collection kept at the Polish Institute and Sikorski Museum reveal the involvement of the Ukrainian Bureau in London in disseminating information about the Great Famine (Holodomor) outside the USSR borders. In terms of engagement, the publicity campaign was second in scope only to the campaign concerning the so-called "pacification" of Eastern Galicia in 1930. With a very modest staff at its disposal, yet thanks to the extensive involvement of its director, this institution became one of the few to campaign effectively to inform Western European society about the terror, political repressions, and the famine-catastrophe in Ukraine during the 1930s.

Archives

Archiwum Akt Nowych w Warszawie, Ambasada RP w Londynie, sygn. 1254, 1437.

Biblioteka Narodowa w Warszawie, Towarzystwo Naukowe im. T. Szewczenki, mkf. 68694

Instytut Polski i Muzeum im. gen. Sikorskiego w Londynie, Biuro Ukraińskie w Londynie 1931–1939: Kolekcja 433, sygn. 1–2, 4–6, 14–14a, 16, 140, 198–199, 205, 297.

The National Archives in London, Security Service, KV 2/1239, KV 2/1240

---

[90] IPMS, BU, sygn. 199, 331, *Українське Бюро до Українського Комітету Допомоги Голодуючим України в Люксембурзі*, Лондон, 24.08.1934.

[91] *II Rzeczpospolita wobec ruchu prometejskiego*, vol. 4, ed. P. Liber, Warsaw 2013, 292.

[92] IPMS, BU, sygn. 2, k. 41–42, *З діяльности празького представництва Українських Бюр в Лондоні та Женеві 1.X.1933 — 1.X.1934*, Прага, жовтень 1934.

[93] IPMS, BU, sygn. 205, 56, *Anglo-Ukrainian Committee*; AAN, Ambasada RP w Londynie, sygn. 1437, s. 100. *R. Smal-Stocki do E. Raczyńskiego*, Warszawa, 01.05.1935.

Bibliography

Breitman, Richard, Barbara McDonald, and Severin Hochberg, eds. *Advocate for the Doomed: The Diaries and Papers of James G. McDonald, 1932–1935,* Bloomington: Indiana University Press, 2009.

"Aktsiia dopomohy v Angli." *Dilo*, no. 264, October 8, 1933, 2.

"Angliiska presa pro holod na Kubani." *Dilo*, no. 227, August 31, 1933, 4.

"Angliiska presa pro holod na Ukraïni." *Dilo*, no. 244, September 17, 1933, 3.

Arsenych, Petro I. "Urodzhentsi Prykarpattia — diisni ta zvychaini chleny NTSh (1873–1989)." *Prykarpatskyi visnyk NTSh*, no. 3 (2009): 233–34.

Bochkovskyi Olgerd Ipolit, *Vybrani pratsi ta dokumenty*, T. III (Kyiv: Ukraina Moderna, Dukh i Litera, 2020), 77–142.

"Byimo u velykyi dzvin na tryvohu!" *Dilo*, August 14, 1933, 1.

"Grandfather" of Marine Aviation Dies in Mass." *Windward Marine*, January 27 (1956), 5.

Bruski, Jan Jacek, ed. *Hołodomor 1932–1933. Wielki Głód na Ukrainie w dokumentach polskiej dyplomacji i wywiadu.* PISM: Warsaw, 2008.

Liber, Pawel, ed. *II Rzeczpospolita wobec ruchu prometejskiego*, vol. 4. Centralne Archiwum Wojskowe Instytut Polski i Muzeum im. gen. Sikorskiego: Warsaw, 2013.

Kravets, Roman. "Iakiv Makohin." *Ukraïnska Dumka*, December 3, 2011, 8.

Kuśnierz, Robert. "Propaganda radziecka w okresie Wielkiego Głodu na Ukrainie (1932–1933)." *Dzieje Najnowsze* 4 (2004): 29–46.

— *Ukraina w latach kolektywizacji i Wielkiego Głodu (1929–1933).* Wydawnictwo Adam Marszałek: Toruń, 2005.

Kyselivskyi, Volodymyr Iu. "Ukraïnska sprava u Angli." *Dilo*, January 24, 1935, 2–3.

Martynowych, Orest T. "A Ukrainian Canadian in London: Vladimir J. (Kaye) Kysilewsky and the Ukrainian Bureau, 1931–40." *Canadian Ethnic Studies* 4/5 (2015): 263–88.

Paprocki, Stanisław Józef. "Zjazdy Mniejszościowe. IX. Kongres Mniejszości Narodowych w Bernie." *Sprawy Narodowościowe* 5 (1933): 590–97.

"Pogrom włościan ukraińskich na pograniczu rumuńsko-sowieckim." *Wiadomości Ukraińskie*, March 3, 1932, 2.

"Pomer Iakiv Makohin, vidomyi diiach i metsenat," *Svoboda*, January 17, 1956, 1.

"Presove Biuro v Londoni i komunistychna robota." *Ukraïnske Slovo*, April 21, 1935, 1.

"Propaganda ukraińska w Anglji." *Biuletyn Polsko-Ukraïnski* 35 (1936), 356.

"Protyaktsiia bilshovykiv v anhliiskii presi." *Dilo*, October 19, 1933, 2.

Rudnytska, Milena. *Statti, lysty, dokumenty*, uporiad. M. Diadiuk. Lviv, 1998.

Serbyn, Roman. "Photographic Evidence of the Ukrainian Famines of 1921–1923 and 1932–1933." *Holodomor Studies*, no. 2 (2010): 63–94.

Skakun, Roman. *Patsyfikatsiia: polski represi 1930 roku v Halychyni.* Lviv, 2012.

"Sprawy kulturalno-oświatowe i społeczne. Ridna Szkoła. — Proświta. — Akcja antysowiecka. — Wszechukraiński kongres." *Sprawy Narodowościowe* 5 (1933), 553.

"Tajne mafie ukraińskie", *Słowo Narodowe*, December 17, 1937, 3.

"The Catholic Relief Committee for Russia: An Appeal." *The Tablet*, October 6, 1934, 12.

"The Famine in the Soviet Union." *The Tablet*, February 16, 1935, 21.

Carynnyk, Marco, Lubomyr Y. Luciuk, and Bohdan S. Kordan, eds. *The Foreign Office and the Famine: British Documents on Ukraine and the Great Famine of 1932–1933*, Kingston, Ont. Vestal, 1988.

"The Great Famine." *The Ukrainian Weekly*, September 4, 1983, 7.

Tsehlynskyi, M. "Sprava z Makohonom." *Robitnycha Hromada*, no. 4 (1937): 12–16.

"Ukraïnske Biuro v Zhenevi perestalo isnuvaty." *Chas*, December 2, 1936, 3.

"Ukraïnskyi Hromadskyi Komitet Dopomohy Strazhdalnii Ukraïni." *Dilo*, July 28, 1933, 1.

United States Census, 1910, https://familysearch.org/pal:/MM9.3.1/TH-1942-25141-44442-61?cc=1727033.

"Vidbudetsia vystavka mystetskoï spadshchyny Iakova ta Suzanny Makohin-Rozumovskykh." *Svoboda*, December 16, 1978, 1.

Vogl, Josef. "Alexander Wienerberger — Fotograf des Holodomor." In *Dokumentationsarchiv des österreichischen Widerstandes*, 2015, 259–72.

Zięba, Andrzej A. "Jacob Makohin i jego Ukraińskie Biuro Prasowe (1931–1939)." *Biuletyn Informacyjny Południowo-Wschodniego Instytutu Naukowego* 1 (1995): 65–67.

— *Lobbing dla Ukrainy w Europie międzywojennej. Ukraińskie Biuro Prasowe w Londynie raz jego konkurenci polityczni (do roku 1932).* Cracow, 2010.

— *Ukraińcy w Kanadzie wobec Polaków i Polski, 1914–1939.* Cracow, 1998.

The Ukrainian Famine of 1932–33 in the Russian Émigré Discourse of the Interwar Period[1]

Mykola I. Soroka

Introduction

The Ukrainian famine of 1932–33, known as the Holodomor, has been the focus of much attention in the study of Ukrainian history as well as in comparative famine studies.[2] Various sources have been analyzed, including British, Italian, Polish, American, and Canadian materials. Surprisingly little attention has been paid to sources of the large and active Russian emigration in the interwar period. The purpose of this study is to show how the Ukrainian famine of 1932–33 was presented and interpreted in the Russian émigré discourse of the interwar period.

The specifics of the Russian-Ukrainian relationship have determined the methodological approach of this study. The Russian émigré discourse, which viewed Ukraine through an imperial prism and was critical of Ukrainian separatism, was quite consistent in exposing the totalitarian nature of the new Soviet state and thus serves as a valuable and reliable source on the Holodomor in Ukraine. The discourse indicates that famine was unleashed most brutally in Ukraine and in the Kuban region and North Caucasus, territories with large Ukrainian populations. This study also contributes to the literature on Russian-Ukrainian relations, which can be important in understanding the evolution of the values and identities of the two Slavic groups and the current conflict in Ukraine.

I will start with the identification of the famine in the Russian émigré press and then move on to its most prominent aspects as presented through foreign accounts, references to the Soviet press, an analysis of the famine in the broad context of the first Five-Year Plan, and global challenges and the efforts of the Russian émigrés to recognize the tragedy. I will end with the national Ukrainian dimension of the famine, which the Russian émigrés largely framed in the context of their imperial perception of Ukraine. The materials I examined in preparing this study include archival documents

---

[1] This paper is based on a presentation delivered at the Canadian Association of Slavists annual conference at Brock University, May 24, 2014. I acknowledge support of the Holodomor Research and Education Consortium (HREC) at the Canadian Institute of Ukrainian Studies, University of Alberta, which made this study possible, as well as the assistance of my colleagues Jars Balan and Serge Cipko, whose expertise in the study of the Holodomor was invaluable for my work.

[2] The most recent large-scale study was organized by HREC (www.holodomor.ca).

and correspondence of Russian émigrés (from politicians to ordinary people), reports of eyewitnesses, letters, visual materials (maps and caricatures), analytical accounts from the Russian émigré press and publications, reports based on evidence of foreign correspondents, and references to the Soviet press.

I argue that Russian émigrés were among the best-informed and competent sources on the famine. At least three factors contributed to their effectiveness: (1) Russian émigrés were in contact with people in their homeland and watched developments there closely; (2) many were highly qualified to provide analysis, including prominent politicians, scholars, and journalists; and (3) living abroad, they were able to take advantage of numerous foreign sources.

The Russian Émigré Press

The Russian émigré press played a unique role in revealing the reality of the Soviet Union and specifically in calling attention to the famine. Its role and reception are best described in an editorial by the newspaper *Poslednie novosti*: "Only the Russian émigré press has provided accurate information about the USSR thus far, although the West, under the influence of Soviet propaganda, did not really trust it. ... But now the situation has really changed, and they speak more about the famine."[3] Among the most prominent Russian émigré periodicals of the interwar period were the Paris-based newspapers *Poslednie novosti (Les dernières nouvelles), Vozrozhdenie (La Renaissance), and Mladorosskaia iskra* (Etincelle russe); *Dni* (Berlin and Paris); *Novoe russkoe slovo* (New York); and the journals *Sovremennye zapiski, Novyi grad, Chasovoi* (Paris); *Sotsialisticheskii vestnik* (Berlin and Paris); and *Volia Rossii* (Prague and Paris). These publications represented a broad spectrum of political views — liberal-democratic, social-democratic, socialist-revolutionary, conservative, and monarchical — that reflected in essence the perceptions and attitudes of the majority of Russian émigrés to the famine in the USSR and Ukraine. Geographically, these publications were located and published in the major Russian émigré centres of Paris, Prague, and Berlin, as well as New York. The most authoritative was the Paris-based daily *Poslednie novosti* (1920–40, print 30,000), which was read by émigrés from the former Russian Empire

[3] *Poslednie novosti*, April 7, 1933. Yuri Semenov from the major newspaper *Vozrozdenie* also spoke about the importance of the Russian émigré press, pointing to two major sources of information, Soviet publications and personal letters (November 3, 1933).

scattered in Europe, North and South America, and the Far East; it also found its way to the USSR and was read by Stalin.[4]

News and Letters

The Russian émigré discourse reported news about the famine on an almost daily basis. Information from these media show that the famine enveloped the whole Soviet Union, with the most severe outbreak occurring in Ukraine as well as the Kuban and North Caucasus, areas densely populated by Ukrainians. "The most difficult is the situation in Ukraine, where a poor harvest last year and new procurements have resulted in a real famine," reported *Vozrozhdenie*.[5] The situation was later illustrated with maps published by Russian publishers.

A similar map was printed in *Famine in Russia* by Aleksander Markov,[6] reprinted in the English edition (New York, 1934).[7]

Although information on food shortages in the Soviet Union had appeared earlier, recognition that a famine was taking hold became clearer in the summer of 1932. On June 12, 1932, *Vozrozhdenie* mentioned "the catastrophic dimensions of the famine in Ukraine" after Molotov and Kaganovich had visited Ukraine's capital Kharkiv and some information had appeared in the Soviet press. On July 1, 1932, *Poslednie novosti* published a letter from Ukraine in which an anonymous author compared the current catastrophe to the famine in the Volga region in 1921. The author despaired that by February, all bread had been consumed and that people were eating the livestock. Malnourishment eventually affected the peasants' ability to conduct spring and summer work in the fields (only 30 percent of the winter crops were sown), which would presumably affect the winter crops. The author complained that nothing could be found at the market and that people with bread were being robbed. "It is hard to say what to expect, but it's clear that never has it been as difficult as it is now, and the times ahead will be even more difficult."

An abundance of such letters appeared in the Russian émigré press, first-hand proof of the severe and man-made nature of the famine. Three more letters were published in *Poslednie novosti* in the same month, on July

---

[4] Its editor-in-chief was Pavel Miliukov, a leading historian and politician and former Minister of Foreign Affairs in the Russian Provisional Government before the Bolshevik coup. The newspaper provided information daily about developments in the Soviet Union and globally from various sources. It also contained a regular editorial column with thoughtful analyses of current events. For more detail, see S. A. Aleksandrov, *Lider rossiiskikh kadetov P. N. Miliukov v emigratsii* (Moscow, 1996), 82.

[5] *Vozrozhdenie,* July 9, 1932.

[6] *The Russian Economic Bulletin,* 1933, no. 9.

[7] *Poslednie novosti,* July 29, 1933.

12, 1932, in the section "Letters from there." Interestingly, two came from Ukraine and a third from Crimea, which was a part of the Russian Federation at that time but more closely tied with agriculture in Ukraine. By the end of 1932, thirty to forty people were dying per day in Poltava, reported *Novoe russkoe slovo* on December 12, 1932.

Although these letters came from various parts of the USSR, the majority were from Ukraine and areas with large Ukrainian populations. Some letters were even published in Ukrainian, such as the one from the Poltava region.[8] Sometimes Ukrainian words were preserved in the original. For example, a Mrs. Stebalo, who visited her homeland in 1933, reported that children were crying "Khliba, khliba!"[9] Even in letters from Russia, the writers recognized that the situation in Ukraine was the most catastrophic.

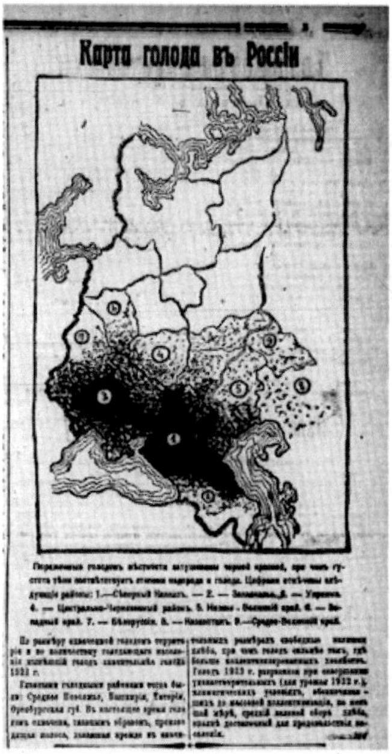

Fig. 1. Map of the famine in Russia.

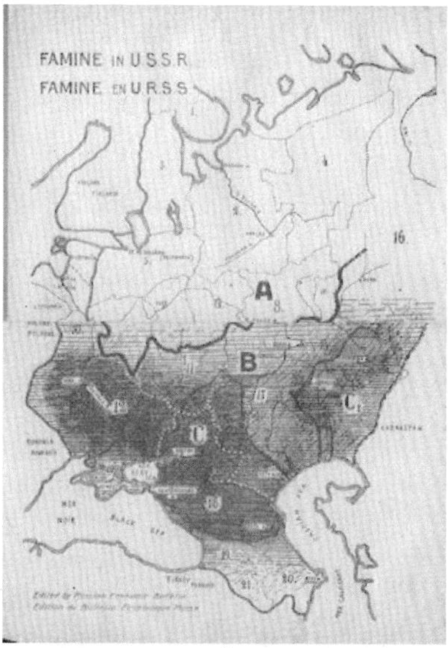

Fig. 2. Famine in the USSR (repr. Eng. edn. as Famine in Russia).

[8] *Poslednie novosti*, April 13, 1933.

[9] Published first in *Le Matin*, reprinted in *Poslednie novosti*, August 30, 1933. The Ukrainian-language original is also preserved in a letter published in *Vozrozhdenie*, April 9, 1933, under the title "Children are Killed and Eaten in Ukraine."

In a letter from Moscow complaining about the shortage of bread in the Soviet capital, the author wrote: "But in Ukraine, Russia's breadbasket, which used to supply bread to the whole world, the famine is even worse."[10] Under the title "The Famine in Ukraine," *Vozrozhdenie* reported that people were barely surviving the winter and were now eating straw mixed with potato powder, and that over one million had left their homes in search of food (July 18, 1932).[11]

The first cases of cannibalism featured in the Russian émigré press were associated with Ukraine. On October 22, 1932, *Vozrozhdenie* described child victims of cannibalistic acts committed by parents and strangers. A peasant woman named Zakharchenko from the village of Kharkivka killed her son in order to feed her other offspring. Children who disappeared were feared to have been victims of cannibalism. *Novoe russkoe slovo* informed the Russian émigré community in the United States about similar cases in the article "Cannibalism in Ukraine," based on a letter full of Ukrainian words (March 18, 1933).

The Russian émigré press published reports of eyewitnesses who managed to escape the "Soviet paradise" to neighboring countries such as

Fig. 3. – "Religion is the opiate of the people! Celebration of Easter is prohibited." (poster) – "Just try prohibiting people from fasting!" (caption)

[10] *Poslednie novosti*, April 22, 1933.
[11] *Poslednie novosti*, April 9, 1933.

Poland and Romania. The escapees to Romania provided information about the famine in Ukraine in July 1932.[12] By mid-1933, it claimed that about ten million people had died as a result of the famine in the USSR, most of them in Ukraine, the Caucasus, and the Volga region.[13] The fact that there were many Ukrainians among the famine victims outside the Ukrainian SSR was known to the Russian émigrés, in particular from the book *Facts about Ukraine*.[14] A reviewer in *Poslednie novosti*, however, criticized the book, claiming that it had exaggerated the number of Ukrainians living in the Don region, North Caucasus, and Crimea (August 17, 1933).

Foreign accounts in the Russian émigré discourse

Accounts by foreign journalists, tourists, and employees who worked and travelled in the Soviet Union comprised another important source of information about famine in the USSR. Scattered across Europe, Russian émigrés had access to numerous foreign publications and public presentations from the UK, Germany, France, the USA, Austria, Poland, and Switzerland and frequently referred to their perceptions of events in the USSR.[15] Among numerous foreign eyewitnesses of the famine were prominent figures such as the former British MP René Smith; Gareth Jones, secretary to the former British PM Lloyd George; the American professor Richard Sallett;[16] the prominent German journalist Richard Levinson; and German diplomat Dr. Otto Schiller, whose impressions were published originally in other newspapers. Despite Soviet propaganda and efforts to restrict the movements of foreigners inside the country, they became keen eyewitnesses of the drama unfolding before their eyes.

One of the first accounts to circulate came from the former British MP René Smith, who visited the Soviet Union and in distinguishing Ukraine as the site of the most severe chaos, predicted the famine.[17] Another authoritative voice was Martin Moore, a correspondent of *The Daily*

---

[12] *Vozrozhdenie*, July 18, 1932.
[13] *Novoe russkoe slovo*, July 11, 1933.
[14] *Fakty pro Ukrainu* (London, 1933).
[15] This list includes the British newspapers *The Times, The Sunday Times, The Sunday Express, The Daily Telegraph, The Daily Express, The Daily Mail, The Observer, The British United Press, The Morning Post, The Christian Science Monitor, The Manchester Guardian*, and *The News Chronicle*, as well as the German *Vossische Zeitung, Kolnische Zeitung, Berliner Tageblatt, Stuttgarter Tageblatt, Frankfurter Zeitung,* and *Neue Freie Presse*, the French *Le Temps, Le Petit Parisien, L'Écho de Paris,· Journal de Debates, Candide, La Republique,* and *Le Matin*, the American *New York Herald Tribune, Chicago Tribune*, and *Forverts* (Jewish), the Austrian *Reichpost*, Polish *Molwa* and *Kuryer Ilustrowany,* and the Swiss *Journal de Geneve*.
[16] *Novoe russkoe slovo*, July 11, 1933.
[17] *Poslednie novosti*, November 3, 1932.

Telegraph, who wrote a series of letters presented in *Poslednie novosti.* He also envisaged famine in Ukraine, the North Caucasus, the Volga region, and Western Siberia. He noted that despite some success in industry development, the Soviet agricultural system was failing, as peasants were not interested in collectivization and opposed it passively *en masse.*[18] A correspondent of *The Times* defined the situation as "a war against the village."[19] A German correspondent noticed that peasants saw "the proletarian dictatorship" as an enemy that they resisted through all possible means.[20]

Of special interest were reports and lectures of experts who had recently visited the Soviet Union. On February 16, 1933, *Poslednie novosti* published "Reports about Russia," which featured a public discussion of the situation in the USSR by the French Senator Victor Boreau (former Minister of Agriculture) and a professor of psychiatry, A. Mari, who had recently visited the Soviet Union. They described witnessing how the Soviet state made farmhands out of peasant farmers and argued that Soviet agriculture was doomed. Their speeches were followed by presentations by Alexander Guchkov, former Chairman of the Third Duma and Minister of War in the Russian Provisional Government, and Manuil Margulies, a doctor and lawyer.

Another witness, the American Dr. Billy Durant, had to interrupt his visit to the Soviet Union because his wife could not stand watching the suffering of the people there. He stated that he "could not expect such tyranny and depriving of basic rights of people in the twentieth century." Published in *The Saturday Evening Post,* his impressions were immediately reported in *Novoe russkoe slovo* (December 15 and 16, 1932; January 2, 1933), and an announcement that he would speak in New York about his visit to the USSR appeared in that paper.[21] In an editorial, *The Morning Post* referred to new domestic "passport" regulations in the USSR that limited the social mobility of the population as "Soviet slavery."[22]

Foreign accounts became more frequent in the spring of 1933, when it was difficult to hide the fact of mass starvation. One of the most shocking and trustworthy accounts came from Gareth Jones. Initially published by the *Daily Express,* his articles were immediately reprinted in Russian émigré newspapers such as *Poslednie novosti* and *Vozrozhdenie.*[23] Jones's

---

[18] Ibid., November 23, 25 and 26, 1932.
[19] Ibid., January 26, 1933.
[20] Ibid., February 2, 1933.
[21] *Vozrozhdenie,* January 15, 1933.
[22] Ibid., January 22, 1933.
[23] They were published in both newspapers on April 7 and 12, 1933; in *Novoe russkoe slovo,* on April 24, 1933.

revelations were an important sign for Russian émigrés that information about the famine had finally made its way to people in the West. "The valuable observations of an Englishman who managed to travel through Russian villages in one of the most fertile Russian regions and saw the consequences of Stalin's agricultural policies, which have totally ruined the Russian peasantry, supports entirely our account of Stalin's collectivization presented in the Russian press abroad."[24] Although Jones's depictions of famine were based on his travels in the Kharkiv region of Soviet Ukraine, the periodical framed them as "Russian villages," reflecting the imperial Russian view of the editors.

With a reference to *Forvets*, *Vozrozhdenie* presented an account of a correspondent of the German newspaper *Berliner Tagetblatt*, Paul Scheffer, who was initially sympathetic to the Soviet cause but changed his mind after Stalin's government began forced collectivization. Scheffer was apparently the first Western journalist banned from the Soviet Union, in 1929, for telling the truth.

The territorial disproportionality of the famine was also pointed out by a *Sunday Times* correspondent in Moscow, who reported that the most affected areas were Ukraine and the Northern Caucasus, noting that there was no shortage of food in Western Siberia, the Upper Volga region, and the Central provinces.[25] Malcolm Muggeridge of *The Morning Post,* who compared the famine in Ukraine and North Caucasus to humanitarian catastrophes he witnessed in India and Belgium, where people had abandoned their home villages due to cholera and war, wrote that he had never seen as abandoned a place as Ukraine. Writing that it was difficult to believe in the scale of the tragedy at that time of immense technological progress, he spoke in terms of an evil that had settled in this land: "It seems that nothing will grow here ever. It seems that the peasant is being eradicated with all his roots from his soil, like a plant, and is wandering as an anxious shadow through those places where he had enjoyed his life and been happy."[26]

---

[24] *Poslednie novosti*, April 7, 1933. In 2015, the Kashtan Press published *Tell Them We Are Starving: The 1933 Diaries of Gareth Jones* by Lubomyr Luciuk, which provides facsimiles of three pocket notebooks that the journalist filled with his observations during a three-week stay in the USSR in March 1933, as well as transcriptions of the contents.

[25] *Vozrozhdenie,* May 8, 1933.

[26] Ibid., June 7, 1933. Translation (mine) of the published Russian translation of Muggeridge's original English quote.

Fig. 4. Stalin: "The Soviet government takes all measures so that the number of hungry people decreases every day."

At the same time, the Russian émigré press was critical of Walter Duranty of the *New York Times*, who symbolized servility to the Soviet regime. An entire editorial in *Vozrozhdenie* was devoted to Duranty's attempts to burnish the Soviet image after the revelations of Gareth Jones. The newspaper focused on Duranty's falsehoods and deviations from the facts that were intended to convince the Western audience that "there is no famine at all."[27] On the other hand, the Russian émigré press acknowledged his sporadic revelations about displacement and the high death rate in Ukraine.[28] The Russian newspaper characterized as "idiotic rubbish" the writings of the editor and owner of the *Vancouver Sun*, Robert Cromie, who wrote pathetic paeans to the Soviet Union: "If there is a country that really

[27] *Novoe russkoe slovo*, December 7, 1932; *Vozrozhdenie*, April 26, 1933.
[28] "Ieshche o golode," *Vozrozhdenie*, October 6, 1933.

does something and does it well, it is the USSR. I praise the Soviet leaders and Soviet chiefs. ... Russia will be flourishing soon."[29]

Important news was also reported through Jewish channels in the Soviet Union. In particular, eyewitness accounts from Ukraine were transmitted to Tel Aviv and found their way to the Russian émigré press there as well as elsewhere.[30] The Jewish press in the US, UK, and other countries reported on the difficult situation for Jews, except for those individuals who had found government jobs, particularly in "southern Russia."[31] Unlike during the 1921 famine, when Jews had received help from various Jewish organizations abroad, in 1932–33 it became much more difficult as the Soviet government denied there was famine and imposed restrictions on communicating with foreign countries.[32] Moreover, reports in *Novoe russkoe slovo* claimed that a significant part of humanitarian aid sent from abroad was confiscated by the authorities.[33] In some cases, money was seized by means of "inquisition tortures" that aroused protests from Jewish groups, headed by the poet Khaim Bialik.[34]

The Soviet press

The Russian émigré discourse also made numerous references to the Soviet press regarding the famine. Although the Soviet government did not admit there was a famine or publish any materials on the matter, attentive readers were able to read between the lines. "Soviet newspapers provide rather valuable data for those who have learned to read them and evaluate their numbers and facts critically. Sorting through "low-hanging fruit, eyewashing, the ignorance of prominent and ordinary tourists and traps of Soviet propaganda, one nevertheless can discover fresh and interesting details," noted S. Fedorovich.[35] It was actually possible to follow the dynamics of wheat procurement through Soviet newspapers, to which the Russian émigré press referred and commented on a regular basis.

---

[29] *Vozrozhdenie* (July 29, 1933) gives a reference to his article in *News Chronicle* (Vancouver). More on the Canadian involvement see Cipko, Serge. *Starving Ukraine: The Holodomor and Canada's Response* (University of Regina Press, 2018).

[30] *Novoe russkoe slovo*, December 12, 1932.

[31] "Southern Russia" was usually referred in the Russian historical imagination as Ukraine.

[32] *Vozrozhdenie*, September 5, 1932.

[33] About 80 percent of the aid was confiscated, according to an eyewitness in a letter to *Novoe russkoe slovo* ("About Parcels and Money Drafts through the Torgsin," December 8, 1932; see also "Where Do Packages from Abroad Confiscated by the Soviet Custom Office Go?" December 14, 1932).

[34] *Novoe russkoe slovo*, January 21, 1933.

[35] *Poslednie novosti*, May 6, 1933.

Taking into account the Soviet press, Russian émigrés made important observations that helped to explain the nature of the tragedy unfolding in the USSR. Especially interesting were accounts by prominent Soviet officials such as Mikhail Kalinin, Mendel Khataievich, and Lazar Kaganovich. During the course of collectivization, they identified the "petit bourgeois attitude" of peasants as a serious obstacle to the implementation of the party line in agriculture. "The survival of possessiveness is deeply rooted among the peasants, and as soon as one has the chance to steal from the state, he would do it, obviously," said Khataievich, a member of the Politbureau of the Communist Party of Ukraine.[36] They explained failures in agriculture by the intrigues of the so called kulaks and raised the question of "a socialist reeducation of the peasants."[37] The famine, according to Kalinin, was part of a learning process in the construction of a communist society. Referring to the "insufficient or hardly sufficient" grain supply in Ukraine and North Caucasus, he stressed that the famine was "just revenge" on those collective farms that had not worked hard enough: "Collective farmworkers have learned a good lesson this year. For some it was quite a severe lesson."[38] Kalinin distinguished a category of peasants who joined the collective farms "with the clear purpose of corrupting and demoralizing them," against whom the government had to wage a decisive war.[39] Thus, Kaganovich advised Communists who were sent to enforce collectivization to be vigilant in uncovering class enemies.[40] This belligerent rhetoric might come from Stalin's speech at a plenary meeting of the Central Committee of the CPSU, where he allegedly said it would be necessary "to destroy several millions of the kulaks."[41] The idea that "getting rid of an excessive number of mouths" was an option for solving the food problem and would be desirable for the party was also voiced in a number of issues of *Poslednie novosti*.[42][43]

The Soviet government could have helped the starving with grain aid offered by Western countries and charitable organizations. Even if it made food purchases, they were transported mainly to cities but not to villages, argued a *Chicago Tribune* correspondent.[44] Certainly, the cities were seen as

---

36 Ibid., November 28, 1932.

37 Ibid., November 28, 1932; December 31, 1932 (with reference to *Pravda* December 27, 1932; *Vozrozhdenie*, June 21, 1933.

38 *Vozrozhdenie*, June 26, 1933.

39 *Poslednie novosti*, February 5, 1933.

40 Ibid., March 28, 1933.

41 *Poslednie novosti*, February 14, 1933.

42 See editorial for November 28, 1932 and an issue for May 29, 1933.

43 *Poslednie novosti*, September 10, 1932.

44 Reported in *Poslednie novosti*, June 6, 1933.

bastions of the proletariat, as opposed to the conservative peasants who had to be emancipated, this time in the new communist manner.

The Russian émigré press referred to the Soviet press in every issue, including *Pravda, Izvestiia, Sotsialisticheskoe zemledelie, Za industrializatsiiu, Za kommunisticheskoe prosveshchenie, Ekonomicheskaia zhizn', Znamia Rossii.* The news revealed that something might not be quite right in the Soviet Union. Problems with grain procurements were euphemistically hidden under titles such as "Bor'ba za urozhai"[45] [Fight for the harvest], "Bor'ba za khleb na Ukraine"[46] [Fight for bread in Ukraine] or "Gde khleb"[47] [Where is the bread]. An author in *Vozrozhdenie* referred to *Izvestiia* in writing about how the Bolsheviks had recognized the famine in Ukraine for the first time, if only by calling it "a difficult food situation in a number of collective farms in the Ukrainian SSR."[48] The Soviet press provided pieces of the puzzle of information that when merged with materials coming from eyewitnesses and foreign journalists, formed a picture of the avoidable famine that had begun in the summer of 1932.

Industrialization, Collectivization and the Five-Year Plan

Industrialization and collectivization were seen as major factors in the accomplishment of the Five-Year Plan of socialist construction, which would bring the young country to historic heights. By 1932, it was clear that the plan was not realistic and could not be fully achieved. *Vozrozhdenie* referred to *Pravda* in stating that the Bolshevik government had failed to increase the production of oil, coal, as well as food and both heavy and light industrial products,[49] which led to the further failure of many projects and imbalances in the Soviet economy, causing a political crisis. The Soviet state was unable to pay its international financial credits.[50] Russian émigré periodicals were full of titles such as "Full Collapse in the USSR,"[51] "Soviet Chaos,"[52] and "The Collapse of Soviet Industrialization."[53] The slogan "The Five-Year Plan in Four Years!" had been dropped, they wrote, adding that some would be happy if it could be finished in six years.[54] Furthermore,

---

[45] *Poslednie novosti,* July 14, 1932.
[46] Ibid., July 18, 1932.
[47] Ibid., November 2, 1932.
[48] *Vozrozhdenie,* July 21, 1932.
[49] Ibid., July 6, 1932.
[50] *Vozrozhdenie,* April 6, 1933.
[51] Ibid., July 9, 1932.
[52] Ibid., December 30, 1932.
[53] *Novoe russkoe slovo,* April 12, 1933.
[54] Ibid., December 4, 1932.

some analyses showed that despite collectivization, all grain harvests except for 1930 were lower than in 1913.[55]

Russian émigrés placed the crisis in the Soviet Union in the broad context of the world economy, recent developments in agriculture, the role of new machinery, and industrialization.[56] It was noted that the world economic crisis, which began in 1929, had been overcome by 1932.[57] Russian émigrés undermined the Soviet myth that economic crises were natural only in capitalist societies; on the contrary, they stressed in what deep crisis the Soviet Union found itself. Moreover, the long depression in the West affected considerably investments in the Soviet economy.[58]

Collectivization was seen as a major reason for the crisis. On December 20, 1932, *Poslednie novosti* published a report titled "Perelom v Sovetskoi Rossii" based on public presentations by Aleksandr Markov and Pavel Miliukov in Paris.[59] They explained the failure of the Five-Year Plan by "an underwater stone"—that is, the passive opposition of the peasants. Despite numerous efforts by the Soviet authorities to instill new Communist ideals, peasants opposed forced collectivization, unwilling to part with their traditions of individual farming.[60]

Годы	Посѣвная въ милл. га площадь въ	Урожай хлѣбов въ милл. тоннъ	Урожайность на 1 га въ центн.	На 1 голову населенія цент.
1913	102.0	81,6	8,0	6,5
1928	92.4	71,5	7,7	4,8
1929	95	71.7	7,5	4,6
1930	105,6	87,4	8,5	5.5
1931	102,0	67,0	6,3	4,7
1932	98.2	62,0	6,3	3,8

Fig. 5. Comparison of grain harvests between 1913 and 1928–32.

[55] Published in *Vozrozhdenie*, July 3, 1933.

[56] A number of book reviews were published in the Paris-based Russian émigré journal *Sovremennye zapiski* (1920–40), including *Krizis sel'skogo khoziaistva v SSSR* by Aleksandr Markov (Paris, 1933) (1933, vol. 51), *Ideia planirovaniia i itogi piatiletki* by S. Prokopovich (Paris, 1934) (1934, vol. 55), *Die Bilanz des Ersten Funfjahrplanes der Sovetwirtschaft* by Otto Auhagen (Breslau, 1933) (1934, vol. 55) and *World Agriculture and the Depression* by Vladimir Timoschenko (Ann Arbor, 1933) (1934, vol. 55). A number of analytical accounts appeared in the Christian-oriented journal *Novyi grad* in 1932–33, including articles by Petr Savitskii and Sergei Gessen. Savitskii published a book, *Voprosy industrializatsii* (Berlin, 1932), reviewed in *Novoe russkoe slovo* (December 24, 1932).

[57] *Vozrozhdenie*, January 6, 1933.

[58] *Novoe russkoe slovo*, January 2, 1933.

[59] *Novoe russkoe slovo* published this report on January 3, 1933.

[60] Ibid., July 20, 1933.

While granting that industrialization in the USSR had met with some success, Boris Brutskus, the leading economist of *Sovremennye zapiski,* called the Five-Year Plan a failure, used mainly to advance industry and the military by exploiting the peasantry and boasting of the advantages of socialism while proving ineffective in management. He concluded that "the famine was the result of the forced implementation of the plan."[61] *Novoe russkoe slovo* referred to the *Daily Telegraph* journalist Martin Moore, who argued that the Soviet leadership exploited the peasantry to reach their goals: "For the sake of new industrial constructions, the country has reached its limit, so that people were not interested in anything except food."[62]

In view of the failure of the first Five-Year Plan and collectivization, most Russian émigré activists as well as other experts came to the conclusion that the Soviet Union was in a serious political crisis with no clear way forward. Many believed that passive peasant opposition would gradually undermine the Bolshevik regime. But while some were inclined to believe that this would finally lead to the demise of Bolshevism, others were not so sure. In an editorial, N. Timashev spoke about "the exhaustion of Bolshevism." Comparing it to the crisis in 1921, the author said that "the current concessions [from the Bolsheviks] engender only a sense of their weakness and the necessity of further pressure." This, in his opinion, would lead to a positive solution: "Logic says that the existing revolutionary situation will finally result in a revolution liberation, constructive and national."[63] Kerenskii, editor-in-chief of *Dni,* agreed that something like the New Economic Policy introduced by Lenin to save the Bolshevik regime in 1921 was not possible at this juncture. The peasantry would not trust it, while the Bolsheviks had to adhere to their ideological principle of socialist construction, making no concessions. This deadlock would be resolved only in a violent conflict, and the famine was its manifestation.[64] He was quite naïve to expect that Soviet youth, who largely embraced the Soviet endeavor and later became disillusioned by it, might now change the situation.[65]

The Russian émigrés actually perceived this conflict as a war, "a peasant war," accompanied by passive opposition, spontaneous protests, and armed struggle. This concept was articulated in the military newspaper *Chasovoi* with a reference to V. Levitskii and his presentation in Gallipoli. The author emphasized that the main battle was occurring in Ukraine and

---

[61] Boris Brutskus, "Vzlet i raspad Sovetskogo planovogo khoziaistva," *Sovremennye zapiski,* 51 (1933): 417–31.

[62] *Novoe russkoe slovo,* December 1, 1932.

[63] *Vozrozhdenie,* July 10, 1932.

[64] *Vozrozhdenie,* October 25, 1932.

[65] Ibid., September 5, 1933.

the North Caucasus.[66] Kerenskii used the term "civil war," which in its third phase was waged against the workers and peasants (the war against landowners and capitalists had been the first phase, and against new business and middle-class people, the second).[67]

In his presentation at the Russian Central Federation on December 27, 1932, A. M. Kritskii put the current struggle in the broad historical context of the Soviet regime's ongoing attack on the peasantry. The first attack had occurred in the early 1920s, which the peasantry had won despite significant losses. Collectivization was seen as a second attack, which brought initial success to the regime followed by a sudden setback as peasants lost motivation when forced to perform labor. This had led to a political crisis in the Kremlin and the introduction of punitive measures, including the decree of the death penalty for the theft of socialist property. Kritskii saw 1933 as a breakthrough year that would bring about a horrible famine and a peasant uprising that would put an end to the Soviet regime. Commenting on Stalin's speech in early January 1933, an editorial in *Vozrozhdenie* was even more optimistic that "nothing can save the Communist regime" and that "a revolution is the only way to solve the problem."[68] The inevitability of the collapse of the Soviet regime was articulated by Georgii Fedotov, one of the most prominent Russian philosophers, in his article "Padenie sovetskoi vlasti."[69]

Following the logic of events, even foreign journalists and diplomats expressed some optimism that a new revolution would bring new people to power, including specialists, workers, and some Communist leaders who had become disillusioned in past Soviet practice.[70] Referring to the French *Le Temps, Vozrozhdenie* noted that there could be two solutions: the peasant movement would either smash the regime or initiate radical changes (December 30, 1932). According to Polish sources, economic collapse would lead to a political one: "Like a fire in the steppe, the revolutionary movement against the Soviet regime is taking on momentum quickly and openly in the army and even in the ranks of Communist Party

---

[66] *Chasovoi*, September 1933, no. 108–9: 3. See also: *Vozrozhdenie*, December 7, 1932.

[67] *Novoe russkoe slovo*, March 22, 1933.

[68] *Vozrozhdenie,* January 10, 1933. How optimistic some Russian emigres were can be confirmed by an announcement in *Vozrozhdenie* (March 7, 1933): "V. M. Levitskii will speak on 'The Struggle in Russia' at the Gallipoli meeting March 10, at 21:00. Content: Failures of the communists in the national republics of Transcaucasus. The struggle in the Ural region. News from the Don and Kuban. Victory of the cossacks on the grain front. 'Infamous' betrayals of local party members. Progress of the armed conflict. Tactics of the 'enemy': Peasants preparing to bury socialist agrarian culture. Zigzags of the authorities. The significance of current events. Free entry."

[69] *Novyi grad*, 1932, no. 5: 10–20.

[70] *Vozrozhdenie*, January 26, 1933.

members, largely among communist youth, not to mention peasantry and the working class."[71] The Russian émigré press actually supported the assumption that a civil war was already being waged in the Soviet Union. With a reference to the Italian diplomatic service, they reported that the war enveloped the Kuban and Don regions and destroyed the railway connection to the Black Sea, where Italian ships were waiting to transport wheat abroad.[72]

Besides their accounts in the Russian émigré press, Russian émigré experts were engaged in other projects in which they found a forum to speak about Soviet affairs and the famine. One of the most authoritative sources on the famine in the USSR was *The Russian Economic Bulletin*, a monthly periodical published in French in Paris by a group of professors of the Russian Commercial Institute. Articles in the bulletin devoted to the state of agriculture in the USSR included "The Agricultural Policy of the Soviets and Its Results" by A. Markov (October 1932, no. 1), "The Wheat Crop" by N. Popov (November 1932, no. 2), "What is Socialist Agriculture in the USSR" by M. Peroff (January 1933, no. 4), and "Soviet Wheat Harvest in 1932" by M. Gregorovich (February 1933, no. 5).

Markov's extensive study, "Famine in Russia," stands as an important document, which showed "indisputably that Soviet Russia is in the grip of a severe famine."[73] Professor Markov drew his conclusions from various sources, including letters of eyewitnesses, letters from foreigners residing in the USSR,[74] expert reports (made by Drs. Schiller and Auhagen), and attentive perusal of the Soviet press. He argued that "the present famine is not a sudden phenomenon but the result of Soviet policy over a series of years" and that "collectivization is the principal cause of the catastrophe." Markov also suggested that the reduction of the population was a part of the socialist reconstruction of the country "to attain a balance between a decreased volume of food products and consumption." He found it paradoxical that areas with rich soil such as Ukraine, the Kuban region and North Caucasus suffered most of all and explained it by the fervent opposition to collectivization. Due to its significance, Markov's work was translated into English and published by the Committee for the Relief of Famine in Russia in New York (1934).[75] In France N. S. Timashev, a journalist at *Vozrozhdenie,*

[71] Ibid., March 19, 1933.

[72] See *Vozrozhdenie*, February 2, 1933; *Novoe russkoe slovo*, February 12, 1933.

[73] *The Russian Economic Bulletin*, 1933, no. 9, 2.

[74] *The Russian Economic Bulletin* published many of these letters in 1933, no. 7; others appeared in *Entente Internationale contre la Troisieme Internationale tt. Documentation*, July-August, 1933.

[75] Reviews of Markov's study were published in the Russian émigré press. See *Vozrozhdenie*, April 6, 1933.

produced another important study. Published in the journal *Le Monde slave*, it provided evidence that the famine was not due to weather conditions but to the reckless agrarian policies of the Bolsheviks.[76]

A report prepared by the Bureau on Russian Economy at the University of Birmingham in the UK also confirmed that the famine in the USSR was occurring not because of unfavorable meteorological conditions. Referring to the Soviet press, the report said that the famine "had been prepared gradually and evolved progressively, and that it was the result of the general economic policy implemented by the Soviet government for a number of years." *Vozrozhdenie* noted that the famine in the USSR was a major event not only for Russians but, in terms of its consequences, perhaps for the whole world. The author emphasized that the report was especially important for foreigners "who often do not have accurate knowledge about the reasons and nature of the agrarian catastrophe in the USSR."[77]

Russian émigrés noted that not only knowledge but also a more consistent policy on the part of Western countries would have helped the Soviet peasantry in their struggle with the cold-blooded state. They were critical of the West's myopic politics of collaboration with the Soviet regime, which had indirectly contributed to the tragedy: "First of all, Western Europe and America should stop helping the Bolsheviks so that they will not have an upper hand over the Russian peasantry and Russia."[78] A similar call came from Kerenskii during a public lecture in Prague, organized largely for a local audience.[79] He emphasized his position in an open letter published in *The Times*, in which he suggested to participants of an economic conference in London the idea of creating an international commission to investigate the real economic situation in the USSR.[80]

Some foreigners who visited the Soviet Union were critical of the position of their governments, which continued providing financial support to the USSR. As one American visitor put it, "many Americans and in particular the newspaper *New York Herald* have to finally open their eyes and to see things as they are."[81] Sen Bris of the French *Journal* expressed this view after an international conference in London: "The strangest thing is that everyone knows about it [the famine], no one in London objected to revealing this incredible scandal. It was high time to show the world the total failure of Soviet methods. But instead, all governments jump on the

[76] See review in *Vozrozhdenie*, October 26, 1933.
[77] Ibid., January 4, 1933.
[78] *Vozrozhdenie*, January 15, 1933.
[79] *Novoe russkoe slovo*, March 22, 1933.
[80] Ibid., June 25, 1933.
[81] *Vozrozhdenie*, January 15, 1933. As was known, *New York Herald* was quite sympathetic to the Soviet Union for some time.

mirages of Soviet requests and issue credits in a rush to the regime, which has doomed 160 million to total misery."[82] Speaking about "an entirely unbelievable situation that had occurred in a European country in 1933," a correspondent of *The Daily Telegraph* called the politics of silencing the famine in the USSR criminal, with a reference to Pontius Pilate washing his hands. Speaking about the famine he witnessed during his travels in Ukraine, he said: "There are certainly some people who pretend they are deaf because of political or commercial considerations. But these people cannot be considered true representatives of the British nation."[83]

The collaboration of Western governments with the Soviet Union was connected with Soviet efforts to conceal the fact of the famine and in particular to achieve recognition of the USSR by the USA. With the intensification of the famine in the summer of 1933, all foreign journalists were summoned to a meeting with the Soviet authorities, where they were instructed not to leave the Moscow district without special permission.[84] As a correspondent of *The Observer* noted, these travel restrictions were concerned first of all with Ukraine and the North Caucasus, the regions which were suffering most.[85]

Fig. 6. – "Do you see: we have a real America here." (Soviet official) – "Yes, yes all that's missing is the Statue of Liberty." (Herriot).

Russian émigré efforts

As is well known, many people in the West were fooled into believing in the success of Soviet economic advances, both in industry and agriculture.[86] The Russian émigré discourse was

[82] *Vozrozhdenie*, August 2, 1933.
[83] "Ieshche o golode v SSSR." *Vozrozhdenie*, September 10, 1933.
[84] *Vozrozhdenie*, August 12, 1933.
[85] Ibid., September 4, 1933.
[86] *Sovremennye zapiski*, 1933, vol. 51.

instrumental in unmasking Soviet propaganda. An example that specifically concerned Russian émigrés in France was the visit of the former French prime minister Édouard Herriot to the USSR in August-September 1933, a time when millions had already perished as the result of the famine. Herriot visited industrial sites such as the DniproHES (Dnipro Hydroelectric Station) and enjoyed a reception by the Ukrainian government. Herriot was impressed with the new harvest and Ukraine's potential in agriculture, asserting that France had been deceived by stories of a famine in the USSR. *Poslednie novosti* was enraged by Herriot's ignorance: "Following his statements made in oppressed Ukraine that is dying out because of the famine, one cannot help but be dismayed: this is a man who may rule France again one day."[87] K. I. Zaitsev contributed with a brochure in French, *Herriot in Russia*, in which he showed a detailed itinerary of the French guest and argued that Herriot's uncritical admiration was intended to promote closer French-Russian ties.[88, 89]

The Russian émigrés also brought to light the methods used by Soviet authorities for the purposes of propaganda. "One should not underestimate the results achieved by the Bolsheviks through advertising tourism. Along with a few visitors who are able to perceive deception and see something, there are many people, unreflective and trusting, and simply fools who are the easy prey of Soviet propaganda," noted an author in the article "About Travelling in the USSR."[90] "They show what they want to show," commented the former Chair of the Russian Provisional Government Aleksandr Kerenskii about Herriot and other foreigners who visited the USSR, who, he said, "conceded to praise the system, which they do not understand at all."[91][92][93]

Recognizing the ideological harm caused by Soviet tourism, the author took a pragmatic approach, proposing rhetorically that Soviet tourists travel abroad, when the only way for them to travel would be by "swimming across the Dnister River or crawling under barbed wire and gun-shots." At the same time, the Russian émigré press reported on Soviet propaganda about life in the West, especially in connection with the economic depression. *Novoe*

---

[87] *Poslednie novosti*, August 31, 1933.

[88] See review on this publication in *Vozrozhdenie*, December 7, 1933.

[89] *Poslednie novosti*, August 27, 1933.

[90] *Vozrozhdenie*, September 2, 1932.

[91] Ibid., September 5, 1933. The American journalist G. Lang wrote about his impressions of "*a-la* Potemkin staging of receptions of foreign delegations" in *Sotsialisticheskii vestnik* (September 10, 1933), 14–15.

[92] *Poslednie novosti*, August 18, 1932. This caricature describes the attitudes of Soviet authorities to foreign tourists.

[93] Ibid., September 7, 1933. This caricature depicts the first humans, Adam and Eve, with their simple way of life.

russkoe slovo*, for example, referred to its allegations concerning the disappearance of dogs in the USA and Canada and special brigades to clean the streets from people who had died from hunger.[94]

Worth noting are the efforts of prominent Russian émigré individuals who sought to bring the famine to the attention of the international community. On March 12, 1933, a meeting of Russian émigré groups produced a resolution in New York in which they condemned the new wave of terror by the Soviet government against its own people, leading to famine, and called on American society to defend the great principle of freedom and democracy.[95] On October 5, 1933, a group of activists that included Aleksnadr Kerenskii, the former head of the Russian Provisional government, Pavel Miliukov, and the prominent writer Mark Aldanov sent telegrams to the Chair of the Council of the League of Nations Johan Mowinckel (who was also Prime Minister of Norway) and to the Red Cross in Geneva in appreciation of their "stance in defence of the population of Russia affected by the famine."[96]

On October 22, 1933, a coordinated appeal to people in Western Europe and America was published by Russian émigrés to raise awareness of "the

Fig. 7. "When everything turns to dust, all that's left is to blow it into the eyes of foreigners."

[94] *Novoe russkoe slovo*, December 14, 1932.
[95] Ibid., March 14, 1933.
[96] *Poslednie novosti*, October 6, 1933.

severe tragedy in the Russian lands under the Communist rule." "It is the logical result of Soviet politics. Being continuously at war with their own people and brutally suppressing any attempts of resistance, the Soviet authorities have not acknowledged the famine, did not help their citizens, and did not count its victims. And there are many millions so far."[97] Among others, the appeal was signed by General Yevgenii Miller, Aleksandr Guchkov, and the philosopher and editor Petr Struve. Other Russian émigrés joined the list later, including Metropolitan Yevlogii, members of the Federation of Russian Social Organizations and Unions in Bulgaria, and many others. A Famine Relief Committee was established in Yugoslavia to raise funds among parishioners.[98] In Warsaw, Russian émigré groups organized a similar committee and sent their concerns to the International Red Cross, US President Franklin Roosevelt, and former US President and chair of the American Relief Administration (ARA) Herbert Hoover.[99] The Russian Red Cross sent an appeal to the International Red Cross, its national branches and other international organizations.[100] In addition to general appeals, the Russian émigré press reported on the needs of specific ethnic groups, including Jews and Germans. One letter sent from Odesa in Yiddish to a charitable organization was published in *Vozrozhdenie*.[101] The newspaper also featured information about an initiative of Dr. Mattisen who published a call in *Stuttgarter Tagblatt* to raise money for German colonists in "southern Russia."[102] *Novoe russkoe slovo* wrote about 357 destitute German escapees from Ukraine and the Volga region who had managed to return to their homeland and were settled in a special camp.[103]

The Russian émigré press also described international efforts to help people in the Soviet Union to cope with the famine. They in particular wrote about an appeal by Archbishop of Vienna Theodor Innitzer to the international community and the establishment of the Famine Aid Committee to help thousands of people facing death by hunger in the USSR.[104] Especially praised were efforts by Prime Minister Mowinkel, of Norway and Chair of the League of Nations, who referred specifically to the famine in Ukraine. He was approached about addressing the issue at the League of Nations by a member of the Ukrainian government in exile,

---

[97] It was published on the same day in *Poslednie novosti* and *Vozrozhdenie*.
[98] *Vozrozhdenie*, October 29, 1933.
[99] Ibid.
[100] Ibid., November 13, 1933.
[101] Ibid., June 24, 1933.
[102] Ibid., June 28, 1933.
[103] *Novoe russkoe slovo*, July 21, 1933.
[104] "Uzhasy goloda v SSSR." *Vozrozhdenie*, August 23, 1933 (with reference to *The Morning Post*); *Vozrozhdenie*, October 18, 1933.

Oleksandr Shulhyn, among others. As a result, the League of Nations in effect recognized the facts of the famine and passed on materials to the International Red Cross for further action.[105] The journal *Christianity in the XX Century* (no. 41) was quoted as reporting that there were about 200,000 letters confirming the famine in the USSR and asked that donations be sent to their office in Geneva.[106]

The Russian émigré audience was also informed of actions undertaken by Ukrainian émigrés to help their brethren in Soviet Ukraine, including a pastoral appeal by Greek-Catholic Metropolitan Andrei Sheptyts'kyi and other clerics. It was announced at a meeting of the Ukrainian Committee in Vienna that "the catastrophic famine in Ukraine, the bread-basket of Europe, was a tool of the Bolsheviks to destroy the Ukrainian people."[107] There was even an attempt at collaboration between Russian and Ukrainian Orthodox organizations in Poland, which, however, was quickly brought to a halt by the refusal of the Synod of the Russian Orthodox Church in Poland to remove the anathema on the Ukrainian hetman Ivan Mazepa it had imposed in 1709.[108] An anti-Russian message was issued by Ukrainian MPs in the Polish parliament, who were wary of close Polish-Russian collaboration.[109]

The Ukrainian question

The Ukrainian question was never far from the center of the Russian émigré discourse, as it was directly related to their conception of the Russian Empire and identity. This question gained a new impetus after 1932 for a number of reasons: the Kremlin-generated famine that was most severe in Ukraine; the destruction of the Ukrainian intelligentsia and peasantry and cleansing of the Ukrainian Communist Party; and the new role that Ukraine could potentially play on the European map after Hitler's rise to power in Germany.[110] On November 18, 1932, *Vozrozhdenie* published the article "Ukraine instead of Russia" by Yevgenii Sablin, former Russian ambassador to the UK, in which he responded to a campaign initiated by Volodymyr

---

[105] "Golod v Rossii." *Vozrozhdenie*, October 1, 1933 (with reference to *Le Matin*).

[106] *Vozrozhdenie*, October 15, 1933.

[107] Ibid., November 2, 1933.

[108] *Novoe russkoe slovo*, December 16, 1932. The report was titled "Ukrainian Chauvinism."

[109] *Vozrozhdenie*, November 5, 1933.

[110] A number of publications in the Russian émigré press focused on the German interest in promoting the Ukrainian card, especially in view of the unpredictable German-Soviet relationship (see *Vozrozhdenie*, July 20, 1933). To be sure, Hitler referred to the famine in the USSR in his anticommunist rhetoric (*Vozrozhdenie*, October 26, 1933), and his name was mentioned among the most popular leaders in the USSR who might bring change (*Chasovoi*, 1933, no. 108–9).

Korostovets (the program was published in a bulletin of Lloyds Bank).[111] Sablin recognized the civilizational underpinning of the campaign aimed at the creation of a "European and independent Ukrainian state" as a counterbalance to "Asian Russia."[112] The author noted that "nationalistic tendencies are on the rise in Russia now... and the possibility of separatist outbreaks is quite high." He agreed with Prince A. Volkonskii that "there is no way back to the past" and proposed an accommodation of local interests, but he could not get beyond the imperial paradigm, proposing creation of "an empire that would be an attractive dream to all of its constituent parts." The author of an editorial in the same issue supported Korostovets idea of invading the Soviet Union to help overthrow the Bolshevik regime on the whole Soviet territory. To a great extent, the Ukrainian question remained, according to Anton Denikin, a "border question."[113] The Union for the Protection of Russian Freedom and Democracy, a Russian émigré group in the USA, called on all Russian people [sic] regardless of their nationality, religion, and party affiliation to stand against the "internationalist and featureless" USSR and build a new free Russia.[114]

Initially Russian émigrés did not relate Ukrainian separatism to the political crisis in the USSR. An editorial in *Vozrozhdenie* pointed out that branches of the Ukrainian Communist Party were headed by non-Ukrainians such as Khataevich, Terekhov, Stroganov, Veger, and Maiorov. "The issue is not ethnic struggle but spreading 'party betrayal' to the middle ranks of the party," said the author. He, however, did not rule out the possibility that an ethnic factor might come into play: "If there is ethnic conflict in the USSR now, it is no doubt pushed to the side by a general mobilization against Stalin's tyranny, hated equally by all people."[115]

In this light, Russian émigrés considered "the end of forced Ukrainization" or "super-Ukrainization" as "a victory of life over intricately designed and anemic actions." Criticizing the Bolsheviks' initial concessions to national impulses in the creation of a proletarian culture, the Russian émigrés now acknowledged Bolshevik measures to curtail that "unnatural"

---

[111] In 1934 and 1935, Sablin referred to Korostovets a few times in his correspondence with Vasilii Maklakov, former Russian ambassador to France. See *Chemu svideteli my byli Perepiska byvshikh tsarskikh diplomatov, 1934–1940. Sbornik dokumentov v dvukh knigakh*, Book 1: 1934–1937 (Moscow, 1998).

[112] A similar civilizational comparison was voiced by Andrii Livytskyi, president of the UNR government-in-exile, in his interview to *Le Matin*, which was reported in *Vozrozhdenie* (November 2, 1933). *Novoe russkoe slovo* referred to *Komsomol'skaia pravda* regarding the "counter-revolutionary environment" in Ukraine, in which Ukraine was distinguished as a western country and Great Russia as an eastern one (May 10, 1933).

[113] *Posledniie novosti*, December 20, 1938.

[114] *Novoe russkoe slovo*, May 7, 1933.

[115] *Vozrozhdenie*, February 14, 1933.

process.[116] They argued that Bolshevik intentions were tactical, used "as demonstrative slogans designed for local and foreign simpletons but not for the 'Red Chief,' who even forbade mention of this in his secret directives." The Russian émigrés found cause for reiteration of old imperial clichés and denial of the existence of the Ukrainian people: "By efforts of the Russian people living in Little Russia and New Russia, the criminal attempt of the Bolsheviks to split the Russian people was stopped, we believe, forever."[117]

In 1933, the Russian émigrés often referred to "Ukrainian nationalism"[118] as written about in the Soviet press, and they followed closely the cleansing of the Communist Party of Ukraine. The first reference was published in *Vozrozhdenie* on February 7, 1933, in which the central Bolshevik government put the full blame on the Ukrainian Communists for their failure to provide grain procurements and strengthen collective farms. It also reported on the appointment of Pavel Postyshev as Second Secretary and member of the Politburo of the Communist Party of Ukraine and identified him as "a carrier of real power and Moscow proxy." In one of the reports about the cleansing of the Ukrainian Communist Party, they noted that in Kyiv region about 75 percent of candidates for district commissions responsible for the cleansing were "filtered out" as unreliable and affiliated with "Petlurites" and bourgeois and nationalist elements.[119] The Russian émigrés responded positively to the dismissal of Mykola Skrypnyk, a leading Ukrainian Communist blamed for the rise of nationalism in Ukraine.[120] Linguistic changes imposed by new Moscow plenipotentiaries that were made in order to bring the Ukrainian language closer to the Russian would reflect "the unity of the Russian language" (implying that there is no separate Ukrainian language) and its premier status in the modern age, contrary to the "incomprehensible and useless Ukrainian language, which does not open access to any treasure house of culture."[121]

---

[116] *Vozrozhdenie* reported on measures taken by the new leadership of the Communist Party of Ukraine to curtail "forced Ukrainization of the Great Russian and Jewish population under the influence of nationalistic elements" (May 5, 1933). Speaking about "sabotage" on the linguistic front, the newspaper was in line with the Soviet *Za kommunisticheskoe prosveshchenie*, stating that "all linguistic changes are being removed and that the orthography will follow the Russian language as closely as possible" (July 8, 1933).

[117] *Vozrozhdenie*, July 9, 1933.

[118] See "Ukrainian Nationalists," *Novoe russkoe slovo*," May 16, 1933.

[119] *Novoe russkoe slovo*, June 28, 1933.

[120] Ibid., July 10, 1933. Referring to various speculations, the newspaper claimed that the Ukrainian politician was in contact with Alfred Rosenberg and plotted to kill Stalin (July 30, 1933).

[121] Ibid. I addressed this topic in another article, "Issues of Modernity, Nation, and Language and the Ukrainian Question in Russian Émigré Discourse during the Interwar Period," *Australian Slavonic and East European Studies* 25, no. 1–2 (2011): 61–77.

Russian émigrés were greatly concerned with any ideas of territorial changes and the creation of an independent Ukrainian state, which were spreading at that time. Besides internal factors of "a Ukrainian threat" (caused by the Bolsheviks themselves through the politics of Ukrainization), they identified an external factor engendered by the Polish-German relationship, aimed at moving the Polish border further east.[122] *Vozrozhdenie* referred to a German-Italian meeting in Locarno where discussions included the possibility of a division of Poland and the USSR to create a common federation of Belarus, Lithuania, and Ukraine.[123] New concerns for the Russian émigrés were aroused in the UK when a group of Hetman Skoropadsky's supporters headed by Korostovets initiated a campaign of political and financial support for an independent Ukrainian state.[124] While in 1932 they spoke only of "rumors,"[125] a year later they made their case for geopolitical changes as a result of the famine. "It is hard to say how serious is the movement in Ukraine, which scares the Bolsheviks so much. It is quite possible that people who are suffering from chronic hunger and losing any hope of improving their lives under the Communist regime dream of liberators from abroad regardless of who they are."[126] In this light, Russian émigrés pointed to the galvization of Ukrainian émigré groups abroad, in particular in Paris, Prague, and Warsaw, considered a major potential divisive factor in Russia.[127]

The Russian émigrés recognized "the Ukrainian separatist movement" as a part of the anti-communist movement in the USSR and its potential for future developments. However, this future would depend on the direction of Russia after the demise of the Bolsheviks, according to a discussion in the émigré journal *Znamia Rossii*: "If the revival of Russia starts from the centre, then separatism will have fewer chances than if Russia is liberated from its peripheries to the centre." One of the greatest obstacles to the revival of Russia, according to an editorial in *Vozrozhdenie*, were Ukrainian émigré separatists who wanted to give Ukraine international prominence, which, the editorial stated, Russian émigrés should prevent as before.[128]

The Russian émigrés were equally concerned with any organized support to promote a Ukrainian state. In particular, they reported on

---

[122] An editorial, "Germany and Poland Encroach on Ukraine," appeared in *Novoe russkoe slovo* on June 2, 1933.

[123] *Vozrozhdenie*, March 14, 1933.

[124] See "Ukrainian Separatists Looks for Support among English Capitalists," *Novoe russkoe slovo*, June 2, 1933.

[125] *Vozrozhdenie*, July 3, 1932.

[126] "The Bolsheviks to Face the Ukrainian Question," *Vozrozhdenie*, December 1, 1933.

[127] N. Khrabrov, "Razdel Rossii." *Novoe russkoe slovo*, March 20, 1933: 3–4.

[128] "Ukrainskii vopros," *Vozrozhdenie*, December 22, 1933.

financial aid from American Ukrainians to support the Berlin-based journal *East-European Correspondence* and *The Ukrainian Service Press Newsletter*, as well as efforts to target influential British individuals and institutions, including support for the London-based journal *The Investigator*, edited by Korostovets.[129] Especially troublesome for the Russian émigrés were attempts to approach Jews who had suffered from pogroms during the Ukrainian revolution. S. Varshavskii complained about a Czech publisher, producer of a Ukrainian calendar with a map of "Great Ukraine," which included territories of "Little-Russian provinces," "New Russia," the North Caucasus, Crimea, Eastern Galicia, and Ciscarpathian (Subcarpathian) Rus. This concept of "Great Ukraine" was actively debated and attacked in the Russian émigré discourse until World War II.

But did the Russian émigrés perceive the famine in Ukraine as differing from famine in other regions? It is critical to understand that Russian émigrés regardless of their political affiliation were largely anti-Ukrainian, criticized the politics of Ukrainization, and denied Ukraine's right to independence. Yet despite these attitudes, the Russian émigré discourse acknowledged that the famine was most severe in Ukraine and on territories with large Ukrainian populations.[130] The point here is that since they considered Ukraine a Russian territory, there was no need to disguise the fact that the famine raged on what for them was Russian soil.

Nevertheless, a close reading of the Russian émigré press reveals references to the national aspect of the tragedy in Ukraine and Stalin's attitude toward Ukrainians. While failures in grain procurement on the Russian territories could be explained by class opposition, in Ukraine such failures were exacerbated by so-called "national deviations." *Poslednie novosti,* reflecting on an atmosphere in Ukraine of dislike of the Russian presence, referred to "chauvinistic *chastushki*," "graffiti in washrooms," and "nationalistic propaganda at institutions."[131] The newspaper even claimed that Ukrainian Communists were to blame for a "separatist bias" and "unwillingness to give the prescribed amount of grain to the centre."[132]

Furthermore, an editorial in *Poslednie novosti* asserted that the Soviet authorities hated Ukraine and the North Caucasus for their consistent opposition to collectivization.[133] That opposition was explained in part by the national character of Ukrainians, who had historically developed a more individualistic mode of farming. As a peasant from Bila Tserkva put it: "Our

---

129 *Vozrozhdenie*, August 1, 1933.

130 *Poslednie novosti*, November 21, 1932.

131 *Poslednie novosti*, April 7, 1933.

132 Ibid., July 19, 1932.

133 Ibid., November 28, 1932.

Ukrainian man did not get used to working the land according to instructions. Collective farms will fail because they contradict the nature of the Ukrainian people."[134] In contrast, Miliukov, reflecting on the idea of collectivization, spoke about the historical "strong roots" for collective farming in Great Russia.[135]

The émigré newspaper *Vozrozhdenie*, in an attempt to explain the causes of the famine, stated that "famine is a weapon of the Soviet government...used to destroy the disobedient population and for resettlement." Speaking about the Kuban and North Caucasus regions, the newspaper referred to an eyewitness of the famine who claimed that "the Kremlin consciously supported the extinction of the population in these regions: "The Cossack population made much trouble for the Soviet authorities from the very beginning. They have been active in opposition to collective farms and, according to Moscow, are the core of the counterrevolution in the future. Neither executions nor exile to the North made any changes. A famine came to the rescue of the government, and it decided to make use of it. How the physical destruction of the disobedient population of the North Caucasus would be beneficial to the Politburo was evident from the fact that People's Commissariats had already prepared a program of resettlement of peasants from the Black Earth region of Russia to newly vacated households."[136] Referring to the French journal *Revue des Deux Mondes* (by P. Pignon), *Vozrozhdenie* argued that "the Soviet government mostly capitalized on the famine in Ukraine and North Caucasus, the richest lands, in order to suppress their autonomous aspirations."[137]

Russian socialists in emigration (Mensheviks) maintained that it was not collectivization per se that had caused the famine but how the collected grain was distributed. A. Yugov in his article "Golod bez neurozhaia" claimed that the harvest was larger in 1931 and 1932 in comparison to 1928 and 1929, when there was no famine. This led the author to conclude that the Soviet authorities had distributed the harvest disproportionately so that some regions suffered, first of all Ukraine, while lessening food problems in other regions.[138] Although Yugov was right about the "disproportional distribution," his non-socialist critics claimed that the famine was the result of "a socialist experiment."[139] The main point of the

---

[134] Ibid., April 7, 1932.

[135] D. I. Meisner, *Mirazhi i deistvitel'nost' (Zapiski emigranta)* (Moscow, 1966): 163.

[136] *Vozrozhdenie*, June 29, 1933.

[137] Ibid., September 17, 1933.

[138] A. Yugov, "Golod bez neurozhaia," *Sotsialisticheskii vestnik*, August 25, 1933: 6–12.

[139] See "Golod ot sotsializma," *Vozrozhdenie*, August 31, 1933.

Mensheviks was that the USSR had digressed from the socialist path and in fact was building state capitalism.[140] But they agreed that forced labor was not effective for an economy. Some were reminded of feudal times, with dependence on a suzerain, regular tributes to the Kremlin, and the lack of rights for the subjects.[141]

This national dimension of the famine became especially evident after the cleansing of the Communist Party of Ukraine in 1933. An editorial in *Poslednie novosti* referred to the Soviet press in describing the necessity of fighting "Ukrainian chauvinism," which allegedly had penetrated all spheres of life—villages, libraries, schools, and even government offices. The author expressed deep concern that "the failure of collectivization, famine in villages, and the collapse of the Five-Year Plan had evoked the galvization of anticommunist propaganda." In Ukraine, this failure of the Soviet leadership had reinvigorated the "anti-Moscow agitation of Ukrainian nationalists."[142] This is actually what worried Russian émigrés the most. They assumed that the Soviet image of Petlurites might be exaggerated but that it might also encourage the growth of nationalistic tendencies, which would be dangerous not only for the Soviet authorities but also for Russia.[143] Referring to "nationalistic deviations" in Ukraine as articulated by Pavel Postyshev, the newly appointed leader of Ukrainian communists, the editorial concluded: "It seems that Moscow has now realized where this play with Ukrainization would lead her... Enemies of Russia who are ready to help Ukrainian nationalism can capitalize on the results of this work."[144] The only way to overcome this danger of separatism, the author suggests, is to construct economic policies that would be tolerable for the population. Russian émigrés were skeptical of "foreign fascists" who allegedly fostered separatism in the Soviet Union, as claimed by the Soviet authorities. They claimed it was the Bolsheviks "who engendered and strengthened it by implementing Communist recipes. The more the Bolsheviks stick to power, the more the seeds of separatism will grow."[145]

To conclude, as one of the best-informed sources on developments in the Soviet Union, the Russian émigrés maintained that famine was most severe in Ukraine and in territories with large Ukrainian populations in the Kuban region and North Caucasus. Russian émigrés depicted this human catastrophe as the result of the totalitarian nature of the first socialist state

[140] They presented their views mainly in *Sotsialisticheskii vestnik*. See D. Dalin, "Preodolenie kapitalizma v SSSR," April 30, 1932: 9–11, etc.
[141] *Novoe russkoe slovo*, May 13, 1933.
[142] *Poslednie novosti*, April 15, 1933.
[143] Ibid., June 28, 1933.
[144] *Poslednie novosti*, June 28, 1933.
[145] "Separatizm," *Vozrozhdenie*, December 30, 1933.

and its politics of forced industrialization during the first Five-Year Plan. But they also reflected on the national dimension of events in Ukraine and neighboring regions and on the use of the famine as a political tool. The émigrés singled out Ukrainian dormant nationalism, conceptions of freedom, individualism and civilizational orientation, and its unique geopolitical situation. While sympathetic to human losses regardless of national affiliation, the Russian émigrés supported Soviet actions that were aimed at quelling the national aspirations of Ukrainians. Perceiving the Soviet Union as one cultural-historical space, the émigrés viewed Ukraine within the imperial framework of Russian continuity and feared that the famine could invigorate "separatist" aspirations.

Bibliography

Brutskus, Boris. "Vzlet i raspad Sovetskogo planovogo khoziaistva." *Sovremennye zapiski* 51 (1933): 417–31.

Chasovoi

Chemu svideteli my byli Perepiska byvshikh tsarskikh diplomatov, 1934–1940. *Sbornik dokumentov v dvukh knigakh*. Book 1: 1934–1937 (Moscow, 1998).

Cipko, Serge. *Starving Ukraine: The Holodomor and Canada's Response.* University of Regina Press, 2018.

Entente Internationale contre la Troisieme Internationale tt. Documentation, July-August, 1933.

Khrabrov, N. "Razdel Rossii." *Novoe russkoe slovo*, March 20, 1933, pp. 3–4.

Meisner, D. I. *Mirazhi i deistvitel'nost' (Zapiski emigranta.* Moscow, 1966, p. 163.

Novoe russkoe slovo

Poslednie novosti

Soroka, Mykola. "Issues of Modernity, Nation and Language and the Ukrainian Question in Russian Émigré Discourse during the Interwar Period." *Australian Slavonic and East European Studies* 25, no. 1–2 (2011): 61–77.

Sotsialisticheskii vestnik

Sovremennye zapiski

The Russian Economic Bulletin

Vozrozhdeniia

New Research Perspectives

The Meaning of the Holodomor of 1932–33: From Collective Reproduction to Individual Reconstruction of Mental Trauma

Larysa Zasiekina

I. Introduction

The Great Famine (Holodomor) in Ukraine was a genocide organized by the Soviet-Russian government. Its aim was to kill ethnic Ukrainians and subdue their national culture and national identity. Norman Naimark argues that the collective research of a substantial group of scholars has resulted in a consensus that the Holodomor corresponds to the general pattern exhibited by genocides and could be further examined as a "Soviet Genocide of Ukraine."[1] The death or deportation of millions of Ukrainians in 1932–33 resulted in what has been termed a collective, historic, and identity trauma.[2] It is a *collective trauma*, since it aimed to affect the whole group rather than individuals.[3] Gilad Hirschberger argues that a collective trauma is aligned rather with collective memory than with a historical event.[4] It affects not only the direct survivors but also the development of national identity in their descendants. Moreover, a collective trauma might have a negative effect on individuals who are relatively distant from the trauma in space and time, but who share national values and traditions. Together, survivors and their offspring attempt to reconstruct the meaning of the tragedy, a process that can be crucial for the survival of the group and the development of its collective identity. Collective trauma evokes an existential threat in survivors, which then drives a search for meaning in the collective trauma and the

---

[1] Norman Naimark, "How the Holodomor Can Be Integrated into Our Understanding of Genocide," *East/West: Journal of Ukrainian Studies 2*, no. 1 (2015): 117–32.

[2] Brent Bezo and Stefania Maggi, "Living in "survival mode:" Intergenerational transmission of trauma from the Holodomor genocide of 1932–1933 in Ukraine," *Social Science & Medicine* 134, no. 6 (2015): 87–94.

[3] Gillian Eagle and Debra Kaminer, "Continuous traumatic stress: Expanding the lexicon of traumatic stress," *Peace and Conflict: Journal of Peace Psychology* 19, no. 2 (2013): 85.

[4] Gilad Hirschberger, "Collective trauma and the social construction of meaning," *Frontiers in Psychology* 10, no. 8 (2018): 1441.

construction of a "*trans*-generational identity" as a robust predictor of "freedom, independence and group security."[5]

The Holodomor in Ukraine can also be termed an *identity trauma*, since it is closely connected with collective trauma and includes discrimination, invalidation and a psychological attack on the group of people.[6] The Holodomor is associated with a continuous assault on the Ukrainian population, and has a combined ethnic (national identity, national culture, national language) and class (peasants) dimension. Famine as a *historic trauma* is aligned with genocide during a certain historical period and a struggle for physical and psychological survival.[7] Braitman et al. connect a collective, historic and identity trauma with moral injury.[8] Psychological distress is felt when individuals perpetrate, witness, or fail to prevent actions that transgress their core moral or ethical beliefs.

Evidence consistently suggests that collective, historic, and identity traumas develop in people a survival mode. It is represented by negative emotions, inner states, and trauma-based behavioral strategies in survivors—all of which affect the well-being of their direct descendants.[9] Despite the existence of a survival mode as a result of physical and psychological attacks on a group, there remains a paucity of evidence concerning the negative impact of the Holodomor on emotions, inner states, and trauma-based behavioral strategies in survivors. There is also little published data on the famine as a deep mental trauma and moral injury.

A particular concern in a collective, historic, and identity trauma is its impact on people at the individual, family, and community-society levels.[10] The trauma at the community-society level is reproduced by collective memory as preserved in Ukrainian archival collections, while at the individual and family levels memory can be examined through interviews with Holodomor survivors. Psychotrauma at the individual level is aligned with cognitive and emotional distortions in the survivor's personality. However, the links between the study of the Holodomor and transgenerational mental trauma as a predictor of emotional distress in

---

[5] Victor Béliveau, "Memory and Trauma in International Relations. Theories, Cases and Debates," Erica Resende and Dovile Budryte (New York: Routledge, 2014).

[6] Ibrahim Aref Kira, "Taxonomy of trauma and trauma assessment," *Traumatology* 7, no. 2 (2001): 73–86.

[7] Joseph P. Gone, "Colonial genocide and historical trauma in Native North America: Complicating contemporary attributions," in *Colonial Genocide in Indigenous North America* (Durham: Duke University Press, 2014), 273–89.

[8] Abby L. Braitman, et al. "Psychometric properties of a Modified Moral Injury Questionnaire in a military population," *Traumatology* 24, no. 4 (2018): 301.

[9] Ibrahim A. Kira, et al., "Measuring cumulative trauma dose, types, and profiles using a development-based taxonomy of traumas," *Traumatology* 14, no. 2 (2008): 62–87.

[10] Bezo and Maggi, op. cit.

survivors and their offspring is highly undeveloped. Therefore, the study of the Holodomor as a mental trauma should be examined in the broader context of other genocides, particularly the Holocaust.

A large and growing body of literature has investigated negative emotional states in Holocaust survivors and their children, notably anxiety, guilt toward personal happiness, and mistrust.[11] Traditionally, it has been argued that traumatic experience at the family level has a poor impact on family relationships, mostly in mother-child role reversal.[12] Evidence of this research indicates that there are specifically organized family patterns which are not pathological, but nonetheless require further explanation. Moreover, a mother's successful coping strategies with trauma are one of the principal factors of a child's well-being; otherwise, the child is modeling the mother's cognitive and emotional distortions and behavioral patterns.

Several studies of traumatic memory aligned with the Holodomor at the *individual and family levels* have investigated the fact that the offspring of Holodomor survivors express specific emotions and inner states (horror, fear, mistrust, sadness, ethnic-related shame, anger, stress and anxiety), and trauma-based coping strategies (overeating, intrinsic selfishness and indifference to others, overemphasis on food). The trauma-based coping strategies are aligned with a strong fear of the possible recurrence of hunger in the future and are expressed in seeking security linked to food.[13] This is in line with Brom's idea that any genocide is a severe traumatization and is aligned with a strong fear of recurrence, which has a poor impact on the survivor's identity.[14] Therefore, the strategies for coping with this fear have an effect on communication patterns in the family and on behavioral strategies of the survivors and their direct descendants.

Community-society trauma is aligned with a loss of identity, culture, and values. Evans-Campbell highlights the need to examine the trauma at this level, since it is less understood as compared with the individual and family levels.[15] Rat-Horenczyk et al. suggest that research in a macro framework that combines the individual, family, and community-society levels could

---

[11] Dan Bar-On, et al., "Multigenerational perspectives on coping with the Holocaust experience: An attachment perspective for understanding the developmental sequelae of trauma across generations," *International Journal of Behavioral Development* 22, no. 2 (1998): 315–38.

[12] Irit Felsen, and H. Shmuel Erlich, "Identification patterns of offspring of Holocaust survivors with their parents," *American Journal of Orthopsychiatry* 60, no. 1.4 (1990): 506–20.

[13] Claude M. Chemtob, et al., "Cognitive-behavioral treatment for severe anger in posttraumatic stress disorder," *Journal of Consulting and Clinical Psychology* 65, no. 1 (1997): 184.

[14] Danny Brom, Kfir Revital, and Haim Dasberg, "A controlled double-blind study on children of Holocaust survivors," *The Israel Journal of Psychiatry and Related Sciences* 38, no. 1 (2001): 47.

[15] T. Evans-Campbell, "Historical trauma in American Indian/Native Alaska communities: A multilevel framework for exploring impacts on individuals, families, and communities," *Journal of Interpersonal Violence* 23(3), 316–38.

improve the healing of traumatized children.[16] Together, these studies provide important insights into genocide as a mental trauma at the individual, family, and community-society levels. However, no previous study has investigated the mental trauma and moral injury of the Holodomor within a multilevel framework.

To date, the research on genocide as a psychotrauma consists of clinical and non-clinical studies. Clinical research aims to explore the psychological impact of genocide on survivors and their descendants. It constitutes a form of therapy dealing with emotional distress. A considerable amount of literature has been published on non-clinical research, which aims to examine the impact of psychotrauma on the well-being of survivors and their everyday life. Much of the current literature on the Holodomor pays particular attention to survivors and their descendants in non-clinical samples.[17] A major advantage of a non-clinical sample is the broad context of research, notably the focus on psychological traits, psychopathology, family relationships, and psychological symptoms.

Of particular concern is the comparison of the Holodomor with other genocides. Naimark points out that the Holodomor should be examined within the broader context of genocide as "a persistent historical phenomenon."[18] A number of studies have postulated a convergence between the Holodomor and other genocides in the context of intergenerational traumatic effect. Evidence consistently suggests the presence of a developed anger as a personality trait and a vulnerability to PTSD and other psychiatric disorders in the direct descendants of Holocaust survivors,[19] ethnic-related shame in the descendants of the Armenian genocide,[20] suicidal thoughts in the direct descendants of Canadian First Nations.[21] and attempts to forget the sufferings of the past and deny traumatic memory in the direct descendants of the Famine during 1959–61 in China.[22, 23]

---

[16] Ruth Pat-Horenczyk, Danny Brom, and Juliet M. Vogel, eds. *Helping Children Cope with Trauma: Individual, Family and Community Perspectives* (New York: Routledge, 2014).

[17] Bezo and Maggi, op. cit.

[18] Norman M. Naimark, "How the Holodomor Can Be Integrated into our Understanding of Genocide," *East/West: Journal of Ukrainian Studies* 2, no. 1 (2015): 117–32.

[19] Dan Bar-On, et al. op. cit.

[20] Hatsantour Karenian et al., "Collective trauma transmission and traumatic reactions among descendants of Armenian refugees," *International Journal of Social Psychiatry* 57, no. 4 (2011): 327–37.

[21] Brenda Elias et al., "Trauma and suicide behaviour histories among a Canadian indigenous population: an empirical exploration of the potential role of Canada's residential school system," *Social Science & Medicine* 74, no. 10 (2012): 1560–69.

[22] Lucien Bianco, "Comparing the Soviet and Chinese Famines: Their Perpetrators, Actors, and Victims," *East/West: Journal of Ukrainian Studies* 3, no. 2 (2016): 51–74.

Previous studies have also explored the similarity between the Holodomor and the Great Irish Famine.[24] However, research has established that survivors of the National Hunger in Ireland and their direct descendants experienced mixed feelings of anger, providentialism, guilt, and misunderstanding, which are different from the feelings of Holodomor survivors.[25]

The factors that enable us to compare the Holodomor with other historical traumas remain speculative, partly because much information was concealed by the Soviet government and even some governments of post-independence Ukraine. Previous research has established that genocide might be organized according to two scenarios, notably ethnic cleansing and starvation.[26] The Holocaust and Armenian genocides represent purely ethnic cleansing, while the Holodomor might represent genocide through starvation, although its aim was also ethnic cleansing. It has now been well established by a variety of studies that the Holodomor was an artificial or man-made famine, which, as compared with the Great Irish Famine (also known as the Irish Potato Famine), was not determined by the lack of a harvest, but was purposefully organized by the Soviet-Russian government. Moreover, the Great Irish Famine was fully documented at the level of community-society, but there is a great paucity of information concerning its impact on the Irish people at the family and individual levels.[27]

When one considers the confidentiality of the aggressive Soviet-Russian policy against the ethnic Ukrainian population and peasants, which included attempts to conceal the truth of the tragic events, research on collective traumatic memory of the Holodomor at the individual, family, and community-society levels might help provide a deeper insight into this collective, historic, and identity trauma.

The aim of my present research is to explore the Holodomor as a historic, collective, and identity mental trauma at the individual, family, and community-society levels with survivors of 1932–33 using semi-structured interviews. Hirschberger argues that collective trauma leads to a crisis of

---

[23] Susanne Weigelin-Schwiedrzik, "Trauma and memory: the case of the Great Famine in the People's Republic of China (1959–1961)," *Historiography East and West* 1, no. 1 (2003): 39–67.

[24] Christian Noack, Lindsay Janssen, and Vincent Comerford, eds., *Holodomor and Gorta Mór: Histories, Memories and Representations of Famine in Ukraine and Ireland* (London: Anthem Press, 2012).

[25] Bezo and Maggi, op. cit.

[26] Gillian Eagle and Debra Kaminer, "Continuous traumatic stress: Expanding the lexicon of traumatic stress," *Peace and Conflict: Journal of Peace Psychology* 19, no. 2 (2013): 85.

[27] Nocak, Janssen, and Comerford, op. cit.

collective meaning aligned with collective identity.[28] Therefore, memory recollection in Holodomor survivors within a multilevel framework can offer a deeper understanding of the Holodomor's meaning as it is formed in collective memory many years after this tragic event.

II. Methods

Considering the importance of a macro-level framework in examining the Holodomor and its psychological impact on survivors, the current research will test the following hypotheses (H):

H (1) There are differences in the memory recollection of Holodomor survivors at the individual, family, and community-society levels.

H (2) There is a difference in how the meaning of the Holodomor is formed through the study of archival collections and through the study of individual traumatic memory of survivors.

Participants

A non-clinical sample of the 25 survivors in Ukraine was recruited for semi-structured interviews. The participants and the researcher were not previously acquainted. The inclusion criterion for participants was their personal history as Holodomor survivors. A survivor was defined as a person who witnessed these tragic events and belongs to a family that experienced hunger in 1932–33. Interviewing the participants took place in 2003–5. Their average age was 82.5. There were 17 females and 8 males (see Table 1). The participants represented different oblasts in Ukraine, specifically Chernihiv (6), Dnipro (formerly Dnipropetrovsk) (5), Donetsk (2), Kharkiv (3), Kyiv (3), Poltava (2), Sumy (2), Vinnytsia (1), and Zhytomyr (1) and were recruited with formal letters asking them to take part in the interview. The researcher then called the participants and explained the aim of the interview. Consent forms were obtained, and the participants were asked take part in the interviews, during which they could talk freely about the events, with a major focus on their thoughts and feelings. All interviews were then transcribed and analyzed.

---

[28] Gilad Hirschberger, "Collective trauma and the social construction of meaning," *Frontiers in Psychology* 10, no. 8 (2018): 1441.

Procedure

Meaning of the Holodomor at the community-society level

The study applies Grounded Theory for qualitative analysis of interviews.[29] The methodology of Grounded Theory in our research includes three stages, namely, a pre-analysis stage, aimed at a preliminary search for similar categories in interviews; an analysis of within-case and cross-case study, aimed at exploring similarity and difference in interviews; and a codification of the main categories. The procedure of Grounded Theory contains successive steps, in particular gathering data, coding, categorizing, developing categories, and generating theory. For coding, the data are broken down, compared, and then placed in categories. Similar data are placed in similar categories, and different data create new categories.[30]

The coding in Grounded Theory is of primary importance, and includes three main aspects, particularly the situation, the main actions or interactions of the people in the situations, and the consequences of the actions. To follow these aspects consistently, the search for situations in our research was aligned with the main subjects (actors) in the situations, their main actions (descriptive categories represented as propositions), and the consequences (conceptual categories). During axial coding, the researcher works to capture the links between categories and their subcategories. The purpose is to delineate and capture relationships on which the axis of the category is being focused.

According to the procedure, first we defined the main actors of these events, and united them in subject categories (Stalin, party officials, secret police units, regular troops, peasants, NKVD, village council); second, we defined the descriptive categories, in particular the main propositions, which were aligned with the subjects; and finally, the descriptive categories were generalized and put into wider conceptual categories based on a broader meaning of the Holodomor. Furthermore, the number and content of descriptive categories led to their evaluation in terms of connotative meaning, notably good/bad, weak/strong, active/passive. In this way the core concepts of collective memory of the Holodomor of 1932–33 were explored at the community-society level.[31]

---

[29] Anselm Strauss and Juliet M. Corbin. Grounded Theory Methodology: An Overview, in *Handbook of Qualitative Research* ed. N.K. Denzin and Y.S. Lincoln (Chapter 17, pp. 273–85) (Thousand Oaks, CA: Sage, 1994).

[30] Diane Walker and Florence Myrick, "Grounded theory: An exploration of process and procedure," *Qualitative Health Research* 16, no. 4 (2006): 547–59.

[31] Larysa Zasiekina and Serhii Zasiekin, *Psykholinhvistychna Diahnostyka [Psycholinguistic Diagnostic*] (Lutsk: Vezha Publishers of Lesya Ukrainka Volyn National University, 2008)

Meaning of the Holodomor at the individual/family level

LIWC (Linguistic Inventory Word Count) analysis assesses individual interviews and explores the main psychologically meaningful categories. LIWC as a software tool is based on the conceptual framework proposed by Tausczik and Pennabaker to select word meanings linked to attentional focus, emotionality, social relationships, thinking styles, and individual differences.[32] The current study applies LIWC to discovering the experience of the Holodomor and its meaning at the individual/family levels as represented by the thoughts and emotions of survivors. Since the interviews were collected and transcribed in Ukrainian, the study applies the Ukrainian version of LIWC analysis.[33] The study applies the Spearman rank-order correlation coefficient, SPSS26 to examine association between length of traumatic narrative (word count) and other psychologically meaningful categories, in other words to assess the most frequent psychologically meaningful categories in the traumatic narrative of Holodomor survivors.

III. Results

First, we checked the control items (subject, descriptive categories, and conceptual categories) according to Grounded Theory. Second, we examined the psychologically meaningful categories, defined by LIWC. Table 1 illustrates the demographic information of the sample. Table 2 indicates the main subjects, descriptive categories (subjects' actions expressed in propositions), and conceptual categories as the Holodomor's meaning at the community-society level. The distribution of subjects was calculated by the number of propositions. Connotative meaning shows the main characteristics of the subjects in terms of good/bad, weak/strong, active/passive. Table 3 illustrates the distribution of the main psychological categories in traumatic narratives of Holodomor survivors, the mean indices of distribution of the main psychological categories in normal everyday speech in autobiographical narrative and Cronbach's alpha α to indicate the internal consistency for each category suggested by Tausczik and Pennabaker.[34]

---

[32] Yla R. Tausczik, and James W. Pennebaker, "The psychological meaning of words: LIWC and computerized text analysis methods," *Journal of Language and Social Psychology* 29, no. 1 (2010): 24–54.

[33] S. Zasiekin, N. Bezuglova, A. Hapon, V. Matiushenko, O. Podolska, and D. Zubchuk, "Psycholinguistic aspects of translating LIWC dictionary," *East European Journal of Psycholinguistics*, 5, no. 1 (2018): 121–31.

[34] Tausczik and Pennabaker, op. cit.

Table 4 shows the correlations (the Spearman rank-order correlation coefficient rs) between word count and psychologically meaningful categories in traumatic narratives.

Table 1. Descriptive information for the individuals-survivors of the Holodomor (n=25) sample.

	Survivors	
	Frequency	**Percentage**
Gender	17/8	68.0/32.0
Female/male		
Marital status		
Single	16	64.0
Married	5	20.0
Divorced	4	16.0
Ethnicity		
White	25	100.0
Occupational status		
Full-time worked		
Part-time worked	2	8.0
Student		8.0

Retired		
Unemployed	23	92.0
Age		
	Mean (SD)	Min-Max
	82. (3.4)	76–84

Table 2. Sample of data analysis: subjective, descriptive and conceptual categories.

Subjects (thematic categories)	Descriptive categories (propositions)	Conceptual categories (meaning of Holodomor)	Connotative meaning	Percentage
Stalin	p1: organized forced collectivization; p2: in 1929 instituted the policy of all-out collectivization	forced collectivization	negative, strong, active	31.4%
	p3: was determined to crush all vestiges of Ukrainian nationalism;	crushing of Ukrainian nationalism		
	p4: in 1932 raised Ukraine's grain procurement quotas by forty-four percent	rise of grain procurement quotas		
	p5: condemned millions of peasants to death by starvation	condemnation of peasants to death by starvation		

<table>
<tr><td rowspan="3">Communist Party, secret police units, regular troops</td><td>p1: waged a merciless war of attrition against the peasants
p2: confiscated forcibly even indispensable seed grain from peasant
p3: suspect those who did not appear to be starving of hoarding grain.</td><td>war of attrition against peasants</td><td rowspan="3">negative, strong, active</td><td rowspan="3">32.4%</td></tr>
<tr><td>p4: showed who is the master in the Soviet Union</td><td>demonstrating power</td></tr>
<tr><td>p3: executed or deported any man, woman, or child caught taking even a handful of grain from a collective farm</td><td>execution and deportation</td></tr>
<tr><td rowspan="2">Peasants</td><td>p1: resist collectivization
p2: refused to give up their grain</td><td>resistance</td><td rowspan="2">positive, passive, weak</td><td rowspan="2">11.2%</td></tr>
<tr><td>p3: before they died, often lost their senses and ceased to be human beings</td><td>sufferings</td></tr>
<tr><td>NKVD</td><td>p1: prevented peasants from leaving their village;
p2: introduced a system of internal passports</td><td>policy against peasants</td><td>negative, passive, strong</td><td>6.4%</td></tr>
</table>

They (head of village council, accountant, secretary)	p1: defined the cause of death p2: explained the death as diphtheria outcome p3: have never thought that father could go abroad and talk about the Holodomor p4: did not like to let the victim go away	village council's actions against peasants	negative, active, strong	18.6%

Table 3. Results of LIWC data analysis.

Categories	Frequent words in Holodomor survivors' traumatic narratives	Normal Speech	Personal Interviews	Internal consistency (corrected α)
Personal pronouns	I, them, her	13.37	20.99	0.67
I	I, me, mine	7.03	2.50	0.81
We	we, us, our	0.87	1.16	0.82
You	you, your	4.04	0.38	0.70
He/she	she, her, him	0.77	0.16	0.85
They	they, their, them	0.65	0.47	0.78
Affective processes	terrified, cried	6.54	0.42	0.57
Positive emotions	love, care	5.31	0.07	0.64
Negative emotions	hurt, ugly, nasty, disgustful	1.19	0.29	0.55
Anxiety	worried, fearful, afraid	0.14	0.02	0.73

Anger	hate, kill, annoyed	0.36	0.04	0.53
Sadness	crying, grief, sad	0.23	0.09	0.70
Social processes	neighbor, talk, they, accountant, village council, secretary	10.42	4.94	0.86
Family	mother, daughter, children, grandmother, sister, father, home, orphan, parents	0.31	2.03	0.88
Friends	comrade	0.37	0.04	0.60
Female references	girl, her, mom	0.55	1.45	0.87
Male references	boy, his, dad	0.80	0.01	0.87
Cognitive processes	cause, know, ought	12.21	9.10	0.92
Insight	think, know	2.46	0.62	0.84
Causation	because, effect	1.45	3.06	0.67
Perceptual processes	look, heard, feeling	2.11	0.80	0.55
See	view, saw, seen	0.78	0.07	0.84
Hear	listen, hearing	0.63	0.51	0.77
Feel	feel, touch	0.61	0.11	0.65
Biological processes	eat, blood, pain	1.23	0.80	0.71
Body	cheek, hands, stomach, spit	0.31	0.13	0.87

Health	clinic, pill, hunger, diphtheria	0.38	0.18	0.37
Ingestion	eat, bread, wheat, potatoes	0.35	0.36	0.78
Past focus	ago, did, talked	3.78	1.30	0.64
Present focus	today, is, now	15.28	1.74	0.66
Future focus	may, will, soon	1.45	0.04	0.68
Space	down, in, thin	5.86	7.07	0.83
Time	end, until, season	4.28	2.17	0.79
Work	field, hard work, land, agriculture	2.87	0.24	0.69
Home	kitchen, bed	0.34	0.63	0.83
Religion	lord, altar, church, priest	0.14	0.00	0.91
Death	bury, coffin, kill, hunger, exhaustion	0.04	0.29	0.79

Table 4. Correlations (the Spearman rank-order correlation coefficient rs) between word count and psychological meaningful categories in traumatic narratives (n = 25).

Variables	**Word Count**	**Family**	**Female**	**Home**	**Death**
Word Count	–	.390*	.333*	.363*	.335*
Family	.390*	–	.769**	.477*	.118
Female	.333*	.769**	–	.497*	0.210
Home	.363*	477*	.497*	–	-.117
Death	.335*	.118	0.210	-.117	–

Note. *= p <.05, **= p <.01

IV. Discussion

With respect to the first hypothesis, it was found that subjects (actors), and also descriptive and conceptual categories as markers of the community-society level, differ from the psychologically meaningful categories represented in the survivors` narratives (see Table 2). In particular, subjects, descriptive and conceptual categories convey mostly cognitive information that is aligned with dates, names, and main agents of the tragic events. The connotative meanings, with reference to all subjects, indicate that the most active negative agents are Communist Party, secret police and Stalin. These results corroborate the findings from previous works that have shown the leading negative role of these subjects in the artificial famine of 1932–33. Thom argues that Stalin's policy aimed at collectivization and "de-kulakization," considered the peasant question in the broader context of the national issue, and organized mass starvation to prevent any resistance to his policy.[35] Moreover, during the war against the peasants, Stalin made changes in the membership of the Communist Party and removed communists who sympathized with the kulaks. Therefore, Stalin strengthened his own power and the power of the Communist Party to crush the peasantry physically and morally, including its identity, values and beliefs.

The previous findings also support the idea that peasants made attempts to survive and protect their families. However, despite their efforts, they were too weak to protect themselves, because the Soviet government's punitive measures were ruthless. These results are consistent with the findings of Wemheuer that "starving populations seldom rebel during a peak of famine."[36] The results of the research also indicate the negative role of village councils and their representatives. The initial attempts of local governments to retain the grain and ease the situation with starvation was defined as counter-revolution and was mercilessly opposed.[37]

Therefore, the representatives of the council, in particular the collective farm leaders, secretaries, and accountants, took action against the peasants.

The present results dealing with the community-society level are significant in at least two major respects. First, the main subjects, and the descriptive and conceptual categories, fit the reproduction of collective memories as represented in archival collections and corroborate the main facts of the Holodomor as presented in Ukrainian historiography. Second,

---

[35] Françoise Thom, "Reflections on Stalin and the Holodomor," *East/West: Journal of Ukrainian Studies* 2, no. 1 (2015): 81–92.

[36] Felix Wemheuer, *Famine Politics in Maoist China and the Soviet Union* (Yale University Press, 2014).

[37] Stanislav Kul'chyts'kyi, Marta D. Olynyk, and Andrij Wynnyckyj, "The Holodomor and its consequences in the Ukrainian countryside," *Harvard Ukrainian Studies* 30, no. 1/4 (2008): 1–13.

the meaning of the Holodomor at the community-society levels does not explain the psychological impact of the Holodomor on survivors and their emotional distress after experiencing mental trauma and moral injury. To develop a full picture of the Holodomor's meaning in collective memory, additional research was needed at the individual and family levels.

Regarding the second hypothesis, the current study found (Table 3) that Holodomor survivors use the pronoun "we" more frequently as compared with normal speech. This finding is consistent with that of Kowalski, who found that the frequency of the first-person pronouns "I" and "we" increases when the individual is the victim of an event.[38] Recent research also shows that people who feel a strong pain and negative emotions use first-person pronouns more frequently.[39] One unanticipated finding was that the Holodomor survivors use the pronoun "I" less frequently. A possible explanation for this might be that the focus on the pronoun "I" is linked to the sense of personal responsibility for the traumatic event, which is often associated with post-traumatic stress disorder (PTSD).[40] Therefore, we can assume that Holodomor survivors are aware of the real cause of the famine and blame the Soviet government and its representatives for this tragedy.

Another possible explanation is that the pronoun "we" expresses belonging to a collectivist rather than to an individualist culture and, therefore, prioritizes in-group goals.[41] Thus, the observed increase in the use of the pronoun "we" could be attributed to the importance of this tragedy as a common experience. Moreover, the group is rather family than community. This conclusion is in line with the higher frequency of the category *family* as compared with normal speech, and the diminished frequency of the category *friends*. The interesting finding is that the category *family* is represented mostly by females. Therefore, the Holodomor is associated with women's suffering, notably with a mother, grandmother, sister. The predominant role of the category of family, as compared with community, is consistent with the low frequency of the category *social processes*. This finding broadly supports the work of other

[38] Robin M. Kowalski, ""I was only kidding!": Victims' and perpetrators' perceptions of teasing," *Personality and Social Psychology Bulletin* 26, no. 2 (2000): 231–41.

[39] Stephanie Rude, Eva-Maria Gortner, and James Pennebaker, "Language use of depressed and depression-vulnerable college students," *Cognition & Emotion* 18, no. 8 (2004): 1121–33.

[40] Larysa Zasiekina, Shelia Kennison, Serhii Zasiekin, and Khrystyna Khvorost, "Psycho-linguistic markers of autobiographical and traumatic memory," *East European Journal of Psycholinguistics* 6, no. 2 (2019): 119–33.

[41] W. B. Gudykunst, Y. Matsumoto, S. Ting-Toomey, T. Nishida, K. Kim & S. Heyman, "The influence of cultural individualism-collectivism, self construals, and individual values on communication styles across cultures," *Human Communication Research* 22(4) (1996): 510–43.

studies in this area that link Ukrainians with individualist culture and with the primary importance of family relationships.[42]

Another important finding of the research is that the categories of affects, negative emotions, anxiety, sadness and feelings are less frequent in survivor narratives as compared with normal speech. This is inconsistent with the results of previous research, which shows that Holodomor survivors express great fear, anger, and sadness towards the events.[43] The results from recent research also indicate that a higher frequency of emotional words show more immersion in the traumatic event, which leads to increased experience of physical pain.[44] A possible explanation for these results may be the lack of an adequate coping strategy when dealing with these traumatic events. This results in attempts to avoid the traumatic narrative, the accumulation the negative experience inside the individual, and the bursting forth of the experience in emotional expressions.

Avoidance of traumatic recollection is one of the symptoms of PTSD.[45] This finding broadly supports the work of other studies in this area, which relate prevention of PTSD to traumatic narratives that deal with detailed experiences, feelings and emotions that are aligned with the traumatic event, instead of avoiding traumatic memories and denying sufferings.[46] Therefore, Holodomor survivors demonstrate avoidance of recollecting events and expressing feelings about them in order to decrease the physical and emotional pain linked to their traumatic memory.

Our assumption on avoidance as a PTSD symptom is also strengthened by another finding concerning the low frequency of the category of *time.* Traumatic memory mediated by PTSD is characterized by a loss of time, the absence of border connection between past and present. Therefore, getting stuck in time whilst describing a traumatic event has a poor impact on the length of the traumatic narrative (word count) and spontaneous self-expression in terms of feelings and emotions. These results corroborate the findings of a great deal of previous work on the strong relationship between PTSD and poor temporal processing.[47]

---

[42] Naimark, op. cit.

[43] Bezo and Maggi, op. cit.

[44] Emily A. Holmes, and Corin Bourne, "Inducing and modulating intrusive emotional memories: A review of the trauma film paradigm," *Acta Psychologica* 127, no. 3 (2008): 553–66.

[45] American Psychiatric Association, "American Psychiatric Association. Diagnostic and Statistical Manual of Mental Disorders, Washington DC", 2013.

[46] James W. Pennebaker, "Putting stress into words: Health, linguistic, and therapeutic implications," *Behaviour Research and Therapy* 31, no. 6 (1993): 539–48.

[47] Carmelo M. Vicario and Kim Felmingham, "The Perception of time is underestimated in adolescents with anorexia nervosa," *Frontiers in Psychiatry* 9, no. 4 (2018): 121.

The low frequency of the *time* category is accompanied by the higher frequency of the category *space* as compared with normal speech. *Space* in the traumatic narratives of Holodomor survivors is represented mostly by the categories *home and family*. This finding supports evidence from our previous observations of the predominant role of family and close relatives rather than community in the experience of these tragic events. The current study found a high frequency of the category *death*, which is consistent with the literature on the Holodomor as the physical and psychological destruction of Ukrainians.[48] This finding is also in line with the psychological definition of trauma, which includes death *per se*, or "extreme death anxiety, as a central component of this psychological phenomenon."[49]

One unanticipated finding was that the category *religion* was not widely represented in the traumatic narratives of Holodomor survivors. This finding is contrary to previous studies which have suggested that starvation, notably in the Great Irish Famine, is aligned with providentialism.[50] Therefore, Holodomor survivors were aware of the famine of 1932–33 as an artificial and man-made starvation and connected it with the Soviet government.

Another important finding suggests a significant positive correlation of word count in traumatic narratives and the categories of *family, female, home, and death* (see Table 4), which supports our previous findings and is consistent with the literature. It can therefore be assumed that the Holodomor experience is aligned with family, in particular the experience of female family members, and results in fear of death and high mortality. Regarding the hypothesis of the current research, we can infer that there are differences in Holodomor survivors' memory recollection at the individual, family, and community-society levels. In particular, the meaning of the Holodomor at the community-society level fits the evidence of the Holodomor as a genocidal assault on the Ukrainian people. However, there is a difference in the way the Holodomor is understood in archival collections and in the individual traumatic memories of survivors. The results of individual memory recollection indicate intimate personal experience, which is not represented at the community-society level and needs further research.

---

[48] Bezo and Maggi, op. cit.

[49] Hirschberger, op. cit.

[50] Nocak, Janssen, and Comerford, eds., op. cit.

V. Conclusion

The purpose of the current study was to determine the experience of Holodomor survivors at the community-society, individual, and family levels. One of the more significant findings to emerge from this study is that traumatic memory *recollections at the community-society level are associated with factual (cognitive) information* and are consistent with the main evidence in archive collections. The Holodomor survivors' experience at the community-society level is represented by the main subject, descriptive and conceptual categories, which reconstruct the sequence of tragic events during the famine of 1932–33. The research has also shown that *only individual memory recollection in Holodomor survivors can give a deeper insight into the sense of mental trauma and moral injury.* The investigation of psychologically meaningful categories in traumatic narratives has shown that Holodomor survivors do not easily express their feelings and emotions, in order to avoid traumatic memory. An implication of this is the possibility that they have continuous PTSD even after more than 75 years have passed. The evidence from this study suggests that the Holodomor experience at the individual and family levels is closely aligned with the family, female members of the family, home experience, and fear of death and high mortality. Taken together, these findings suggest the leading role of the family. These have significant implications for understanding how Holodomor survivors witnessed the genocide, experienced family grief, and did not trust the community. The study also raises important questions about the nature of women's suffering and their experience during the famine. However, broader research is needed to determine how men and women experienced the event differently.

A limitation of this study is that it was not possible to assess PTSD and moral injury with psychometric measures. Therefore, it is only assumed that the Holodomor survivors suffered PTSD. Large randomized controlled trials and purposeful large samples of offspring of Holodomor survivors could provide more definitive evidence of mental trauma and moral injury and could give a deeper insight into the transgenerational transmission of collective traumatic memory at the individual, family, and community-society levels.

Bibliography

American Psychiatric Association. "American Psychiatric Association. Diagnostic and Statistical Manual of Mental Disorders, Washington DC" (2013).

Bar-On, Dan, et al. "Multigenerational perspectives on coping with the Holocaust experience: An attachment perspective for understanding the developmental sequelae of trauma across generations." *International Journal of Behavioral Development* 22, no. 2 (1998): 315–38.

Béliveau, Victor. "Memory and Trauma in International Relations. Theories, Cases and Debates," Erica Resende and Dovile Budryte. New York: Routledge, 2014.

Bezo, Brent, and Stefania Maggi. "Living in "survival mode:" Intergenerational transmission of trauma from the Holodomor genocide of 1932–1933 in Ukraine." *Social Science & Medicine* 134, no. 6 (2015): 87–94.

Bianco, Lucien. "Comparing the Soviet and Chinese Famines: Their Perpetrators, Actors, and Victims." *East/West: Journal of Ukrainian Studies* 3, no. 2 (2016): 51–74.

Braga, Luciana Lorens, Marcelo Feijó Mello, and José Paulo Fiks. "Transgenerational transmission of trauma and resilience: a qualitative study with Brazilian offspring of Holocaust survivors." *BMC Psychiatry* 12, no. 1 (2012): 134.

Braitman, Abby L., et al. "Psychometric properties of a Modified Moral Injury Questionnaire in a military population." *Traumatology* 24, no. 4 (2018): 301.

Brom, Danny, Revital Kfir, and Haim Dasberg. "A controlled double-blind study on children of Holocaust survivors." *The Israel Journal of Psychiatry and Related Sciences* 38, no. 1 (2001): 47.

Borysenko, Leonid. Ukrainian culture: individualism or collectivism? *Frontier Problems of Modern Psychology (conference proceedings)*. Kherson: Gelvetika, 2016, 59–63.

Chemtob, Claude M., et al. "Cognitive-behavioral treatment for severe anger in posttraumatic stress disorder." *Journal of Consulting and Clinical Psychology* 65, no. 1 (1997): 184.

Eagle, Gillian, and Debra Kaminer. "Continuous traumatic stress: Expanding the lexicon of traumatic stress." *Peace and Conflict: Journal of Peace Psychology* 19, no. 2 (2013): 85.

Elias, Brenda, et al. "Trauma and suicide behaviour histories among a Canadian indigenous population: an empirical exploration of the potential role of Canada's residential school system." *Social Science & Medicine* 74, no. 10 (2012): 1560–69.

Evans-Campbell, Teresa. Historical trauma in American Indian/Native Alaska communities: A multilevel framework for exploring impacts on individuals, families, and communities. *Journal of Interpersonal Violence*, 23(3) (2008): 316–38.

Felsen, Irit, and H. Shmuel Erlich. "Identification patterns of offspring of Holocaust survivors with their parents." *American Journal of Orthopsychiatry* 60, no. l.4 (1990): 506–20.

Gone, Joseph P. "Colonial genocide and historical trauma in Native North America: Complicating contemporary attributions." *Colonial Genocide in Indigenous North America* (2014). Durham: Duke University Press, 2014, 273–89.

Gudykunst, W. B., Y. Matsumoto, S. Ting-Toomey, T. Nishida, K. Kim & S. Heyman (1996). "The influence of cultural individualism-collectivism, self construals, and individual values on communication styles across cultures". *Human Communication Research,* 22(4), 510–43.

Hirschberger, Gilad. "Collective trauma and the social construction of meaning." *Frontiers in Psychology* 10, no. 8 (2018): 1441.

Holmes, Emily A., and Corin Bourne. "Inducing and modulating intrusive emotional memories: A review of the trauma film paradigm." *Acta Psychologica* 127, no. 3 (2008): 553–66.

Karenian, Hatsantour, et al. "Collective trauma transmission and traumatic reactions among descendants of Armenian refugees." *International Journal of Social Psychiatry* 57, no. 4 (2011): 327–37.

Kira, Ibrahim Aref. "Taxonomy of trauma and trauma assessment." *Traumatology* 7, no. 2 (2001): 73–86.

Kira, Ibrahim A., et al. "Measuring cumulative trauma dose, types, and profiles using a development-based taxonomy of traumas." *Traumatology* 14, no. 2 (2008): 62–87.

Kowalski, Robin M. ""I was only kidding!": Victims' and perpetrators' perceptions of teasing." *Personality and Social Psychology Bulletin* 26, no. 2 (2000): 231–41.

Kul'chyts' kyi, Stanislav, Marta D. Olynyk, and Andrij Wynnyckyj. "The Holodomor and its consequences in the Ukrainian countryside." *Harvard Ukrainian Studies* 30, no. 1/4 (2008): 1–13.

Naimark, Norman M. "How the Holodomor Can Be Integrated into Our Understanding of Genocide." *East/West: Journal of Ukrainian Studies* 2, no. 1 (2015): 117–32.

Noack, Christian, Lindsay Janssen, and Vincent Comerford, eds. *Holodomor and Gorta Mór: Histories, Memories and Representations of Famine in Ukraine and Ireland.* London: Anthem Press, 2012.

Ogienko, V. "Post-traumatic stress disorder and collective trauma in ego-documents and testimonies of the Holodomor." *American Journal of Fundamental, Applied & Experimental Research* 4, no. 11 (2018): 62–76.

Pat-Horenczyk, Ruth, Danny Brom, and Juliet M. Vogel, eds. *Helping Children Cope with Trauma: Individual, Family and Community Perspectives*. New York: Routledge, 2014.

Pennebaker, James W. "Putting stress into words: Health, linguistic, and therapeutic implications." *Behaviour Research and Therapy* 31, no. 6 (1993): 539–48.

Rimé, Bernard, et al. "When collective memories of victimhood fade: Generational evolution of intergroup attitudes and political aspirations in Belgium." *European Journal of Social Psychology* 45, no. 4 (2015): 515–32.

Rude, Stephanie, Eva-Maria Gortner, and James Pennebaker. "Language use of depressed and depression-vulnerable college students." *Cognition & Emotion* 18, no. 8 (2004): 1121–33.

Strauss, Anselm, and Juliet M. Corbin. *Grounded Theory Methodology*: An Overview. In N. K. Denzin & Y. S. Lincoln eds., Handbook of Qualitative Research (Charpter 17, pp. 273–285). Thousand Oaks, CA: Sage, 1994.

Strauss, Anselm, and Juliet M. Corbin. *Grounded Theory in Practice*. Thousand Oaks, CA: Sage, 1997.

Tausczik, Yla R., and James W. Pennebaker. "The psychological meaning of words: LIWC and computerized text analysis methods." *Journal of Language and Social Psychology* 29, no. 1 (2010): 24–54.

Thom, Françoise. "Reflections on Stalin and the Holodomor." *East/West: Journal of Ukrainian Studies* 2, no. 1 (2015): 81–92.

Vicario, Carmelo M., and Kim Felmingham. "The Perception of time is underestimated in adolescents with anorexia nervosa." *Frontiers in Psychiatry* 9, no. 4 (2018): 121.

Walker, Diane, and Florence Myrick. "Grounded theory: An exploration of process and procedure." *Qualitative Health Research* 16, no. 4 (2006): 547–59.

Weigelin-Schwiedrzik, Susanne. "Trauma and memory: the case of the Great Famine in the People's Republic of China (1959–1961)." *Historiography East and West* 1, no. 1 (2003): 39–67.

Wemheuer, Felix. *Famine Politics in Maoist China and the Soviet Union*. Yale University Press, 2014.

Zasiekin, S., N. Bezuglova, A. Hapon, V. Matiushenko, O. Podolska, and D. Zubchuk. "Psycholinguistic aspects of translating LIWC dictionary." *East European Journal of Psycholinguistics* 5, no. 1 (2018): 121–31.

Zasiekina, Larysa, and Serhii Zasiekin. "Psykholinhvistychna Diahnostyka [Psycholinguistic Diagnostic]." Lutsk: Vezha Publishers of Lesya Ukrainka Volyn National University (2008).

Zasiekina, Larysa, Shelia Kennison, Serhii Zasiekin, and Khrystyna Khvorost. "Psycholinguistic markers of autobiographical and traumatic memory." *East European Journal of Psycholinguistics* 6, no. 2 (2019): 119–33.

Reactions to the 1932–33 Holodomor by Ukrainians in Interwar Europe: New Discoveries and Sources

Mirosław Czech and Ola Hnatiuk

Our paper brings together two aspects: a summary of research to date and identification of the problem, both of which, in our opinion, require extensive study. The basic lacuna that we indicate is the lack of studies devoted both to the Ukrainian relief effort on the part of community, political, and church organizations and to similar international efforts undertaken by religious and community organizations of various countries, religious denominations, and nations. In this paper we focus attention on the European dimension, although we realize that actions on the American continent were of considerable importance and have been much better studied.

Study of the relief effort must take account of the broader international context and the politics of the countries in which it was organized. This means putting the subject of "The Holodomor in the Context of European Politics in the Early 1930s" on the agenda. This subject is an integral and important component of the Ukrainian question in European politics of the interwar period.

As has been shown by documents published thanks to the "archival revolution" of the 1990s and 2000s, Stalin was guided by exceptionally ideological notions of inevitable conflict among capitalist states; hence the contradictory nature of his policy between 1932 and 1934. On the one hand, he relied on the system of collective security and struggle against fascism (symbolized by the diplomacy of Maksim Litvinov, commissar of foreign affairs from 1930 to 1939), which was, however, a tactical move. On the other hand, in strategic terms he sought to divide the world and set one state against another.[1] He made the basic elements of domestic policy dependent on the strategic aims of the USSR in the international arena, as was particularly apparent in the first half of the 1930s.

---

[1] There is a rich literature on this subject, to name only Timothy Snyder, *Bloodlands: Europe between Hitler and Stalin* (Basic Books, 2010). See also a recent paper: Sergei Sluch, "Stalin i Gitler, 1933–1941: Raschety i proschety Kremlia," in *Stalin i nemtsy: Novye issledovaniia,* ed. Iu. Tsaruska, trans. from the German T. G. Van'iat, scholarly ed. S. Z. Sluch (Moscow: ROSSPEN, 2009), 89–90.

An analysis of the international political context of the Holodomor makes it possible to take a new look at the reasons for its occurrence, as well as to indicate the factors conducive to the culmination of its most tragic phase in the summer of 1933. It is also important to take note of assistance to various ethnic and religious groups of the Soviet population.

1. The international context

1.1. The Soviet front on the Prosna and the Warta

Between 1932 and 1934 the political situation in east-central Europe was very dynamic. This was associated with the crisis of the Versailles system, further worsened by the world economic crisis (the Great Depression). Two states, Germany and Poland, were particularly important to the development of the domestic and foreign political situation in Europe. Germany's importance derived from its economic potential, which Europe needed to exploit if it was to overcome the crisis and develop normally. Poland's importance lay in its geopolitical role as a stabilizing factor in European politics generally and, in particular, in the alliances of France, the chief guardian of the Versailles system. The Franco-Polish alliance was meant to prevent a potential German threat and restrain the USSR. In this paper we will focus mostly on the triangle Germany-USSR-Poland. We realize, however, that the whole issue is not limited to that dimension.

In the Weimar Republic the program of boundary revision, especially of the Po-lish corridor—the territories of East Pomerania that belonged to the Second Polish Republic and divided West Pomerania from East Prussia, both of which belonged to Germany — was an element of general political consensus. The Treaty of Rapallo (the German-Soviet political alliance of 1922, with a secret annex on cooperation in the military sphere) provided for revision of the system established by the Paris Peace Conference and the satisfaction of German interests. In German foreign policy, the "Rapallo line" remained relevant even after Hitler's accession to power until the beginning of 1934.[2] At that time, a declaration of non-aggression was signed by Germany and Poland, which entailed a reconfiguration (revision) of the system of European interstate alliances in general and, in particular, the culmination of the "Rapallo line" in German-Soviet relations. From the German viewpoint, the declaration was to bring about an alliance with Poland, incentivized by the recognition of "Warsaw's interests in Soviet

[2] In the opinion of the Russian scholar Sergei Sluch, Stalin did not want a withdrawal from the Treaty of Rapallo. For him, even the annulment of military cooperation with the Third Reich in May 1933 could have been an element of pressure on Hitler to prevent him from refusing to maintain the current level of partnership in military technical cooperation (Sluch, "Stalin i Gitler," 86).

Ukraine." It is worth noting that Hitler officially recognized those particular interests of Poland until March 1939.[3]

For Stalin, the signing of the German-Polish declaration came as a surprise, all the more because, since 1932, a policy of maximum rapprochement with Poland had been followed on his orders. On April 1, 1932, by resolution of the Politburo, the Bureau of International Information, headed by Karl Radek, was established as an adjunct to the Central Committee of the All-Union Communist Party (Bolshevik).[4] The Bureau was endowed with broad authority in foreign policy: it received all available information about the international situation from government structures and special services, had the right to contact foreign politicians and dispatch its own agents, and reported directly to Stalin. From mid-1932 to early 1934 the Bureau concentrated on "political and military strategic problems of mutual relations in the Moscow-Warsaw-Berlin triangle."[5]

Of course, various scenarios of political development were considered, given that, in parallel with Stalin's signing of the non-aggression pact with Poland in July 1932, he confirmed a plan for war with Poland presented to him by Mikhail Tukhachevsky at the beginning of 1932. The plan was an element of an impressive program for the development of the Red Army, including motorization and acquisition of heavy aviation and tanks, as many as 10,000 by the following spring. This would be several times greater than the number of tanks in the armies of all the European states. The rearmament of the Red Army was to be accompanied by a change of its structure: mechanized divisions were to become the nucleus of the armed forces, and the army's system of recruitment was to be reformed. The strategy of waging war was adjusted accordingly: the Red Army was to be prepared for rapid offensive operations far beyond enemy lines. And on the Western Front the main adversary was Poland,[6] which was to be "destroyed." At the end of 1932 Tukhachevsky declared to Stalin that he was ready to carry this out.[7]

---

[3] The most recent monograph on the subject is Krzysztof Rak, *Polska—niespełniony sojusznik Hitlera* (Warsaw: Bellona, 2019), 197–245. Its value lies in the author's comprehensive study of German diplomatic documents. See also *Deklaracja polsko-niemiecka o niestosowaniu przemocy z dnia 26 stycznia 1934 r. z perspektywy Polski i Europy w siedemdziesiątą rocznicę podpisania*, ed. Mieczysław Wojciechowski (Toruń: Centrum Edukacji Europejskiej, 2005).

[4] O. N. Ken, "Karl Radek i Biuro mezhdunarodnoi informatsii TsK VKP(b), 1932–34 gg.," *Cahiers du Monde Russe* 44, no. 1 (2003): 135–77.

[5] Ibid., 151.

[6] In a letter of February 25, 1935, addressed to Kliment Voroshilov, Tukhachevsky criticized the new operational plan developed under the direction of the head of the General Staff of the Red Army, Aleksandr Yegorov. Tukhachevsky's critique was prompted by what he considered inadequate attention to changes in the European political situation brought about by the German-Polish declaration of January 26, 1934, on non-aggression. He believed that the

The specter of war truly seemed to be hovering over Europe at the time, as shown by the deterioration of the political situation in Germany and the de facto agreement between France and Britain to revise the borders of Germany and Italy.[8] Given this unfavorable international configuration, in April 1932 Józef Piłsudski also adopted a "peace-loving policy" with regard to the USSR, entrusting its implementation to two close collaborators, Ignacy Matuszewski and Bogusław Miedziński.[9] Owing to this rapprochement with the USSR, Piłsudski felt sufficiently safe in the east not to refute information about Poland's preparations for a "preventive war" against Germany that was widely disseminated in the world press, especially in Germany. In actual fact, Piłsudski was not planning any war at all.[10]

Moscow, for its part, decided to profit by harping on the subject of "preventive war." In March 1933 a representative of the Kremlin proposed that the Polish leadership make an anti-German alliance with France and, in the event of a German-Polish war, receive weapons and matériel from the USSR, for "today the front of the Soviet Union runs along the Prosna and the Warta," that is, the rivers that constituted the Polish-German boundary at

---

declaration included a secret military agreement providing for an alliance of the two states and therefore directly threatened the USSR with a confrontation with their armies.

"Tukhachevsky made a reminder that 'the hitherto valid strategic plan of war in the West had the goal of destroying the Polish state under the assumption that:

1. Finland, Estonia and Latvia, in all likelihood, will maintain neutrality, at least for the initial period of the war.
2. Germany is temporarily well disposed to the USSR and sharply hostile to Poland, and, if it does not advance against the latter, it will draw its [Poland's] forces away to defend the Danzig corridor, and, by its [Germany's] disposition on the borders of East Prussia, it will constitute a threat to the rear of the Polish army as our Western front advances.
3. Poland will not manage to occupy Lithuania until the advance of our Western front is under way.
4. Romania advances against us together with Poland.
5. Romania cannot offer Poland support on the approaches to Warsaw because their geographic locations are disconnected. Those countries can be attacked separately.'"

As cited in Sergei Minakov, "Voennaia ėlita 20–30-kh godov XX veka," *Russkoe slovo* (Moscow, 2004), 419.

[7] Lennart Samuel'son, *Krasnyi koloss: Stanovlenie voenno-promyshlennogo kompleksa SSSR 1921–1941,* trans. from the English I. S. Davidian (Moscow: AIRO-XX, 2001), 155–56; O. N. Ken, *Mobilizatsionnoe planirovanie i politicheskie resheniia (konets 1920—seredina 1930-kh godov)* (St. Petersburg: Izd-vo Evrop. Un-a v S.-Petersburge, 2002), 202–65.

[8] This, in particular, is how the Italian initiative of the Pact of Four (March 1933) was interpreted—as a "new concern of great states" to govern Europe. Poland and the USSR came out resolutely against the pact (Rak, *Polska,* 101–19).

[9] Ken, "Karl Radek," 151–52.

[10] Rak, *Polska,* 126.

the time. In reply, the official *Gazeta Polska* declared Poland's readiness to cooperate with the USSR and the countries of the Little Entente.[11]

The price of a potential Soviet-Polish alliance was also understandable: Poland would refrain from showing any interest in "internal matters of the USSR." Toward the end of May 1933 Radek discussed plans for a trip to Poland with a Polish representative (he spent sixteen days there in July), warning that any Polish activity on the territory of the Ukrainian SSR "would be described by us as conscious or unconscious execution of German plans in the East."[12] The warning was heard in Warsaw: Poland did not come out in defense of starving Ukrainians, or even of its own compatriots, even though Polish diplomacy correctly appraised the dimensions of the catastrophic famine and accurately identified Stalin's desire to make use of it in order to put an end to the Ukrainian national movement.[13]

1.2. The front and security behind the lines

The mention of a "Soviet front" on the Prosna and the Warta should be understood as a variant of a long-held Bolshevik plan for the "destruction of the Polish state." The role of Ukraine in this plan, from the military viewpoint, was to serve as a deep and especially reliable rear area of the USSR[14] so that in the event of Soviet "fraternal assistance to the Polish people," the Poles would not be able to count on a Ukrainian uprising.

Understanding the political and military strategy of the USSR in 1932–34 makes it possible to take a new look at Stalin's goals in programming the Great Famine. He well remembered the experience of 1919–22, when powerful peasant uprisings forced Lenin to make concessions to the Ukrainians. At the beginning of 1930 Bolshevik fears of a Ukrainian uprising forced Stalin to publish the article "Dizzy with Success" in *Pravda* on March 2 and suspend collectivization in the Ukrainian SSR for more than half a year.[15]

Similar fears underlay Stalin's directive of August 11, 1932, to the Politburo, which initiated the Holodomor: "Set yourself the goal of turning

---

[11] Ken, "Karl Radek," 155.

[12] Ibid., 158–59.

[13] *"Nas, Polaków, nie ma kto bronić..." Represje wobec Polaków w Związku Sowieckim w latach 1935–1938 na materiałach MSZ i wywiadu wojskowego Drugiej Rzeczypospolitej,* ed. with introduction by Robert Kuśnierz (Łomianki: Wydawnictwo LTW, 2018).

[14] "Informacja Karola Radka skierowana do Stalina o nowym etapie stosunków polsko-sowieckich," December 3, 1933, Moscow, in *Geneza Paktu Hitler-Stalin: Fakty i propaganda,* ed. Bogdan Musiał and Jan Szumski (Warsaw: Instytut Pamięci Narodowej. Komisja Ścigania Zbrodni przeciwko Narodowi Polskiemu, 2012), 123–24.

[15] O. N. Ken and A. I. Rupasov, *Politbiuro TsK VKP(b) i otnosheniia SSSR s zapadnymi sosednimi gosudarstvami. Problemy. Dokumenty. Opyt kommentariia,* part I, *1928–1934* (St. Petersburg: Evropeiskii dom, 2000), 482–533.

Ukraine into a fortress of the USSR, a real model republic, within the shortest possible time. Do not spare money for this purpose." For, he maintained, "If we do not correct the situation in Ukraine immediately, we could lose Ukraine. Bear in mind that Piłsudski is not drowsing, and his network of agents in Ukraine is many times stronger than [Stanislav] Redens or [Stanislav] Kosior think. Also keep in mind that within the Communist Party of Ukraine (500,000 members, ha-ha) there is no lack (yes, no lack!) of rotten elements, active and latent Petliurites and direct agents of Piłsudski. As soon as the situation gets worse, these elements will not hesitate to open a front within (and outside) the Party, *against* the Party."[16]

In 1932–33, compared with the period of forced collectivization, Moscow's position in the international arena was considerably stronger. True, the grandiose plans for the rearmament of the Red Army had been realized only in part (only one-quarter of the planned 10,000 new tanks for the army had been produced by the spring of 1933),[17] but the armed forces of the USSR had still become the strongest in Europe. In its relations with Germany the USSR maintained the Rapallo line, simultaneously developing friendly relations with Poland and France. Consequently, no one considered intervening in Soviet internal affairs. Moscow managed to attract the United States with the prospect of economic cooperation, also possibly with the prospect of a partnership against Japan (the US's and USSR's main rival in the Far East). On the other hand, for large circles of left and liberal public opinion, red Moscow was the only hope of stopping Hitler. The USSR could now propose terms more favorable to its interests to other states.

2. International assistance in the political game

2.1. Soviet flirtation with Nazi Germany

The preceding survey of the political situation in the Soviet-Polish-German triangle was required as preparation for a clearer exposition of our theses on the reaction of Ukrainians outside the USSR to the Holodomor and the place of the relief campaign in that reaction.

Given memories of the Polish-Bolshevik War of 1920 and Piłsudski's plans in connection with that war to support the independence of Dnipro Ukraine, Poland was regarded by the USSR, Germany, and other states as

---

16 "Pis'mo I. Stalina L. Kaganovichu, 11 avgusta 1932 g.," in *Stalin i Kaganovich: Perepiska, 1931–1936 gg.*, comp. O. V. Khlevniuk, R. U. Devis, L. P. Kosheleva, E. A. Ris, L. A. Rogovaia, Federal'naia arkhivnaia sluzhba Rossii; Rossiiskii gosudarstvennyi arkhiv sotsial'no-politicheskoi istorii (Moscow: ROSSPEN, 2001). Translation cited from *The Holodomor Reader*, comp. and ed. Bohdan Klid and Alexander Motyl (Edmonton and Toronto: Canadian Institute of Ukrainian Studies Press, 2012), 239–40.

17 Samuel'son, *Krasnyi koloss*, 157–61.

the country with the greatest interest in the Ukrainian question. But Poland remained silent about the Holodomor, which was one of the aims of Kremlin policy with regard to Warsaw. To cite Stalin's words, there was no one to defend the "rotten elements, the conscious and unconscious Petliurites," for Piłsudski himself was the first to refrain from that.

The situation was initially different in Germany, where the Holodomor was discussed openly, although concern was expressed first and foremost for starving ethnic Germans.[18] In research on the Holodomor there is no greater taboo subject than the silence of the West or even its utter denial of the death of millions by starvation. The reason was supposedly fear of the consequences of Hitler's accession to power and his inhumane ideology.

But Stalin himself did not fear Hitler's coming to power. Until mid-1934 he did not regard the Führer as an independent politician and considered the Nazi regime a temporary phenomenon.[19] Therefore, he did all he could to continue the "Rapallo line," even in concert with Hitler.[20] Inhumane ideology was no obstacle to Stalin then or later, in 1939. He regarded the socialists, particularly the Second International, as much more serious enemies than Hitler. And the Kremlin began to change this attitude only in mid-1934.[21]

In June and early July 1933 mass actions were conducted in Germany to support starving compatriots in the USSR, and an exhibition of "hunger letters" and photographic materials was organized. The official Soviet representative in Germany responded with a protest: "This is a mendacious campaign that has nothing to do with the real situation in the USSR.... I pointed out to Neurath [the German foreign minister] the weighty

---

[18] Although "The Holodomor and the Third Reich" has been acknowledged as a subject for decades, no published research on it has yet appeared. It does not figure even in Frank Golczewski's authoritative monograph on the Ukrainian question in German politics from 1914 to 1939. Cf. Frank Golczewski, *Deutsche und Ukrainer, 1914–1939* (Paderborn: Ferdinand Schöningh, 2010).

[19] Sluch, "Stalin i Gitler," 85. See also Stanisław Żerko, *Polityka zagraniczna Niemiec 1933–1939* (Poznań: Instytut Zachodni, 2005), 99.

[20] According to Lenin, "skillful manipulation of the antagonisms among the capitalist powers could temporarily prevent the imperialist states from uniting to smash the Soviet regime." The Treaty of Rapallo with Weimar Germany represented the foremost achievement of that strategy. See Teddy J. Uldricks, "Stalin and Nazi Germany," *Slavic Review* 36, no. 4 (December 1977): 599.

[21] G. M. Adibekov, L. A. Rogovaia, and comp. K. K. Shirinia, *Politbiuro TsK RKP(b)–VKP(b) i Komintern 1919–1943: Dokumenty* (Moscow: ROSSPĖN, 2004), 14, 689. In March 1933, at an extraordinary session of the Plenum of the Executive Committee of the Communist International, Dmytro Manuilsky, the general secretary of the Comintern, emphasized that the "destruction of social democracy" remained their goal (p. 679).

consequences to which that campaign will lead if he does not manage to prevent it."[22]

The protest yielded instant results: two days later Joseph Goebbels, the minister of education and propaganda, issued a directive emphasizing that "[t]he government requests that accounts from Soviet Russia be concluded, as the publications have already achieved the desired effect."[23] The directive was carried out in Germany in the course of the next year.[24]

At the same time, Germany and the USSR agreed that assistance from German community and religious organizations would be supplied to the German population of the USSR through the network of Torgsin stores. The Soviets made every effort to interfere with this action[25] but, owing to the initiative of individuals and organizations, assistance to Germans was provided on a large scale. Some 40 to 60 percent of the German minority benefited from assistance,[26] which continued until May 1934. At that point it was declared "Hitlerite," and thus hostile, in the Ukrainian SSR.[27] In the following year it was forbidden completely, mass repressive measures were undertaken against the German minority, and tens of thousands of Germans were deported from the Ukrainian SSR to Kazakhstan.

The USSR permitted assistance to the starving population on the basis of the "like to like" principle, that is, "one's own" were to help "one's own."

---

[22] "Telegramma Polnomochnogo Predstavitelia SSSR v Germanii v Narodnyi Komissariat Inostrannykh Del SSSR, 3 iiulia 1933 g.," in *Dokumenty vneshnei politiki SSSR*, vol. 16 (Moscow: Izdatel'stvo politicheskoi literatury, 1970), 402–3.

[23] Iaroslav Papuha, *Zmova movchannia: Stavlennia Zakhodu do Holodomoru* (Lviv: Vydavets' Oleh Filiuk, 2018), 177.

[24] Levko Chykalenko, head of the Committee to Aid the Starving in Ukraine attached to the Ukrainian Central Committee in Warsaw, reported to Polish intelligence in early 1934 that behind the scenes of the conference of the Interdenominational and International Committee to Aid the Starving in the USSR, which took place in Vienna in mid-December 1933, a disheartening impression was made by reports that "in both Poland and Germany, owing to the direction of foreign policy, which is useful to the Soviets, propaganda concerning the action to aid the starving is being seriously hindered. It was indicated that in Germany it has been forbidden to call meetings and organize public lectures." As cited in *Hołodomor 1932–1933: Wielki Głód na Ukrainie w dokumentach polskiej dyplomacji i wywiadu,* comp. and ed. Jan Jacek Bruski (Warsaw: Polski Instytut Spraw Międzynarodowych, 2008), 550.

[25] See "Lyst nachal'nyka politviddilu Akkarzhans'koï MTS Spartakivs'koho nimets'koho natsional'noho raionu Odes'koï oblasti M. Polians'koho sekretariu TsK KP(b)U S. V. Kosioru pro 'hitlerivs'ku dopomohu' naselenniu raionu ta propozytsiï shchodo prypynennia tsiieï aktsiï. 21 kvitnia 1934 r.," in *Nimtsi v Ukraïni 20–30-ti rr. XX st.: Zbirnyk dokumentiv derzhavnykh arkhiviv Ukraïny,* comp. L. V. Iakovleva, B. V. Chyrko, and S. P. Pyshko (Kyiv, 1994), 175–78.

[26] "Z dopovidnoï zapysky holovy DPU V. Balyts'koho TsK KP(b)U pro vplyv natsionalistychnykh orhanizatsii i konsul'stv Nimechchyny na nimets'ke naselennia Ukraïny ta nadannia iomu 'hitlerivs'koï dopomohy,' 22 travnia 1934 r.," in *Nimtsi v Ukraïni 20–30-ti rr. XX st.,* 181.

[27] Ibid., 180.

Germans from Germany helped Germans in the USSR, Mennonites throughout the world helped Mennonites,[28] Quakers helped Quakers, Jews helped Jews,[29] Russians helped Russians, and Ukrainians helped Ukrainians.[30] Stalin exploited this form of assistance as an element of interstate relations with states in which assistance committees were active. It became a pretext for subsequent repressive measures against national groups once the Kremlin declared that assistance itself constituted evidence of "counterrevolutionary" and "espionage" activity of a given national group.

Kremlin policy and the current international situation contributed to formulating assistance as a humanitarian activity on the model of assistance provided to the starving during the famine of 1921–22. It was Ukrainians outside the USSR who undertook this initiative. In Lviv, the Ukrainian Social Committee for Rescuing Ukraine was established on July 24, 1933, and it became the coordinating body for Ukrainian committees in various countries, notably Poland, Czechoslovakia, France, the United States, and Canada. Ukrainian parliamentary deputies in Romania, who worked closely with the Galicians, showed considerable activity. The Ukrainian Socialist Radical Party and the Ukrainian Social Democratic Party formed their own committees in Poland. The Petliurist Ukrainian Central Committee in Warsaw and its branches throughout Poland set themselves apart at the demand of the Polish authorities,[31] but the Association of Ukrainian Émigrés in Paris cooperated with the Lviv committee, as did the European Association of Ukrainian Organizations Abroad, established in 1931 by the Organization of Ukrainian Nationalists.

On the international level, the Interdenominational and Interethnic Committee to Help the Starving in the USSR, initiated by Cardinal Theodor Innitzer of Vienna in August 1933 at the behest of Metropolitan Andrei Sheptytsky, attempted to coordinate the relief action.

But the International Red Cross, which had provided a great deal of assistance in 1921–22, offered none this time, although its leadership was requested to do so by the Council of the League of Nations. The request was

---

[28] Colin Peter Neufeldt, "The Fate of Mennonites in Ukraine and the Crimea during Soviet Collectivization and the Famine (1930–1933)," PhD diss., University of Alberta, 1999.

[29] *"Posledniaia glava": Agro-dzhoint v gody Bol'shogo terrora* (Kyiv: Dukh i Litera, 2012) (see especially the list of victims of the Great Terror, 295–341).

[30] Vasyl' Mudryi, *Lykholittia Ukraïny* (Lviv, 1933); Andrii Zhuk, *Riatunkova aktsiia dlia Velykoï Ukraïny* (Lviv, 1933). In his article "Holod na Ukraïni," Olgerd Bochkovsky noted: "There are special national organizations, for example, Russian, German and Jewish, that inform the world about the misfortune of their countrymen under the Soviets and help them." On the same model, "an all-Ukrainian national rescue effort began in Lviv in the summer that is naturally directed first and foremost toward the Ukrainian population threatened with death by starvation under the Soviets."

[31] *Hołodomor 1932–1933: Wielki Głód na Ukrainie*, lii, 547.

issued as a result of the discussion of famine in the USSR, particularly in Ukraine, by the Council on September 27, 1933. Moscow did not agree to the provision of assistance because, as Soviet diplomats insisted, "there was no famine" in the USSR. Moscow could behave insolently because no member state of the League initiated consideration of the matter: it was put forward only by Ukrainian parliamentarians from Poland and Romania, as well as international and Ukrainian organizations cooperating with them.

2.2. The Ukrainian relief effort in European countries

Volodymyr Kysilevsky's diary for the years 1931–39 may be regarded as something of a "guidebook" to the Ukrainian question in European politics of the 1930s, informing the world about the Holodomor, and the relief effort. At the time, Kysilevsky was director of the Ukrainian Bureau in London, founded by the Ukrainian émigré Yakiv Makohin, who had come to the United States early in the twentieth century. The bureau worked with particular urgency during the Holodomor, informing the Western public and politicians and doing all it could to support international and relief efforts to help the starving.[32]

Kysilevsky visited Vienna at the turn of the years 1933–34 (after the conference of Cardinal Innitzer's committee on December 16–17, 1933), and there he met with the cardinal, his deputy Ewald Ammende (general secretary of the International Congress of National Minorities and author of a book on the Holodomor illustrated with photographs by Alexander Wienerberger),[33] and the Rev. Myron Hornykevych, secretary of the committee and parish priest in Vienna. He discussed avenues of cooperation with them and spoke separately with another member of the committee, the chief rabbi of Vienna, Dr. David Feuchtwang, about involving Jewish organizations in Austria and Britain in the relief effort.

"The rabbi," he wrote, "received me with extraordinary friendliness. We spoke at first about matters of the relief efforts, then went on to political subjects.... With regard to relief efforts, he asked me to direct the attention of the London Jewish organizations to the need for getting in touch with similar organizations in Vienna."[34]

---

[32] The activity of the Ukrainian Bureau in London is the subject of another paper in this issue (Roman Wysocki's "The Ukrainian Holodomor and the Informational Work of the Ukrainian Bureau in London during 1932–34," 252–75).

[33] Ewald Ammende, *Muss Russland hungern?* (Vienna: Braumüller, 1935); English ed.: *Human Life in Russia* (London: Allen & Unwin, 1936).

[34] Volodymyr Kysilevs'kyi, *Shchodennyk 1931–1939*, entry for January 9, 1934. The diary is being prepared for publication in the series "Ukraine-Europe. 1921–1939." The original is preserved in Library and Archives Canada (Ottawa).

The unique aspect of the relief effort of 1933–34 was the successful coordination of the activity of Ukrainian, German, Jewish, and Russian émigré organizations in providing humanitarian assistance to the starving in the USSR—this despite pressure from the Soviets and European governments under their influence, as well as left and liberal public opinion.

Such cooperation required a common ethical, intellectual, and political denominator. On the Ukrainian side, it was formulated by Olgerd Ipolyt Bochkovsky, a Ukrainian sociologist and political and community activist living in Prague. He was a Social Democrat and a member of the Foreign Delegation of the Ukrainian Social Democratic Labor Party, which belonged to the Second International.

In 1933–34 Bochkovsky published two open letters to Édouard Herriot[35] and an essay titled "Spineless Europe."[36] In the following year, the Lviv newspaper *Dilo* (The Deed) carried his article "The Moral Inflation of Our Age," in which he generalized the moral lesson of the Holodomor for European civilization, pointing out its universal character.[37] In January 1934 Bochkovsky published "Famine in Ukraine" for the use of the Ukrainian Bureau. Translations into Western languages were planned, but ultimately the project was not carried out. Significant for us, however, are the conclusions that Bochkovsky wanted to set before Western public opinion.

"The world," he asserted, after a thorough enumeration of publications about the Holodomor in the world press, "was not badly informed about the catastrophic famine in the land of Soviets. It is another matter that it did not react actively to this disaster; it did not give actual assistance to the population dying en masse on that side of the Soviet border."

He named the key problem facing the Old Continent at the time of the Holodomor: "Previously Europe would react to what happened and how. Now it is mainly interested in where something happened and to whom. Depending on that, it either remains silent or reacts. A crime ceases to be a crime, a wrong a wrong, oppression, violence depending whether they occurred, for example, in Moscow or Berlin, on this or that side of the Soviet border."[38]

He reacted with particular indignation to Édouard Herriot's contention that the "campaign with the invented famine in Ukraine" came from Berlin: "This is unheard-of and unexampled slander. This is a slap in the face to hundreds of thousands of victims of this year's famine in Ukraine! This is an

[35] Ol'gerd Ipolyt Bochkovs'kyi, *Vybrani pratsi ta dokumenty*, vol. 1 (Kyiv, 2018), 105–16.
[36] Ibid., 117–21.
[37] Ol'gerd Ipolyt Bochkovs'kyi, "Moral'na infliatsiia nashoï doby," *Dilo*, nos. 292–94, October 31–November 2, 1934.
[38] O. I. Bochkovs'kyi, "Bezkhrebetna Ievropa," *Vybrani pratsi*, 1:118.

insult, never justified in any way, to the tragic condition of national misfortune in Soviet Ukraine!"[39]

"The task of this publication," explained Bochkovsky in the article "Famine in Ukraine," "is to cast light in general on the catastrophic famine in the Ukrainian lands under the Soviets in 1933 and to draw attention to the circumstance that it is not accidental but that...*the famine will definitely be repeated in 1934*."

This observation is important as part of an answer to the question about the true meaning of the relief action for inhabitants of the USSR. What is paramount is that assistance actually reached part of the Soviet population, including people of various nationalities and denominations. The extent to which the efforts to inform the world about the famine and the relief effort, in particular—Ukrainian, international, and interdenominational—helped put a stop to the Holodomor in the summer of 1933 has not been determined. However, we do know that the fact of the death of millions became too obvious and that the regime needed enough farmers to sow grain in 1933; therefore, Stalin began to wind down the famine in the spring of 1933. Stalin's invitation to Édouard Herriot to visit the USSR (he was there from August 26 to September 9, 1933) was partly Moscow's reaction to the voices of Ukrainians outside the USSR raised in protest, the pastoral letter of the hierarchy of the Greek Catholic Church titled "Ukraine in Its Death Agony," the formation of relief committees, and the efforts to inform the international community. Earlier, Stalin had felt no need to organize such "Potemkin spectacles." There were more general reasons for this invitation, one of them being the need to improve Soviet-French relations; both sides were interested in this. Thus, Herriot helped Stalin to cover up the famine.[40]

For an appropriate presentation of the reaction of Ukrainians outside the USSR to the Holodomor, it is important to note that in parallel with the action concerning the famine in Greater Ukraine, preparations were being made for the convocation of an All-Ukrainian National Congress. It was intended to unite and consolidate all Ukrainian national forces and political groupings in order to create an all-national representation in the international arena.[41]

---

[39] Ibid., 1: 111.

[40] Iryna Dmytrychyn, *Le voyage de Monsieur Herriot: Un épisode de la Grande Famine en Ukraine* (L'Harmattan, 2018); see also this author's article on "The *Voyage Enchanté* of Édouard Herriot" in this publication, p. 216-33.

[41] Preparations for the convocation of the congress were not completed before the outbreak of war, but the process of preparation itself was important for the evolution of the Ukrainian question in the international arena and the associated development of Ukrainian politics and political thought in the democratic parties of Galicia, Bukovyna, and the emigration. For basic

2.3. Domestic Ukrainian factors in the relief effort

Bochkovsky noted the decisive significance of the suicides of Mykola Khvylovy and Mykola Skrypnyk for the initiation of the Ukrainian relief effort.[42] Similar views were expressed by Milena Rudnytska.[43] It is important to emphasize this because the reaction of Ukrainians outside the USSR was conditioned not only by the international political situation but also by domestic Ukrainian factors: the assessment of Ukrainian-Russian relations (imperial center and national periphery) and the situation of the Ukrainian people in the USSR by Ukrainian political actors and church hierarchs in Galicia in cooperation with the bulk of the political emigration.

For the Soviets, the reaction of Ukrainians throughout the world to the Holodomor presented a serious challenge; accordingly, Moscow had to resort to a variety of measures to suppress it, especially pressure on Poland to forbid the activity of relief committees.

In 2016 the Foreign Intelligence Service of Ukraine granted public access to the archives of the Soviet special services, especially the civilian intelligence service of the GPU/OGPU in the years 1925–32, confirming that for the Moscow leadership the Ukrainian question was particularly important and was considered politically integral, with no distinction between the Ukrainian SSR and Western Ukraine and the political emigration. Soviet intelligence sought to penetrate all Ukrainian political groupings, obtain confidential information, and neutralize those of their actions that the Kremlin considered dangerous to itself. The Soviets took a particular interest in contacts of Ukrainian political parties and groupings with foreign governments, special services, and armies. And, naturally, Moscow sought by every measure, with the assistance of its subordinates in

---

information on the preparations for the congress, see O. B. Potikha, "Konsolidatsiia ukraïns'kykh politychnykh syl v ramkakh vseukraïns'koho natsional'noho konhresu (1933–1935)," *Intelihentsiia i vlada*, no. 38 (2018): 170–82.

[42] O. I. Bochkovsky: "The suicides had a clearly political and demonstrative character against Soviet policy in Ukraine and utterly convinced everyone that the historical Muscovite-Ukrainian dispute had just reached its great climax under the current Moscow regime— which, breaking sharply with its previous courting of Ukraine, had now embarked on an open and merciless campaign to destroy the liberation struggle of the Ukrainian people in the USSR, renouncing no means, indifferent to the mass death by starvation of the Ukrainian population, ruined and exhausted by the unheard-of exploitation of the Moscow center."

[43] Milena Rudnytska remarked that "news of Skrypnyk's suicide [on July 7] has just become evidence for all that something unspeakable is going on beyond the Zbruch, and it is this news in particular that has roused Ukrainian society on this side to come out actively in defense of the threatened life of the Ukrainian people." As cited in *Milena Rudnyts'ka—statti, lysty, dokumenty*, comp. Myroslava Diadiuk (Lviv, 1998), 405–6.

Kharkiv and, from 1934, Kyiv, to prevent the unification of the Ukrainian political community outside the USSR.[44]

The culmination of efforts by Ukrainians abroad to inform the world was to be the Day of Mourning planned for October 29, 1933. A week before that date, however, Mykola Lemyk shot an official of the Soviet consulate in Lviv, Aleksei Mailov, and the Polish authorities availed themselves of that pretext to forbid mass activity on squares and streets throughout Galicia. A similar prohibition had been issued earlier by Romania.[45] But that was not enough for Moscow, for in July and August it had already directed Warsaw's attention to the activity of "anti-Soviet forces" in Galicia. In mid-November, in conversation with the Polish foreign minister, Józef Beck, the Soviet plenary representative Vladimir Antonov-Ovseenko declared: "In Little Poland there are several dozen and perhaps even more organizations of district committees alone. Those organizations arose in the process of the anti-Soviet campaign, and I do not understand how one can combat the anti-Soviet campaign without destroying the very organizations that are leading and organizing that campaign."[46]

The issue of prohibiting the activity of committees to aid the starving did not die down until early 1934.[47] Moscow interpreted the absence of such a ban as an attempt by the Polish authorities "to support and inflame anti-Soviet and even interventionist attitudes in Western Ukraine for any eventuality."[48]

An element of pressure on Poland was the preparation for a public trial of the so-called Ukrainian Military Organization (UVO) that supposedly still existed in the USSR. The "Trial of the UVO" was meant to be an exact copy of the trial of the "Union for the Liberation of Ukraine" of 1930, that is, a settling of accounts with the "Petliurists." The "Trial of the UVO" was meant to provide cover for the extermination of Galicians in the Ukrainian SSR and to encourage the Poles to root out the Ukrainian movement in Galicia. It was

---

[44] https://szru.gov.ua/news/galuzevij-derzavnij-arhiv-szru/dialnist-ukrainskoi-politicnoi-emigracii-u-mizvoennij-period-1920–1930-h-rokiv-u-dokumentah.

[45] Papuha, *Zmova movchannia*, 186.

[46] "Zapis' besedy sovetnika Polnomochnogo Predstavitelia SSSR v Pol'she s Ministrom Inostrannykh Del Pol'shi Bekom. 17 noiabria 1933 g.," in *DVP SSSR*, 16: 660–62. See also "Rozmowa ambasadora Jerzego Potockiego w Ankarze z Woroszyłowem, 6 listopada 1933 roku." "He [Kliment Voroshilov] drank with me to the Marshal's health and then made reference, with some irritation, to the Ukrainians, and to the fact that in Lviv there had been a murderous assault on the Soviet consulate. In this connection, he expressed surprise that Poland is so lenient with the Ukrainians and has not dealt with them severely enough, inasmuch as in Soviet Russia they are kept on a tight leash." Original Polish text in *Hołodomor 1932–1933...*, 680–81.

[47] "Pis'mo Polnomochnogo Predstavitelia SSSR v Pol'she chlenu Kollegii Narodnogo Ko-missariata Inostrannykh Del SSSR B. S. Stomotiakovu. 1 dekabria 1933 g." in *DVP SSSR*, 16: 698.

[48] Ken and Rupasov, *Politbiuro TsK VKP(b)*, 394.

also a means of discrediting the relief effort and intimidating Ukrainians who received assistance from abroad. In the autumn of 1933 a new motif was added to the "Trial of the UVO"—the complete destruction of Ukrainian national communism as personified by Mykola Skrypnyk. By the same token, this would be the destruction of the remains of Ukrainian autonomy in the USSR. The process of destruction culminated with the joint plenum of the Central Committee and the Central Control Committee of the Communist Party (Bolshevik) of Ukraine, which took place on November 18–22, 1933.[49] It is important to note that initially the defendants in the "Trial of the UVO" were accused of belonging to a "network of Polish agents." In the autumn, when German-Polish negotiations on the signing of a non-aggression pact entered their final stage, the charge against the defendants was changed to membership in a "Polish-German" network.[50]

This confirms yet again that the successive waves of repression against the Ukrainian national movement in the 1930s must be studied in relation to goals pursued by Stalin in the international arena at a given moment and the current status of the Ukrainian question in European politics.

3. Conclusions and postulates

We have presented the subject articulated in the title only in point form. Such were the views and conclusions that arose in the course of our work on successive volumes of the publication series "Ukraine. Europe, 1921–1939." The discovery of a certain quantity of sources hitherto unused by historians reveals the tremendous potential of archival collections outside Russia and Poland for the study of the Holodomor and its international dimension.

First, it is necessary to restore the memory of those who provided assistance, not only to give due recognition to those who showed humanity at a difficult time and to preserve their memory. The point is also that relief efforts offered a practical alternative to the politics of the day, with their imperialism and totalitarian ideologies covered up by clamorous slogans about social progress and universal, class, or racial happiness.

Second, it has to be shown that remaining silent or even denying the catastrophic famine of the Ukrainian people was the policy of European states regardless of their prevailing social order. Democratic, authoritarian, and totalitarian countries alike kept silent about the genocide of Ukrainians. They did so for a variety of reasons, but maintaining good relations with the Soviets was always the motive.

[49] Oleksandr Rubl'ov, *Zakhidnoukraïns'ka intelihentsiia u zahal'nonatsional'nykh politychnykh i kul'turnykh protsesakh (1914–1939)* (Kyiv: Instytut istoriï NANU, 2004), 355–433.
[50] Ibid., 389–91.

Third, the study of the international context of the Holodomor offers eloquent proof that by 1932–34, Stalin, along with Hitler, was a principal creator of European politics. Ukraine occupied the key position in his political and military strategy; hence his program, adopted in mid-1932, of turning it into a "veritable fortress" and "model Soviet republic," one element of which was to starve to death millions of Ukrainians and annihilate party and government cadres.

Fourth, the question of shared responsibility of Western states for the Holodomor takes its place on the agenda—a question raised as long ago as 1958 by Milena Rudnytska as a student of the Holodomor.[51]

Fifth, the Ukrainian question must be included *in full measure* in the history of interwar Europe, for that is the only way to gain an understanding not only of the tragedy of the Holodomor but also of Europe's descent into the abyss of World War II. The configuration of international politics in 1932–34 is strongly reminiscent of the situation in 1939, when Stalin invited Hitler to renew the "Rapallo line," the configuration of European politics depended on Poland, and everyone endeavored to use Ukraine as a bargaining chip, for its place in Hitler's strategy determined the direction of his expansion—to strike East or West?

In order to give well-founded answers to these questions, it is necessary to study archival collections, first and foremost those of aid committees and individual organizations that provided assistance to people in the USSR. For the study of the international context of the Holodomor and its place in European politics, particularly valuable sources are German, Polish, Austrian, British, French, Italian, American, Canadian, and Romanian archives, as well as the archives of international organizations, especially the League of Nations and the International Congress of National Minorities, the Vatican archives, the archives of the Second International, and the editorial offices of newspapers that wrote most about the famine. Especially important from our point of view are the archival collections of particular individuals: Cardinal Theodor Innitzer, Ewald Ammende, Alexander Wienerberger, Johan Mowinckel, Édouard Herriot, Robert Seton-Watson,

---

[51] Milena Rudnytska returned to the question of (the lack of) reaction to the Holodomor a quarter-century after she, along with other Ukrainian politicians, had tried in vain to convince various European forums, especially the League of Nations and the Congress of National Minorities, to come out in defense of those who had died of starvation. A series of her publications in the newspaper *Svoboda* (Jersey City) from July 16 to August 9, 1958 (reprinted in *Milena Rudnyts'ka: Statti, lysty, dokumenty,* 380–433) was meant to be the beginning of a larger work. As far as is known, she did not manage to realize that idea. Milena Rudnytska's son, Ivan Lysiak Rudnytsky, informed Jerzy Giedroyc about it in letters of January 16, 1966, and December 13, 1967. See *Iezhy Gedroits' ta ukraïns'ka emihratsiia: Lystuvannia 1950–1982 rokiv* (Kyiv: Krytyka, 2008), 531 and 546.

Sir Lewis Namier, Mary Sheepshanks, Rhys Davies, and the British politicians and scholars who belonged to the Anglo-Ukrainian Society.

Studies of the Holodomor have concentrated mainly on such questions as revealing its scope and geography, as well as the organization of the repressive system built by the Kremlin to suppress Ukraine by means of famine. The national aspect of the catastrophic famine has been studied, creating a strong basis for classifying the Holodomor as genocide of the Ukrainian people.

The time has now come to study world reaction to the death by starvation of millions of Ukrainians and other peoples inhabiting the USSR, as well as to describe the relief efforts. It is also time to analyze the place of the Holodomor in European politics of the 1930s, which can already be called extraordinarily important.

This is also relevant to the evolution of present-day European and world politics. Those who want a return to the 1930s are growing in strength. The international context of the Holodomor is an eloquent testimony to the tragically high price paid by Europe and the world for renouncing values in politics, for the "-moral inflation" of their age.

Translated from the Ukrainian by Myroslav Yurkevych

Archives

Haluzevyi derzhavnyi arkhiv sluzhby zovnishn'oi rozvidky Ukrainy

Bibliography

Ammende, Ewald. *Muss Russland hungern?* Vienna: Braumüller, 1935.

Berdykhovs'ka, B. (Berdychowska), ed. *Iezhy Gedroits' ta ukraïns'ka emihratsiia: Lystuvannia 1950–1982 rokiv.* Trans. Ukrainian Research Institute, Harvard Univ. Kyiv: Krytyka, 2008.

Bochkovs'kyi, Ol'gerd Ipolyt. "Moral'na infliatsiia nashoï doby." *Dilo*, 292–94. October 31–November 2, 1934.

— *Vybrani pratsi ta dokumenty*, vol. 1. Kyiv: Dukh i Litera, 2018.

Bruski, Jan Jacek, ed. *Hołodomor 1932–1933: Wielki Głód na Ukrainie w dokumentach polskiej dyplomacji i wywiadu.* Warsaw: Polski Instytut Spraw Międzynarodowych, 2008.

Dmytrychyn, Iryna. *Le voyage Enchenté de Monsieur Herriot: Un épisode de la Grande Famine en Ukraine*. Paris: L'Harmattan, 2018.

Dokumenty vneshnei politiki SSSR, vol. 16, 402–3. Moscow: Izdatel'stvo politicheskoi literatury, 1970.

Golczewski, Frank. *Deutsche und Ukrainer, 1914–1939.* Paderborn: Ferdinand Schöningh, 2010.

"Informacja Karola Radka skierowana do Stalina o nowym etapie stosunków polsko-sowieckich," December 3, 1933, Moscow. In *Geneza Paktu Hitler-Stalin: Fakty i propaganda,* edited by Bogdan Musiał and Jan Szumski 123–24. Warsaw: Instytut Pamięci Narodowej. Komisja Ścigania Zbrodni przeciwko Narodowi Polskiemu, 2012.

Ken, O. N., and Rupasov, A. I. *Politbiuro TsK VKP(b) i otnosheniia SSSR s zapadnymi sosednimi gosudarstvami. Problemy. Dokumenty. Opyt kommentariia,* part I, *1928–1934*. St. Petersburg: Evropeiskii dom, 2000.

Ken, O. N. *Mobilizatsionnoe planirovanie i politicheskie resheniia (konets 1920—seredina 1930-kh godov)*. St. Petersburg: Izd-vo Evrop. Un-a v S.-Peterburge, 2002.

— "Karl Radek i Biuro mezhdunarodnoi informatsii TsK VKP(b), 1932–34 gg.," *Cahiers du Monde Russe* 44, no. 1 (2003): 135–77.

Kuśnierz, Robert, ed. *"Nas, Polaków, nie ma kto bronić..." Represje wobec Polaków w Związku Sowieckim w latach 1935–1938 na materiałach MSZ i wywiadu wojskowego Drugiej Rzeczypospolitej.* Łomianki: Wydawnictwo LTW, 2018.

Kysilevs'kyi. Volodymyr. *Shchodennyk 1931–1939*, entry for January 9, 1934.

Milena Rudnyts'ka—statti, lysty, dokumenty, edited by Myroslava Diadiuk. Lviv: 1998.

Minakov, Sergei. *Voennaia ėlita 20–30-kh godov XX veka.* Moscov; Russkoe Slovo, 2004.

Mitsel, Mikhail. *"Posledniaia glava": Agro-dzhoint v gody Bol'shogo terrora,* Kyiv: Dukh i Litera, 2012.

Mudryi, Vasyl'. *Lykholittia Ukraïny*. Lviv: Dilo, 1933.

Neufeldt, Colin Peter. "The Fate of Mennonites in Ukraine and the Crimea during Soviet Collectivization and the Famine (1930–1933)." PhD diss., University of Alberta, 1999.

Nimtsi v Ukraïni 20–30-ti rr. XX st.: Zbirnyk dokumentiv derzhavnykh arkhiviv Ukraïny, comp. L. V. Iakovleva, B. V. Chyrko, and S. P. Pyshko, 175–78. Kyiv: Institut IstorIYi NAN UkraYini, 1994.

Papuha, Iaroslav. *Zmova movchannia: Stavlennia Zakhodu do Holodomoru*. Lviv: Vydavets' Oleh Filiuk, 2018.

Politbiuro TsK RKP(b)–VKP(b) i Komintern 1919–1943: Dokumenty. Comp. G. M. Adibekov, L. A. Rogovaia, K. K. Shirinia. Moscow: ROSSPĖN, 2004.

Potikha, O. B. "Konsolidatsiia ukraïns'kykh politychnykh syl v ramkakh vseukraïns'koho natsional'noho konhresu (1933–1935)" *Intelihentsiia i vlada*, no. 38 (2018): 170–82.

Rak, Krzysztof. *Polska—niespełniony sojusznik Hitlera*. Warsaw: Bellona, 2019.

Rubl'ov, Oleksandr. *Zakhidnoukraïns'ka intelihentsiia u zahal'nonatsional'nykh politychnykh i kul'turnykh protsesakh (1914–1939)*. Kyiv: Instytut istoriï NANU, 2004.

Samuėl'son, Lennart. *Krasnyi koloss: Stanovlenie voenno-promyshlennogo kompleksa SSSR 1921–1941.* Translated by I. S. Davidian. Moscow: AIRO-XX, 2001.

Sluch, Sergei. "Stalin i Gitler, 1933–1941: Raschety i proschety Kremlia". In *Stalin i nemtsy: Novye issledovaniia,* edited by Iu. Tsaruska, trans. from the German T. G. Van'iat, scholarly edited by S. Z. Sluch. Moscow: ROSPĖN, 2009.

Snyder, Timothy. *Bloodlands: Europe between Hitler and Stalin*. New York: Basic Books, 2010.

Uldricks, Teddy J. "Stalin and Nazi Germany." *Slavic Review* 36, no. 4 (December 1977): 599.

The Holodomor Reader, comp. and ed. Bohdan Klid and Alexander Motyl. Edmonton and Toronto: Canadian Institute of Ukrainian Studies Press, 2012.

Wojciechowski, Mieczysław, ed. *Deklaracja polsko-niemiecka o niestosowaniu przemocy z dnia 26 stycznia 1934 r. z perspektywy Polski i Europy w siedemdziesiątą rocznicę podpisania*. Toruń: Centrum Edukacji Europejskiej, 2005.

Zhuk, Andrii. *Riatunkova aktsiia dlia Velykoï Ukraïny*. Lviv, 1933.

Żerko, Stanisław. *Polityka zagraniczna Niemiec 1933–1939*. Poznań: Instytut Zachodni, 2005.

Our Authors

Olga Andriewsky is an associate professor in the Department of History at Trent University. She teaches and researches in the area of late Imperial and Soviet history. Professor Andriewsky has written numerous articles on identity and politics in late Imperial Russia and is the author of "Towards a Decentered History: The Study of the Holodomor and Ukrainian Historiography" (*Contextualizing the Holodomor*).

Andrii Bolianovskyi is a senior scholarly associate at the Ivan Krypiakevych Institute for Ukrainian Studies, National Academy of Sciences of Ukraine (Lviv). He has studied the methodology and literature of genocide studies at the US Holocaust Memorial Museum in Washington, D.C. (2016/2017). While in Washington, he also collected documents on Soviet policy in Ukraine at the US National Archives and Records Administration (NARA). He is the author of *Foreign Military Formations within the German Armed Forces, 1939–1945* (in Ukrainian, Lviv, 2013).

Serge Cipko is assistant director for research at the Canadian Institute of Ukrainian Studies, University of Alberta. He is the author of *Starving Ukraine: The Holodomor and Canada's Response; Ukrainians in Argentina, 1897–1950: The Making of a Community; St. Josaphat Ukrainian Catholic Cathedral, Edmonton: A History (1902–2002)*, and co-author (with Glenna Roberts) of *One-Way Ticket: The Soviet Return-to-the-Homeland Campaign, 1955–1960.*

Mirosław Czech is a historian who graduated from the University of Warsaw. He has served as a deputy to the Parliament of the Republic of Poland (1993–2001) and was a columnist for the newspaper *Gazeta Wyborcza* in the period 2005–2016. He is currently the coordinator of the book series "Ukraine. Europe, 1921–1939."

Iryna Dmytryczyn is a historian of French-Ukrainian relations and a translator of Ukrainian contemporary literature in France. She is the head of the Department of Ukrainian Studies at the Institut des Langues et Civilisations Orientales in Paris. She is the author of a biography of Hryhorii Orlyk (2005) and has published a book about Édouard Herriot's trip to Ukraine (2018). She is currently exploring the French archives about Ukraine in the first half of the twentieth century.

Gennady Estraikh is a professor at the Skirball Department of Hebrew and Judaic Studies at New York University, where he also directs the Shvidler Project for the History of the Jews of the Soviet Union. Born in Zaporizhzhia, Ukraine, he was Managing Editor of the Moscow Yiddish literary journal *Sovetish Heymland* (Soviet Homeland) from 1998 to 1991. He received his doctorate from the University of Oxford. His fields of expertise are Jewish intellectual history, Yiddish language and literature, and Soviet Jewish history.

Paolo Fonzi is an assistant professor at the University of Eastern Piedmont, Vercelli. He received his PhD both at the University of Naples (Federico II) and at the Humboldt University of Berlin. He has conducted extensive research on the history of National Socialism, focusing on the economic policy of the Third Reich and World War II. In 2016 he held the Shklar Research Fellowship at the Ukrainian Research Institute, Harvard University, where he conducted a project on the "German Perception of the Great Famine in Ukraine and Northern Caucasus (1932–33)," under the supervision of Prof. Andrea Graziosi.

Inna Gogina has a master's degree in Classical Philology from Moscow State University, a master's degree in Public Administration from California State University, Northridge, and a MLIS degree from San José State University. Her studies focused on information organization, digital services, and emerging technologies. She has worked at the USC Shoah Foundation—The Institute for Visual History and Education, University of Southern California, in a variety of capacities since 1999. She has authored entries describing the national archival systems of Bulgaria, Czech Republic, Hungary, Poland, Slovakia, Slovenia, and Ukraine in The International Directory of National Archives (Rowman & Littlefield, 2018).

Ola Hnatiuk is a professor at the University of Warsaw and Kyiv-Mohyla Academy. Vicepresident of the PEN International—Ukrainian Centre, she served in the Polish diplomatic corps (2006–2010). Dr. Hnatiuk is the recipient of numerous awards, including Polonia Restituta (the highest award given by the Polish state), the Antonovych Foundation Award for fostering Polish-Ukrainian cultural cooperation, and the Pruszynski Polish PENClub Award. She is the author of several books, including *Farewell to Empire: Ukrainian Debates on Identity* (2003). Her most recent book *Courage and Fear* (2015) received awards in Ukraine and Poland and was published in 2020 by Academic Study Press and HURI.

Olga Klymenko is a research associate at the Holodomor Research and Education Consortium, Canadian Institute of Ukrainian Studies, University of Alberta. She is currently working on a project of digitization of the Maniak Collection, a collection of letters of witnesses to the Holodomor written in 1988–89.

Hiroaki Kuromiya currently teaches history at Indiana University (USA). His research interest is modern Eurasian history. His published books include *Freedom and Terror in the Donbas: A Ukrainian-Russian Borderland, 1870s–1990s* (1998), *The Voices of the Dead: Stalin's Great Terror in the 1930s (2007), Conscience on Trial: The Fate of Fourteen Pacifists in Stalin's Ukraine, 1952–1953 (2012),* and *The Eurasian Triangle: Russia, the Caucasus, and Japan, 1904–1945* (2016, co-authored with Georges Mamoulia).

Colin P. Neufeldt is a professor of history at Concordia University of Edmonton, Canada. His research focus is the history of Mennonites in Eastern Europe and the Soviet Union. His most recent publications include *The Public and Private Lives of Mennonite Kolkhoz Chairmen in the Khortytsia and Molochansk German National Raĭony in Ukraine (1928–1934)* and "Collectivizing the Mutter Ansiedlungen: The Role of Mennonites in Organizing Kolkhozy in the Khortytsia and Molochansk German National Districts in Ukraine in the Late 1920s and Early 1930s." Colin and his family live in Edmonton, Alberta, where he practices law.

Myroslav Shkandrij, EDITOR, has taught Slavic Studies at the University of Manitoba (from 1987), Calgary, and Ottawa. He is a Professor Emeritus at the University of Manitoba. His research has focused on Ukraine's cultural history: the cultural flowering of the 1920s, the avant-garde, nationalism, and Jewish-Ukrainian relations. His books include *Russia and Ukraine: Literature and the Discourse of Empire* (2001; in Ukrainian 2004), *Jews in Ukrainian Literature: Representation and Identity* (2009), *Ukrainian Nationalism: Politics, Ideology, and Literature, 1929–1956* (2015), and *Avant-garde Art in Ukraine: Contested Memory, 1910–1930* (2019).

Mykola Iv. Soroka received his candidate of philological sciences degree at Taras Shevchenko National University of Kyiv (1995) and PhD in Modern Languages and Cultural Studies at the University of Alberta (2005). He is the author of the monographs Visual Poetry in Ukrainian Literature in the End of the 16–18 Centuries (Kyiv, 1997) and Faces of Displacement: The Writings of Volodymyr Vynnychenko (McGill UP, 2012). He worked at the Canadian Institute of Ukrainian Studies at the University of Alberta (2007–15) and is now an independent scholar. His recent publications explore

Ukrainian-Russian cultural contacts of the interwar period in emigration, and issues of modernity, displacement, and travel in Ukrainian literature.

John Vsetecka is a PhD candidate in the Department of History at Michigan State University, where he works on issues of violence, memory, and famine in Soviet Ukraine. His dissertation project, entitled "In the Aftermath of Hunger: Coming to Terms with Famine in Soviet Ukraine, 1933–1988," examines how those Ukrainians who survived the famine attempted to make sense of the event and come to terms with what happened in 1932–33. His work is aimed at gaining a better understanding of how the famine created lasting repercussions that continued to influence, disrupt, and affect the lives of many well after the famine officially ended. He is also the founder and current co-editor of H-Ukraine, a scholarly page dedicated to Ukrainian Studies, which is part of the larger online H-Net platform.

Roman Wysocki is a lecturer at the Institute of History at Maria Curie-Sklodowska University in Lublin, Poland. He holds a PhD from the same university. He is the author of three books as well as articles on Polish-Ukrainian relations between the two World Wars, and on Ukrainians and Belarusians in Poland. His areas of interest include Ukrainian political thought, Polish-Ukrainian history in the twentieth century, Ukrainian emigrants in Poland, reactions to the Holodomor, and the Orthodox Church in Poland.

Larysa Zasiekina is professor and vice-president for research and international affairs at Lesya Ukrainka Eastern European National University in Lutsk, Ukraine. Her research areas are individual and collective trauma and transgenerational transmission of psychological trauma associated with genocide, notably the Holodomor and the Holocaust. She is the founder and director of the Ukrainian Psychotrauma Center, which attracts leading international specialists in trauma and resilience treatment and research. She is the recipient of Fulbright and Chevening awards and has been a visiting professor in the US.

Index